SO-BJZ-820

JESUS THE EXORCIST

A Contribution to the Study of the Historical Jesus

GRAHAM H. TWELFTREE

HENDRICKSON PUBLISHERS

Hendrickson Publishers, Inc.
P. O. Box 3473
Peabody, Massachusetts 01961-3473

Printed in the United States of America
ISBN 1–56563–146–3

JESUS THE EXORCIST: A CONTRIBUTION TO THE STUDY OF THE HISTORICAL JESUS, by Graham H. Twelftree © 1993 J. C. B. Mohr. All rights reserved. Hendrickson Publishers' edition reprinted by arrangement with:

J. C. B. Mohr (Paul Siebeck), P. O. Box 2040, 72010 Tübingen.

This book may not be reproduced, in whole or in part, in any form (beyond that permitted by copyright law) without the original publisher's permission. This applies particularly to reproductions, translations, microfilms and storage and processing in electronic systems.

232.95
T917j

L. I. F. E. Bible College
LIBRARY
1100 COVINA BLVD
SAN DIMAS, CA 91773

To
my parents
Eric and Iris Twelftree
as a
token of
my appreciation

046729

L. I. F. E. Bible College
LIBRARY
1100 COVINA BLVD
SAN DIMAS, CA. 91773

Preface

Although I take full responsibility for the contents of this study I am very conscious of the debt I owe to others. The late Professor George Caird, when principal of Mansfield College, Oxford, introduced me to the world and critical study of the New Testament. I remain grateful for his encouragement and patience with a beginner and am deeply sorry he is not still with us. I cannot say how much I appreciated Professor James Dunn's supervision of an earlier version of this study which was submitted to the University of Nottingham as a Ph. D. degree dissertation. He gave generously of himself and of his time. His love of the New Testament text and enthusiasm for discovering both the intention of the ancient writers and their significance for the present has had a considerable and lasting impact on me. I continue to value his scholarship, friendship and critical Christian faith.

Librarians at Nottingham University, Pastor Trevor Zweck and Ruth Strelan of Luther Seminary (Adelaide), Dr. Lawrence McIntosh of Ormond College (Melbourne), .Val. Canty of Parkin-Wesley College (Adelaide) and Margery Kirschke of the State Library of South Australia are to be thanked for their willing and forbearing help. I am indebted to and wish to thank those who have read parts or various drafts of the whole of this material; especially Professor David E. Aune, Canon Anthony E. Harvey, Professor Howard C. Kee, Rev'ds. Robert Morgan and Philip Muston, Professor Harold Remus, Dr. Stephen H. Travis, Professor Edwin Yamauchi and Professors C. Kingsley Barrett and John Heywood Thomas (examiners of the thesis), as well as many others. Their comments have greatly helped improve the final product. I have also appreciated the help and support of Professors Martin Hengel and Otfried Hofius, as well as Georg Siebeck, Ilse König and the staff of J.C.B. Mohr (Paul Siebeck). Thanks is also due to those who have typed various stages of this study — particularly to Wendy Jettner.

The literal translations of the Greek text at the beginning of each section of chapter III are my own. In order to handle the ever increasing volume of secondary literature, relevant to chapter III, I have not attempted to repeat the material cited by Joachim Gnilka and Rudolf Pesch in their commentaries on Mark's Gospel. Also, the bibliography of secondary sources is only able to contain a selection of the literature.

I could not have undertaken this project without the complete support of my parents — thank you, Mum and Dad! Please accept this volume as a token of my gratitude. Then, again, to Barbara my wife, I tender my gratitude for her love, help and patience. Our children, Catherine and Paul, continue to be long-suffering and hope that the completion of this project will help make good the promise of more time together as a family.

Adeladie 1991   Graham H. Twelftree

Contents

Abbreviations IX

I

§ 1   The Debate   1

II
Exorcism and Exorcists in First Century Palestine

§ 2   Materials   13
§ 3   Exorcism and Exorcists   22
§ 4   Conclusions   48

III
Jesus the Exorcist: The New Testament Data

§ 5   Gospel Research   53
§ 6   The Demoniac in the Synagogue (Mark 1.21 – 8)   57
§ 7   The Gadarene Demoniac (Mark 5.1 – 20)   72
§ 8   The Syrophoenician Woman's Daughter (Mark 7.24 – 30)   88
§ 9   The Epileptic Boy (Mark 9.14 – 29)   91
§ 10 The Beelzebul Controversy
      (Mark 3.22 – 7 and Matthew 12.22 – 30/Luke 11.14 – 23)   98
§ 11 The Temptations
      (Mark 1,12, 13 and Matthew 4.1,2,11/Luke 4.1, 2, 13)   114
§ 12 Jesus' Answer to John the Baptist
      (Matthew 11.2 – 6/Luke 7.18 – 23)   118
§ 13 The Disciples' Mission(s) (Mark 6.7 – 12,30/Matthew 10.1 – 15/
      Luke 9.1 – 6; 10.1 – 11,17 – 20)   122
§ 14 The Brief Summary Reports   128

IV
Jesus the Exorcist

§ 15 Historical Method   130
§ 16 Was Jesus an Exorcist?   136
§ 17 Jesus as an Exorcist   143
§ 18 Distinctive and Unique Features of Jesus' Methods   157
§ 19 Miracle and Message in Jesus' Ministry   166
§ 20 Conclusions   172

V
As Others Saw Him

§ 21 Introduction   175
§ 22 Jesus' Audience   176
§ 23 Messiah?   182
§ 24 Magician?   190
§ 25 Necromancer?   208
§ 26 Ḥasid?   209
§ 27 Conclusion   213

VI
Jesus the Exorcist: His Self Understanding

§ 28 Introduction   216
§ 29 Exorcism and Eschatology   217

VII

§ 30 Conclusions   225

Bibliography   229
Indexes   249

Abbreviations

For abbreviations see *Journal of Biblical Literature* 107 (1988) 579—96. Other abbreviations are as follows.

CC　　　　H. Chadwick *Origen: Contra Celsum* (Cambridge: Cambridge University Press, 1980).

DNTT　　　C. Brown (ed.) *The New Interantional Dictionary of NT Theology* 3 vols. (Exeter: Paternoster, 1975—1978).

ERE　　　　J. Hastings (ed.) *Encyclopedia of Religion and Ethics* 13 vols. (Edinburgh: T & T Clark, 1908ff.).

Hennecke　E. Hennecke *New Testament Apocrypha* 2 vols. (London: SCM, 1973 and 1974).

HSE　　　　L. Gaston *Horae Synopticae Electronicae* (Missoula: Scholars Press, 1973).

ND　　　　G.H.R. Horsley, (ed.) *New Documents Illustrating Early Christianity* (Macquarie University: The Ancient History Documentary Research Centre, 1981—).

I

§ 1 The Debate

"Men kicked woman to death in attempt at exorcism, court told.

A preacher and his friend went berserk and kicked a mentally unstable woman to death as they tried to rid her of Judas Iscariot's evil spirit, the Central Criminal Court was told yesterday.

During the 'exorcism' John Sherwood and Anthony Strover punched Miss Beatrix Rutherford, aged 31, unconscious and then kicked and jumped on her stomach, it was alleged.

Mr Strover was said to have told the police that as they tried to chase the devil out of her, Miss Rutherford spoke in a strange voice which claimed to be the spirit of Judas Iscariot."[1]

Press reports such as this, popular interest in the occult, and renewed interest in Christian deliverance, have generated considerable discussion on exorcism with the Church.[2] However, there is by no means a consensus of opinion within the Church on the place or the form exorcism should take in the twentieth century. For example, the Bishop of Exeter's report on exorcism recommended that "every diocesan bishop should appoint a priest as diocesan exorcist."[3] On the other hand, in an open letter to the Archbishops, the bishops and members of the General Synod of the Church of England, Reverend Don Cupitt and Professor G.W.H. Lampe wrote: ". . . we believe that the Church of England is in danger of making a serious error of judgment. . . We believe that exorcism should have no official status in the Church at all . . ."[4]

The different views represented in these two quotations — and the spectrum of opinions between them — usually seek the support of the

---

1 *The Times* (London) 4 September 1980, 2.

2 Cf. the "Barnsley Case" *The Times* (London) 26 March 1975, 4; 27 March 1975, 6 and G.H. Twelftree *Christ Triumphant: Exorcism Then and Now* (London: Hodder and Stoughton, 1985) chaps. I and V. See also the bibliographies in John Richards *But Deliver Us From Evil* (New York: Seabury, 1974) 222–40; and *Exorcism, Deliverance and Healing: Some Pastoral Guidelines* (Nottingham: Grove Books, 1976) 24.

3 Dom R. Petitpierre (ed.) *Exorcism. The Report of a Commission Convened by the Bishop of Exeter* (London: SPCK, 1972) 26. For other church "reports" see Richards *Exorcism* 3 n. 2.

4 D. Cupitt and G.W.H. Lampe "Open Letter on Exorcism" reprinted in D. Cupitt *Explorations in Theology* 6 (London: SCM, 1979) 50–3, quotation from 50.

New Testament, especially the reported activities of Jesus.[5] Therefore, in the current debate on exorcism, the student of the New Testament has a weighty responsibility to elucidate the data in the Gospels in relation to Jesus and exorcism.

The Gospel of Mark has as one of its key questions: Who is Jesus? [6] And, ever since Mark wrote his Gospel, Christians have been writing and rewriting the story of Jesus, attempting to explain for their readers Jesus' identity. However, Schweitzer showed us that, in attempting to depict Jesus for our contemporaries, we too often merely create an image of him after the likeness of our own cultural and theological predispositions.

In the Gospels the earthly Jesus has, at times, been obscured behind, and at least partly identified with, the early Christians' view of the risen Christ. The problem is that in trying to see again the Jesus of Nazareth — so important to early Christianity — we strip away the first century cultural and Christian garb only to replace it with the comfortable clothes of our own culture. In relation to the nineteenth century study of the life of Jesus, Schweitzer's words are apt:

> "It loosed the bands by which He had been riveted for centuries to the stony rocks of ecclestiastical doctrine, and rejoiced to see life and movement coming into the figure once more, and the historical Jesus advancing, as it seemed, to meet it. But He does not stay; He passes by our time and returns to His own."[7]

Yet, we must still attempt to discover anew the historical Jesus — the founder of Christianity — in order that our age may see and understand him more clearly. To follow Käsemann:

> ". . . defeatism and scepticism must [not] have the last word and lead us on to a complete disengagement of interest from the earthly Jesus. If this were to happen, we should either be failing to grasp the nature of primitive Christian concern with the identity between the exalted and the humiliated Lord; or else we should be emptying that concern of any real content, as did the docetists."[8]

---

5   E.g. J.H. Crehan in Petitpierre (ed.) *Exorcism* 11–15; Cupitt *Explorations* 6, 51 and K. Grayston "Exorcism in the NT" *Epworth Review* 2 (1975) 90–4.

6   E.g. 1.27; 2.7; 4.41; 6.3; 14.16; and 8.7–9. Cf. J.D. Kingsbury *The Christology of Mark's Gospel* (Philadelphia: Fortress, 1983) 80–9.

7   A. Schweitzer *The Quest of the Historical Jesus* (London: Black, 1910) 397. Cf. D.C. Duling *Jesus Christ Through History* (New York: Harcourt Brace Jovanovich, 1979); J. Pelikan *Jesus through the Centuries* (New Haven and London: Yale University Press, 1985). On scholars continuing to cast Jesus after the fashion of their own christologies, see E.A. Johnson "Images of the Historical Jesus in Catholic Christology" *Living Light* 23 (1986) 47–66.

8   E. Käsemann "The Problem of the Historical Jesus" in *Essays on NT Themes* (London: SCM, 1964) 45–7. Cf. V.A. Harvey *The Historian and the Believer* (London: SCM, 1967) 4, 6. On the recent move away from excessive scepticism regarding historicity see C.A. Evans "Jesus of Nazareth: Who Do Scholars Say That He Is? A Review Article" *Crux* 23 (1987) 15–19.

This book presupposes that the life, ministry and passion of Jesus of Nazareth were — and remain — of fundamental significance to the life of the Church.[9] In turn, therefore, the search for the historical Jesus is an important enterprise for scholars who wish to serve the Church.[10]

Thus, the present study is an attempt to make a modest contribution to our understanding of the historical Jesus; to sketch a picture of the historical Jesus in his ministry of exorcism. In other words, this study seeks to determine if the historical Jesus was an exorcist and then to answer the three-part question: If Jesus was an exorcist, What did the first reports of his activities as an exorcist contain? How would he have been viewed by those who saw him at work? And, how did he understand his ministry of exorcism?

If we turn to the Synoptic Gospel writers, even a brief survey reveals how important exorcism was for them. For example, of the thirteen healing stories of Jesus in Mark's Gospel — 1.29–31, 40–5; 2.1–12; 3.1–6; 5.21–43; 7.31–7; 8.22–6; 10.46–52 and 1.21–8; 5.1–20; 7.24–30; 9.14–29 — the last four mentioned are exorcism stories. This makes exorcism the most numerous category of healing story in Mark. Also, even though (apart from Matthew 12.22/Luke 11.14) Matthew and Luke provide no extra detailed stories of exorcism they, like Mark, agree that exorcism was an important aspect of Jesus' ministry and go so far as to suggest that Jesus' dealings with the demon-possessed is of central significance in understanding Jesus and his ministry. At least this is the case on a first reading of Matthew 12.28/Luke 11.20 (see §10 below).

This importance of the miracles for the Evangelists' portrayal of Jesus, as well as the presentation of the Christian Gospel itself, was reflected in the eighteenth and nineteenth century scholarly preoccupation with miracles. Representing the mood of his time Ludwig Feuerbach (1804—72) put it sharply: "The specific object of faith . . . is miracle; faith is the belief in

---

9 Cf. R.R. Niebuhr *Resurrection and Historical Reason* (New York: Scribner, 1957) 146; C.F.D. Moule *The Phenomenon of the NT* (London: SCM, 1981) 77; J.P. Mackey *Jesus the Man and the Myth* (London: SCM, 1985) 2–3.

10 See also M.J. Borg "What Did Jesus Really Say?" *BibRev* 5 (1989) 18–25; J.H. Charlesworth "Research on the Historical Jesus Today . . ." *Princeton Seminary Bulletin* 6 (1985) 98: "What do I consider the central task of the New Testament scholar? It is to seek what can be known about the life and teachings of Jesus of Nazareth." Cf. J.H. Charlesworth *Jesus Within Judaism* (London: SPCK, 1988) 9. It is well known that the term "historical Jesus" is an ambiguous one. J.M. Robinson *A New Quest of the Historical Jesus* (London: SCM, 1959) defines the term "historical Jesus" as "What can be known of Jesus of Nazareth by means of the scientific methods of the historian" (26). But the earthly Jesus – like any other figure in history, lost to us – is the Jesus of Nazareth as he actually was, whereas Christ is reached through faith and doctrine (28). More recently, see J.P. Meier "The Historical Jesus: Rethinking Some Concepts" *TS* 51 (1990) 3–24.

miracle; faith and miracle are absolutely inseparable."[11] For Hermann Reimarus (1694—1768), however, whose notorious 'Fragments' were published posthumously by Gotthold Lessing between 1774 and 1778, the substance of Christianity were the principal articles of faith in the Kerygma: ". . . spiritual deliverance through the suffering and death of Christ; resurrection from death in confirmation of the sufficient suffering of Christ; and, the return of Christ for reward and punishment, as the fruit and consequence of the deliverance."[12] Miracles, he goes on to say, are not essential, not least because of Jesus' criticism of those who sought assurance in signs and wonders. But Reimarus stands apart from those who followed him.[13] For, as post-Enlightenment people attempted to subject their world views to the critical eye of reason and scientific knowledge, the concept of miracle became more and more a focus of attention and difficult for scholars to accept.[14]

So, in various ways, the major contributors to the nineteenth century search for the historical Jesus sought to remove the miraculous from the centre of the theological stage. Heinrich Paulus (1761—1851), who exemplified the rationalist approach in New Testament scholarship, offered rationalistic explanations for the miracles. For example, the feeding of the five thousand is explained by suggesting that, on seeing the hungry multitude, Jesus said to his disciples, "We will set the rich people among them a good example, that they may share their supplies with the others." According to Paulus, Jesus then began to distribute his own provisions, and those of the disciples. Soon, as the example was followed, every one had plenty.[15] The main interest and objective of Paulus' enterprise was to show that miracles need no longer be an obstacle to faith for the intelligent person.

The most important contribution to the nineteenth century debate about the miracles came from D.F. Strauss (1808—74). In his two volume *The Life of Jesus* (1835), he faced head-on the problem of miracle, proceeding not by seeking 'what actually happened' but by examining the narratives.[16] He postulated that much of the New Testament, including the miracle stories, should be understood as, and placed in one of a number of

11 L.A. Feuerbach *The Essence of Christianity* (New York: Harper & Row, 1957) 126.
12 C.H. Talbert (ed.) *Reimarus: Fragments* (London: SCM, 1971) 229–30.
13 B.F. Meyer *The Aims of Jesus* (London: SCM, 1979) 30, who also cites material from Reimarus not in the above English translation.
14 Cf. J.D.G. Dunn "Demythologizing – The Problem of Myth in the NT" in I.H. Marshall (ed.) *NT Interpretation* (Exeter: Paternoster, 1977) 289.
15 From Schweitzer *Quest* 52, cf. 57.
16 D.F. Strauss *The Life of Jesus* (Philadelphia: Fortress, 1973).

categories of, *myth*.[17] Myths which related directly or indirectly to Jesus Strauss designated 'evangelical' myths. In turn, these were of two kinds. On the one hand, there were *pure* myths, like the transfiguration, which had no foundation in a historical event in the ministry of Jesus. On the other hand, the *historical* myth "has for its groundwork a definite individual fact which has been seized upon by religious enthusiasm, and twined around with mythical conceptions culled from the idea of the Christ." As examples of this category of myth Strauss gave the "saying of Jesus such as that concerning 'fishers of men' or the barren figtree, which now appear in the Gospels transmuted into marvellous histories."[18]

Strauss' *Life* unleashed a torrent of criticism, directed primarily at the way he approached myth and the problem of miracle. As Schweitzer put it: "Scarcely ever has a book let loose such a storm of controversy."[19] Nevertheless, the significant and long term results were, to continue with Schweitzer, that "With Strauss begins the period of the non-miraculous view of the Life of Jesus. . . The question of miracle constantly falls more and more into the background."[20]

However, in the early part of his lectures, "The Essence of Christianity", delivered in the winter semester of 1899—1900, Adolf Harnack (1851—1930) attempted a protest at this fear of treating the miracles. He put it: "Not Strauss only, but many others too, have allowed themselves to be frightened by them [the miracles] into roundly denying the credibility of the Gospels." Yet, was not Harnack still under the spell of Strauss when he said that miracles did "not possess the significance for that age which, if they existed, they would possess for ours," and "that Jesus himself did not assign that critical importance to his miraculous deeds which even the evangelist Mark and the others all attributed to them"?[21]

---

17 "The myth, in its original form, is not the conscious and intentional invention of an individual but a production of the common consciousness of a people or religious circle, which an individual does indeed first enunciate, but which meets with belief for the very reason that such individual is but the organ of this universal conviction. It is not a covering in which a clever man clothes an idea which arises in him for the use and benefit of the ignorant multitude, but it is only simultaneously with the narrative, nay, in the very form of the narrative which he tells, that he becomes conscious of the idea which he is not yet able to apprehend purely as such." *New Life of Jesus* (London: 1865) I, 206. Quoted by Dunn in Marshall (ed.) *NT Interpretation* 303 n. 22.

18 Strauss *Life* 87. Cf. Peter C. Hodgson's "Introduction" to *Life* xxxviff. Strauss did not escape the rationalism he criticised, for, in relation to our subject, he said, "that Jesus cured many persons who suffered from supposed demonical insanity or nervous disorder, in a psychical manner, by the ascendancy of his manner and words" (*Life* 436).

19 Schweitzer *Quest* 97; cf. 97–120 on Strauss' opponents and supporters.

20 Schweitzer *Quest* 111.

21 A. Harnack *What is Christianity?* (London: Williams and Norgate, 1901) 24, 25 and 28–9.

This attempt, exemplified by Harnack, to shrug off the problem of miracle was thwarted by Bultmann in his denial that myth and Gospel could be separated.[22] In Bultmann's view the element of myth could not be eliminated from the Gospel. Rather, myth was to be *demythologized*: its meaning interpreted for twentieth century people. This approach to the problem of miracle, along with the view that a modern person "does not acknowledge miracles because they do not fit into [the rational order of the universe],"[23] meant that, in Bultmann's assessment of the life of Jesus, miracles received less attention than might have been expected in the light of the Gospel data. For example, in *Jesus and the Word*, Bultmann's 'life' of Jesus, he devotes only about five pages to 'miracles'. He says there, "Most of the wonder tales contained in the gospel are legendary, at least they have legendary embellishments."[24]

In the last decade there has been a renaissance of interest in research related to the historical Jesus. This is evidenced not only in the literature,[25] but also in the inauguration of the Historical Jesus Section of the Society of Biblical Literature in 1981 and the Jesus Seminar founded by Robert Funk in 1985.[26]

However, in contrast to the great interest in Jesus as a teacher, the low profile of the treatment of the miracle stories in the Gospels as well as in the treatment of the historical Jesus, has continued to the present day.[27]

---

22   R. Bultmann "NT and Mythology" (1941) in H.W. Bartsch (ed.) *Kerygma and Myth* (London: SPCK, 1957) 3.

23   R. Bultmann *Jesus Christ and Mythology* (New York: Charles Scribner's Sons, 1958) 37–8.

24   R. Bultmann *Jesus and the Word* (London and Glasgow: Collins/Fontana, 1958) 124.

25   E.g. I.W. Batdorf "Interpreting Jesus since Bultmann: Selected Paradigms and their Hermeneutic Matrix" in K.H. Richards (ed.) *SBLSP* (Chico: Scholars Press, 1984) 187–215; M.J. Borg *Conflict, Holiness and Politics in the Teachings of Jesus* (Lewiston, NY: Mellen, 1984); D. Oakman *Jesus and the Economic Questions of His Day* (Lewiston, NY: Mellen, 1986); M.J. Borg *Jesus, A New Vision: Spirit, Culture and the Life of Discipleship* (San Francisco: Harper & Row, 1987); D.J. Harrington "The Jewishness of Jesus: Facing Some Problems" *CBQ* 49 (1987) 1–13; R. Horsley *Jesus and the Spiral of Violence: Popular Jewish Resistance in Roman Palestine* (San Francisco: Harper & Row, 1987); Charlesworth *Jesus within Judaism* 9–29 and Appendix 5; M.J. Borg "A Renaissance in Jesus Studies" *TToday* 45 (1980) 280–92. Further, see the following bibliographies and bulletins: W.G. Kümmel "Jesusforschung seit 1965: Nachträge 1975–1980" *TR* 47 (1982) 136–65, 348–83; W.S. Kissinger *The Lives of Jesus: A History and Bibliography* (New York and London: Garland, 1985); W.G. Kümmel "Jesusforschung seit 1981, I. Forschungsgeschichte, Methodenfragen" *TR* 53 (1988) 229–49; L.J. White *Jesus the Christ* (Wilmington: Glazier, 1988); P. Hollenbach "The Historical Jesus Question in North America Today" *BTB* 19 (1989) 11–22; W.G. Kümmel "Jesusforschung seit 1981, II. Gesamtdarstellungen" *TR* 54 (1989) 1–53.

26   See Hollenbach *BTB* 19 (1989) 11–13 and the new journal *Forum* (Bonner, MT) 1 (1985).

27   P.W. Hollenbach "Recent Historical Jesus Studies and the Social Sciences" in K.H. Richards (ed.) *SBLSP* (Chico: Scholars Press, 1983) 66: "Most contemporary study of the historical Jesus focuses almost wholly on him as a teacher of ideas with the almost

Consonant with this has been the particular neglect, in scholarly study, of the exorcism stories in the Gospel traditions.

Richard H. Hiers, among others, has pointed out that in more recent times the exorcism stories and associated themes in the New Testament have been neglected in scholarly New Testament work. He mentions Schweitzer, Bultmann, Morton Enslin and Pannenberg as sharing this neglect.[28] Hans Conzelmann's famous *RGG* article,[29] which reviewed the then current position in the life of Jesus research, offers no treatment of the miracles or of the exorcism traditions associated with Jesus.

This neglect is also noticeable in the 'lives' of the so-called New Quest. For example, Bornkamm's emphasis is on the words of Jesus and his authoritative ministry. There is a token mention of Jesus' activities,[30] but the works — including miracles and exorcisms — play no signifcant role in Bornkamm's Jesus.[31] The same neglect of exorcism and associated themes can be noticed in, for example, the works of Gustaf Aulen, B.F. Meyer, John Marsh, as well as Leonard Goppelt's *Theology*.[32] In *Jesus and Judaism* E.P. Sanders has a very brief, though important, section on 'Miracles and Crowds' (chap. 5) in which he includes some discussion of exorcism. We shall interact with Sanders in the course of this study. Yet, in Sanders' concluding thumb-nail sketch of Jesus, only the miracles in general and not the exorcisms of Jesus in particular are treated.[33]

---

total omission of his actions and involvements in the material side of life." Cf. Hollenbach *BTB* 19 (1989) 12. On miracles of Jesus and the historical Jesus see K. Kertelge "Die Überlieferung der Wunder Jesu und die Frage nach dem historische Jesus" in K. Kertelge (ed.) *Rückfrage nach Jesus. Zur Methodik und Bedeutung der Frage nach dem historischen Jesus* (Freiburg–Vienna: Herder, 1974) 174–93.

28 R.H. Hiers "Satan, Demons, and the Kingdom of God" *SJT* 27 (1974) 35 and n. 2. Cf. Hollenbach *BTB* 19 (1989) 14.

29 H. Conzelmann *RGG* (3rd. ed.) III cols. 619–53, *Jesus* (Philadelphia: Fortress, 1973).

30 G. Bornkamm *Jesus of Nazareth* (London: SCM, 1960) chap. 8.

31 Cf. Hiers *SJT* 27 (1974) 35 n. 2. For some recent reviews on "historical–Jesus studies" see, e.g. Hollenbach in Richards (ed.) *SBLSP* (1983) 61–78; W.B. Tatum *In Quest of Jesus* (London: SCM, 1983) part two; Batdorf in Richards (ed.) *SBLSP* (1984) 187–215; Kissinger *The Lives of Jesus*.

32 See G. Aulen *Jesus in Contemporary Historical Research* (London: SPCK, 1976); Meyer *The Aims of Jesus*; J. Marsh *Jesus in His Lifetime* (London: Sidgwick and Jackson, 1981); L. Goppelt *Theology of the NT* 2 vols. (Grand Rapids: Eerdmans, 1981 and 1982). See also the following recent studies of Jesus which give little or no attention to the exorcism stories: A.E. Harvey *Jesus and the Constraints of History* (London: Duckworth, 1982); J. Riches *Jesus and the Transformation of Judaism* (New York: Seabury, 1982); J. Breech *The Silence of Jesus: The Authentic Voice of the Historical Man* (Philadelphia: Fortress, 1983); G.W. Buchanan *Jesus: The King and his Kingdom* (Macon: Mercer University Press, 1984); Horsley *Spiral of Violence*; H. Braun *Jesus – der Mann aus Nazareth und seine Zeit* (Gütersloh: Mohn, 1988); B.L. Mack *A Myth of Innocence* (Philadelphia: Fortress, 1988).

33 E.P. Sanders *Jesus and Judaism* (London: SCM, 1985) 319.

So, despite the apparent importance of Jesus' exorcistic activity in the Synoptic tradition, the present state of New Testament research on the life of Jesus appears still to be under the spell of Strauss when it comes to this aspect of the reports of Jesus' ministry. This is probably because the exorcism stories are seen to form part of the miracle tradition in the Gospels. Also, they carry special difficulties in that exorcism stories presuppose a belief in the existence of demons or evil spirits. For the vast majority of twentieth century people such a belief is no longer possible nor necessary in the face of the advance in our knowledge of our world.[34]

Over against this general neglect there have been a few specific studies that have taken up the theme of miracles, including exorcism, in the Gospels. One of the most formidable studies is that by H. van der Loos in which he has a large section on 'Healing of the Possessed'.[35] However, it is mainly a compendium of the views of others with little historical-critical analysis.

There are four other studies which, while contributing to this study, are fundamentally different in purpose from it. First, Gerd Theissen's *Miracle Stories of the Early Christian Tradition* (Edinburgh: T & T Clark, 1983) is an attempt to develop "the methods of classical form criticism by way of an analysis of one Synoptic literary form," namely the miracle story. Second, H.C. Kee sets out the two aims of his *Miracle in the Early Christian World* as follows. He wishes

". . . to offer a critique of what have been, for the past century and more, the prevailing historical methods in the study of religion; and to propose a historical method which more faithfully portrays and interprets religious phenomena in their

---

34 See Twelftree *Christ* chap. V, also P.L. Berger *The Heretical Imperative* (London: Collins, 1980) and E. Yamauchi "Sociology, Scripture and the Supernatural" *JETS* 27 (1984) 169–92. Cf. Schweitzer *Quest* 111, "Scientific theologians of the present day who desire to show their 'sensibility,' ask no more than that two or three little miracles may be left to them – in the stories of childhood, perhaps, or in the narratives of the resurrection. And these miracles are, moreover, so far scientific that they have at least no relation to those in the text, but are merely spiritless, miserable little toy–dogs of criticism, flea–bitten by rationalism, too insignificant to do historical science any harm, especially as their owners honestly pay the tax upon them by the way in which they speak, write, and are silent about Strauss."

35 H. van der Loos *The Miracles of Jesus* (Leiden: Brill, 1965) 339–414. Many of the other studies of the miracles have given only a low priority to the exorcism stories. E.g. A. Fridrichsen *The Problem of Miracle* (Minneapolis: Augsburg, 1972) 102ff.; A. Richardson *The Miracle Stories of the Gospels* (London: SCM, 1941) parts of chap. III; F. Mussner *The Miracles of Jesus* (Notre Dame: University of Notre Dame Press, 1968) 41ff.; R.H. Fuller *Interpreting the Miracles* (London: SCM, 1963) 29–37. For a survey of work on the miracles of Jesus, including detailed criticism of Fuller *Miracles* and G. Schille *Die urchristliche Wundertradition. Ein Beitrag zur Frage nach dem irdischen Jesus* (Stuttgart: Calwer, 1967) see K. Kertelge "Zur Interpretation der Wunder Jesu. Ein Literaturbericht" *BibLeb* 9(1968) 140–53.

original setting and which seeks to develop safeguards against imposing modern categories on ancient data."[36]

Third is *The Miracles of Jesus and the Theology of Miracles* by René Latourelle, which is dominated not by a historical but a theological concern: a hermeneutic of the signs of credibility of the Christian faith. His direct purpose, says Latourelle, "is to tackle the question of the signs that reveal and accredit Jesus as Son of the Father."[37]

Fourth, in a recent book, *Human Agents of Cosmic Power in Hellenistic Judaism and the Synoptic Tradition* (Sheffield: JSOT, 1990), Mary Mills calls into question writing off the tradition of Jesus' ability to command spiritual forces as the views of ignorant and undeveloped humanity. Her concern is not so much with a detailed historical investigation into the traditions of Jesus as an exorcist but with the background to Jesus' control of the cosmic forces and their significance for Mark and Luke.

The present book differs from these studies. It is not a comprehensive theological study of Jesus' miracles or his background but an examination of his reported ministry of exorcism from a historical perspective.

In *The Significance of the Synoptic Miracles* (London: SPCK, 1961), James Kallas has also recognized the central significance of the miracle stories in the Gospels and has, in turn, seen the importance of the exoricism stories in Jesus' cosmic struggle. Nevertheless, Kallas does not critically examine the exorcism stories nor does he clarify our knowledge of the historical Jesus the exorcist.[38]

Geza Vermes also acknowledges the importance of the exorcism stories in understanding the historical Jesus (*Jesus the Jew* [London: Collins, 1973]). Yet, his very brief treatment of this aspect of Jesus' ministry does not do justice to the Synoptic data. In chapter V I will examine Vermes' suggestion that Jesus was simply a Palestinian Ḥasid.

In *Hellenistic Magic and the Synoptic Tradition* (London: SCM, 1974), John Hull gives considerable attention to the exorcism stories in the Synoptic Gospels. He uses Hellenistic magical traditions in an attempt to throw new light on the Synoptic Evangelists' portrayal of Jesus, especially as a miracle-worker. However, I will question whether or not Hull's concentration on Hellenistic magical traditions to the virtual exclusion of the Jewish traditions gives an accurate view of the background against

---

36 H.C. Kee *Miracle in the Early Christian World* (New Haven and London: Yale University Press, 1983) 1.

37 R. Latourelle *The Miracles of Jesus* (New York: Paulist, 1988) 1.

38 J. Kallas *The Significance of the Synoptic Miracles* (London: SPCK, 1961) chaps. 5 and 6. The same is to be said of, e.g. R. Leivestad *Christ the Conqueror* (London: SPCK, 1954); J.M. Robinson *The Problem of History in Mark* (London: SCM, 1957).

which this aspect of the Gospel traditions is to be interpreted. I will also question the perspective of Fiebig who sets Jesus' miracles against an exclusively rabbinic milieu.[39] As this study proceeds, it will become apparent that matters of detail also need correction in Hull and Fiebig. In relation to the Hellenistic background to the exorcism stories I shall also be asking if Bultmann is correct in saying that folk stories or miracle stories and miracle motifs have come from the Hellenistic milieu into the Synoptic oral tradition.[40]

In contrast to these studies, what follows is an attempt to press behind the Jesus of the Evangelists to the Jesus of history. Also, this study differs from Hull's work in that I want to concentrate on Jesus and exorcism rather than the whole miracle tradition associated with Jesus. Further, Hull's work also raises the question of an appropriate first century Palestinian definition of magic. I shall investigate magic in relation to Jesus as an exorcist in chapter V.

Another study that pays more attention to Jesus and exorcism than most contemporary studies of Jesus is *Jesus the Magician* (London: Gollancz, 1978) by Morton Smith. Smith examines the Gospel material to try and show that Jesus' contemporaries considered him a magician. Because it so directly cuts across our study I will be discussing this book at some length in chapter V where I will be asking: Would those who saw Jesus perform an exorcism have considered him to be a magician?

In the light of the purpose of this study and what I have said so far I will need to do two things. In the first place, I will need to reconstruct the background against which Jesus' ministry of exorcism would have been viewed by his contemporaries. Secondly, I will need to make an attempt at recovering the historical Jesus the exorcist. This will involve trying to sketch a picture of this aspect of the historical Jesus, as well as attempting to see how Jesus understood himself in relation to his exorcisms. I will also attempt to see whether I can say how Jesus' audience assessed and understood him as an exorcist.

Therefore, in chapter II, I shall begin by addressing the question: What notions of exorcism and exorcists would probably have been available to Jesus and his audience in first century Palestine? In chapter III, the principal data in the Gospels on Jesus and exorcism will be examined in order to attempt to indentify material that can probably be traced back to

---

39 P. Fiebig *Jüdische Wundergeschichten des neutestamentlichen Zeitalters* (Tübingen: Mohr, 1911) 71ff.

40 R. Bultmann *History of the Synoptic Tradition* (Oxford: Blackwell, 1963) 231, cf. 38; cf. M. Dibelius *From Tradition to Gospel* (Cambridge and London: Clarke, 1971) chaps. V and VI.

the ministry of the historical Jesus. This analysis will form the basis for the next three chapters where I will be sketching out a picture of the historical Jesus the exorcist (chap. IV), seeing if I can say how his contemporaries saw him (chap. V) and, finally (chap. VI), attempting to discover how Jesus understood himself in relation to his exorcisms and what significance, if any, he gave to them.

Before I begin, we need to note two subjects which are closely allied to our own. First, demonology and demon-possession. In contrast to exorcism, these themes have been dealt with relatively well, both in the ancient world and in relation to Jesus and I have dealt more fully with them in *Christ Triumphant: Exorcism Then and Now* (London: Hodder and Stoughton, 1985).[41] Therefore, apart from occasional necessary references, I will not give my attention to demonology and demon-possession.[42] In any case, the New Testament in general, and the Gospel writers in particular, show little interest in demons for their own sake.

Another area that is related to, but outside the scope of this study is the question of exorcism in our own time. Before we can approach this question — not least because of the place of the canon in the construction of modern theology and practice — we have to deal thoroughly with the Jesus tradition in relation to our theme. That is the purpose of this book. Nevertheless, I readily concur with a sentence in Harnack's preface to the English edition of *What is Christianity?*: ". . . this I know: the theologians of every country only half discharge their duties if they think it enough to treat of the Gospel in the recondite language of learning and bury it in

---

41 To my knowledge the most important literature on demonology and demon-possession is: F.C. Conybeare "The Demonology of the NT" *JQR* 8 (1896) 576–608, 9 (1897) 59–114, 444–70, 518–603; M. Dibelius *Die Geisterwelt im Glauben des Paulus* (Göttingen: Vandenhoeck & Ruprecht, 1909); T.K. Oesterreich *Possession Demonological and Other* (London: Kegan Paul, Trench, Trubner, 1930); B. Noach *Satanas und Soteria* (København: Gads, 1948); E. Langton *Essentials of Demonology* (London: Epworth, 1949); S. Eitrem *Some Notes on the Demonology of the NT* (Osloae: Brøgger, 1950); O. Bücher *Dämonenfurcht und Dämonenabwehr* (Stuttgart: Kohlhammer, etc., 1970); W. Kirchschläger *Jesu exorzistisches Wirken aus der Sicht des Lukas: Ein Beitrag zur lukanischen Redaktion* (Klosterneuberg: Osterreichisches Katholisches Bibelwerk, 1981) 45–54; E. Ferguson *Demonology of the Early Christian World* (New York: Mellen, 1984); E. Yamauchi "Magic or Miracle? . . ." in D. Wenham and C. Blomberg (eds.) *Gospel Perspectives* 6 (Sheffield: JSOT, 1986) 115–20; W. Kirchschläger "Engel, Teufel, Dämonen. Eine biblische Skizze" *BLit* 54 (1981) 98–102; P.L. Day *An Adversary in Heaven* (Atlanta: Scholars Press, 1988). Cf. the bibliographies in J.Z. Smith "Towards Interpreting Demonic Powers in Hellenistic and Roman Antiquity" *ANRW* II.16.1 (1978) 425–39 and E. Schillebeeckx *Christ* (London: SCM, 1980) 499–500. Also see J.D.G. Dunn and G.H. Twelftree "Demon-Possession and Exorcism in the NT" *Churchman* 94 (1980) 215–19; W. Wink *The Powers: Naming the Powers* vol. 2 (Philadelphia: Fortress, 1986) 9–68.

42 Hence we shall not be dealing here with passages like Matt 12.43–5/Luke 11.24–6.

scholarly folios."[43] Therefore, in *Christ Triumphant*, I have attempted to take the next step. There, at a more popular level, I have sought to apply some of the results of this study to the question, Should exorcism be part of the ministry of the twentieth century Church?[44]

As I have just intimated, before we can better understand the historical Jesus the exorcist we need to understand particular aspects of the cultural setting in which Jesus' ministry was exercised and the range of options open to Jesus as exorcist. That is our task now.

---

43 Harnack *Christianity?* Preface.
44 See also G.H. Twelftree "The Place of Exorcism in Contemporary Ministry" *Anvil* 5 (1988) 133–50. Cf. J. Kremer "Besessenheit und Exorzismus. Aussagen der Bibel und heutige Problematik" *BLit* 48 (1975) 22–8; J.K. Howard "New Testament Exorcism and its Significance Today" *ExpTim* 96 (1985) 105–9.

II
Exorcism and Exorcists in First Century Palestine

§ 2 Materials

According to the programme just outlined our first task is to set out the background against which we shall examine and understand the historical Jesus, particularly with regard to his reported ministry of exorcism. However, before going any further we need to discuss: What is meant by the term, exorcism? and What material should be used to provide an appropriate background to understanding Jesus as an exorcist?

What is meant by the term exorcism? The view of the vast majority of Church leaders and theologians can probably be summed up in a sentence from the Church of Scotland's 'Report of the Working Party on Parapsychology' (May 1976): "We believe that it (exorcism) effects nothing that cannot be accomplished by expeditious use of medical skills, the latter including prayer, blessing and such healing procedures as the pastoral agent may have at his disposal" (paragraph 36).

However, regardless of whether or not this is correct, we cannot use our twentieth century presuppositions to determine the understanding of people in the first century AD. We require a definition of exorcism which would have been understood in a first century milieu and will, in turn, enable us to assemble appropriate material to provide a background to the stories and sayings associated with Jesus. Therefore, we furnish the following working definition.

> *Exorcism was a form of healing used when demons or evil spirits were thought to have entered a person and to be responsible for sickness and was the attempt to control and cast out or expel evil spiritual beings or demons from people.*[1]

Our definition omits reference to specific techniques for, as we shall see in this and the next chapter, the techniques varied from a few words of command to a full cultic ceremony.

Our definition also omits reference to exorcism of evil spirits from places. It is probable that the parable of the Strong Man (Matthew 12.29/ Luke 11.21—2, see §10 below) and the story of the return of the evil spirit with seven other evil spirits to a clean swept house (Matthew 12.43—5 /Luke 11.24—6) reflect ancient views on the possession of places, as well as

---

1 For other definitions of exorcism see, e.g. Eitrem *Notes* 20 and 57; C.H. Ratschow *RGG* (3rd. ed.) II cols. 832ff.; L Mendelsohn *IDB* II, 199; J.M. Hull *IDBSup* 312.

the possession of people. However, apart from these references, there is no interest in either the Jesus tradition or in the rest of the New Testament in the possession of places and so our definition and focus in this study will only be on exorcism in relation to people.[2]

Our other preliminary question is, What material should be used in an attempt to set Jesus the exorcist within his own milieu?[3] Two further questions are involved in making this decision.

First, should only Palestinian or Jewish material be used? We have noted (§1 above) that some recent works related to our theme have greatly concentrated on either the 'Hellenistic' or the 'Jewish' milieu of Jesus and earliest Christianity.[4] Such a rigid approach is now seen to rest on doubtful premises.[5] And, there is ample evidence to support the idea that Palestine, and not least Galilee, was far from insulated from the outside world.[6] For example, Senzo Nagakubo studied the funerary inscriptions at Beth She'arim (a post-biblical Jewish village about 15 kilometres west of Nazareth), and concluded that it is impossible to say that the Jews of the Diaspora were any more or less Hellenized than those from Palestine.[7]

---

2 Twelftree *Christ* 175–6.
3 Harrington *CBQ* 49 (1987) 13, "Our increased understanding of the diversity within Palestinian Judaism in Jesus' time makes it difficult to know precisely what kind of Jew Jesus was and against which background we should try to interpret him." More broadly see J.D. Crossan "Materials and Methods in Historical Jesus Research" *Forum* 4 (1988) 3–24.
4 On the history of the use of the labels "Hellenistic" and "Jewish" in NT scholarship see A.F.J. Klijn "The Study of Jewish Christianity" *NTS* 20(1973–4) 419–31; M. Hengel *Judaism and Hellenism* 2 vols. (London: SCM, 1974) I, 1ff.
5 See Hengel *Judiasm and Hellenism* I, 1ff.
6 See S. Safrai "Relations between the Diaspora and the Land of Israel" in S. Safrai and M. Stern (eds.) *The Jewish People in the First Century* 2 vols. (Assen: Van Gorcum and Philadelphia: Fortress, 1974 and 1976) I, 184–215; S. Freyne *Galilee from Alexander the Great to Hadrian* (Wilmington: Glazier and Notre Dame: University of Notre Dame Press, 1980) chap. 2 and E.M. Meyers and J.F. Strange *Archeology, the Rabbis and Early Christianity* (London: SCM, 1981) chap. 2, esp. p. 43.
7 In Meyers and Strange *Archeology* 102. Great trade routes passed through the area along which came exotic cultures and their *Weltanschauung* and artifacts (see G.A. Borrois "Trade and Commerce" *IDB* IV, 677–83), foreign powers had founded cities in Palestine (V. Tcherikover *Hellenistic Civilization and the Jews* [New York: Atheneum, 1977] chap. 2; E. Schürer *The History of the Jewish People in the Age of Jesus Christ* 3 vols. [Edinburgh: T & T Clark, 1973–1987] II, 85–183), the country was often administered by foreigners (note the Zeno Papyri, C.C. Edgar *Zeno Papyri* 5 vols. [Hildesheim and New York: Georg Olms, 1971], see also M. Smith *Palestinian Parties and Politics that Shaped the OT* [New York and London: Columbia University Press, 1971] 59–60, 67ff.), and Jews returning from the Diaspora also contributed to the Palestinians' contact with surrounding culture (J. Jeremias *Jerusalem in the Time of Jesus* [London: SCM, 1969] chap. 3; Smith *Parties* 71–2). Importantly for us, the literary activity of the period indicates the Palestinians were well aware of the "outside world" (Hengel *Judaism and Hellenism* I, chap. 2; M. Hengel *Jews, Greeks and Barbarians* [London: SCM, 1980] 115–6; J.N. Sevenster *Do You Know Greek?* [Leiden: Brill, 1968]).

Further, Hengel went so far as to say that: "From about the middle of the third century BC *all Judaism* must really be designated '*Hellenistic Judaism*' in the strict sense . . ."[8]

However, there were differences between diaspora Judaism and Palestinian Judaism which cannot be obliterated. Fergus Millar says no reader of inter-testamental Jewish literature, and of the Dead Sea Scrolls in particular

> "will be readily disposed to assent without severe qualifications to the proposition that Palestinian Judaism was as Hellenistic as that of the Diaspora . . . what we should emphasize is the uniqueness of the phenomenon of an original and varied non–Greek literary activity developing in a small area only a few miles from the Mediterranean coast."[9]

In addition, not only is there a distinction between Palestinian culture and the rest of the Hellenistic world but Galilean culture had its own distinctive characteristics (see §22 below). Indeed, as even Hengel is aware, the Maccabean Revolt and the attitudes and practices of the Qumran Essenes and the Pharisees are clear signs that not all Palestinian Jews so readily accepted imported cultures.

For the purposes of our study this means that the material we use to provide a background to Jesus' ministry of exorcism cannot be limited to that of Palestinian origin or even to Jewish material alone. Nevertheless, it also means that we need to pay particular attention to Palestinian material and traditions that may help us understand exorcism in first century Galilee.

The second problem, relating to the question of what material we should use, is that of dating. It is essential that each story, idea or body of tradition which is of potential value in contributing to our study can be reasonably established as part of the intellectual currency of first century Palestine. This applies to material that antedates and is contemporary with Jesus as well as later literature. For this material often contains themes and ideas that predate the literature in which they are now found. But, herein lies the problem of ascertaining which ideas belong to the time of publication of the literature and which ideas can be traced back to the times referred to in the literature.[10] This problem, though evident

---

8 Hengel *Judaism and Hellenism* I, 104 (his emphasis). Cf. M. Hengel *The 'Hellenization' of Judaea in the First Century after Christ* (London: SCM and Philadelphia: Trinity Press International, 1989); S. Liebermann *Greek in Jewish Palestine* (New York: Jewish Theological Seminary, 1942) and *Hellenism in Jewish Palestine* (New York: Jewish Theological Seminary, 1962). Cf. the criticism of Hengel by L.H. Feldman "How Much Hellenism in Jewish Palestine?" *HUCA* 57 (1986) 83–111.

9 F. Millar "The Background of the Maccabean Revolution: Reflections on Martin Hengel's 'Judaism and Hellenism' " *JJS* 29 (1978) 9.

10 Cf. G. Vermes *Jesus and the World of Judaism* (London: SCM, 1983) chap. 6 on the

elsewhere, is particularly apparent when dealing with exorcism stories *within* the New Testament that are *not* reported as part of Jesus' activity.[11]

In response to these problems of suitable material and dating I argued in chapter II of *Christ Triumphant* that *1 Enoch*, Tobit,[12] *Jubilees*,[13] the Qumran Scrolls,[14] Josephus,[15] Philo of Alexandria,[16] Pseudo-Philo's *Liber Antiquitatum Biblicarum (LAB)*,[17] the magical papyri,[18] Lucian of Samosata,[19] Apollonius of Tyana[20] and rabbinic literature[21] can, with varying

---

issues and problems involved in using later Jewish material to help reconstruct the world of the historical Jesus. See also Harrington *CBQ* 49 (1987) 13.

11   See the stories of the Jewish exorcists mentioned in the Beelzebul Controversy (Matt 12.27/Luke 11.9; the Strange Exorcist (Mark 9.38/Luke 9.49) and the sons of Sceva (Acts 19.13–20) all of which we will discuss below. We will need to be aware of the distinct possibility that these stories have been reshaped in the light of the Jesus stories and the interests of the early Church.

12   On texts, translations and literature see M.E. Mills *Human Agents* (Sheffield: JSOT, 1990) chap. 6 and notes.

13   On texts, translations and literature see Charlesworth *OTP* 2, 35–142.

14   On texts, translations and literature see B. Jongeling (et al.) (eds.) *Aramaic Texts from Qumran* I (Leiden: Brill, 1976) 77–81, 123–5; J.A. Fitzmyer *The Dead Sea Scrolls: Major Publications and Tools for Study* (Atlanta: Scholars Press, 1990); J.A. Fitzmyer and D.J. Harrington *A Manual of Palestinian Aramaic Texts* (Rome: Biblical Institute, 1978) 3; G. Vermes *The Dead Sea Scrolls: Qumran in Perspective* (London: SCM, 1982) 66–8.

15   On texts, translations and literature see H. St. J. Thackeray (et al.) (eds.) *Josephus* LCL, 10 vols. (Cambridge, MA: Harvard University Press and London: Heinemann, 1926–65); L.H. Feldman *Scholarship on Philo and Josephus, 1937-61* (New York: Yeshiva University, 1963); H. Schreckenberg *Bibligraphie zu Flavius Josephus* (Leiden: Brill, 1968); L.H. Feldman *Josephus, a Supplementary Bibliography* (New York: Garland, 1986).

16   On texts, translations and literature see R. Williamson *Jews in the Hellenistic World: Philo* (Cambridge: Cambridge University Press, 1989) 307–9.

17   On texts, translations and literature see Charlesworth *OTP* 2, 297–377; Cf. D.J. Harrington "A Decade of Research on Pseudo–Philo's Biblical Antiquities" *JSP* 2 (1988) 3–12.

18   On texts, translations and literature see H.D. Betz (ed.) *The Greek Magical Papyri in Translation* (Chicago and London: University of Chicago Press, 1986). The role of the magical papyri for our study is confirmed by similar magical material being discovered at Qumran. See 4QTherapeia (H.C. Kee *Medicine, Miracle and Magic in NT Times* (Cambridge: Cambridge University Press, 1986) Appendix. On the debate on the nature and value of this text see J.H. Charlesworth *The Discovery of a Dead Sea Scroll (4QTherapeia)* (Lubbock, TX: Texas Tech University Press, 1985); J. Naveh "A Medical Document or a Writing Exercise? The So–called 4Q Therapeia" *IEJ* 36 (1986) 52–5. Even if this document was a writing exercise, as Naveh argues, it may still be useful in illustrating first century Palestinian beliefs about healing.

19   On texts, translations and literature see H.D. Betz *Lukian von Samosata und das Neue Testament* (Berlin: Akademie–Verlag, 1961); A.M. Harmon (et al.) *Lucian* 8 vols. (London: Heinemann, New York: Macmillan and Putnam and Cambridge, MA: Harvard University Press, 1913–67).

20   On texts, translations and literature see §3 n. 4 below.

21   On texts, translations and literature see Schürer *History* II, 314–80. See also J. Neusner *A History of the Jews in Babylonia* (Leiden: Brill, 1968) III, 110–26, "Torah, Medicine and Magic"; M.J. Geller "Jesus' Theurgic Powers: Parallels in the Talmud and Incantation Bowls" *JJS* 28 (1977) 141–55.

degrees of ease and reliability, be used to provide material to reconstruct first century understandings of spirits, demons, possessions, magic, healing, healers, exorcism and exorcists.[22] These materials were able to provide a broad backdrop to Jesus' ministry of exorcism and the ministry of the early churches as represented in the New Testament. However, our inquiry here is more narrow; it focuses on the historical Jesus as an exorcist who lived and worked only in Palestine, principally in Galilee. Therefore, while drawing on some of the conclusions reached in *Christ Triumphant*, we need to be more particular in the sketching of an appropriate backdrop for Jesus the exorcist of Galilee in northern Palestine.

As well as these materials, three other bodies of material command our attention briefly before we can proceed. That is, the Prayer of Nabonidus, the Testament of Solomon and data from the New Testament Apocrypha are generally thought to be useful for an enterprise such as ours.

1. *The Prayer of Nabonidus* (4QPrNab or 4QsNab),[23] coming from the Qumran Scrolls, is certainly appropriate comparative material for the understanding of the historical Jesus. The entire fragment of 4QPrNab reads:

"The words of the prayer uttered by Nabunai king of Babylon, [the great] king, [when he was afflicted] with an evil ulcer in Teiman by decree of the [Most High God]

'I was afflicted [with an evil ulcer] for seven years . . . and an exorcist pardoned my sins. He was a Jew from among the [children of the exile of Judah, and he said], 'Recount this in writing to [glorify and exalt] the Name of [the Most High God'. And I wrote this]

'I was afflicted with an [evil] ulcer in Teiman [by decree of the Most High God]. For seven years [I] prayed to the gods of silver and gold, [bronze and iron], wood and stone and clay, because [I believe] that they were gods . . .' "[24]

In this Prayer Vermes[25] had translated גזר as 'exorcist' rather than 'diviner'.[26] While this might be irreproachable linguistically,[27] it is not the

---

22 For an appropriate cautionary note on using later material to reconstruct the milieu of Jesus see Kee *Miracle* 211, 288 and Kee *Medicine* 78.

23 On texts, translations and literature see Vermes *Perspective* 72–3; M.E. Stone (ed.) *Jewish Writings of the Second Temple Period* (Philadelphia: Fortress and Assen: Van Gorcum, 1984) 35–7; F.M. Cross "Fragments of the Prayer of Nabonidus" *IEJ* 34 (1984) 260–4.

24 From G. Vermes *The Dead Sea Scrolls in English* (Harmondsworth: Penguin, 1978) 229. Jongeling (et al.) *Aramaic Texts* I, 123 add a fragment to this text but it is so mutilated that its contents cannot readily be reconstructed or interpreted and so does not affect our discussion.

25 See also A. Dupont-Sommer *The Essene Writings from Qumran* (Oxford: Blackwell, 1961) 322 n. 3, 177ff.; A. Dupont-Sommer "Exorcismes et guérisons dans les écrits de Qumran" *VTSup* 7 (1959) 246–61; Fitzmyer and Harrington *Manual* 3.

26 See J.T. Milik " 'Prière de Nabonide' et Autres écrits d'un cycle de Daniel Fragments Araméens de Qumrân 4" *RB* 63(1956) esp. 409; Jongeling (et al.) *Aramaic Texts* I, 128; Cross *IEJ* 34 (1984) 263–4.

27 See Dupont-Sommer *VTSup* 7 (1960) 246–61.

most natural translation of the term. The noun, literally 'diviner', occurs in Daniel 2.27,[28] and it is probably this translation, rather than 'exorcist', that is to be preferred here.[29] Also, there is no suggestion in the Prayer that the writer had an exorcism in mind. There is no doubt that the גזר is involved in a healing, but there is no mention of an evil spirit or its departure, simply that the Jewish exile pardoned the king's sins. Thus, the Prayer of Nabonidus was probably not understood as an exorcism story and therefore will be excluded from consideration when we attempt to reconstruct a first century Palestinian understanding of exorcism and exorcists.

2. *The Testament of Solomon.*[30] This haggadic-type folk legend about Solomon's building of the Temple in Jerusalem being frustrated by the demon Ornias is headed:

"Testament of Solomon, Son of David, who subdued all the spirits of the air, of the earth, and under the earth; . . . (this tells) what their authorities are against men, and by what angels these demons are thwarted"[31] (Greek title; cf. 15.13–15).

In view of this description of the contents of the Testament of Solomon, it is hardly surprising that this pseudepigraphon is used to help construct the background to New Testament demonology and exorcism.[32] But, the key question is, How legitimate is this?

There are frequent and continuous thematic and vocabulary contacts with, and echoes of, the New Testament. The introductions and footnotes of Conybeare and Duling identify these contacts.[33]

The writer seems to be so familiar with, and reliant upon the New Testament that it is most probable that the Testament of Solomon was written by a Jewish Christian depending on various traditions including the New Testament.[34]

---

28 Jongeling (et al.) *Aramaic Texts* I, 128; A. Lacocque *The Book of Daniel* (London: SPCK, 1979) 42.

29 Yamauchi in Wenham and Blomberg (eds.) *Gospel Perspectives* 6, 121 and n.258.

30 On texts, translations and literature see Charlesworth *The Pseudepigrapha and Modern Research With a Supplement* (Chico: Scholars Press, 1981) 197–202; D. Duling "The Testament of Solomon: Retrospect and Prospect" *JSP* 2 (1988) 87–112 and "The Testament of Solomon" in *OTP* 1, 958–9; Schürer *History* III.1, 372–9. References and translation are from Duling in *OTP* 1.

31 Duling says in a note (e) here, "The Gk. verb *katargeo* is translated throughout *T. Sol.* as 'I thwart.' It can mean 'I make ineffective,' 'I make powerless,' or 'I abolish,' 'I wipe out,' 'I set aside.' " On the various recensions of the introduction (B [MSS P Q] is quoted here) see C.C. McCown *The Testament of Solomon* (Leipzig: Hinrichs, 1922) 99 and Duling in *OTP* 1, 960.

32 Cf. e.g. J.M. Hull *Hellenistic Magic and the Synoptic Tradition* (London: SCM, 1974) 67–9.

33 Conybeare *JQR* 11(1898) 5f.; Duling in *OTP* 1, 960–87.

34 Cf. McCown *Solomon* 108f.. Cf. Conybeare *JQR* 11 (1898) 7. On the evidence of one word M. Gaster concluded that the Testament was a translation of an Hebrew original

Like most hellenistic-Jewish 'magical' literature, the Testament has an international quality so that it is not possible to reach any certain conclusions about the Testament's place of origin.[35] Neverthelsss, although it is difficult to trace, the popular tradition about Solomon was growing in Palestine and it is generally agreed that much of this Testament reflects aspects of first century Judaism in Palestine.[36]

Dating the Testament is difficult because of the lack of explicit reference to historical events other than the story line and the prophecies. However, scholarly opinion has followed McCown who argued that the Testament of Solomon should be dated in the early third century AD, yet incorporating first century material.[37] Thus, the Testament of Solomon is an important witness primarily to exorcism in a part of the post-Apostolic Church with reflections of earlier times.[38]

In turn, we need to conclude that it is only with care that the Testament can be used to provide data for understanding exorcism in first century Palestine (see further §3 below). This applies to those parts of the Testament which are clearly reliant on the New Testament. However, because of its possible relatively late date, other elements will also need to be shown to be more ancient than the document itself.[39]

3. *The New Testament Apocrypha.*[40] There are a number of exorcism stories in this literature which are often cited as appropriate background material to the canonical Gospel exorcism stories.[41] But, the late date, the

---

(M. Gaster "The Sword of Moses" *JRAS* (1896) 155, 170, reprinted in *Studies and Texts in Folklore, Magic, Mediaeval Romance, Hebrew Apocrypha and Samaritan Archeology* 3 vols. (New York: KTAV, 1971) 1, 294, 309; cited by Duling in *OTP* 1, 939 n. 12 and Schürer *History* III.1, 374 n. 50). But, McCown pointed out that, although the author had used materials that had Semitic origins, the language of the Testament as it now stands – similar in language and style to the NT – was koine Greek (McCown *Solomon* 40, 43; followed by Duling in *OTP* 1, 939).

35 So also McCown *Solomon.*

36 Cf. Duling in *OTP* 1, 942 and 5. On traditions in Palestine associating Solomon and demons see 944 n. 62.

37 McCown *Solomon* 105-8; cf. A.–M. Denis *Introduction aux pseudépigraphes grecs d'Ancien Testament* (Leiden: Brill, 1970) 67; and Charlesworth *Pseudepigrapha and Modern Research* 198; J.H. Charlesworth *The OT Pseudepigrapha and the NT* (Cambridge: Cambridge University Press, 1985) 32 and 150 n. 13.

38 An exception to this dating is Preisendanz who suggested that the original Testament was from the first or second century AD. See K. Preisendanz "Salomo" *PWSup* 8 (1956) col. 689 and *Eos. Commentarii Societatis Philologae Polonorum* 48 (1956) 161-2.

39 Contrast the rather uncritical use of the *T. Sol.* by Mills *Human Agents* chap. 4.

40 Literature: Hennecke II, 167f., 259, 390, 425f.; D.R. MacDonald (ed.) *The Apocryphal Acts of Apostles* Semeia 38 (Decatur: Scholars Press, 1986) and J.H. Charlesworth *The NT Apocrypha and Pseudepigrapha: A Guide to Publications, with Excursuses on Apocalypses* (Metuchen, NJ: American Theological Library Association and Scarecrow, 1987).

41 E.g. Bultmann *History* 221ff.; Dibelius *Tradition* 89, 106. Note the crirticisms of Bultmann and Dibelius by Kee *Medicine* 73-9.

fantastic elements in the stories and the obvious dependence upon the New Testament cast grave doubt on the direct usefulness of this material for our purposes.

Thus, while ideas may not have been thought by the publishers of this material to reflect their own times, they may have considered that the 'fantastic' elements they included were appropriate to the apostolic age and so happily worked them into the material. That is, while the publishers may not have expected exorcists of their own time to behave as portrayed in the Apocryphal Acts, they may have felt (perhaps wrongly) that the Apostles would have so behaved.[42]

Nevertheless, a survey of the exorcism stories in the New Testament Apocrypha reveals a few points which confirm the continuation of some techniques of exorcism that had been used during, and even before, the New Testament period. This helps us to substantiate a number of parts of the picture of exorcism in the New Testament period which will emerge from our investigation of more relevant data. That is, first, there was the notion that the demons and the exorcist must, sometimes willingly, confront each other. Secondly, the exorcist, often only in general terms, was believed to need to address or abuse the demon. Thirdly, the personal force of the exorcist (verbally relying on some outside puissance or what we will call a power-authority) was thought to be sufficient to affect success without mechanical or physical aids. Fourthly, the conversation between demon and exorcist, and fifthly, the 'conversion' of the sufferer were also elements of the exorcisms.

In the toppling of a statue as 'proof' of the success of the exorcist in the *Acts of Peter* (2.4.11), we probably have a practise reflecting the period of the publication of the Acts rather than an earlier time. The use of prayer, and the exchange of old clothes for new ones in the *Acts of Andrew*, probably reflect notions involved in exorcism over a long period of time in antiquity. Apart from this, the writers seem to offer us no reliable material as background information to the stories of Jesus. What they seem to do, for the most part, is project back notions and speeches which they felt appropriate to the Apostles they sought to venerate.

Conclusion. From our brief discussions on material which might be an appropriate resource for sketching a backdrop for Jesus the exorcist we

---

42 Cf. E.R. Dodds *The Greeks and the Irrational* (Berkeley: University of California Press, 1971), ". . . If a particular supernatural phenomenon, alleged to occur spontaneously among civilized people in recent times, is *not* attested at any other time and place of which we have adequate knowledge, the presumption is thereby increased that it does not occur as alleged, unless clear reason can be shown why it remained so long unnoticed" (158).

have to exclude the *Prayer of Nabonidus*. Only with care can the Testament of Solomon be used, for it is a witness primarily to exorcism in the third century Church. On the New Testament Apocrypha we have just concluded that its greatest value is in confirming the continuation of some techniques of exorcism that were used in first century Palestine. Apart from these documents, we are able to use *1 Enoch*, Tobit, *Jubilees*, the Qumran Scrolls, Josephus, Philo of Alexandria, Pseudo-Philo's *Liber Antiquitatum Biblicarum*, the magical papyri, Lucian of Samosata, Apollonius of Tyana and the rabbinic literature (see further chap. II of my *Christ Triumphant*).

§ 3 Exorcism and Exorcists

We can now proceed to ask, what would have been believed about exorcism and exorcists in first century Palestine?

Surveying the available material reveals that a variety of exorcists and forms of exorcism would have been known and used in Palestine around the time of Jesus.[1] But, from the variety, a pattern or series of clear options or parameters for exorcism and exorcists emerges.

The data show that an exorcism was thought to be successful as a result of the interplay of three factors: (1) the *exorcist*, (2) a source of *power-authority* and (3) *the ritual or form of application* of that power-authority against the offending spiritual being. The range of kinds of exorcists and forms of exorcism arose out of the varying understanding of importance of these three factors. I will take soundings at the edges of these options to illustrate the two basic kinds of exorcism and exorcists that would have been familiar to Jesus' audience. In these soundings we will see, in particular, that the importance of the source of power-authority varied.

1. *Some exorcisms were thought to be successful because of the exorcist who performed them.* That is, the charismatic force of the exorcist was believed to be sufficiently powerful so that what he said or did was of little or no importance in his success; his mere presence and command were sufficient to send the demon scurrying. The literature bears witness to two kinds of such figures as exorcists: historical exorcists and legendary exorcists.

(a) Historical charismatic figures[2]

(i) I will begin with the *rabbinic literature* for it provides us with insights into the kinds of historical charismatic exorcists in first century Palestine. Tradition places Ḥanina ben Dosa, the devout miracle worker, in the pre-70 AD period. If not a Galilean, he was certainly active there (*j.*

---

1 Cf. K. Thraede "Exorzismus" *RAC* VII (1969) 44–117.
2 On the "charismatic type" see especially S. Freyne "The Charismatic" in G.W.E. Nickelsburg and J.J. Collins (eds.) *Ideal Figures in Ancient Judaism: Profiles and Paradigms* (Chico: Scholars Press, 1980) 233–58 and literature cited.

Ber. 1.9d; *j. Ma'aś. Š.* 5.56a; *b. Ber.* 34b; *Eccl. Rab.* 1). We have no exorcism story associated with him. However, there is the story of interest to us of Ḥanina out walking one evening when he was met by Agrath, the queen of the demons. She said: "Had they not made an announcement concerning you in heaven, 'Take heed of Ḥanina and his learning,' I would have put you in danger." Ḥanina replies, "If I am of account in heaven, I order you never to pass through settled regions" (*b. Pesaḥ.* 112b).[3] After pleading for leniency Agrath is granted freedom on Sabbath and Wednesday nights. In the context of our study it is to be noted that the basis of Ḥanina's preternatural power-authority to order the demon is not in what he says or does but in his standing in heaven, that is, his relationship with God.

(ii) Also from the Jewish material, mention can be made of a story about the fourth generation tannaitic rabbi Simeon ben Yose. A demon, Ben Temalion, is said to enter the Emperor's daughter. When Rabbi Simeon arrived he called out to the demon "Ben Temalion, get out! Ben Temalion, get out!" The story says that as he said this the demon left the girl (*b. Me'il.* 17b). The success of this exorcism is thought to depend entirely on the charismatic force of the exorcist.

(iii) *Apollonius of Tyana* was a historical charismatic figure, close in time and type to Jesus, who was also thought to be a successful exorcist because of his charismatic power. It is worth commenting on him in some detail because of the time in which he lived and because he exercised a peripatetic mission like Jesus, though the travels of Apollonius extended through many countries.

The fame of this wandering Neo-Pythagorean sage, who died c.AD 96—98 rests on a biography of him by Flavius Philostratus (c.AD 170—c.245). *The Life of Apollonius of Tyana* was written about AD 217 at the suggestion of the Empress Julia Domma, wife of Septimus Severus in whose circle of philosopher-friends Philostratus moved (*Life* 1.3).[4]

3　Contrast B.M. Bokser who says "Sources indicate that some first and second–century Jews, like their non–Jewish contemporaries, believed that individuals could achieve special abilities that made them closer to God." "Recent Developments in the Study of Judaism 70–200 C.E." *SecCent* 3 (1983) 30 (my emphasis). Cf. B.M. Bokser "Wonder-Working and the Rabbinic Tradition. The Case of Ḥanina ben Dosa" *JSJ* 16 (1985) 42–92, especially 92. Note Acts 3.2 where the apostles are said to disown the idea that they healed by their own power or piety (*eusebeia*).

4　On texts, translations and literature: G. Petzke *Die Traditionen über Apollonius von Tyana und das NT* (Leiden: Brill, 1970) 239ff. and E.L. Bowie "Apollonius of Tyana: Tradition and Reality" *ANRW* II.16.2 (1978) 1652–99; R.J. Penella *The Letters of Apollonius of Tyana: A Critical Text With Prolegomena, Translation and Commentary* (Leiden: Brill, 1979); M. Dzielska *Apollonius of Tyana in Legend and History* (Rome: L'erma, 1986). See also n. 5 below.

As this *Life* is about a century removed from its subject there is the same kind of problem as in the Gospels — the relationship between the 'historical' Apollonius and the stories about him.[5] How far then the *Life* represents views apparent in Philostratus' time and how far it represents earlier views is difficult to determine. In relation to our particular study on exorcism I will note a few points Philostratus makes which may give us some idea how he handled the exorcism stories of Apollonius.

In *Life* 7.39 Philostratus says that Apollonius tells Damis of the people he finds discredited and condemned by nature and law: those who ask vast sums of money for their feats and those who sell boxes containing bits of stones, which people wear to gain success. In *Life* 8.7 Philostratus has the sage dissociate himself from those who get men to believe that the unreal is real and to distrust the real as unreal and thereby seek to gain vast fortunes. Thus, as we would expect, Philostratus portrays Apollonius as a poor philosopher, neither misleading people, nor asking reward for his activities.

But, in at least two ways Philostratus opens up the way for portraying Apollonius as a miracle worker. First, in *Life* 1.2, Philostratus mentions the apparently well known story of how Anaxagorus at Olympia, in a time of severe drought, predicted rain, the fall of a house, and stones being discharged from heaven. Then, Philostratus complains that those who accept the works of Anaxagorus as the result of his wisdom rather than his

---

5   This is particularly evident in the interesting points of contact the *Life* has with the formation of the Gospels, in that Julia Domma placed in the hands of Philostratus some memoirs by Damis, a disciple of Apollonius (*Life* 1.3). Philostratus was also able to use a history of the career of Apollonius at Aegae by Maximus an admirer (*Life* 1.3), as well as many letters of Apollonius that were in circulation and various treatises of the sage which have not survived. Finally, Philostratus had been able to travel to cities where Apollonius was honoured – especially to Tyana where there was a temple specially dedicted to the cult of Apollonius. (F.C. Conybeare *Philostratus: The Life of Apollonius* LCL, 2 vols. [Cambridge MA: Harvard University Press and London: Heinemann, 1948] I, vi.) However, a difficulty for the historian seeking the historical Apollonius is that Damis, the favourite disciple, may only be an invention of the author. (The view of e.g. F. Täger *Charisma: Studien zur Geschichte des antiken Herrscherkultes* [Stuttgart: Kohlhammer, 1960] 203–5; E.R. Dodds *Pagan and Christian in an Age of Anxiety* [Cambridge: Cambridge University Press, 1965] 59; J. Ferguson *The Religions of the Roman Empire* [Ithaca: Cornell University Press, 1965] 180ff.; M. Hengel *The Charismatic Leader and His Followers* [Edinburgh: T & T Clark, 1981] 27; W. Speyer "Zum Bild des Apollonius von Tyana bei Heiden und Christen" *JAC* 17 [1974] 49 and more recently Kee *Miracle* 256.) For, as Kee points out, the material allegedly originating from Damis contains historical and geographical anachronisms. To mention one example; Damis is said to visit Ninevah and Babylon. However, they had been in ruins since the third and fourth centuries BC (*Miracle* 256–7). On the unreliability of Philostratus see the last chapter in W.R. Halliday *Folklore Studies: Ancient and Modern* (Ann Arbor: Gryphon Books, 1971) and further on the debate see Bowie *ANRW* II.16.2 (1978) 1653–71.

wizardry are the very same people who would wish to discredit Apollonius for the same kind of activities. Second, the method of Philostratus is to represent Apollonius as somewhat sceptical — so that his miracles will seem more probable.[6] Thus, Apollonius refuses to believe that trees are older than the earth (*Life* 6.37; cf. 3.45 and 5.13) and Philostratus voices his own doubt about Apollonius raising a dead girl (*Life* 4.45).

What implications do these factors have for Philostratus' handling of the individual exorcism stories? First, we can agree with Conybeare that "the evident aim of Philostratus is to rehabilitate the reputation of Apollonius, and defend him from the charge of having been a charlatan or wizard addicted to evil and magical practices."[7] It also probably means that Philostratus will at least heighten the simplicity of Apollonius' technique. Further, if Philostratus wants to align Apollonius with the great philosopher-miracle-workers of the past then the miracles of Apollonius may well be presented as spectacular. With these things in mind we turn to two stories of interest to us in Philostratus' *Life*.

There is a well-known exorcism story in the *Life* which concerns a young lad who interrupts Apollonius while he is speaking in Athens in the king's portico (4.20). Apollonius looked at the young lad and, as if possessing some preternatural insight into the boy's life, said: "It is not yourself that perpetrates this insult, but the demon, who drives you on without knowing it." At Apollonius' gaze the demon cried out, screamed and "swore that he would leave the young man alone and never take possession of any man again." But, Apollonius reprimanded him and ordered him to quit (ἀπαλλάττεσθαι) the youth and to give some definite proof that he had done so. The devil said that he would throw down a nearby statue. The statue moved gently and then fell down, the result of which was a hubbub and a clapping of hands with wonder by the crowd. The lad rubbed his eyes as if he had just woken. The lad is also described as "coming to himself" (ἀλλ' ἐπανῆλθεν ἐς τὴν ἑαυτοῦ), a phrase already shown to be associated with exorcism by Josephus (*Ant.* 8.49). The story ends with a report that the young lad fell in love with the austerities of the philosophers, put on their cloak, took off his old self, and modelled his life upon that of Apollonius (*Life* 4.20).

Can we suggest which parts of this story may have come from the reports of those who saw this incident take place, and which have been appended? The distress of the demoniac, and the simple technique of

---

6 R.M. Grant *Miracle and Natural Law in Graeco-Roman and Early Christian Thought* (Amsterdam: North-Holland, 1952) 74.

7 Conybeare *Philostratus* 1, viif. and xii. We can note also that Conybeare suggests that Damis may have, "Like the so-called *aretologi* of the age, set himself to embellish the life of his master, to exaggerate his wisdom and his supernatural powers" (xii).

Apollonius are elements of exorcism stories that are found associated with other exorcists of the period (see below). But, the episode of the toppling statue is much like that of the destruction of a statue in the apocryphal *Acts of Peter* 2.4.11 (see above). So, our only other parallel to this feature is also late and from material which is quite an unreliable indication of notions of exorcism in the time of Jesus (cf. above). Thus, we probably cannot use this element in the Apollonius story to help us understand exorcism in the first century. Nevertheless, this kind of proof may stem from the more simple kind of proof of disturbing a bowl of water which Josephus mentions (*Ant*. 8.49). The demon saying he would not take possession of anyone again reflects the view of Mark 9.25 and *Antiquities* 8.47, but does not seem dependent on them. Therefore, it probably represents a widely held view of what took place in an exorcism.

The end of the story — the young man's following the austerity of the philosopher — is so obviously in line with Philostratus' objective to portray Apollonius in this way (see above). We cannot be sure, therefore, that it does not come from Philostratus' own hand.

Another story in the *Life* deals with a mother who petitions Apollonius for her 16 year old son who for two years had been possessed by a devil (3.38). The mother says that the demons drive the boy into deserted places and that the boy has lost his former voice for another which is deep and hollow in tone. She says that she has wept and torn her cheeks as well as reprimanding her son — but to no avail, for the boy does not know her. The woman says that she is also frightened of the demon and, because of its threats to her of steep places, precipices and the death of her son, she has not brought the boy to Apollonius. Finally, Apollonius says: " 'Take courage, for he will not slay him when he has read this.' Upon this Apollonius took out a letter from his pocket and gave it to the woman . . ." The letter, it appears, was addressed to the demon and contained threats (ἀπειλή) of an alarming kind. There is no indication of the efficacy of the letter. All we are told is that on reading the letter the demon would not kill the boy.

This story is, again, clearly intended to enhance the reputation of Apollonius, for the incident occurs during a discussion between the sage and some Indian wise men. Also, the conclusion to the series of stories, of which this is one, reads: "With such lore as this then they surfeited themselves, and they were astonished at the many-sided wisdom of the company, and day after day they asked all sorts of questions, and were themselves asked many in turn" (3.40).

This story tells us of an exorcism at a distance by a wandering charismatic, of talking demons and of the use of a written incantation to rid the boy of the demon. Both of these things would have been widely and well known in the ancient world and, apart from its setting, Philostratus may not have altered this story much. These elements, as well as the distress of the demoniac and the simple technique of Apollonius, are probably those which would represent notions of exorcism in first century Palestine. Finally, although he is writing during and expressing views of the early third century, it is pertinent to note, in relation to our discussion of magic in §24 below, that according to his digression in *Life* 7.39, Philostratus considers none of the techniques or methods of Apollonius to be related to magic or wizardry, but to be miracles. For Philostratus, magic is a commercial enterprise involving the manipulation of forces to produce feats for a fee, while miracles are performed by someone who was divine (θεία) and superhuman (καὶ κρείττων ἀνθρώπου) (7.38).[8]

(iv) Another example of historical charismatic figures, who were in some cases exorcists, are the *wandering philosophers, healers and exorcists*. Some of the exorcists and healers of the period were probably attached to pagan temples (see n.32 below), but peripatetic healers were also common in the New Testament era.

First, writing as far back as the fourth century BC in *The Republic*, Plato tells of wandering priests.

> "Mendicant priests and soothsayers come to the rich man's door with a story of a power they possess by the gift of heaven to atone for any offence that he or his ancestors have committed with incantations and sacrifice, agreeably accompanied by feasting. If he wishes to injure an enemy, he can, at a trifling expense, do him a hurt with equal ease, whether he be an honest man or not, by means of certain invocations and spells which, as they profess, prevail upon the gods to do their bidding . . ." (364b–365a).[9]

There is no certainty here that these wandering divines included exorcism in their repertoire. Nevertheless, Plato's description establishes the antiquity of travelling priests who were thought to be able to exercise control over preternatural beings.

Secondly, Origen, quoting Celsus, who is probably to be assigned to the period AD 177—80[10] writes of

> " . . . sorcerers who profess to do wonderful miracles, and the accomplishments of those who are taught by the Egyptians, who for a few obols make known their sacred law in the middle of the market–place and drive daemons out of men and blow away diseases and invoke the souls of heroes . . ." (*CC* I.68).

---

8 Cf. Kee *Miracle* 260–1, 264.

9 Further and for other examples see W. Burkert "Craft Versus Sect: The Problem of Orphics and Pythagoreans" in B.F. Meyer and E.P. Sanders (eds.) *Jewish and Christian Self-Definition* III (Philadelphia: Fortress, 1982) 4–8.

10 See H. Chadwick *Origen: Contra Celsum* (Cambridge: Cambridge University Press, 1980) xxviii.

So, with Plato's comments in mind, we have evidence of an ancient and widespread tradition of wandering religious individuals who included the control of spiritual beings among their activities. The sorcerers of whom Origen writes were obviously exorcists. It is said that they "blow away diseases" so it is possible that blowing on the sufferer was part of their method of exorcism.

Thirdly, another example of historical charismatic figures who were wonder-workers are the Cynics.[11] There is evidence of a long tradition of wandering Cynic philosophers in Palestine, at least one of whom we know had a reputation for wonder-working. Antisthenes of Athens (c.455—c.360 BC), a devoted pupil of Socrates, was considered to be founder of the Cynics (Diodorus Siculus 15.76; Diogenes Laertius *Lives of Eminent Philosophers* 1.15, 19; 6.13, 103—5). Diogenes says that they did away with logic and physics and devoted their whole attention to ethics (*Lives* 6.103). Concentrating on virtue (ἀρετή) at the expense of an elaborate philosophical system (*Lives* 6.104—5), what distinguished them was their dress and habits. Diogenes said: "They also hold that we should live frugally, eating food for nourishment only and wearing a single garment. Wealth and fame and high birth they despise. Some at all events are vegetarians and drink cold water only and are content with any kind of shelter or tubs . . ." (Diogenes *Lives* 6.104).

It is coming to be recognized that Cynicism was an important aspect of the world of Jesus and the origins of Christianity.[12] Dio Chrysostom, whose travels as a Cynic philosopher included the eastern Mediterranean country areas and towns, said that Cynics were on every street corner in

---

11 On the Cynics and Cynicisms see D.R. Dudley *A History of Cynicism from Diogenes to the Sixth Century A.D.* (Hildesheim: Georg Olms, 1967); H.W. Attridge *First Century Cynicism in the Epistle of Heraclitus* (Missoula: Scholars Press, 1976); E. O'Neil *Teles (The Cynic Teacher)* (Missoula: Scholars Press, 1977); A.J. Malherbe *Moral Exhortation: A Greco-Roman Sourcebook* (Philadelphia: Westminster, 1986) and F.G. Downing *Jesus and the Threat of Freedom* (London: SCM, 1987). See also A.J. Malherbe "Self—Definition among Epicurians and Cynics" in Meyer and Sanders (eds.) *Self—Definition* III, 49—50; A.J. Malherbe " 'Gentle as a Nurse'. The Cynic Background to 1 Thess ii" *NovT* 12 (1970) 203—17.

12 See, e.g. F.G. Downing "Cynics and Christains" *NTS* 30 (1984) 584 and n. 2 who mentions Theissen, Malherbe and Attridge as seeing the relevance of the Cynic's points of contact with Christianity. Cf. F.G. Downing "The Social Contexts of Jesus the Teacher: Construction or Reconstruction" *NTS* 33 (1987) 439—51, who says that "Cynic ideas and the Cynic life—style (in its considerable varieties) could well have been available for Jesus to adopt and adapt and for his first followers to recognize and make sense of; and he might well not have been the first Jew from Galilee to attempt a marriage of these ideas with his own native Judaism" (449). F.G. Downing "Quite Like Q. A Genre for 'Q': The Lives of Cynic Philosophers" *Biblica* 69 (1988) 196—225. See also the cautionary note sounded by C.M. Tuckett "A Cynic Q?" *Biblica* 70 (1989) 349—76 and the critical evaluation of Theissen by R.A. Horsley *Sociology and the Jesus Movement* (New York: Crossroad, 1989) esp. 47, 116—9.

cities such as Alexandria (*Discourse* 32.2, 9—11). But, more importantly, there are striking parallels between Cynicism and the Christian traditions.[13] For example, Seneca's saying ". . . good does not spring from evil, any more than figs grow from olive trees" (EM LXXXVII.25) calls to mind the sayings in, for example, Matthew 7.16—17/Luke 6.43—5. Cynics debated the nature of blessedness; Epictetus saying that it lay in a right relation with deity (*Discourses* 3.20.15). And, the way the Gospels portray Jesus and John the Baptist as speaking sharply to and rebuking people can be paralleled in the Cynic's style of public speaking.

Of particular interest to us is the fact that Diogenes Laertius includes in his list of Cynics Menedemus, a third century BC pupil of Echecles from Asia Minor. He says Menedemus, "had attained such a degree of audacity in wonder-working (τεϱατεία) that he went about in the guise of a Fury ('Εϱινύς), saying that he had come from Hades to take cognizance of sins committed, and was going to return and report them to the powers down below" (*Lives* 6.103).[14] We have, then, in the Cynic tradition, an example of a wonder-working philosopher whose activities were said to include taking cognizance of people's sins (see also Peregrinus below).

In his *Lives of Eminent Philosophers*, Diogenes Laertius gives evidence of two Cynics living in the area around Galilee. Menippus of Gadara was by descent a Phoenician who lived in the first half of the first century BC.[15] Among his writings was one piece on Necromancy (*Lives* 6.101). In turn, Menippus influenced Meleager of Gadara (born in c.140 BC), who grew up and was educated at Tyre (Athenaeus *Deipnosophists* 4.157b; 11.502c).[16] He wrote poetry and popular philosophical essays. He had an intimate knowledge of Greek epigrams and made a collection of them in his *Garland*. He died in old age in c.70 BC.

From Lucian of Samosata's *The Passing of Peregrinus* we learn of Peregrinus, a Cynic from Mysia (c.AD 100—c.165). At one stage he was suspected of strangling his father. So Lucian says: ". . . when the affair had been noised abroad, he condemned himself to exile and roamed about going to one country after another. It was then that he learned the wondrous lore of the Christians, by associating with their priests and scribes in Palestine." He soon became a

---

13 For other examples see Downing *NTS* 30 (1984) 584—93. While Seneca was a Stoic, his creed was similar to the Cynics (Dudley *Cynicism* 120).

14 Further see *PW* 15.794—5.

15 Diogenes Laertius *Lives* 6.29, 95, 99—101; *PW* 15.888—93. H.D. Rankin *Sophists, Socratics and Cynics* (Beckenham, Kent: Croom Helm, 1983) 229—48.

16 Lucian of Samosata was also influenced by Menippus. See Lucian *Menippus or the Descent into Hades* and *Icaromenippus or the Sky-Man*. Cf. P. Whigham *The Poems of Meleager* (London: Anvil, 1975), bibliography.

"prophet, cult–leader, head of the synagogue, and everything else, all by himself. He interpreted and explained some of their books and even composed many, and they revered him as a god, made use of him as a lawgiver, and set him down as a protector, next after that other, to be sure, whom they still worship, the man who was crucified in Palestine because he introduced this new cult into the world" (*Peregrinus* 10–11).

Although imprisoned for this he was, with the aid of Christians, released to roam about living off the wealth of the Christians. However, he was later rejected by the Christians, according to Lucian, because he ate forbidden food (*Peregrinus* 16).

In Peregrinus, we have an example of a wandering Cynic living on the margins of Palestinian society just a few decades after the time of Jesus. His and other Cynics' charismatic life-styles were close to the Christian tradition, and probably, in turn, to that of Jesus in Palestine. This is seen in the ease with which Peregrinus moved in and out of Christianity.[17]

The Cynic tradition in Palestine carries through and beyond the time of Jesus. A number of sources, including Eusebius, testify to a Cynic, Oenomaus of Gadara who lived in the second century AD.[18] Although the sources do not say that the wandering Cynics were exorcists, that at least Menedemus was a wonder-worker means that exorcism might have been part of their activities. In any case, the Cynics are important to us as evidence of wandering historical figures involved in wonder-working in Palestine.

Fourthly, in the New Testament itself we have examples of some wandering priests who were exorcists; in the story of the *sons of Sceva* in Acts 19.13—19.[19]

It cannot be claimed that we have direct evidence of exorcism in first century Palestine, for the story is set in Ephesus. However, as the exorcists

---

17 G. Theissen "Wanderradikalismus" *ZTK* 7 (1973) 245–71 and "Itinerant Radicialism: The Tradition of Jesus Sayings from the Perspective of the Sociology of Literature" *Radical Religion* 2 (1975) 87. See also his *The First Followers of Jesus* (London: SCM, 1978) Part One.

18 *PW* 17.2249.

19 Literature: E. Haenchen *The Acts of the Apostles* (Oxford: Blackwell, 1971) 564 and 6 and R.E. Oster, Jr. *A Historical Commentary on the Missionary Success Stories in Acts 19.11-40* (Ph.D. Thesis, Princeton Theological Seminary, 1974) bibliography. É. Delebecque "La mésaventure des fils de Sévas selon ses deux versions (*Actes* 19, 13–20) *Revue des Sciences Philosophiques et Théologiques* 66 (1982) 225–232; W.A. Strange "The Sons of Sceva and the Text of Acts 19:14" *JTS* 38 (1987) 97–106; S.R. Garrett *The Demise of the Devil: Magic and the Demonic in Luke's Writings* (Minneapolis: Fortress, 1989). Luke's story of Paul's driving out a spirit of divination from a slave girl (Acts 16.16–18), though an entirely Christian exorcism, is a further example of a wandering exorcist being successful by using the name of a renowned exorcist as a power–authority. See further, E.R. Dodds "Supernormal Phenomena in Classical Antiquity" in his *The Ancient Concept of Progress and Other Essays in Greek Literature and Belief* (Oxford: Clarendon, 1973) 195–200; Twelftree *Christ* 93–4.

are said to be Jews (19.13), as well as peripatetic, they probably represent notions on exorcism in the wider world including Palestine. Our discussion of the Cynics (see above) further confirms this point.

Who were these exorcists in Acts? Our answer depends on the way we resolve the textual difficulties in 19.14. If we follow the Western text, as we most probably should, the verse begins ἐν οἷς καί — probably meaning "at this juncture" a second group of exorcists, the sons of Sceva, were involved in the story. The Western text also says that Sceva was a priest, not a high priest, and the number of his sons is not mentioned. It is not said that Sceva was a Jew.[20] This means that a travelling troupe of Gentile exorcists was plying its trade in Ephesus at the time.

On the other hand, in the majority text of Acts 19.14 only one group of exorcists is assumed to be involved in the story and Luke says they were sons of Sceva a chief priest. A possible difficulty here is that Josehpus, who records the names of the chief priests from the first century BC to the abolition of the office in AD 70, does not mention a Sceva as a high priest.[21] So, it has been suggested, for example, that Sceva may have been a renegade Jew holding the office of high priest in the imperial cult.[22] But, there is no evidence, or sufficient reason, that this was the case for Sceva. Further, this would be the only New Testament reference to a pagan priest. Also, Schürer thought that "high priests" were members of a few privileged families from which the high priests were taken.[23] However, Schürer mistranslates the Mishnah passages, and the passages from Josephus and Acts are unclear in relation to Schürer's thesis.[24] Further, these "high priests" in Acts 19 cannot even be retired ruling priests because they do not appear in Josephus' list.

Rather, in view of Josephus' calling "high priests" people who had never been ruling high priest, and a high priest living in Galilee before AD 70,[25] as well as the New Testament using ἀρχιερεύς in the plural 64 times (even though there was only one high priest at a time), the term would have meant not ruling priests but prominent or high ranking priests.[26] There is no difficulty in accepting the idea that Sceva was a high priest in

---

20 See further Strange *JTS* 38 (1987) 97–106.
21 Josephus *Ant.* 20.224–51. For a list of high priests see Jeremias *Jerusalem* 377–8 and Schürer *History* II, 229–32.
22 B.E. Taylor "Acts xix.14" *ExpTim* 57 (1945–6) 222.
23 E. Schürer *A History of the Jewish People in the Age of Jesus Christ* II, 1 (Edinburgh: T & T Clark, 1901) 204 on the basis of Josephus *War* 6.114; Acts 4.6; *m. Ketub.* 13.1–2; *m. Ohol.* 17.5.
24 Jeremias *Jerusalem* 175–7.
25 See Jeremias *Jerusalem* 176 and n. 87.
26 Cf. Jeremias *Jerusalem* 178; B.A. Mastin "Sceva the Chief Priest" *JTS* 27 (1976) 405–6.

this sense. In turn, this means that the "sons of Sceva" would also have been high priests.[27]

That there were *seven* sons has been seen to be a difficulty not least because of ἀμφότεροι ("both" or "two") in verse 16.[28] However, it is more difficult to explain how ἑπτά ("seven") came to be part of the text than to assume that it is original. Further, ἀμφότεροι can mean not only "both" but "all".[29]

It is possible that Sceva's seven "sons" were not brothers but members of a guild of exorcists.[30] This view can be supported by noting that in Matthew 12.27 (Luke 11.19) "the sons" would most naturally refer not to the physical sons of Jesus' critics but to members of a group. Also, in the Jerusalem Talmud (*j. Šeqal.* 4.48a) a group of high priests officiating at the ceremony of the Red Heifer are called "sons of the high priest".[31]

Regardless of whether Luke wrote of one or two groups of exorcists here they are described as peripatetic exorcists (19.13). This could be to distinguish them from the exorcists who would have been attached to the Ephesian pagan temple[32] of Artemis, a goddess associated with, among many other things, healing.[33]

These "door to door" exorcists had taken up the name of Jesus into their incantations. The form in which they used it is interesting: "I adjure you by Jesus whom Paul preaches." This form, "I adjure you by . . .," is very common in the magical papyri (e.g. PGM IV.3007—86). However, I can find no instance of this term in incantations prior to its use in the

---

27 On geneological descent as the requirement for membership of the priesthood see Schürer *History* II, 239–43.

28 See B.M. Metzger *A Textual Commentary on the Greek NT* (London and New York: United Bible Societies, 1975). On the textual difficulties in this pericope see F.J. Foakes Jackson and K. Lake (eds.) *The Beginnings of Christianity* 5 vols. (London: Macmillan, 1920–33) IV, 241; MM 28; F.F. Bruce *The Acts of the Apostles* (London: Tyndale, 1952) 359; and Metzger *Commentary* 470–2.

29 See BAGD and Haenchen *Acts* 564 n. 5.

30 F.J. Foakes Jackson *The Acts of the Apostles* (London: Hodder and Stoughton, 1931) 179 n. 1.

31 See further Jeremias *Jerusalem* 177 and n. 90.

32 See C.T. Newton *Essays on Art and Archeology* (London: Macmillan, 1880) 136–209, esp. 151 and 163; D.G. Hogarth *Excavations at Ephesus* (London: British Museum, 1908); W.J. Woodhouse *ERE* X, 302ff.; E.M. Yamauchi *The Archeology of NT Cities in Western Asia Minor* (Grand Rapids: Baker, 1980) 102–109; Homer *Iliad* 5.77; 16.234, 605; Pausanias ii.xii.2; Origen mentions exorcists at work in the market place, *CC* I.68; III.50.

33 Hogarth *Ephesus* 232, 238. Ephesus was renown for its "magical" tradition. Note particularly the "Ephesian Grammata"; see C.C. McCown "The Ephesian Grammata in Popular Belief" *Transactions and Proceedings of the American Philological Association* 54 (1923) 128–40. See further E.M. Yamauchi "Magic in the Biblical World" *TynBul* 34 (1983) 173 n. 14. Cf. R.E. Oster *Bibliography of Ancient Ephesus* (Metuchen: Scarecrow, 1987).

New Testament: Mark 5.7 and here in Acts. The term is, of course, commonly used in other contexts prior to the first century AD. For example, 1 Kings 22.16 (LXX) has ". . . the king said to him, 'How often shall I *adjure* you, that you speak to me truth in the name of the Lord?' " The general meaning of ὁρκίζω is clear; to adjure or implore someone, or more correctly to cause to swear by someone (cf. Joshua 6.26; §7 below). Its particular meaning in the context of an exorcist's incantation is made plain with reference to earlier incantations. In Babylonian exorcisms and incantations the climax of an exorcism was very often indicated by the line:

"By Heaven be thou exorcised!
By Earth be thou exorcised"

— by which "it is indicated that the powers of Heaven and earth shall lay the demon under a *tapu*,"[34] ban, or supernatural restriction. That this is the way in which ὁρκίζω should be approached is made all the more likely by the fact that in the magical papyri ὁρκίζω is also placed at the climax of the incantations, at the point where the supernatural is called upon to act on behalf of the exorcist.[35]

If these conjectures are correct then what the exorcists in Acts 19 were doing in using ὁρκίζω was not imploring[36] the demons to leave because of Jesus, but rather using Jesus' name to put a supernatural restriction on the demons.

It has been suggested that the formula — "I adjure you by the Jesus whom Paul preaches" — is of the type in which the exorcist recited the history of the invoked god in order to impress and terrify the demon.[37] This is an important question as it relates to the methods exorcists used in the New Testament period.

It can readily be documented that exorcists' incantations included, usually at the beginning, a brief history of the god under whose aegis they worked. For example, Origen says that Christians get their power to subdue demons "by the name of Jesus with the recital of the histories about him" (*CC* I.6).[38]

But, in Acts 19.13, the phrase "Jesus whom Paul preaches" (κηρύσσει —

---

34 R.C. Thompson *The Devils and Evil Spirits of Babylon* 2 vols. (London: Luzac, 1903 and 4) II, XLI.

35 See, e.g. H.I. Bell (et al.) "Magical Texts from a bilingual Papyrus in the British Museum" *Proceedings of the British Academy* 17 (1931) 254f. and 266.

36 Contra, e.g. D.E. Nineham *Mark* (Harmondsworth: Penguin, 1969) 153; E. Schweizer *The Good News According to Mark* (London: SPCK, 1971) 114; Loos *Miracles* 386.

37 W.L. Knox "Jewish Liturgical Exorcisms" *HTR* 31 (1938) 195; Oster *Acts* 54ff.

38 See also *CC* III.24; IV.34 and PGM IV.3034ff.; *LAB* 60 (both quoted below); *Apostolic Constitutions* VIII.7.

present tense) does not easily fit the form of a history. Notably, the travelling exorcists are not said to mention the past, powerful activities of their source or power-authority. Rather, what they are doing is identifying Jesus as he is presently known.

That we are justified in thinking that this is a formula of identification rather than glorification can be shown from other places where the name of Jesus is mentioned along with an identificatory phrase.[39] For example, Justin Martyr says: "So now we who believe on Jesus our Lord who was crucified under Pontius Pilate exorcise all the demons and evil spirits, and thus hold them subject to us" (*Dial.* 76.6; see also 30.3; 85.2; *Apology* 1.6; Irenaeus *Adversus Haereses* 2.32.4).

Although parts of these references appear credal or are, in parts, statements of belief, details appended to the name of Jesus are probably best understood as identificatory. In each case Pontius Pilate is the reference. This strengthens the present case, for early Christian writers assumed that statements they made about Jesus could be checked in the apocryphal *Acts of Pilate.*[40]

So, to conclude this point, it is probable that Acts 19.13 is to be understood in the light of these identificatory passages rather than, say, those like *LAB* 60 which have histories of the power-authority as part of the incantation. Thus, "I adjure you by the Jesus whom Paul preaches" was the exorcists' method of unmistakably identifying a (perhaps) previously obscure, now recently known powerful *name* as a power-authority for use in exorcism. And, this understanding is further confirmed by verse 15, the demons' successful defence: "But the evil spirit answered them, 'Jesus I know, and Paul I know; but who are you?' "[41]

In short, Acts 19.13—19 tells us that the exorcists were using incantations, unaided by cultic performances, to put a supernatural restriction on demons. Their source of power-authority was the name of a renowned exorcist whose aid was sought through a careful identificatory formula. And, finally, the demons made a successful self-defence. We turn, now, from looking at historical charismatic figures, to those which were literary creations.

---

39 Cf. R.H. Conolly " 'The Meaning of ἐπίκλησις': A Reply" *JTS* 25 (1924) esp. 346–51.

40 Cf. F. Scheidweiler in Hennecke I, 444f. See also Justin *Apology* 1.35; cf. 1.48; Eusebius *History of the Church* 1.9.3; Tacitus *Annals* 15.44. See also Acts 4.10 which seems to contain both elements of "identification" and "glorification".

41 Our case is not, I think, substantially altered if Luke is responsible for ὃν Παῦλος κηρύσσει as we would still be dealing with notions about exorcism in the first century. On demons attacking holy men see P. Brown "The Rise and Function of the Holy Man in Late Antiquity" *JRS* 61 (1971) 88.

(b) *Legendary or non 'historical' charismatic figures*

Some of the 'exorcists' known to us from the New Testament era are legendary figures in the literature. Thus, not only from the various historical figures but also from the legendary accretions around these figures we can learn something of views on exorcism and exorcists in first century Palestine. Solomon and David are the two most important figures in this category.[42]

(i) *Solomon*.[43] It is in the *Testament of Solomon* that the legend of Solomon is most developed, portraying him not so much as an exorcist, but as a controller of demons.

Keeping in mind what we concluded in §2 above about the difficulty of using the Testament of Solomon to provide background material against which to view the historical Jesus the exorcist, we can ask: What does the Testament of Solomon tell us about exorcism in Palestine in the first century through its treatment of Solomon?

First, in the Greek title, Solomon is described as the one who "subdued all the spirits of the air, of the earth, and under the earth." The origin of this power-authority is described early in the Testament, just after Solomon discovered that Ornias the demon had stolen wages and provisions of the men building the Temple.

"When I, Solomon, heard these things, I went into the Temple of God and, praising him day and night, begged with all my soul that the demon might be delivered into my hands and that I might have authority over him. Then it happened that while I was praying to the God of heaven and earth, there was granted me from the Lord Sabaoth through the archangel Michael a ring which had a seal engraved on precious stone. He said to me, 'Solomon, Son of David, take the gift which the Lord God, the highest Sabaoth, has sent to you; (with it) you shall imprison all the demons, both female and male, and with their help you shall build Jerusalem when you bear this seal of God·' " (1.5–7).

---

42 Other names, e.g. Moses, Daniel, Jonah, Abraham and Jacob, were all names taken up into incantations, See J. Gager *Moses in Greco-Roman Paganism* (Nashville: Abingdon, 1972); C. Bonner *Studies in Magical Amulets Chiefly Graeco-Egyptian* (Ann Arbor: University of Michigan Press, 1950) 171, 272f.; E.R. Goodenough *Jewish Symbols in the Greco-Roman Period* 13 vols. (New York: Pantheon Books for the Bollingen Foundation, 153–68) II, 223f., 226; C. Bonner "The Story of Jonah on a Magical Amulet" *HTR* 41 (1948) 31–7.

43 For literature on the legendary status of Solomon's magical wisdom in late antiquity see Schürer *History* III.1, 375–9. Compare, Nag Hammadi Codex IX.3.70 ". . . the one who built Jerusalem by means of the demons . . . " (J.M. Robinson [ed.] *Nag Hammadi Library in English* [San Francisco: Harper & Row, 1988] 458); S. Giversen "Solomon und die Dämonen" in M. Krause (ed.) *Essays on the Nag Hammadi Texts in Honour of Alexander Böhlig* (Leiden: Brill, 1972) 16–21; D.C. Duling "The Eleazar Miracle and Solomon's Magical Wisdom in Flavius Josephus's *Antiquitates Judaicae* 8.42–49" *HTR* 78 (1985) 1–25; Mills *Human Angents* chap. 4. J. Bowman "Solomon and Jesus" *Abr-Nahrain* 23 (1984–5) 1–13, depends heavily on late material for his sketch of the legendary Solomon, and therefore does not produce a reliable sketch against which to view Jesus and his dealing with the demons.

Like   Hanina   ben   Dosa's,   the   legendary   Solomon's   ability   to   control
demons   is   seen   to   be   a   gift   from   God,   or   at   least   arising   out   of   his
positive relationship with God.

Secondly, the Testament is carried forward by a series of conversations
between   Solomon   and   various   demons.   This   confirms   what   we   see   from
other   literature   that   it   was   believed   that   demons   and   exorcists   engaged   in
conversations   (see,   e.g.   Philostratus   *Life*   4.20;   *b. Pesah.*   112b),   and   the
conversations   in   the   Testament   of   Solomon   do   not   seem   to   be   modelled
directly on those in the New Testament.

The   Testament   of   Solomon   is,   as   we   noted   above   in   §2,   an   important
witness,   primarily   to   exorcism   in   a   part   of   the   post-Apostolic   Church.
Nevertheless,   it   does   yield   some   information   that   is   of   help   to   us   in   the
first   century   Palestine.   The   success   of   exorcism   was   thought   to   depend   on
the   exorcist   —   on   what   he   says   and   does.   We   see   from   the   Testament   that
conversations   between   demons   and   exorcists,   amulets,   the   key   importance
of   knowledge   of   the   demon's   name,   the   use   of   potions   and   appropriate
strong   names   in   the   exorcists'   incantations   persisted   through   the   New
Testament   era   into   the   period   represented   by   this   present   document.

Josephus   also   venerates   Solomon   as   a   skilled   exorcist.   In   the   story   of
Eleazar   the   Jewish   exorcist   freeing   a   man   possessed   by   demons,   it   is   said
that   a   ring   which   had   under   its   seal   one   of   the   roots   prescribed   by   Solomon   was   used.   As   the   man   smelled   it   the   demon   was   drawn   out   through
the   man's   nostrils.   When   the   man   fell   down   Eleazar   adjured   (ὁρκίζω)   the
demon   not   to   come   back,   speaking   Solomon's   name   and   reciting   incantations composed by Solomon (*Ant.* 8.46—9).

Two   views   of   exorcism   are   entwined   in   this   story.   At   one   level   there   is
the   story   and   the   notions   of   exorcism   revolving   around   the   exorcism
performed   by   Eleazar.   We   shall   deal   with   these   in   a   moment   when
discussing   exorcisms   which   were   successful   because   of   what   was   said   and
done   rather   than   who   performed   the   exorcism.   The   other   level   is   the   use
to which Josephus puts the story: his reflections on Eleazar's exorcism.

Josephus   says   that   this   event   revealed   the   understanding,   wisdom   and
"greatness   of   nature"   of   Solomon   and   how   God   favoured   (θεοφίλεια)   him
(*Ant.* 8.49). A little earlier Josephus says: "And God granted him knowledge
of   the   art   used   against   demons"   (8.45).   Thus,   Josephus   understood   Solomon
to   have   been   successful   as   an   exorcist   because   God   favoured   him   and   had
given   him   knowledge   of   how   to   control   evil   spirits.   In   other   words,
Josephus   believed   it   was   Solomon's   charismatic   force,   based   on   his
standing with God that enabled him to control demons (cf. *Ant.* 8.182, 190).[44]

---

44   Cf. Duling *HTR* 78 (1985) 13–14. See further and for literature S.V. McCasland "Portents
     in Josephus and in the Gospels" *JBL* 51 (1932) 323–35; G. Delling "Josephus und das

(ii) *David.* Josephus also venerated David as an exorcist. In *Antiquities* 6.166—9, Josephus retells the story in 1 Samuel 16 as an exorcism. He says Saul was beset by strange disorders and evil spirits which caused him suffocation and strangling which physicians could not heal (6.166). David is found and, by singing his songs and playing his harp, drives out (ἐξέβαλεν, 6.211) the evil spirits and demons so that Saul is restored to himself (καὶ ποιῶν ἑαυτοῦ γίνεσθαι τὸν Σαοῦλον, 6.168).

Josephus does not explicitly tell the reader why David is successful as an exorcist. However, by implication, David is described when Samuel says that God is looking for a king: "one who in full measure is distinguished by this (virtue of soul), one adorned with piety, justice, fortitude and obedience, qualities whereof beauty of soul consists" (6.160). Then, a little later, Samuel exhorts David to be righteous and obedient to God's commandments for in this way he would be a successful king (6.165).

Josephus says that the Deity (τὸ θεῖον) abandoned Saul and passed over to David, who, when the divine Spirit (θείου πνεύματος) entered (εἰς) him, began to prophesy (6.166). Then Saul is said to find the sight and presence of David a pleasure (6.169). And, the songs David sang to restore Saul are said to be his own (6.168). Probably, then, Josephus understood David's success as an exorcist to arise out of his character, obedience to God and having the divine spirit.

An incomplete Psalms Scroll (11QPsᵃ) confirms that the Qumran community also venerated David as being given the ability to control demons:

"David son of Jesse was wise and brilliant like the light of the sun; . . . YHWH gave him an intelligent and brilliant spirit, and he wrote 3,600 psalms and . . . 4 songs to make music on behalf of those stricken (by evil spirits) . . ." (27.2, 3, 4, 10).[45]

Wunderbare" *NovT* 2 (1958) 291–309; O. Betz "Das Problem des Wunders bei Flavius Josephus im Vergleich zum Wunder problem bei den Rabbinen und im Johannesevangelium" in O. Betz, K. Haacker and M. Hengel (eds.) *Josephus-Studien* (Göttingen: Vandenhoeck & Ruprecht, 1974) 23–44; O. Betz "Miracles in the Writings of Flavius Josephus" in L.H. Feldman and G. Hata (eds.) *Josephus, Judaism and Christianity* (Leiden: Brill, 1987) 212–35.

45 For the literature and texts see J.A. Sanders *Discoveries in the Judaean Desert of Jordan IV* (Oxford: Clarendon, 1965); M.H. Goshen–Gottstein "The Psalms Scroll (11QPsᵃ): A Problem of Canon and Text" *Textus* 5 (1966) 22–33; S.B. Gurewicz "Hebrew Apocryphal Psalms from Qumran" *ABR* 15 (1967) 13–20; J.A. Sanders *The Dead Sea Psalms Scrolls* (Ithaca: Cornell University Press, 1967); J.A. Sanders "The Qumran Psalms Scroll (11QPsᵃ) Reviewed" in M. Block and W.A. Smalley (eds.) *On Language, Culture, and Religion* (The Hague: Mouton, 1974) 79–99; F.M. Cross "David, Orpheus, and Psalm 151:3–4" *BASOR* 231 (1978) 69–71; P.W. Skehan "Qumran and Old Testament Criticism" in M. Delcor (ed.) *Qumran: sa piété, sa théologie et son milieu* (Gembloux: Duculot, 1978) 163–82; J. Starky "Le psaume 151 des Septante retrouvé à Qumrân" *Le Monde de la Bible* 6 (1979) 8–10; M. Smith "Psalm 151, David, Jesus, and Orpheus" *ZAW* 93 (1981) 247–53; J. Baumgarten "Concerning the Qumran Psalms Against Evil Spirits" *Tarbiz* 55 (1985–6) 442–6 (in Hebrew); G.H. Wilson "The Qumran Scrolls Reconsidered: Analysis of the Debate" *CBQ* 47 (1985) 624–42; S. Talmon "Extra-

In 11QPsAp[a] we probably have examples of these apocryphal songs by David for those stricken by Satan and his demons (cf. 11QPsAp[a] 1.2; 4.4).[46] Notably, David is said to invoke the tetragrammon in the incantations against Belial and the demons (1.4, 6; 4.4).

So far, we have been dealing with historical as well as legendary figures whose success as exorcists was thought to arise out of their personal charismatic force — out of who they were — rather than out of what they did. We will now take another sounding at the other extreme within the range of options for the first century exorcists.

2. *Some exorcisms were thought to be successful* not because of who performed them but *because of what was said or done* in the ritual or form of application of the power-authority against the offending spiritual being.

(a) The best example of this view of exorcism and exorcists is found in the *magical papyri* which represent the spoken element as well as the directions for the act of an exorcism.[47] Although there is a great variety and age of texts it is possible to detect and reconstruct a picture of exorcists and exorcism in the papyri.

First, the exorcist, following an incantation closely, began by invoking a power-authority. Thus, the incantation PGM V.99—171 begins, "I call you the headless one . . . hear me and drive away this spirit" (cf. P. Warren 25f.; P. Leiden I.348 [22]).

Secondly, descriptive histories to identify the god invoked were used to gain the support of an uncooperative power-authority. Or, sometimes, threats were used for the same purpose. For example, PGM V.247—304 says that if the god does not tell the enquirer what he wants his belly will be eaten by fish!

Thirdly, the exorcist either used the god to expel the demon with a command or called on the god to perform the expulsion (e.g. PGM IV.3033; V.122—33). To do this, it was important to know the name of the demon. In the Testament of Solomon 11.5, for example, Solomon asks a demon its name and he answers: "If I tell you his name, I place not only

---

Canonical Hebrew Psalms from Qumran – Psalm 151" in his *The World of Qumran from Within* (Jerusalem: Magnes and Leiden: Brill, 1989) 244–72.

46 For literature and texts see J.P.M. van der Ploeg "Le Psaume XCI dans une recension de Qumrân" *RB* 72 (1965) 210–17; J.P.M. van der Ploeg "Un petit rouleau de psaumes apocryphes (11QPsAp[a])" in G. Jeremias (et al.) (eds.) *Tradition und Glaube: Das Frühe Christentum in seiner Umwelt* (Göttingen: Vandenhoeck & Ruprecht, 1971) 128–39; É. Puech "*11QPsAp[a]*: Un rituel d'exorcismes. Essai de recontruction" *RevQ* 14 (1990) 377–408.

47 See further and for literature Twelftree *Christ* 39–43; H.D. Betz "The Formation of Authoritative Tradition in the Greek Magical Papyri" in Meyer and Sanders (ed.) *Self-Definition* III, 161–70; H.D. Betz "Introduction to the Greek Magical Papyri" in H.D. Betz (ed.) *The Greek Magical Papyri in Translation* xli–liii. Cf. 4QTherapeia.

myself in chains, but also the legion of demons under me." Although there is the probability of dependence on Mark 5.9, it does confirm and clarify the notion contained there that knowing a demon's name gives the exorcist power over the demon (see §7 below).

Solomon's response to the demon is probably also dependent on the New Testament. Nevertheless, again it does show the persistence of the idea of the use of a strong name. Solomon says: "I adjure you by the name of the God Most High: By what name are you and your demons thwarted?" (11.6). Many of the conversations between Solomon and the demons are designed to set out the "angels" or strong names that can be used to overpower the demons. We have already cited (see §2 above) the stated purpose of the Testament. Hence, in 16.6 for example, Solomon says to a demon: " 'Tell me by what angel you are thwarted.' He replied 'By Iameth' " (note 18.6—37).

Finally, in our reconstruction of exorcism and exorcists in the magical papyri, we see that having used a power-authority to expel the demon, the exorcist sought to protect the sufferer from the demon's return by sending the demons away or by the use of amulets (cf. PGM IV.1248).

In addition to this fourfold pattern of *invocation*, *identification* of the power-authority, *command* and *protection* we may note that, sometimes, physical aids or cultic performances were used. For example, a potion applied to a sufferer, or special sounds or words, like the vowel sounds or the word "Abrasax", are found described in the texts. In the Testament of Solomon 1.6 and 2.9 the wearing of a ring as an amulet is used to control demons (cf. 18.16, [23], 25, etc.). We can be confident of the antiquity of this technique, for the use of amulets was both ancient and widespread.[48] The dependence of the Testament of Solomon on Tobit in 5.7 and 5.9, 10 indicates the persistent belief, throughout the New Testament period, in the efficacy of the incense of fish liver and gall. Finally, we may note that in the magical papyri the exorcist was of little significance compared with what he said or did.

(b) In the story of Josephus we have already mentioned concerning Solomon, where Eleazar is the exorcist, we have another example of an exorcist being of little importance in the success of a cure (*Ant.* 8.46—9, see above). It is what he does and says, and particularly the use of Solomon's name, that is seen to effect the healing.

(c) In this same category of "anonymous" exorcists — successful because of the power-authority they used rather than their own charismatic force — are the *Jewish exorcists* of Matthew 12.27/Luke 11.19. This verse is one

---

48 See Twelftree *Christ* chap. 2 and see further on amulets Yamauchi *TynBul* 34 (1983) 195—9 and notes.

of Jesus' responses to the Pharisees (Luke does not specify the critics) accusing him of casting out demons by Beelzebul: ". . . If I by Beelzebul cast out demons, by whom do your sons cast them out?" If, as will be argued later (§10 below), this saying probably goes back to the historical Jesus it means that we probably have evidence here of exorcists in first century Palestine who were contemporaries of Jesus.

Exactly who "your sons" were has been a matter of debate. Some commentators think that the term is meant in the general sense of "your people".[49] But, others consider "your sons" to be more specific and refer to the disciples or pupils of the Pharisees.[50] However, the reference to the Pharisees in Matthew 12.24 is probably redactional (see §10 below) so that the more general sense of "your people" is to be preferred.

The methods of these Jewish exorcists are not specified beyond the hint that they exorcise *by* (ἐν/ב) someone or something. So, these Palestinian exorcists may have had a simple technique that centred around calling upon, or at least relying upon some power-authority, by which to cast out demons. The context of this verse limits the source of the power-authority to either God or Beelzebul (see §10 below). As the latter is excluded by the context, Jesus is said to assume that God is their source of power-authority. In any case, their technique could not have been entirely unlike that of Jesus for the comparison to have been made. Therefore, we have evidence of first century Jewish exorcists, probably similar to Jesus in their technique, perhaps using the name of God as a source of power-authority for their exorcisms.

(d) *The Strange Exorcist* is also successful because of what he says rather than because of who he is (Mark 9.38—9/Luke 9.49—50[51]). John is said to report to Jesus: "Teacher, we saw a man casting out demons in your name, and we forbade him, because he was not following us." Not a few scholars propose that this story of the so-called Strange Exorcist arose

---

49 E.g. P. Gaechter *Das Mätthaus Evangelium* (Innsbruck–Wien–München: Tyrolia, 1963) 401 and E. Klostermann *Matthäusevangelium* (Tübingen: Mohr, 1971) 109.

50 E.g. P. Bonnard *L'Evangile selon Saint Matthieu* (Paris: Delachaux et Niestle, 1970) 181; F.V. Filson *The Gospel According to Saint Matthew* (London: Black, 1971) 149f.; A.R.C. Leaney *The Gospel According to Saint Luke* (London: Black, 1971) 189; E. Schweizer *TDNT* VIII, 365 n. 215.

51 Literature: R. Pesch *Das Markusevangelium* 2 vols. (Freiburg: Herder, 1976 and 1977) II, 112; J. Schlosser "L'exorciste étranger (Mc, 9.38–39)" *RSR* 56 (1982) 229–39; H. Baltensweiler " 'Wer nicht uns (euch) ist, ist Für uns (euch)!' Bemerkungen zu Mk 9,40 und Lk 9,50" *TZ* 40 (1984) 130–6; E.A. Russell "A Plea for Tolerance (Mk 9.38–40)" *IBS* 8 (1986) 154–60. The story is not in Matthew probably because he cannot conceive of a true charismatic working outside Jesus' circle, see E. Schweizer *The Good News According to Matthew* (London: SPCK, 1976) 364. On textual difficulties in Mark 9.38 see J.M. Ross "Some Unnoticed Points in the Text of the NT" *NovT* 25 (1983) 63–4.

in the early Church.[52] This is an important matter for, if the story arose in the early Church, we may not have evidence of exorcists in Palestine but in another part of the ancient world; the milieu of the Christian(s) responsible for this element of the story.

The case for the early Church origin of this story centres on the vocabulary,[53] supported by the notion that the pericope is assembled around the catch-phrase "in my name".[54] While the pericope may indeed have coalesced around a catch-phrase, it still has to be shown where the source had its origin. The vocabulary which is of particular interest in 9.38 is "in your name" and "he did not follow us". And, the question is whether or not this vocabulary was more likely to have arisen in the post-resurrection community or whether it is quite plausible that such terms would have been used in the pre-Easter Palestinian situation.

(i) The phrase ἐν ὀνόματι,[55] denoting "that which characterizes or accompanies the act, the sphere (according to the Greek manner of thinking) in which it is performed"[56] — has not been found in secular Greek.[57] However, this does not mean that this notion of ἐν ὀνόματι was a Christian innovation. Consider two points. First, this study will show that, independently of the New Testament, the name of someone, usually a god, was efficacious in healing (cf. e.g. 11QPsApᵃ 4.4; Josephus Ant. 8.46f. and PGM IV.3019). Second, Deissmann came across the phrase, without ἐν but with the dative alone — ἔθυσαν τῷ τῆς πόλεως ὀνόματι.[58] In the light of this, Deissmann rightly rejects Cremer's hypothesis that "it was Christianity which first introduced the use of the phrase 'in the name of, etc.,' into occidental languages."[59]

Bultmann says "the use of ὄνομα Jesus in the exorcism of demons could hardly have antedated its use in the Church."[60] The force of this argument is difficult to see. For if Jesus was the successful exorcist the Gospels and later extra-canonical material would have the reader believe he was, it would not be at all surprising if Jesus' contemporaries quickly

---

52 E.g. Bultmann *History* 25 and E. Haenchen *Der Weg Jesu* (Berlin: Töpelmann, 1966) 327.

53 Bultmann *History* 25; V. Taylor *The Gospel According to St. Mark* (London: Macmillan, 1952) 407; H.C. Kee *Community of the New Age* (London: SCM, 1977) 43.

54 W. Grundmann *Das Evangelium nach Markus* (Berlin: Evangelische Verlagsanstalt, 1965) 194.

55 For its use in the NT see BAGD. On the subject of the use of names in magic see D.E. Aune "Magic in Early Christianity" *ANRW* II.23.2 (1980) 1546 n. 164.

56 H. Cremer *Biblio-Theological Lexicon of NT Greek* (Edinburgh: T & T Clark, 1895) 457.

57 BAGD and MM.

58 A. Deissmann *Bible Studies* (Edinburgh: T & T Clark, 1901) 197f. See other possible similar uses of the dative in MM.

59 Deissmann *Studies* 198 quoting Cremer *Lexicon*.

60 Bultmann *History* 25.

took up the use of his name in their exorcisms. We see an example of this in Acts 19.13 where the sons of Sceva are said to be very quick to pick up the name of Paul as a possible source of power-authority (see above). And, in Acts 8.18—19, Simon the sorcerer is said to be very quick in recognizing a potentially useful source of power-authority.

The most reasonable conclusion regarding "in your name" is that the ideas involved in the phrase were not at all new in the early Church but had a history outside it. Of course, the early Church adopted the phrase. Although it came to have special significance for the Church, the phrase would have been a quite natural way of expressing the thoughts of Mark 9.38.

(ii) The other phrase that could indicate a post-Easter origin of this story is "he did not *follow us*". A look at a concordance makes it very clear how "to follow" was used by the early Church. It is worth quoting Kittel at some length, for he summarizes well its use:

"... the connection of the word with the concrete processes of the history of Jesus is so strongly felt and retained that no noun ever came into use corresponding to the concept of discipleship. The NT simply has the active term, because what it was seeking to express is an action and not a concept. On this basis it is no accident that the word ἀκολουθεῖν is used only in the Gospels,[61] that there is agreement as to its uses in all four Gospels, and that they restrict the relationship signified by it to the historical Jesus. In the Epistles other expressions are used (σύν, ἐν) in which the emphasis falls on relationship to the exalted κύριος and His πνεῦμα."[62]

However, Wellhausen has noted that: "The subject of v. 38 is not following Jesus but association with the Apostles."[63] Bultmann takes this as testimony to a post-Easter origin of the saying.[64] But, with overwhelming evidence in favour of "to follow" being used in the sense of following the historical Jesus, in this instance at least, it seems most reasonable to equate "being one of the disciples" with following the earthly Jesus, rather than as being part of the post-Easter community.

(iii) What we have said so far is leading to the conclusion that the origin of this pericope is to be located in the ministry of the historical Jesus. Two further small points help strengthen this conclusion. First, verse 39, which is inseparable from verse 38, most probably goes back to the historical Jesus because of the Semitic manner of the expression.[65] Secondly, in his attempt to apply this pericope to his *post*-Easter situation,

---

61   G. Kittel (*TDNT* I) later on the same page (214) notes Rev. 14.4 as an exception to this. John 11.31 is the only instance in the Gospels of ἀκολουθεῖν being used without Jesus as its object.

62   Kittel *TDNT* I, 214.

63   Quoted by Bultmann *History* 25.

64   Bultmann *History* 25.

65   See further Schlosser *RSR* 56 (1982) 229–39. Note M. Black *An Aramaic Approach to the Gospels and Acts* (Oxford: Clarendon, 1967) 71, 169ff. who argues for an Aramaic

Luke altered Mark's "us" to "you" (Mark 9.40/Luke 9.50). Thus, Mark's form of Jesus' answer was not seen by Luke as directly applicable to the Church after Easter and so perhaps did not have its origin there.[66]

If this is right, then, this small pericope is further evidence of exorcism in first century Palestine by a contemporary of Jesus. But, all that the brief story tells us is that the exorcist, though not a follower of Jesus, was using the name of Jesus, who, as another (more powerful) exorcist, was a source of power-authority for healings.[67]

(e) The *rabbinic material* also provides evidence of the view that exorcism depended on what was said and done. For example, there is a story attributed to the first generation tannaitic rabbi, Johanan ben Zakkai. Zakkai says to a heathen:

> " 'Have you ever seen a man into whom that demon had entered?' He said, 'Yes.' 'What do they do to him?' He replied, 'They take roots, and make a smoke underneath the man, and sprinkle the water on him, and the demon flies away from him' " (*Num. Rab.* 19.8).

In this second section we have been examining examples of exorcisms which were thought to be successful not because of who performed them but because of what was said and done. In the first section we saw that some exorcisms were thought to be successful because of the exorcist who performed the cure. There is one more point to make before summarizing our findings.

3. In rewriting the story of Abraham in Genesis 12—15, the *Genesis Apocryphon* (1QapGen) from the Dead Sea Scrolls gives us an example of an exorcism which comes within the range of options for first century Palestinian exorcists and exorcisms. The exorcism is thought to be successful because of what is said as well as because of the personal force of the exorcist. In particular, column 20 recounts the courtiers' description of Sarah to Pharaoh, and his taking of Sarah as his wife. Abraham then prays for Sarah's protection. Then:

> ". . . during that night the Most High God sent a spirit to scourge him (Pharaoh), an evil spirit to all his household; and it scourged him and all his household. And he was unable to approach her, and although he was with her for two years he knew her not."[68]

---

source behind this small pericope. M. Reiser *Syntax und Stil des Markusevangeliums im Licht der hellenistischen Volksliteratur* (Tübingen: Mohr, 1984) who argues that Semitisms in Mark are restricted to vocabulary and phraseology rather than syntax and style which are largely free from them.

66 Further see Twelftree *Christ* 114–5.

67 On the incredible suggestion of J. Weiss that the Strange Exorcist is Paul see E. Best *Following Jesus* (Sheffield: JSOT, 1981) 84.

68 This, and other quotations from the Dead Sea Scrolls are from Vermes *English* (1987) 255. On texts, translations and literature see §2 n. 14 above.

Eventually, the illness reaches a point where Pharaoh finds it necessary to call all the sages and magicians who, as it turns out, are unable to help him. Finally, when Pharaoh hears that Sarah is not Abraham's sister, as he had been led to believe, but his wife, Abraham is summoned. He is told:

> " '. . . depart and go hence from all the land of Egypt! And now pray for me and my house that this evil spirit may be expelled from it.'
>
> So I prayed [for him] . . . and I laid my hands on his head; and the scourge departed from him and the evil [spirit] was expelled [from him], and he lived."

This is an important and interesting story because, apart from the much earlier story of David in 1 Samuel 16, this is the earliest extant story in our period which relates an individual's ability to control and expel demons in the way we find in the New Testament.

It is also to be noted that the source of power-authority is not to be found in cultic traditions, amulets, incantations, special words or ceremonies. The success of the exorcist is believed to lie in his own prayers.

But, along with the prayer went the laying on of hands. This is probably the first instance of healing through the laying on of hands found in Jewish material.[69]

With the Old Testament rite of blessing through the laying on of hands, the Qumran equation of blessing and health (1QS 4.6), and the notion of the hand being a symbol of power and blessing (Genesis 32.11; Exodus 19.13; Deuteronomy 28.12; 31.29; Judges 2.14; Psalm 90.17; Jeremiah 27.6f.), it is reasonable to see the use of the laying on of hands in healing as a development of Old Testament thinking, rather than as a practice originating from the East.[70]

In the *Genesis Apocryphon* the exorcism is described as follows: "and the evil spirit was expelled (גער)." Primarily on the basis of the use of גער in 1QM 14, where God "expels" Satan's spirits from the elect, H.C. Kee says that: "גער is a technical term for the commanding word, uttered by God or by his spokesman, by which evil powers are brought into sub-

---

69 D. Flusser "Healing Through the Laying-on of Hands in a Dead Sea Scroll" *IEJ* 7 (1957) 107f. See also J. Behm *Die Handauflegung im Urchristentum* (Leipzig: A. Deichert, 1911); K. Grayston "The Significance of the Word *Hand* in the NT" in A. Descamps et R.P.A. de Halleux (eds.) *Mélanges Bibliques en hommage au R.P. Béda Rigaux* (Gembloux: Duculot, 1970) 479–87; W. Heitmüller *Im Namen Jesu* (Göttingen: Vandenhoeck & Ruprecht, 1903); S. Morenz, H.-D. Wendland, W. Jannasch "Handauflegung" *RGG* III, 52–5.

70 The suggestion of Dupont-Sommer *VTSup* 7 (1959) 252 n. 1. L.W. King's collection of a group of Babylonian tablets bear the title "Prayers of the Lifting of the Hand". However, this relates not to the "laying on of hands" but is the universally regarded symbol of invocation of a deity. See L.W. King *Babylonian Magic and Sorcery* (London: Luzac, 1898) xi.

mission, and the way is thereby prepared for the establishment of God's righteous rule in the world."[71] But, Kee is probably introducing too much into the significance of גער in the exorcism story.

First, it is not clear in the *War Scroll* that the driving away of Satan's evil spirits *results* in God's being able to establish his righteous rule in the world. The passage from the *War Scroll* reads:

> "Blessed be the God of Israel
> > who keeps mercy towards His Covenant,
> and the appointed times of salvation
> > with the people He has delivered!
> . . .
> we are the remnant [of Thy people.]
> [Blessed be] Thy Name, O God of mercies,
> > who has kept the Covenant with our fathers.
> In all our generations Thou hast bestowed
> > Thy wonderful favours on the remnant [of Thy people]
> > under the dominion of Satan.
> During all the mysteries of his Malevolence
> > he has not made [us] stray from Thy Covenant;
> Thou hast driven his spirits [of destruction]
> > far from [us]" (1QM 14.5ff.).

This passage does not portray the triumph of the redemptive plan of God, culminating in the overcoming of Belial and the evil spirits.[72] Rather, the driving out or destruction of Satan is simply one of the things for which the people of God praise his name. How Belial is driven out is not made clear.

Secondly, what Kee's interpretation does is to equate exorcism with the defeat of Satan in the Qumran material. However, this is a connection that the Dead Sea Scrolls do not seem to have made. In this passage in the *Genesis Apocryphon* — apart from Kee's interpretation of גער — there is no hint of any wider significance of exorcism. And, in the passage from the *War Scroll*, which we have just quoted, there is no indication that it is through exorcism that God drives the spirits of destruction from the elect.

Thirdly, גער has a range of meanings[73] that extend beyond Kee's alternatives of "rebuke", and "to overcome the enemies of God". On the basis of 1QH 9.11 and Fragment 4, Kee rightly rejects the simple trans-lation "rebuke". But, in the last two pargraphs we have, in effect, also cast doubt on Kee's interpretation of גער as, "to overcome the enemies of God". As others, as well as Kee, have noted, גער is the Semitic equivalent

---

71 H.C. Kee "The Terminology of Mark's Exorcism Stories" *NTS* 14 (1967–8) 235; followed by Pesch *Markus*. I, 123; R.A. Guelich *Mark 1-8:26* (Dallas: Word, 1989) I, 57. See also J.M. Kennedy "The Root *G'R* in the Light of Semantic Analysis" *JBL* 106 (1987) 47–64.

72 As in Kee *NTS* 14 (1967–8) 234.

73 See n. 71 above.

of ἐπιτιμᾶν.[74] Thus, we need to take into account some sense of "to exorcise".[75]

If we take note of the lines previous to line 29 in the *Genesis Apocryphon* we come to a clearer understanding of exorcism at Qumran and how גער should be translated. The reading of 20.26 has been considerably debated. However, following Fitzmyer, it should probably be translated — "the plague will depart from you."[76] This is what is expected to happen in the exorcism. Thus, what is said to have happened in line 29 is probably that the evil spirit left or "departed". One of the possible translations of גער would be to "expel".[77] As this suits the element of "rebuke" in the word,[78] as well as describing the expulsion of the evil spirit, we suggest "rebuking in order to expel" as the best understanding of what the Qumran people thought was happening in exorcism.

Excluding the Prayer of Nabonidus (see §2 above), the Qumran material has one story from which we can draw conclusions about exorcism in first century Palestine. The healing is related to a particular individual and it is told to enhance the reputation of Abraham. As a result of the healing, the King is said to have given many gifts to Abraham (and Sarah) as well as an escort out of Eygpt. However, even though his identity may be less important for the success of the healing than the techniques used — and though Abraham is reported to have used no mechanical or physical aids in his exorcism — he does pray and lay his hands on the sufferer. The Qumran people understood exorcism as expelling an evil spirit. In view of our discussion on exorcism and eschatology in §29, we can note here that the scroll sees no significance in the exorcism outside the particular healing or relief of the sufferer.

4. In summary, in this section (§3), we have noted that (a) Apollonius of Tyana, Rabbi Simeon and Ḥanina ben Dosa attained legendary status in the literature about them, and stories of them contain legendary details. Nevertheless, they are historical figures in that they were probably exorcists in the New Testament period. They were thought to conduct *successful exorcisms because of who they were*. More particularly, Apollonius' success was seen to arise out of his charismatic presence which involved special ability to discern the presence of a demon. The rabbis we have mentioned were thought to be successful also because of their char-

---

74 Kee *NTS* 14 (1967–8) 232 and n. 2; cf. J.A. Fitzmyer *The Genesis Apocryphon of Qumran Cave* I (Rome: Biblical Institute, 1971) 138.

75 Fitzmyer *Genesis Apocryphon* 138.

76 Fitzmyer *Genesis Apocryphon* 138.

77 Cf. G.R. Driver "The Resurrection of Marine and Terrestrial Creatures" *JJS* 7 (1962) 15 and A. Caquot *TDOT* III, 50f.

78 A.A. Macintosh "A Consideration of Hebrew גער" *VT* 19 (1969) 475–9.

ismatic presence. This was seen to arise out of a special standing or relationship with God.[79]

(b) In the magical papyri, the Testament of Solomon, Josephus' story of Eleazar, the Jewish exorcists of Matthew 12.27/Luke 11.19, the Strange Exorcist, the sons of Sceva and rabbinic material, we have stories of exorcisms thought to be successful because of *what was said and done* by the exorcist.

(c) In the Qumran Scroll story of Abraham we have a story that shows that an exorcism could be thought to be successful because of the personal force of the healer as well as what he said or did.

(d) We can also see that, in Plato's mendicant priests and soothsayers, the sons of Sceva, the sorcerers known to Celsus, Apollonius of Tyana, and particularly the Cynics, the peripatetic life-style of a philosopher-wonder-worker would have been familiar to Jesus' audience and observers.

---

79 We can agree with J.Z. Smith "The Temple and the Magician" in J. Jervell and W.A. Meeks (eds.) *God's Christ and his People* (Oslo: Universitetsforlogets, 1977) 238, that the sociological niche that the holy man, in Brown's sense of the term (*The World of Late Antiquity* [London: Thames and Hudson, 1971] 102–3 and *JRS* 61 [1971] 80–101) would later fill, was already being occupied by entrepreneurial figures as early as the second century BC. Cf. G. Theissen *Miracle Stories of the Early Christian Tradition* (Edinburgh: T & T Clark, 1983) 266–7.

§ 4 Conclusions

In this chapter we have been asking and trying to answer the question —
What would have been believed about exorcism and exorcists in first
century Palestine?

In our analysis of the material, which was potentially of help in
answering this question, we have had virtually to exclude the Testament
of Solomon and the New Testament Apocrypha because of their manifest
dependence on the New Testament. All these pieces of literature have
been able to do for this study is confirm the continued existence of a
number of older notions and practices.

1. One of the impressions left by such books as Bultmann's *History of
the Synoptic Tradition* and Hull's *Hellenistic Magic in the Synoptic Tradition* is that there is a great deal of material upon which to draw parallels
to the Synoptic traditions about Jesus and exorcism.

Indeed, before each of these writers, Paul Fiebig had concluded in his
study on Jewish miracle stories in New Testament times that

"1. dies Material zeigt, dass auch in Palästina . . . in der Zeit Jesu . . . Wundergeschichten etwas Geläufiges waren, dass die Juden jener Gegenden und jener Zeit
Wunder von ihren Lehrern erzählten . . . dass also das Milieu, in dem Jesus lebte,
derartig war . . . 2. dass es falsch ist, die Wunder Jesu allein oder vorzugsweise aus
seiner Messianität abzuleiten. Gewiss erwarteten die Juden der Zeit Jesu vom Messias
Wunder, aber sie sagten sie doch auch von ihren Rabbinen aus, ohne dabei an
Messianisches zu denken."[1]

However, one of our conclusions from surveying the Jewish material
must be that there are extremely few stories of, or traditions about,
individual historical exorcists available to help provide a background to
examining the Jesus tradition in relation to exorcism.

From the Jewish material we could only find the brief reference to
rabbi Simeon giving the simple and direct command to a demon: "Ben
Temalion, get out! Ben Temalion, get out!" (*b. Me'il.* 17b).

From other material, only the stories of Apollonius are sufficiently
comparable to be of direct value to us. Thus, we can agree with A.E.
Harvey when he says: "If we take the period of four hundred years

---

1   Fiebig *Jüdische Wundergeschichten* 72.

stretching from two hundred years before to two hundred years after the birth of Christ, the number of miracles recorded which are remotely comparable with those of Jesus is astonishingly small."[2] He goes on to say that it is then significant that later Christian fathers compared and contrasted Jesus with almost legendary figures such as Pythagoras or Empedocles.[3]

However, we have seen that an understanding of exorcism and exorcists in the first century was not limited to what we can discover from stories roughly parallel to the Jesus stories.

2. One of the things Wesley Carr does in *Angels and Principalities* is set out the background to Paul's thought on αἱ ἀρχαὶ καὶ αἱ ἐξουσίαι ("principalities and powers"). He examines Daniel, *1 Enoch* and *Jubilees* and concludes that "the concept of mighty forces that are hostile to man from which he sought relief was not prevalent in the thought world of first century AD."[4] But, in the light of our study so far, can this conclusion be correct?

If we include in our survey of material Tobit, the Qumran Scrolls,[5] Josephus, Philo and Pseudo-Philo's *LAB* it is clear that this conclusion needs some correction. For example, in the Qumran community it was believed that everyone was ruled by one of two spirits. At one point the *Community Rule* or Manual of Discipline scroll says: "Those born of truth spring from a fountain of light, but those born of falsehood spring from a source of darkenss" (1QS 3.9). And, in the eschatological battle, it was expected that the evil spiritual beings would be destroyed.

---

2   Harvey *Constraints* 103. See M. Smith (*Tannaitic Parallels to the Gospels* [Philadelphia: SBL, 1968] 81) who says, having cited Fiebig (see n. 1 above) ". . . as a matter of fact Tannaitic literature contains almost no stories of miracles performed by Tannaim." W.S. Green ("Palestinian Holy Men: Charismatic Leadership and Rabbinic Tradition" *ANRW* II.19.2 [1979] 624) who also quotes Smith, says "Neusner's comprehensive studies of the Pharisees before 70 and his biographical studies of Yohanan b. Zakkai and Eliezer b. Hyrcanus reveal a virtual total absence of such stories . . ." (See J. Neusner *The Rabbinic Traditions about the Pharisees before 70* 3 vols. [Leiden: Brill, 1971] and *Development of a Legend* [Leiden: Brill, 1973]). Green goes on to say: "Indeed, with the sole exception of the Honi–tradition, no miracle stories about Tannaim appear in Mishnah, and of the few such stories which do exist, most occur first in the *gemera*–stratum of the two Talmuds" (625). See also A. Vögtle "The Miracles of Jesus against their Contemporary Background" in H.J. Schultz (ed.) *Jesus in His Time* (Philadelphia: Fortress, 1971) 96–105; L. Sabourin "Hellenistic and Rabbinic 'Miracles' " *BTB* 2 (1972) 305; Kee *Medicine* 80 and *Miracle* 70.
3   Harvey *Constraints* 103.
4   Wesley Carr *Angels and Principalities* (Cambridge: Cambridge University Press, 1981) 43. On page 174 Carr says "the pagan world to which Paul went lacked any sense of mighty, hostile forces that stood over against man as he struggled for survival."
5   Cf. L. Houlden's review of Carr *Angels* in *JSNT* 20 (1984) 120–1.

"[Be brave and] strong for the battle of God! For this day is [the time of the battle of] God against all the host of Satan, [and of the judgement of] all flesh. The God of Israel lifts His hand and His marvellous [might] against all the spirits of wickedness" (1QM 15.end).

Philo can serve us as another example of the first century belief in preternatural forces hostile to man. In a discussion on Genesis 6.1—4, Philo deals with souls, demons and angels. How prevalent they were thought to be is shown when he argues that:

". . . the universe must needs be filled through and through with life . . . The earth has the creatures of the land, the sea and the rivers those that live in water . . .
    And so the other element, the air, must needs be filled with living beings, though indeed they are invisible to us . . ." (*De Gigantibus* 7–8).

That people were afraid of the air being filled with unseen beings is shown by Philo saying that: " . . . if you realize that souls and demons and angels are but different names for the same one underlying object, you will cast from you that most grievous burden, the fear of demons or superstition" (*De Gigantibus* 16).

Clearly, Carr's conclusion is not correct for all writers of the milieu of Paul and the Gospel traditions. Rather, it was widely believed that the world was infested with beings hostile to man, against which protection or relief was sought.[6]

3. Another impression left by the material surveyed in this chapter is that there was a variety of forms of exorcism that would have been known and used in Palestine in Jesus' time. But, as we have tried to show, there may be a pattern which can be deduced in all this evidence.

Some of the texts we surveyed showed that there were, on the one hand, exorcists who were successful because of the particular things they said and/or did. The best example of this is Eleazar (*Ant.* 8.46—9), but we see it represented in the rabbinic material (*Pesiq. R.* 40b) and especially in the magical papyri. Although these examples are all relatively late, the very earliest material — Babylonian and Egyptian — exhibit this same notion of exorcism.[7] That such exorcists were common in our period and

---

6 Cf. D.S. Russell *The Method and Message of Jewish Apocalyptic* (London: SCM, 1964) chap. IX; Twelftree *Christ* chap. II and D.S. Russell *From Early Judaism to Early Church* (London: SCM, 1986) chap. VII. On others critical of Carr see e.g. P.W. Barrett, review *JRH* 12 (1982) 206–7; Wink *Naming the Powers*; Wink's review of Carr *Angels* in *USQR* 39 (1984) 146–50; P.T. O'Brien "Principalities and Powers: Opponents of the Church" in D.A. Carson (ed.) *Biblical Interpretation and the Church: Text and Context* (Exeter: Paternoster, 1984) 110–50; R.A. Wild "The Warrior and the Prisoner: Some Reflections on Ephesians 6.10–20" *CBQ* 46 (1984) 284–5; C.E. Arnold "The 'Exorcism' of Ephesians 6.12 in Recent Research: A Critique of Wesley Carr's View of the Role of Evil Powers in First–Century AD Belief" *JSNT* 30 (1987) 71–87.

7 See Twelftree *Christ* 21–2; Yamauchi in Wenham and Blomberg (eds.) *Gospel Perspectives* 6, 99–103.

that they were often charged with being magicians or sorcerers is indicated by the great number of times sorcery is referred to in Jewish traditions.

Of paramount importance in these exorcisms was the exorcist's knowledge of both the demon he sought to combat and the god or power-authority on whose aid he could rely. In order to impress the demon or the god, the exorcist used prescribed descriptions and histories of the demon and god. Sometimes the exorcist went so far as to identify himself with some other powerful individual — for example Hermes or Moses or even the invoked god as in the magical papyri. Most of these kinds of exorcism involved using the god or power-authority to put a "supernatural restriction" on the demon. In addition, the speaking of special words and sounds was employed so that the demon could be persuaded to leave the person. Sometimes the demon would speak in its defence and plead for leniency (*Jubilees* 10.8; Acts 19.15 and *b. Pesaḥ.* 112b). Usually, the words of exorcists were accompanied by some kind of activity, like burning incense or boiling a special brew. The activities prescribed by some texts were designed not merely to represent what was expected to happen in the exorcism, but to enable the exorcist to transfer the demon from the person to, say, a bowl of water which was then poured away (see further §§7 and 17.7 below). Where the exorcist depended on diagrams or particular words an amulet was sometimes employed.

On the other hand, there seem to have been exorcisms that were successful not because of what was said and/or done but because of who performed them. The earliest evidence of this kind of exorcism is perhaps in 1 Samuel 16 and then in *Jubilees* 10. But, it is in the *Genesis Apocryphon* that we have the earliest extant story in the New Testament period that relates the ability to control and expel demons not to particular words or prayers but to a particular individual's personal force.

At least at the level of story, Tiede[8] has argued for the glorification, in specifically Greek stories, of the combination of the ability to work miracles and wisdom or holiness. But, in *Jubilees* 10 the righteous man, Noah is glorified by relating his ability to control demons (10.5, 17). And, in the *Genesis Apocryphon*, the wise and godly Abraham is credited with healing the king (cols. 19 and 20). Thus, we have the combination of healer and holy individual acclaimed in stories known in Palestine.

The individual who is most often represented in these stories as combining the attributes of wisdom and miracle-working is Solomon. The *locus classicus* of the tradition that associated the wise Solomon with

---

8 D.L. Tiede *The Charismatic Figure as Miracle Worker* (Missoula: Scholars Press, 1972).

miracle-working and especially with exorcism, is *Antiquities* 8.46—9 (cf. the later *T. Sol.*). But, in Palestine in *LAB* 60 and in the Qumran community, as well as in the magical papyri, the wise Solomon was directly linked with exorcism and the ability to control demons.[9]

The shift in the stories from focusing on the technique, as in Tobit, to the individual charismatic healer, as in the Solomon of the Testament of Solomon and Josephus is, most importantly, not confined to these mythical or literary figures. A little later in the first century AD it is reflected in "historical" individuals, as represented by Lucian's Palestinian exorcist, Apollonius, as well as, notably for Palestine, some of the Cynics and rabbis.

The methods of these individual healers in literature and history seem to vary from the mere ". . . Get out!" used by a rabbi, to simple prayer and laying on of hands in the *Genesis Apocryphon*, to the more involved prayers and incantations of *Jubilees* 10 and *LAB* 60. And, finally the success, in the literature (Solomon) or in actual terms (Jesus), of these particular individual healers is reflected in their names being used in "incantational" exorcisms (cf. *Ant*. 8.46—9; Mark 9.38/Luke 9.49 and Acts (16.17; 19.13).

Our next task is to examine the Gospels in the light of this background in order to recover data that will help provide material to sketch a picture of the historical Jesus the exorcist.

---

9   See Twelftree *Christ* chap. II.

III
Jesus the Exorcist: The New Testament Data

§ 5 Gospel Research

So far we have been able to build a picture of one small aspect of the world into which Jesus came. This will provide a basis and background for our investigation of the Gospel data. In this and the next chapter we will examine the Gospel material relating to Jesus and exorcism so that, as far as possible, we can ascertain which elements of this Gospel material might, with reasonable confidence, be traced back to the reports of those who witnessed Jesus as an exorcist.

The questions of historicity and of redaction of Gospel traditions are interrelated. However, for the sake of convenience and clarity, we will deal with them as separately as practicable. Of course, when discussing Christian contributions to a passage we will often find ourselves needing to stray into the problem of historicity — and vice versa.

In this chapter we will examine the Gospel data with a view to identifying Christian modifications to the reports of Jesus' activities as an exorcist. Setting aside this redaction is part of the task in recovering the earliest reliable traditions about Jesus the exorcist.

In the next chapter we will examine these traditions to see what reliable material remains available as data to sketch a picture of the historical Jesus the exorcist.

In chapter V we will try to discover what responses Jesus evoked during his lifetime, as this will further contribute to filling out our picture of the historical Jesus the exorcist.

A preliminary matter which has important implications for any Gospel research is the solution to the Synoptic Problem.[1] In this study we will accept the traditional solution. That is, in the first place, we accept the priority of Mark. In the second place, assuming Mark was written first, there seems at present no other viable alternative in explaining the origin

---

1 The problem and its history is well set out and discussed by W.G. Kümmel *Introduction to the NT* (London: SCM, 1975) 38–80. See also Arthur J. Bellinzoni, Jr. (ed.) *The Two-Source Hypothesis: A Critical Appraisal* (Macon: Mercer University Press, 1985) and F.G. Downing "Compositional Conventions and the Synoptic Problem" *JBL* 107 (1988) 69–85.

of the material found to be common to Matthew and Luke, but not in Mark, than to suppose that there is a common source of tradition, Q, being used by Matthew and Luke.[2] The material which Matthew and Luke have in common can hardly be the limit of the extent of Q: if the treatment of Mark by Matthew and Luke is any indicator then we can be fairly certain of this. Finally, here, we do not assume that there is a literary relationship between Q and Mark, nor a direct literary relationship between Matthew and Luke.

If we accept the traditional solution to the Synoptic Problem then we are faced with the long-standing problem of the redaction and tradition-history of Mark. In recent years much has been done in trying to discover Mark's contribution to, and use of traditional material.[3] The point at which we know so little and where certainty is least assured is in determing what is to be taken as a word or stylistic feature of the last stage(s) of redaction and what is to be taken as being from earlier tradition(s). Up until recently the works of Sir John Hawkins and C. H. Turner[4] have been heavily utilized. But, these studies rely on the simple frequency of occurrence of a linguistic characteristic and do not allow for the possibility that the prominence of a feature may be due to Mark's tradition rather than redaction. Even Lloyd Gaston's useful work (*HSE*) which is a considerable advance on Hawkins, particularly with regard to Matthew,

---

2   On the nature and extent of Q, see, e.g. C.K. Barrett "Q: A Re–examination" *ExpTim* 54 (1942–3) 320 and notes; P. Vassiliadis "The Nature and Extent of the Q Document" *NovT* 20 (1978) 50–60 and notes; Kümmel *Introduction* 67 and notes; J. Delobel (ed.) *Logia: Les Paroles de Jésus – The Sayings of Jesus* (Leuven: Leuven University Press, 1982).

3   See N. Perrin *What is Redaction Criticism?* (London: SPCK, 1970); R.H. Stein "The 'Redaktionsgeschichtlich; Investigation of a Markan Seam (Mc 1 21f.)" *ZNW* 61 (1970) 70–94; and "The Proper Methodology for Ascertaining a Markan Redaction History" *NovT* 13 (1971) 181–98; E.J. Pryke *Redactional Style in the Marcan Gospel: A Study of Syntax and Vocabulary as Guides to Redaction in Mark* (Cambridge: Cambridge University Press, 1978). See the review of Pryke's work by P.J. Achtemeier in *CBQ* 41 (1979) 655–7. Notable is the work of F. Neirynck "The Redactional Text of Mark" *ETL* 57 (1981) 144–62; P. Dschulnigg *Sprache, Redaktion und Intention des Markus-Evangeliums* (Stuttgart: Katholisches Bibelwerk, 1984); J. Schreiber *Der Kreuzigungsbericht des Markusevangeliums Mk 15,20b-41* (Berlin and New York: de Gruyter, 1986) 395–433, Exkurz V, "Tabellen zur Markinischen Vorzugsvokabeln"; D.B. Peabody *Mark as Compsoer* (Macon, GA: Mercer University Press, 1987); F. Neirynck "Words Characteristic of Mark: A New List" *ETL* 63 (1987) 367–74; C.C. Black "The Quest of Mark the Redactor: Why has it been Pursued, and What has it Taught Us?" *JSNT* 33 (1988) 19–39; C.C. Black *The Disciples According to Mark: Markan Redaction in Current Debate* (Sheffield: JSOT, 1989).

4   J. Hawkins *Horae Synopticae* (Oxford: Oxford University Press, 1909); C.H. Turner "Markan Usage. Notes, Critical and Exegetical, on the the Second Gospel" *JTS* 25 (1924) 377–85; 26 (1925) 12–20, 145–56, 225–40, 337–46.

Luke and Q, still does not offer any way of distinguishing between Mark's redaction and tradition, for he also uses simple frequency as an indication of the origin of a feature.[5] The implication of this for our present study is that, in assigning a feature of style, including vocabulary, to a particular level of tradition we should be extremely cautious and avoid depending entirely on mere frequency of occurrence.

In any case, the earliest recoverable traditions are not obtained merely by taking into account the redaction of the Gospel writers. The form critics have established that the Gospel traditions had an oral and probably, in many cases, a written tradition-history before they were known to the Gospel writers. Therefore, we need to take into account not only possible modifications by the Gospel writers but also earlier Christian redaction as we seek to reconstruct the earliest possible reports of Jesus as an exorcist.

We shall now proceed to examine the principal Synoptic pericopes that have to do with Jesus and exorcism, dealing first with those which occur in Mark (1.21—8; 5.1—20; 7.24—30; 9.14—29) and then those in Q (Matthew 12.22—30/Luke 11.14—23 [/Mark 3.22—7]). We shall examine the Temptation narratives (Matthew 4.1—11/Luke 4.1—13 and Mark 1.12—13) because of the suggested connection between this story and the defeat of Satan. We shall examine Jesus' answer to John the Baptist (Matthew 11.2—6/Luke 7.18—23) because, in Luke, it refers to Jesus performng exorcisms, and it may also illuminate Jesus' self-understanding. Finally, we will look at the Disciples' Mission(s) (Mark 6.7—12, 30/Matthew 10.1—15/Luke 9.1—6; 10.1—11, 17—20) because it may also be important in assessing Jesus' understanding of his exorcisms.

Here we must make note of Luke 13.10—17, the story of the healing of the crippled woman, which is unique to Luke.[6] The woman is described as having a spirit of infirmity (πνεῦμα ἔχουσα ἀσθενείας, 13.11) and having been bound by Satan for eighteen years (13.16). However, in the healing, Jesus does not address Satan or the spirit but the woman herself, as in a healing story (13.12). What is effectively a blurring of the distinction between healing and exorcism is most probably to be attributed to Luke. For, in the case of the story of Simon's mother-in-law, a story which Mark

---

5 Gaston *HSE* 12ff. New ground is being broken by some scholars. See particularly W.O. Walker "A Method for Identifying Redactional Passages in Matthew on Functional and Linguistic Grounds" *CBQ* 39 (1977) 76–93 and Black *Disciples*.

6 Bultmann (*History* 12–13) regarded the story as a variant of Mark 3.1–6. To the contrary, see I.H. Marshall *The Gospel of Luke* (Exeter: Paternoster, 1978) 556–7.

has told as a healing, Luke has treated as an exorcism in that an enemy is subdued and caused to flee (Mark 1.29—31/Luke 4.38—9). In the light of this, Luke 13.10—17 will be excluded from our discussion.[7]

---

7 Further, see Twelftree *Christ* 103–4. Cf. J. Wilkinson "The Case of the Bent Woman in Luke 13.10–17" *EvQ* 49 (1977) 195–205; L. Milot "Guérison d'une femme infirme un jour de sabbat (Lc 13.10–17)" *Sémiotique et Bible* 39 (1985) 23–33; J.D.M. Derrett "Positive Perspectives on Two Lucan Miracles" *Downside Review* 104 (1986) 272–87; M.D. Hamm "The Freeing of the Bent Woman and the Restoration of Israel: Luke 13.10–17 as Narrative Theology" *JSNT* 31 (1987) 23–44; Latourelle *Miracles* 194–6; J.B. Green "Jesus and the Daughter of Abraham (Luke 13.10–17): Test Case for a Lucan Perspective on Jesus' Miracles" *CBQ* 51 (1989) 643–54.

Because of its late origin Mark 16.17 ("And these signs will accompany those who believe: in my name they will cast out demons; '. . .'") will not be dealt with in this study. For literature see Pesch *Markus*. II, 544–56; J. Gnilka *Das Evangelium nach Markus* 2 vols. (Zürich: Benziger and Neukirchen–Vluyn: Neukirchener Verlag, 1978 and 1979) II, 352–8; C.S. Mann *Mark* (Garden City: Doubleday, 1986) 672–6.

§ 6 The Demoniac in the Synagogue[1]
Mark 1.21—8 (/Luke 4.31—7)

Our purpose in examining this and subsequent stories is to identify and set aside the Christian redaction in order to help recover the probable earliest reports of Jesus as an exorcist.

We can probably say that this narrative, embracing as it does so many of Mark's themes and being placed first in the public ministry of Jesus, is paradigmatic and programmatic for his story of Jesus.[2] The story reads as follows.

(21) And they went into Capernaum; and immediately on the sabbath entering the synagogue he taught. (22) And they were astonished at his teaching; for he was teaching them as one having authority and not as the scribes.

---

1 Literature: Pesch *Markus*. I, 128; cf. H. Schürmann *Das Lukasevangelium: Erster Teil: Kommentar zu Kap. 1, 1-9, 50* (Freiburg: Herder, 1969) 245; Gnilka *Markus* I, 199; P. Guillemette "Un enseignement nouveau, plein d'autorité" *NovT* 22 (1980) 222–47; G.E. Rice "Luke 4:31–44; Release for the Captives" *Andrews University Seminary Studies* 20 (1982) 23–8; J.F. Strange and H. Shanks "Synagogue Where Jesus Preached Found at Capernaum" *BARev* 9 (6, 1983) 24–31; A Suhl "Überlegungen zur Hermeneutik an Hand von Mk 1,21–28" *Kairos* 26 (1984) 28–38; S. Becker-Wirth "Jesus treibt Dämonen aus (Mk 1, 21–28)" *Religionsunterricht an höheren Schulen* 28 (1985) 181–6. On miracles in Mark see, e.g. K. Tagawa *Miracle et évangile. La pensée personelle de l'évangeliste Marc* (Paris: Universitaires de France, 1966); K. Kertelge *Die Wunder Jesu im Markusevangelium* (München: Käsel, 1970); L. Schenke *Die Wundererzählungen des Markusevangeliums* (Stuttgart: Katholisches Bibelwerk, 1970); D.-A. Koch *Die Bedeutung der Wundererzählungen für die Christologie des Markusevangeliums* (Berlin and New York: de Gruyter, 1975); P. Lamarche "Les miracles de Jésus selon Marc" in X. Léon-Dufour (ed.) *Les Miracles de Jesus selon le Nouveau Testament* (Paris: Seuil, 1977) 213–226; Mack *Innocence* 208–19; B.D. Chilton "Exorcism and History: Mark 1:21–28" in Wenham and Blomberg (eds.) *Gospel Perspectives* 6, 253–71; H. Hendrickx *The Miracle Stories* (London: Geoffrey Chapman and San Francisco: Harper & Row, 1987) 34–62; E. Drewermann *Das Markusevangelium* 2 vols. (Olten und Freiburg: Walter, 1987 and 1988) I, 171–202; A. Stock *The Method and Message of Mark* (Wilmington: Glazier, 1989) 71–7; H. Giesen "Dämonenaustreibungen – Erweis der Nähe der Herrschaft Gottes. Zu Mk 1,21–28" *Theologie der Gegenwart* 32 (1989) 24–37; Guelich *Mark* I, 53–4.

2 Cf. Eitrem *Notes* 8. Kee *Miracle* 161; Gnilka *Markus* I, 86. Also see, A.M. Ambrozic "New Teaching with Power (Mk. 1:27)" in J. Plevnik (ed.) *Word and Spirit: Essays in Honour of David Michael Stanley* (Willowdale Ontario: Regis College, 1975) 114; though I am not sure that he is right in saying that the amazement aroused in the witnesses of Jesus' teaching and mighty works is a theme "dear to Mark's heart".

(23) And immediately there was in their synagogue a man with an unclean spirit (24) and he cried out saying; "What have we to do with you, Jesus of Nazareth? Have you come to destroy us? I know who you are, the Holy One of God." (25) And Jesus rebuked him saying; "Be muzzled and come out of him." (26) And the unclean spirit convulsed him and crying with a loud voice came out of him. (27) And they were all amazed so that they questioned among themselves saying; "What is this? New teaching with authority! And the unclean spirits he commands and they obey him." (28) And the report of him went out immediately everywhere to the whole of the region of Galilee.

The introduction to this story (1.21—2) gives a Sabbath in Capernaum as its setting as well as saying that Jesus did not teach like the scribes. The phrase, "And immediately" (καὶ εὐθύς) joins this introduction to the story proper and gives it a fresh beginning.[3] Using this phrase to join stories and pericopes is not uncommon in Mark (1.12, 23, 29; 6.45; 7.25[?]; 14.43; 15.1) but it is not used to join stories in the two larger passages generally recognized to be pre-Markan complexes (2.1—3.6 and 4.35—5.43).[4] Thus, it is probable that Mark appended the introduction (1.21—2) to the exorcism story.[5] This conclusion does not mean that we should consider the introduction, including the astonishment at one who had an authority unlike the scribes, as unhistorical.[6] In fact, since there is no hint of Jesus ever receiving formal training and since he teaches without formally justifying his utterances, the historicity of verse 22 may be assumed. But, we must set aside the introduction (1.21—2) in our search for the earliest form of the exorcism story.

The end of the pericope (1.27—8) may also contain some redaction we can set aside, for it is in the beginning and end of pericopes that redactors seems to have been most active.[7]

On witnessing the healing the crowd is said to be "astounded" or "amazed" (1.27). Only Mark uses θαμβέομαι (1.27; 10.24, 32), but in neither of the other cases does it seem that Mark is responsible for the idea.[8] But, has Mark added the concept here? Jesus' teaching[9] and even his mere

---

3   K.L. Schmidt *Der Rahmen der Geschichte Jesu* (Darmstadt: Wissenschaftliche Buchgesellschaft, 1964) 50; Taylor *Mark* 175 (though on 171 Taylor is confident that all of this pericope was in Mark's tradition). Cf. K. Kertelge *Die Wunder Jesu im Markusevangelium; Eine redaktionsgeschichtliche Untersuchung* (München: Käsel, 1970) 150f. and n. 58.

4   Taylor *Mark* 91; P.J. Achtemeier "Towards the Isolation of Pre–markan Miracle Catenae" *JBL* 89 (1970) 265–91; Stein *ZNW* 61 (1970) 81 n. 38.

5   Cf. e.g. Schweizer *Mark* 50; H. Anderson *The Gospel of Mark* (London: Marshall, Morgan and Scott, 1976) 89; Pesch *Markus*. I, 119; Guelich *Mark* I, 55.

6   That they are from Mark's hand see, e.g. Kertelge *Wunder* 50.

7   See K. Grobel "Idiosyncracies of the Synoptists in their Pericope–Introductions" *JBL* 59 (1940) 405–10; E. Best *Temptation and Passion* (Cambridge: Cambridge University Press, 1965) 63; Stein *ZNW* 61 (1970) 70f.; Guelich *Mark* I, 55.

8   See Pesch *Markus*. II, 143 and 150–2.

9   Mark 1.22/Luke 4.32; Mark 6.2/Matt 13.54/Luke 4.22; Mark 10.26/Matt 19.25; Mark 11.18/Luke 19.48; Matt 7.28f; 22.33; (Mark 12.34/Matt 22.46/Luke 20.40). Cf. Bornkamm

presence may have had a great impact on his hearers and those around him so that they are said to be afraid, or amazed.[10] At a number of places the crowd is said to be amazed (or afraid) as the result of a *miracle* of Jesus.[11] This is generally thought to be a stereotyped closing motif in the miracle stories, probably taken over from Greek story telling.[12] However, the Jesus tradition shows no consistency in the occurrence of this motif. Matthew (15.31; cf. Mark 7.37) and Luke (9.43a; cf. Mark 9.23/Matthew 17.18) only once each add the motif to their tradition. Mark never adds it to the summary statements;[13] it is present in the exorcism stories at 1.27, and 5.(14), 15 and (17?), but absent at 7.30 and 9.28, perhaps where we (and Luke [9.43a]) would most expect it. Therefore, Mark does not seem particularly interested in adding this motif to the miracle stories in general nor to the exorcism stories in particular.[14] So, to conclude this point, it seems quite probable that at least the mention of the crowd's amazement was part of Mark's tradition at 1.27.[15]

However, the remainder of the conclusion (1.27b—8) about Jesus' new teaching, his authority over demons and his consequent fame, is most probably from Mark's hand. The vocabulary and grammar suggest this.[16] Consequently we must credit Mark, at least at this point, with associating Jesus the exorcist with Jesus the teacher, possibly after the pattern of the wandering Cynics and rabbis, a connection perhaps suggested by the mention of the synagogue in Mark's tradition.

Jesus 144; Loos *Miracles* 129; J.D.G. Dunn *Jesus and the Spirit* (London: SCM, 1975) 381 n. 42.

10 Cf. Dunn *Jesus* 76f..

11 (Mark 1.27/Luke 4.36); Mark 2.12/Matt 9.8/Luke 5.26; 7.16; Mark 4.41/Matt 8.27/Luke 8.25 (Mark 5.14, 17/Matt 8.33, 34)/Luke 8.34, 35, 37; Matt 9.8; Mark 5.20, 43/Matt 9.26/Luke 8.56; Mark 6.51; 7.37/Matt 15.31; 9.33; 12.23/Luke 11.14; Luke 5.9; 7.16.

12 E. Peterson Εἰς Θεός (Göttingen: Vandenhoeck & Ruprecht, 1926) 183–222; Pesch *Markus*. I, 124; Theissen *Miracle* 69–70.

13 Mark 1.32–4; 3.7–12; 6.53–6. On the *Sammelberichte* see H. Sawyer "The Markan Framework" *SJT* 14 (1961) 279–94 and §13 below.

14 Contrast Stein *NovT* 13 (1971) 197 who considers it a Markan term.

15 See R. Pesch "Ein Tag vollmächtigen Wirkens Jesu in Kapharnahum (Mk 1.21–34, 35–39)" *BL* 9 (1968) 118; also Kertelge *Wunder* 51 and 56.

16 Συζητέω (Hawkins *Horae Synopticae* 13; *HSE* 21); διδαχή (Hawkins *Horae Synopticae* 12; E. Schweizer "Anmerkungen zur Theologie des Markus" in *Neotestamentica et Patristica. Eine Freundesgabe Herrn Professor Dr. Oscar Cullman NovTSup* 6 (Leiden: Brill, 1962) 37f.; Best *Temptation* 71f.; Stein *ZNW* 61 [1970] 73; *NovT* 13 [1971] 197; *HSE* 18; Pryke *Style* 136); Γαλιλαία (E. Lohmeyer *Galiläa und Jerusalem* [Göttingen: Vandenhoeck & Ruprecht, 1936] 26; R.H. Lightfoot *Locality and Doctrine in the Gospels* [London: Hodder and Stoughton, 1938] 112; W. Marxsen *Mark the Evangelist* [Nashville: Abingdon, 1969] 4f.). Ὥστε with an infinitive; Pryke *Style* 115ff.. See also J. Brière "Le cri et le secret. Signification d'un exorcisme. Mc 1.21–28" *Assemblées du Seigneur* 35 (1973) 34–46; W. Weiss "*Ein neue Lehre in Vollmacht.*" *Die Streit- und Schulgespräche des Markus-Evangeliums* (Berlin and New York: de Gruyter, 1989).

We will now examine the core of this pericope (1.23—7a) in an attempt to peel away later accretions in order to identify early elements of the story.

The first element of the story is the presence of the demoniac in the synagogue. Some have seen this as an addition to the original report, doubting that a man with an "unclean" spirit should find his way into a synagogue.[17] However, the chaotic and unpredictable character of demon-possession could well mean that, at times, the man showed no adverse symptoms of his condition.[18] Or, perhaps, not until confronted by Jesus was it evident that he was a demonic (cf. Philostratus *Life* 4.20). There is, then, no ground for attributing this element to Christian redaction.

That the man is said to have an *unclean spirit*, rather than a demon, could be an indication of the Semitic origin of this story.[19] However, the phrase is so characteristic of Mark (he has 7 of the 11 occurrences in the Gospels) that it could equally be his. Either way, the story requires that the tradition contains something of the demonic nature of the sickness, however it was expressed.

The man is said "to cry out" (ἀνακράζειν). Ἀνακράζειν is not a synonym for καλεῖν ("to call out"). Apart from its use here and in Luke 8.28, the New Testament uses it in relation to the heightened excitement or anxiety, of an aroused crowd (Luke 23.18), and of terrified men who think they have seen a ghost (Mark 6.49).[20] It is a cry of extreme consternation. There are a number of reasons for thinking that the early Church probably did not need to introduce this element of consternation into the stories of Jesus.

First, Matthew, who is decidedly reticent about the exorcism stories of Jesus,[21] prunes the Markan accounts.[22] Yet, he does not obliterate the consternation of the demoniacs; though in 17.17—18 he removes Mark 9.20, the most grotesque instance. Also, in Mark 5.7 the demoniac κράξας φωνῇ

---

17 See G.A. Chadwick "Some Cases of Possession" *The Expositor* 6 (1892) 275. Cf. P. Pimental "The 'unclean spirits' of St Mark's Gospel" *ExpTim* 99 (1988) 173—5.

18 E.g. 1 Sam 16.16, 23; 18.10; Mark 9.22. For a fuller discussion of the chaotic nature of evil see Twelftree *Christ* chap. V. Philo, *Flaccum* 36, makes a distinction between a certain mad man (τις μεμηνώς) who was easy-going and gentle and those of the fierce and savage kind.

19 See F. Hauck *TDNT* III, 428; cf. E. Klostermann *Das Markusevangelium* (Tübingen: Mohr, 1950) 14; Pimental *ExpTim* 99 (1988) 173—5.

20 See BAGD, LSJ, MM and W. Grundmann *TDNT* III, 898.

21 Matthew is not simply reticent about the exorcism stories because they are *exorcism* stories (as Hull thinks, *Magic* 128—41) but Matthew is so dominated by his Christological objectives that he alters Mark to enhance the reputation of Jesus. See Twelftree *Christ* 123—31.

22 Hull *Magic* 128ff.; H.J. Held in G. Bornkamm, G. Barth and H.J. Held *Tradition and Interpretation in Matthew* (London: SCM, 2nd. ed., 1982) 172—5.

μεγάλῃ, but in Matthew 8.29 this is toned right down to ἔκραξαν, so that the consternation is only barely evident.[23] Therefore, Matthew recognized the consternation of the demoniac as an essential element to an exorcism story.

Secondly, Mark shows no consistent use of this element in his stories. Thus, in 1.23, he has καὶ ἀνέκραξεν as the expression of this consternation; in 3.11 he has προσέπιπτον (cf. 5.33) . . . καὶ ἔκραζον; in 5.6 προσεκύνησεν and in 9.20 συνεσπάραξεν . . . πεσών. This variety of expression shows, at least, no desire on the part of Mark to portray the demons worshipping Jeuss.[24] So, also, Luke pays no particular attention to this element in the exorcism stories (4.33, 41; 8.28; 9.42).

There is a third indicator that the early Church lacked interest in this part of the form of an exorcism story — viz. the lack of consistency in dealing with the consternation of the demoniacs indicates not only that the early Church did not seek to co-opt it into their theological enterprise, but that it did not even seek to draw attention to this factor.

Therefore, we can conclude here that, in so far as the first three Evangelists represent the interests of the early Church, it is quite unlikely that the early Church introduced the consternation of the demoniacs into the form of the stories of Jesus. We will take up the issue of historicity in the next chapter.

In 1.24 the distress of the demoniac is verbalized as "What have you to do with us?" which corresponds to מה־לי ולד (see below).[25]

Fridrichsen maintained that, in these exclamations of the demons, "we have to see a confession *attributed* to the demon and intended to defend Jesus from the accusation of being in alliance with Beelzebul."[26] But, Fridrichsen's theory can easily be dismantled. First, he says that in Mark 1.24 the name of the exorcist is an additional component.[27] Here Fridrichsen has confused form and content. History of religions parallels make it obvious that the name was part of the form of the prescription used in

---

23 See Grundmann *TDNT* III, 898f.; Str–B II, 401.

24 It is possible that, for Mark, the shouting (κράζειν) of the demons is evidence for his case for Jesus' identity. See A.E. Harvey *Jesus on Trial* (London: SPCK, 1976) 23 n. 7.

25 Cf. Josh 22.24; Judg 11.12; 1 Kgs 17.18; *Acts Thom.* 5.45; Taylor *Mark* 174; C.K. Barrett *The Gospel According to St John* (London: SPCK, 1979) 191; *BAGD* "ἐγώ". While nothing stands in the way of Ebstein's suggestion that the plural used by the demon refers to those around Jesus at the time (E. Ebstein *Die Medizin im NT und im talmud* [Stuttgart: Enke, 1903] 60) neither is there anything to support his notion. In fact, in view of the context – Jesus confronting the demoniac – there is no need to see the demon's words referring to anything other than this confrontation.

26 A. Fridrichsen "The Conflict of Jesus with the Unclean Spirits" *Theology* 22 (1931) 125, my emphasis.

27 Fridrichsen *Miracle* 112.

preternatural control.[28] Secondly, the name "Jesus" does not in any way seem to be an intrusion. Not only does it also appear in 5.7 but, as we will see, it is not a name of any particular messianic or christological significance that would be expected to be deliberately added to the tradition. Thirdly, Fridrichsen says that the demon's discourse (1.24) is only long and prolix because it serves an apologetic end.[29] Burkill provides a sufficient reply to this.

> "The address includes but three concise clauses, and if these are read as though they were meant to have apotropaic significance, the two affirmations which folow on the opening question are seen to increase the effectiveness of the utterance of a defensive weapon. Neither assertion is superfluous."[30]

Fourthly, it is unlikely that 1.24 was framed to counter the Beelzebul Charge, as Fridrichsen suggests, for nowhere in Mark is a connection made between the demonic confessions and the Beelzebul Charge.[31] We conclude that the case that the demon's exclamation was attributed to the story to defend Jesus from the Beelzebul Charge cannot stand.

Some years previous to Fridrichsen, William Wrede assumed that the demons were declaring Jesus' messiahship and so brought the demoniacs' utterances into his scheme of the "messianic secret", deleting them from the real history of Jesus.[32] Similarly, others have thought that the demons had supernatural knowledge of Jesus' (true) identity and were declaring this and their defeat to the world.[33] It is true, especially in relation to 3.11, that Mark understood and used the demons' words as messianic confessions. But, why should those responsible for transmitting the Gospel traditions, particularly Mark, choose demons to play such an important part in declaring Jesus' messiahship when they "might have called on kings or other great persons such as philosophers, or angels, or inspired persons, or infants or persons raised from the deal"?[34] In any case, as S.V. Mc-Casland agrees, this "theory is weak because it shows no motive why demons should be anxious to bear testimony to one whom they recognize to be their enemy."[35]

---

28 Twelftree *Christ* 61. See also O. Bauernfeind *Die Worte der Dämonen* (Stuttgart: Kohlhammer, 1927) 13ff.; cf. T.A. Burkill *Mysterious Revelation: An Examination of the Philosophy of St Mark's Gospel* (New York: Cornell University Press, 1963) 78; Hull *Magic*; see also below.

29 Fridrichsen *Miracle* 12f.

30 Burkill *Revelation* 76.

31 Cf. Burkill *Revelation* 75.

32 W. Wrede *The Messianic Secret* (Cambridge and London: Clarke, 1971) 33f. Cf. A.H. Maynard "TI EMOI KAI ΣOI" *NTS* 32(1985) 584; R. Trevijano "El transfordo apocaliptico de Mc 1, 24.25; 5, 7.8 y par." *Burgense* 11 (1970) 117–33. "τι εμοι και σοι"

33 E.g. See H. Seesemann *TDNT* V, 117–8.

34 S.V. McCasland "The Demonic 'Confessions' of Jesus" *JR* 24 (1944) 33.

35 McCasland *JR* 24 (1944) 33.

Any decision regarding the origin of the demon's words in Mark 1.24 (and 5.7) depends to a large extent on the interpretation given to them. Therefore, we need to discuss how the demon's words would have been understood in first century Palestine.

In both Mark 1.24 and 5.7, the reported words of the demons begin in the same way τί ἡμῖν (5.7 has ἐμοί) καὶ σοί? What does this question mean? Although in classical Greek it would mean "What have we in common?", in Mark 1.24 it probably corresponds to Hebrew-Aramaic idiom (מה־לי ולד) and means: "Why are you bothering us?"[36] J.D.M. Derrett has examined the question — with a view to understanding John 2.4 — and says that the phrase is a "protestation that there is not, or should not be, a difference of viewpoint, still less a dispute, between the two personalities."[37] Others take the question to be the demon's defence against Jesus the exorcist.[38]

The question in Mark has parallels in the New Testament era in John 2.4, as well in the Old Testament[39] and in Philo (see below). In the rabbinic literature, Strack and Billerbeck (II, 401) cite only *Pesiqta Rabbati* 5.

Two examples will help us to elucidate its meaning for first century Palestinians. In 2 Samuel 19.16—23 Shimei asks David for forgiveness for cursing and throwing stones at him (2 Samuel 16.5—14). But, Abishai suggested that Shimei be put to death. David replies: "What have I to do with you?", giving the impression that he is asking not to be interfered with. Josephus shows that, in the New Testament era, the phrase in question was understood as a rebuttal or counter-attack. In his rewriting of this story he has David reply: "Won't you be quiet . . .?" (*Ant.* 7.265).

The other Old Testament example of the question, "What have we (or I) to do with you!" is in 1 Kings 17. A widow is providing food and water for Elijah and her son becomes seriously ill. She connects her son's illness with the presence of Elijah, a man of God. She says to Elijah, "What have you against me (τί ἐμοὶ καὶ σοί), O man of God? You have come to me to bring my sin to remembrance, and to cause the death of my son!" (1 Kings 17.18). What the woman attempts to do in these words is to defend her household by a kind of warding off of Elijah from the

36 H.M. Buck "Redactions of the Fourth Gospel and the Mother of Jesus" in D.E. Aune (ed.) *Studies in NT and Early Christian Literature* (Leiden: Brill, 1972) 177; Anderson *Mark* 91.

37 J.D.M. Derret *Law in the NT* (London: DLT, 1970) 241.

38 Bauernfeind *Worte* 3–28.

39 See, e.g. 2 Sam (LXX 2 Kgs) 16.10; 19.22; 2 Kgs (LXX 4 Kgs) 3.13; 2Chr 35.21. See further N. Turner *Grammatical Insights into the NT* (Edinburgh: T & T Clark, 1965) 43–7; Buck in Aune (ed.) *Studies* 177.

situation. Also, in Judges 11.12, Jephthah sent messengers to the King of Ammon in an attempt to avert war. The messengers were to say: "What have you against me (τί ἐμοὶ καὶ σοί), that you have come to fight against my lord?" With this we need to compare a passage in Philo. In *Quod Deus immutabilis sit*, written around the same time as the earliest New Testament documents, Philo uses the 1 Kings passage showing that the phrase (τὶ ἐμοὶ καὶ σοί) was used to ward off evil. He writes: "Every mind that is on the way to be widowed and empty of evil says to the prophet, 'O man of God, you have come in to remind me of my iniquity and my sin' " (*Quod Deus immutabilis sit* 138). Philo has not reversed the notion of "warding off" to one of "welcome" of the man of God, as Bauernfeind thinks[40] for, as Burkill points out,[41] Philo is talking about a God-inspired man, on the remembrance of past iniquities and sins, attempting to keep them in check and from returning to his old ways.[42]

In view of these parallels, it seems best to adopt the view of Bauern-feind, and those who have followed him, that *the words of the demons were most likely understood as defence mechanisms against Jesus the exorcist*.[43] As we proceed we shall find other elements in the words of the demons to confirm this interpretation.[44]

Having concluded that these words of the demon were a defence against Jesus, we can return to the question of their origin. On the one hand, its introduction ("and he cried out saying") would conform to no theological motif in the early Church and the question is certainly appropriate here as a warding off of Jesus the enemy-exorcist. And, importantly, it has a Semitic background. Yet, on the other hand, we have to face the possibility that it has been included to conform to literary conventions. However, the phrase is not used consistently in Mark (cf. 5.7) nor does it not conform to 1 Kings 17.18, the passage which best explains the meaning and purpose of Mark 1.24. Therefore, its early origin seems quite probable. The final decision will have to be made in the context of the whole of verse 24.

Next, we need to ask if Mark or the early Church is likely to have added the name or title "Jesus of Nazareth", either for dogmatic purposes

---

40 Bauernfeind *Worte* 6ff., followed by Pesch *Markus.* I, 122 n. 19.
41 Burkill *Revelation* 77 and n. 14.
42 Cf. Philo *Immut.* 133–9.
43 Bauernfeind *Worte* 3–28; O. Bächli " 'Was habe ich mit Dir zu schaffen?' Eine formelhafte Frage im A.T. und N.T." *TZ* 33 (1977) 79–8. Cf. the critique of Bauernfeind by P. Guillemette "Mc 1, 24 est-il une formule de défense magique?" *ScEs* 30 (1978) 81–96.
44 Cf. Buck in Aune (ed.) *Studies* 177–8 who, after examining the use of the phrase in Epictetus 1.1.16; 1.22.15; 1.27.13; 2.19.16; 2.19.17ff.; 3.22.26, concludes that it always sets up a distance between the two parties involved.

or in order to make it conform to the literary pattern of such formulae. Or, is it a title likely to be original to the earliest story?

From the characters involved in this story we would expect the name "Jesus" to be part of the words of the demons so we will direct our attention to "Nazareth".

Jesus of *Nazareth* is not a term that was of special significance in the early Church as a designation for Jesus. First, Paul does not use the term, nor does any later Christian Greek writer.[45] Secondly, for Matthew (cf. 2.23[46] and 21.11), Luke (Acts 10.38) and John (1.45), the term refers to Jesus' coming from Nazareth in Galilee.[47] Thirdly, when it was used, Ναζαρηνός and Ναζωραῖος were terms restricted to the Palestinian Church.[48] Mark, coming from a community that probably did not use the title, would have no special interest in promoting the term as a title of Jesus.[49]

So, up to this point, we can conclude that there are no obvious dogmatic reasons why Mark or the early non-Palestinian Church would have wanted to introduce the name "Nazareth" into the tradition.

It is possible that the title "of Nazareth" could have been added to the tradition by early Palestinian Christians. However, if Matthew can be taken as an example of a tradition that has passed through early Palestinian Christianity[50] then we have little evidence that it showed particular interest in the title.[51] This conclusion is strengthened if we take Q

---

45 H.H. Schaeder *TDNT* IV, 874.

46 See B. Lindars *NT Apologetic* (London: SCM, 1961) 194ff. and Str-B I, 92.

47 K.H. Rengstorf *DNTT* II, 33.

48 Schaeder *TDNT* IV, 874; cf. Acts 2.22; 3.6 etc.. On the variant terms see D.B. Taylor "Jesus – of Nazareth?" *ExpTim* 92 (1980) 336–7; G. Allan "He shall be Called – a Nazarite" *ExpTim* 95 (1983) 81–2.

49 I assume that Mark was written in the context of a community. See Marxsen *Mark*; Kee *Community*; E. Best *Mark: The Gospel as Story* (Edinburgh: T & T Clark, 1983) chap. XV; Twelftree *Christ* 116 n. 81.

50 For a Palestinian origin of Matthew see G.D. Kilpatrick *The Origins of the Gospel According to St. Matthew* (Oxford: Clarendon, 1946) chap. VII; E. Käsemann "The Beginning of Christian Theology" in his *NT Questions of Today* (London: SCM, 1969) 83; F.W. Beare *The Gospel According to Matthew* (Oxford: Blackwell, 1981) 8. However, many scholars agree that the Gospel was compiled in Syria. See P. Bonnard *L'évangile selon Saint Matthieu* (Paris: Delachaux & Niestlé, 1963) 9–10; Filson *Matthew* 15; D. Hill *The Gospel of Matthew* (London: Marshall, Morgan and Scott, 1972) 48–52; Schweizer *Matthew* 15–17; Goppelt *Theology* I, 213.

51 Matthew drops Ναζαρηνός at 20.30/Mark 10.47; 28.5/Mark 16.6. At 26.69 Matthew does not use Ναζαρηνός (/Mark 14.67) but at 26.71 he uses Ναζωραῖος (/Mark 14.69). At 2.23 Matthew has Ναζωραῖος but the parallel verse in Luke 2.40 does not. At 2.23 Matthew has Ναζαρέτ, the Lukan parallel has Ναζαρέθ (2.39). At 4.13 Ναζαρά (/Mark 1.21/Luke 4.31) and 21.11 Ναζαρέθ (/Mark 11.11/Luke 19.45) have been added to Matthew's sources. At 3.13/Mark 1.9 Ναζαρέτ and at 1.20/Luke 2.4 Ναζαρέθ has been dropped by Matthew. If Matthew is relying on Q at 13.54/Luke 4.16 then he has there dropped Ναζαρά.

to be a Palestinian compilation for it also shows no interest in the designation "Jesus of Nazareth".[52]

Even though PGM VIII.13 ("I know you Hermes, who you are and whence you come and which is your city") comes from the fourth or fifth century, we see from it that the origin of the one being named was probably of importance in Mark 1.24.[53] If Mark or the early Church introduced a name and origin in order to conform to a literary convention or theological motif it is surprising, in this supernatural context, that they should have chosen "Jesus of Nazareth" rather than the more appropriate and theologically pregnant "Son of God", as Mark seems to have done in 3.11 or "Son of David", which Matthew prefers (see §23 below). Thus, there do not appear to be dogmatic reasons why the early Church would want to introduce this particular appellation. Therefore, we can conclude that, so far as we can see, "Jesus of Nazareth" probably does come from the earliest pre-Easter telling of the story.[54]

The next part of the words of the demon is, "Have you come to destroy us?" (ἦλθες ἀπολέσαι ἡμᾶς;). This phrase clearly serves well the early Church's dogmatic purposes. As we will be discussing later, the destruction of evil was expected in the messianic age (e.g. *As. Mos.* 10.1, 3; see §23 below). The early Church took up the theme (Luke 10.18 and Revelation 20.10) and Jesus is portrayed in the Gospels as one who destroys the evil powers (e.g. Matthew 12.28ff./Luke 11.20ff., see §10 below). Yet, neither in Mark, nor in the rest of the New Testament is ἀπόλλυμι used in relation to the ministry of Jesus.[55] Also, ἀπόλλυμι is by no means a word of particular interest to Mark. Nor did any section of the early Church — as represented in the Gospels — think that Jesus' exorcisms were the final or complete destruction of evil (see chap. VI below). And, when we examine the history of religions parallels of addresses to spiritual entities, we find — as we did when discussing the sons of Sceva story in Acts 19 — that the mention of the spiritual entity can involve a description of him, including his activities. In Acts 19.13 the qualification appended to Jesus' name was argued to be designatory or identificatory rather than descriptive (see §3 above). Here, as we will see, the reverse is the case. In Mark 1.24, Jesus is not yet being identified —

52 On the provenance of Q see R.D. Worden "Redaction Criticism of Q: A Survey" *JBL* 94 (1975) 546 who mentions Wellhausen, Harnack, Tödt, Steck and Hoffmann. See also Kümmel *Introduction* 70. On the non-occurrence of "Jesus of Nazareth" in Q see R.A. Edwards *A Concordance to Q* (Missoula: Scholars Press, 1975).

53 See Twelftree *Christ* chap. II.

54 For the Semitic background of "from Nazareth" see W.C. Allen *Matthew* (Edinburgh: T & T Clark, 1912) 16f.

55 On ἀπόλλυμι see H.C. Hahn *DNTT* I, 462; A. Oepke *TDNT* I, 394ff.; Str-B IV, 527 and II, 2.

that comes after "I know . . ." He is being described. A good parallel example of this is PGM IV.3045—49 where God, who is being invoked, is described as the light bringer, invisible, and causes rain to come upon the earth.[56] So, once again, it is reasonable to conclude that this description of Jesus' activity by the demon is part of the original story.

So far, apart from the initial words of general defence, the demon has made known Jesus' origin (Nazareth) and his activity (the demon's destruction) in a continuing effort to over-power Jesus. Now the climax of the defence comes with the "I know" formula — knowledge of Jesus' identity.

There are a number of appropriate parallels to this part of the verse. Note particularly PGM VIII.6f.: "(I know) your name which was received in heaven, I know you and your forms . . ."[57] Statements like these occur in incantations designed to gain control over spiritual beings. And so, from what we have seen so far, this formula is not out of place in its setting in Mark 1.24. Finally, we need not doubt the historical veracity of this phrase for it is in an Hebrew idiom. That is, we have here the prolepsis of the subject of a subordinate clause as in Genesis 1.4 "God saw *the light*, that *it* was good."[58]

However, what should we make of the origin of the phrase "the Holy One of God"? We can begin by noting that "the Holy One" is used in the New Testament in relation to Jesus, albeit rarely ([Luke 1.36]; John 6.69; [Acts 3.14; 4.27, 30]; 1 John 2.20; Revelation 3.7). The term has no recognizable tradition at all as a messianic title and we know of no other instance of the exact title in the period (cf. "holy ones of God" in CD 6.1).[59] The basic intention of the word is to signify that which is marked off from the secular. That is, it denotes the sphere of the divine.[60] Thus, the term is used of beings that belong to this sphere.[61] And, importantly, it is used of human individuals (CD 6.1; Revelation 22.6).[62] In Jeremiah 1.5 the prophet is "sanctified": that is, he belongs to God. In Ben Sirach 45.6,

---

56 Cf. PGM IV.3033ff..

57 See also PGM IV.1500, 2984ff.; V.103ff.; VIII.13; Bauernfeind *Worte* 11f.; R. Reitzenstein *Hellenistische Wundererzählungen* (Leipzig: Teubner, 1963) 124.

58 N. Turner *A Grammar of NT Greek* IV (Edinburgh: T & T Clark, 1976) 16.

59 R. Bultmann *The Gospel of John* (Oxford: Blackwell, 1971) 449 n. 4; W.R. Domeris "The Holy One of God as a Title for Jesus" *Neotestamentica* 19 (1985) 9.

60 See O. Procksch *TDNT* I, 88f.; Bultmann *John* 448 n. 5; H. Seebas *DNTT* II, 224; W.R. Domeris "The Office of Holy One" *Journal of Theology for Southern Africa* 54 (1986) 35-8.

61 Cf. W. Bousset and H. Gressmann *Die Religion des Judentums im Späthellenistischen Zeitalter* (Tübingen: Mohr, 1966) 321 and n. 2; Seebas *DNTT* II, 225f.; cf. also Bultmann *John* 449 n. 5.

62 See Bultmann *John* 449 n. 5; Domeris *Neotestamentica* 19 (1985) 12.

Aaron is called "holy" (cf. Numbers 16.3—5). And, in Psalm 105.16 (LXX), Aaron is referred to as "the holy one of the Lord" (cf. 2 Kings 4.9). These parallels make a Semitic background to Mark 1.24 quite probable,[63] and its status as a genuine reflection of the words of the demon or demoniac high. If this is right then the demon or demoniac was simply identifying Jesus as belonging to God or perhaps being in the service of God as an exorcist.[64]

This completes our investigation into the origin of the various elements of Mark 1.24. It will be apparent that few of the history of religions parallels cited are actually words of demons. In fact, I can find no precise extra-biblical parallels to the "I know" formula. All the precise parallels are, like PGM VIII.13, words addressed to a power-authority in order to gain its aid. Bultmann called attention to this as it related to Bauernfeind's work.[65] Bultmann said that, in Bauernfeind's evidence, the demon appeared in the role of the threatened man who utters the "protective" words, while Jesus takes on the role of the demon. But, in fact this is not quite the case. Rather, in Mark 1.24, the demon appears to be using technical devices which, in the parallels, were used to call up the aid of the power-authority. Thus, the situation is the same in that in both cases control over a powerful preternatural being is sought, in one case for aid, in another to disarm.

The next part of the story, Mark 1.25, has to do with the technique Jesus used to exorcise the demon. In the first part of the verse Jesus is said to ἐπιτιμᾶν the demon. It has been pointed out,[66] that גער, the Semitic equivalent underlying ἐπιτιμᾶν in the LXX, occurs in the Qumran material.[67] We have seen (§3 above) that Kee attempted unsuccessfully to show that it is a technical term and designates the commanding word spoken by God or his representatives at which evil powers are subjugated so that the way is thereby prepared for the establishment of God's rule.[68] We showed in §3 above that גער/ἐπιτιμᾶν in this context can be

---

63 Cf. Judg 16.17(B). See F.C. Hahn *The Titles of Jesus in Christology* (London: Lutterworth, 1969) 233; F. Mussner "Ein Wortspiel in Mark 1:24?" *BZ* 4 (1960) 285–6 and E. Schweizer " 'Er wird Nazoräer heissen' (zu Mc 1.24/Mt 2.23)" in W. Eltester (ed.) *Judentum, Urchristentum, Kirche* (Berlin: Töpelmann, 1964) 90–3 suggest that "Jesus of Nazareth" would have been a play on the words "Holy One of God". Cf. B. Blackburn *Theios Anēr and the Markan Miracle Traditions* (Tübingen: Mohr, 1991) 110 n. 65.

64 Contrast Guelich *Mark* I, 57, following Koch. *Wundererzählungen* 57–61, who suggests that the demons are recognizing the deity of Jesus.

65 Bultmann *History* 209 n. 1.

66 Notably by J.A. Fitzmyer "Some Observations on the *Genesis Apocryphon*" *CBQ* 22 (1960) 284; W.H. Brownlee *The Meaning of the Qumran Scrolls for the Bible* (New York and Oxford: Oxford University Press, 1964) 210 n. 41; Geller *JJS* 28 (1977) 142.

67 1QM 14.10; 1QHf 4.6; 1QapGen 20.28–9.

68 Kee *NTS* 14 (1967–8) 232–46. Cf. Harvey *Constraints* 118.

translated simply as "rebuke in order to expel". Without the theological connotation Kee attempted to associate with ἐπιτιμᾶν, we may take this word as part of the original report of Jesus' exorcism.

Mark 1.25b reports words of Jesus to the demon, "Be quiet and come out of him" (φιμώθητι καὶ ἔξελθε ἐξ αὐτοῦ). Again, the question is — Did these words originate in the early Church?

In relation to φιμώθητι we need to take into account the notion that this injunction to silence may have been part of a "Messianic Secret" constructed by the early Church.[69] From 1.34 it seems that Mark might have understood Jesus' prohibition as a general injunction to silence.[70] However, if the early Church wished to include in this command the more general conception of ceasing to talk about Jesus it is surprising that it did not use σιώπα ("be quiet"), as in 10.48, rather than φιμώθητι, which is so strongly related to "incantational restriction", rather than to "talking".[71] That is, the use of φιμῶτι puts someone in a position where they are unable to operate,[72] whereas the other injunctions in Mark[73] are requests and commands to silence. Further, if by φιμώθητι the publishers of Mark understood the meaning "be silent"[74] then the phrase φωνῆσαν φωνῇ μεγάλῃ is a glaring oversight by them.[75] In other words, φιμώθητι in 1.25 does not fit the pattern of interdictions in the rest of Mark, nor of a conscious reworking at this point[76] and was probably understood in terms of someone or something being bound or restricted.

Further, φιμώθητι is well known in the magical papyri. For example, P. Oslo 1.161f. has: "Remedy to prevent the wrath of a person . . . muzzle

---

69 Wrede *Secret* 34, though see his note 17 there: "The *phimōthēti* is not in itself an indication that Jesus rejects the messianic address, but simply suppresses the demon's self-expression which lies in its words. In 4.39 Jesus uses the same term in addressing the sea. cf. B. Weiss, *Markusevang.*, p. 62; Volkmar, p. 89, is not far short of the mark in seeing it actually as a spell. Nevertheless, according to the parallel, the evangelist seems to mean that Jesus is also repudiating the messianic form of address by his use of the term." (Cf. Wrede *Secret* 145ff.). The comments of Robinson *History* 38 n. 1 are important here. "Wrede, maintains that the reason for silencing demons cannot be their demonic nature, since this explanation would not apply to the silencings following the raising of Jairus' daughter (5.43) and the healing of the deaf-mute (7.36). But Wrede forces this parallel to the expense of ignoring the contrast between the hostility in the commands to the demons and the absence of such hostility in the other cases. Furthermore the basic assumption of Wrede, that all the silencings in Mark must be understood in the same way, is open to serious question, in view of the variety in form and mood of the silencings." Cf. Schweizer *Mark* 55; C. Tuckett (ed.) *The Messianic Secret* (London: SPCK and Philadelphia: Fortress, 1983).
70 Schweizer *Mark* 52 and RSV.
71 See BAGD and LSJ.
72 Cf. Matt 22.34; Lucian *Peregrinus* 15.
73 Wrede *Secret* 34ff.
74 Cf. RSV.
75 Cf. Burkill *Revelation* 89 (and n. 6).
76 Burkill *Revelation* 74.

(φιμωσάται) the mouths which speak against me . . . !⁷⁷ And, in the *defixiones* found at Cyprus, φιμοῦν and φιμωτικόν are equivalent to καταδεῖν ("to bind") or κατάδεσμος (a magical knot) used in incantations.⁷⁸ And, the original meaning of φιμοῦν was "to bind",⁷⁹ sometimes in relation to the tongue.⁸⁰ Thus, in the context of an exorcist's command, φιμώθητι is quite appropriate in Mark 1.25, and φιμόω corresponds to the Aramaic סתם. Therefore, it is most likely part of the primary tradition rather than Christian redaction. Of course, as 1.34 shows — "He did not permit the demons to speak because they knew him" — this command to silence was taken up into Mark's theological programme.⁸¹

Next to consider in Mark 1.25b is Jesus' command, "Come out of him" (ἔξελθε ἐξ αὐτοῦ). The Lukan form of this phrase (4.35) with ἀπό in place of ἐκ is paralleled in PGM IV.3013ff.. With this can be compared PGM IV.1243ff.: ἔξελθε . . . καὶ ἀπόστηθι ἀπὸ τοῦ δεῖνα. Very similar expressions are found in Philostratus' *Life* 4.20 where Apollonius orders the demon to quit (ἀπαλλάττεσθαι) the young lad, and in Lucian's *Philopseudes* 11, where a spell drives out (ἐξελάσας) poison, and in *Philopseudes* 16, where a Syrian drives out (ἐξελαύνει) a demon. And, as we saw in the last chapter, in the Babylonian Talmud (*b. Me'il.* 17b) two rabbis order a demon to leave a girl. In view of all this, and there being no obvious reasons why this command to the demon to leave should have been added to the tradition by the early Church, it is reasonable to assume that this command of Jesus has not been added to the story but belongs to the bedrock of historical tradition.

The next part of the story, Mark 1.26—8, relates the response to Jesus' command, first by the demon, and then in turn, by the crowd.

The demon is said to "tear or convulse (σπαράξαν) the man". Mark, or his tradition, seems to be fairly consistent in including this element in his stories. If 5.13 is included then the element is in all his stories. But, that Mark did not add this violence to the stories of Jesus is clear from the

---

77   Further examples in S. Eitrem *Papyri Osloenses* I (Oslo: Norske Videnskops–Akademi, 1925) 76f.; BDF §346; cf. E. Rohde *Psyche: The Cult of Souls and Belief in Immortality Among the Greeks* (London: Routledge and Kegan Paul, 1925) 604; Eitrem *Notes* 30f.; U. Luz "The Secrecy Motif and the Marcan Christology" in Tuckett (ed.) *The Messianic Secret* 81.

78   Cited by Rohde *Psyche* 603f.; see also A. Audollent *Defixionum Tabellae* (Frankfurt Main: Minerva GmbH, Unveränderter Nachdruck, 1967) 20.5; 25.13; 32.13; cf. Fridrichsen *Miracle* 112.

79   See BAGD; BDF §346; Kertelge *Wunder* 54 and n. 87, (cf. Rohde *Psyche* 327 n. 107 – this word is "the 'binding' whereby the spirit–raiser magically compels the unseen to do his will").

80   See esp. Audollent *Defixionum* 15.24; cf. Wünsch cited in Rohde *Psyche* 327 n. 107.

81   W.C. Robinson "The Quest for Wrede's Secret Messiah" in Tuckett (ed.) *The Messianic Secret* 105.

fact that he shows no particular consistency of interest in its function. Thus, in 9.26—7, the violence could be a means towards portraying Jesus' compassion, but this could hardly be said of 5.13 (the drowning of the pigs), and in 1.27 the violence may have been a vehicle for dramatizing and heightening Jesus' authority.

Further, it is unlikely that any sector of the early Church appended this factor to the Jesus stories. Matthew and Luke's attitude to this violence makes this most probable. Matthew omits the whole of this first story (Mark 1.23—8), and in 8.32 he changes Mark's strong ἐπνίγοντο ("they were suffocated/strangled" Mark 5.13c) to a less violent ἀπέθανον ("they died"). He also omits the violent convulsions of Mark 9.26 (Matthew 17.18). Luke's treatment is also telling of the early Church's embarrassment over this aspect of Jesus' exorcisms. Most noticeable is his addition of "having done him no harm" (4.35) to Mark's reference to "convulsions" and "loud crying".

Thus, in so far as the first three Evangelists represent the attitude of the early Church on this point, it seems unlikely that the early Church introduced this violence into the Jesus tradition and we can take it that, in all probability, it goes back to the earliest report of the event.

The crowd's response is said to be amazement (ἐθαμβήθησαν, Mark 1.27). We have already discussed this and shown that is was most likely part of Mark's tradition and, notably, that the Jesus tradition shows no consistency in the occurrence of this motif. Thus, although we cannot be sure, it quite probably goes back to the original reports of the event.

Finally, by way of summary here, having set aside Christian redaction we can see what can be confidently said to belong to the very first reports of this event. From our discussions the following elements should probably be included: (1) a demoniac is said to confront Jesus in the synagogue at Capernaum, (2) there is a report, faithfully transmitted in Mark, of a dialogue between Jesus and the demoniac and possibly (3) the crowd is said to be amazed.[82]

---

82 Cf. Guillemette *NovT* 22 (1980) 222–47.

§ 7 The Gadarene Demoniac[1]
Mark 5.1—20 (Matthew 8.28—34/Luke 8.26—39)

This story is both the most astounding of the Synoptic exorcism stories and the one with the most textual and history of tradition problems. These difficulties have, in turn, provoked a wide spectrum of opinion on the historicity of this story. For example, some see the story as faithfully reflecting a historical event[2] while others see it as a popular folk tale appended to the authentic Jesus tradition.[3] Some scholars have attempted to apply Levi-Straussian structural exegesis to the passage. For example, Jean Starobinski says that the story in Mark is a psychic event and that the pigs being destroyed in the sea is "manageable only through a purely

---

1 Literature: Pesch *Markus.* I, 29f.; R. Pesch *Der Besessene von Gerasa* (Stuttgart: Katholisches Bibelwerk, 1972); F. Annen *Heil für die Heiden* (Frankfurt: Knecht, 1976); J.D. Kingsbury "Observations on the 'Miracle Chapters' of Matthew 8–9" *CBQ* 40 (1978) 559–73 and notes; Schürmann *Lukas*. I, 479f.; Gnilka *Markus* I, 199; J.D.M. Derrett "Contributions to the Study of the Gerasene Demoniac" *JSNT* 3 (1979) 2–17; R. Girard "Les démons de Gérasa" in *Le Bouc émissaire* (Paris: Grasset, 1982) 233–57; A. Manrique "El endemoniado de Gerasa" *Biblia y Fe* 8 (1982) 168–79; Drewermann *Markus*. I, 360–5; Latourelle *Miracles* 120–1; Guelich *Mark* I, 271–89; Stock *Method* 164–9; R. Detweiler and W.G. Doty (eds.) *The Daemonic Imagination Biblical Texts and Secular Story* (Atlanta: Scholars Press, 1990). On the textual and geographical problems of "Gadara" see G. Dalman *Sacred Sites and Ways: Studies in the Topography of the Gospels* (New York: Macmillan, 1935) 177; T. Baarda "Gadarenes, Gerasenes, Gergesenes and the 'Diatesseron' Tradition" in E. Ellis and M. Wilcox (eds.) *Neotestamentica et Semitica* (Edinburgh: T & T Clark, 1969) 181–97; Marshall *The Gospel of Luke* 336–7; Schürer *History* I, 132–6; J.A. Fitzmyer *The Gospel According to Luke* 2 vols. (Garden City: Doubleday, 1981 and 1985) I, 736–7; J.D.M. Derrett *The Making of Mark* 2 vols. (Shipston-on-Stour: Drinkwater, 1985) I, 99–101; Gnilka *Markus* I, 275.

2 E.g. E. Lohmeyer *Das Evangeliums des Markus* (Göttingen: Vandenhoeck & Ruprecht, 1959) 95–9; Taylor *Mark* 277–85; G. Dehn *Der Gottessohn* (Hamburg: Furche, 1953) 110–114; C.E.B. Cranfield *The Gospel According to Saint Mark* (Cambridge: Cambridge University Press, 1966) 177–80. Strauss, *Life* 430, saw the story as reflecting a historical event but gave a rationalistic explanation for the cause of the fate of the herd of pigs; cf. Mann *Mark* 278.

3 C.G. Montefiore *The Synoptic Gospels* 2 vols. (London: Macmillan, 1909) I, 11; Dibelius *Tradition* 85ff.; F.C Grant *IB* 7, 712; W. Bundy *Jesus and the First Three Gospels* (Cambridge, MA: Harvard University Press, 1955) 243. Cf. Pesch *Markus* I, 282–95; Annen *Heil für die Heiden*.

symbolic interpretation: the fall of the pigs is a *figure* for the fall of rebellious spirits into the abyss."[4] However, as H.C. Kee comments: "The verbal acrobatics are dazzling, but they cannot conceal that the method is not really concerned with the text, but with the 'deep' (= spiritual) meaning."[5] Some interpret the story psychologically[6] while others interpret it in the context of first century demonology.[7] It has also been seen as a Christian midrash inspired by Isaiah 65.1–5.[8] Recently, insights from a sociological approach have been applied to the pericope.[9] This variety of approaches signals to us that we may not yet fully understand the nature of the Jesus tradition, and that we should proceed with caution.

The story of Mark 5 reads as follows.

(1) And they came to the other side of the sea into the country of the Gerasenes. (2) And when he had come out of the boat immediately there met him out of the tombs a man with an unclean spirit, (3) who lived in the tombs, and no longer was any one able to bind him with a chain (4) because he had often been bound with fetters and chains and he had burst from the chains and the fetters he broke, and no one had the strength to subdue him. (5) And continually night and day among the tombs and among the mountains he was crying out and bruising himself with stones. (6) And seeing Jesus from afar he ran and knelt down before him (7) and crying out with a loud voice he said; "What have I to do with you, Jesus Son of the Most High God? I adjure you by God, do not torment me." (8) For he had said to him; "Come out unclean spirit from the man!" (9) And he asked him; "What is your name?" And he said to him; "Legion is my name, because we are many." (10) And he begged him greatly not to send them out of the country. (11) Now there was there on the mountain a great herd of pigs feeding; (12) and they begged him saying; "Send us into the pigs, so that we can enter into them." (13) And he allowed them. And coming out the unclean spirits entered into the pigs, and the herd rushed down the steep bank into the sea, about two thousand, and was drowned in the sea.

(14) And their herdsmen fled and reported it in the city and in the country; and they came to see what it was that had happened (15) and they came to Jesus and saw the demoniac sitting clothed and in his right mind, the one who had the legion, and they were afraid. (16) And those having seen it declared what had happened to the demoniac and about the pigs. (17) And they began to beg him to depart from their borders.

4   J. Starobinski "Le Démoniaque de Gerasa: Analyse litéraire de Marc 5:1–20" in F. Bovon (ed.) *Analyse Stucturale et Exégese Biblique* (Neuchâtel: Delachaux et Niestlé, 1971) 72, quoted by H.C. Kee *Christian Origins in Sociological Perspective* (London: SCM, 1980) 103.

5   Kee *Origins* 103. Note especially 186–7 n. 8.

6   E.g. M.M. Baird "The Gadarene Demoniac" *ExpTim* 31 (1919–20) 189; L. Weatherhead *Psychology, Religion and Healing* (London: Hodder and Stoughton, 1951) 62ff.; T. Hawthorn "The Gerasene Demoniac: A Diagnosis Mark v.1–20. Luke viii.26–39. (Matthew viii.28–34)" *ExpTim* 66 (1954–5) 79–80.

7   Bauernfeind *Worte* 34f.; Burkill *Revelation* 87; J. Jeremias *Jesus' Promise to the Nations* (London: SCM, 1957) 30 n. 5; S. Cave "The Obedience of Unclean Spirits" *NTS* 11 (1964–5) 96f.

8   H. Sahlin "Die Perikope vom gerasenischen Besessenen und der Plan des Markus-evangeliums" *ST* 18 (1964) 159–72.

9   Theissen *Followers* 100–102; Theissen *Miracle*, e.g. 147–8, 254–6.

(18) And as he was entering into the boat, the demoniac begged him that he might be with him. (19) And he did not let him, but he said to him; "Go to your home to your people and tell them how much the Lord has done for you and had mercy on you." (20) And he went away and began to proclaim in Decapolis how much Jesus had done for him, and they all marvelled.

We must face the difficult task of trying to detect what contribution Mark and earlier Christians made to this pericope so that we can set this material to one side in our search for reliable historical data.

It is generally agreed that this pericope belongs to a longer pre-Markan unit (4.35—5.43) which, with few modifications, Mark incorporated in his Gospel.[10]

However, it has long been proposed that two previously separate stories have been brought together in 5.1—20.[11] One suggestion is that one of the stories is the original exorcism and call-story with features in common with the others in Mark (1.23—7; 3.17—19; 4.35—41 and 9.14—29).[12] A second story, once foreign to the Jesus tradition, included the tale of the destruction of a herd of pigs. As well as creating significant difficulties, such a division of the material seems to rest on a number of presuppositions which we need to examine.

Probably the most important presupposition is that the pigs episode is the proof of the success of the exorcism and is out of character with the Jesus tradition, fitting better with the milieu of someone like Apollonius of Tyana or the Eleazar of Josephus rather than with Jesus. However, parallels to the pigs phenomenon are found in Jewish as well as Hellenistic literature. For example, it is found in Josephus *Antiquities* 8.48, Philostratus *Life* 4.20 and *Acts of Peter* 2.4.11.[13]

We have already expressed severe reservations about the use of the Apocryphal Acts in illuminating the New Testament stories of Jesus as they seem often to be dependent upon the New Testament (§2 above). Nevertheless, *Acts of Peter* 2.4.11 and these other storeis bring into relief the nature and function of the pigs episode in Mark 5. First, in contrast to the parallel stories, Jesus the exorcist in Mark 5 makes no request for proof of his success. The proof of a successful cure is the fact that the people find the former invalid now "sitting properly clothed and in his right mind."[14] Secondly, in Mark 5.13 the demons are said to enter into the

---

10   E.g. Taylor *Mark* 94f.. Achtemeier *JBL* 89 (1970) 275f.; Stein *ZNW* 61 (1970) 81 n. 36; Kertelge *Wunder* 112f.. On the larger unit, 4.1—8.26 see N.R. Petersen "The Composition of Mark 4.1—8.26" *HTR* 73 (1980) 185—217.

11   E.g. Montefiore *Gospels* I, 11; Dibelius *Tradition* 88; Bundy *Jesus* 243; D.L. Bartlett *Exorcism Stories in the Gospel of Mark* (Yale: Ph.D. Thesis, 1972) 136ff..

12   Bartlett *Exorcism* 136ff..

13   E.g. Dibelius *Tradition* 89; Duling *HTR* 78 (1985) 6.

14   Dibelius *Tradition* 87.

pigs (εἰσῆλθον εἰς) rather than act upon them as objects as in the stories in the *Acts of Peter* and other parallels. Thirdly, in Mark 5 the demons themselves are said to make the request for leniency to leave the man and transfer to the pigs in preference to being sent out of the region.[15]

This alternative understanding of the pigs incident that we have just mentioned — that the demons were thought to be displaced from the man into the pigs — has convincing parallels. In the Babylonian material exorcists transferred demons from a sufferer to some object.[16] In the Babylonian texts the intention of the exorcist is that the demons are to be transferred to the water in a container with which he has been working a spell, then to be dissipated when the pot is broken and the water poured onto the ground.[17] The Greeks (Plato *Republic* 398a) and Romans (Pliny *Nat. Hist.* 28.86) also believed in the transfer of evil from one person to another and from people to objects. In more recent times, Sir James Frazer reported that in Morocco "most wealthy Moors keep a wild boar in their stables, in order that the jinn and evil spirits may be diverted from the horses and enter the boar."[18]

What these history of religions parallels show is that it is probably more appropriate to view the destruction of the pigs as part of the cure rather than something set up as a deliberate proof of the exorcist's success. That is, the demons were believed to have passed from the man to the pigs and then, possibly, from the pigs to their watery home.

There is a sense in which this aspect of the story is out of character with the other exorcism stories of Jesus, for no other story has such a dramatic ending, nor is Jesus said, anywhere else, to destroy people's livelihood. But, we may only have a few of the exorcism stories which

---

15 Cf. *b. Pesaḥ* 112b; *Jub.* 10.7–9; Bultmann *History* 224 and 422. Of interest is Theissen's comment: "I may perhaps be allowed . . . to put forward a (totally improvable) hypothesis. The possessed are clearly in the power of spirits of the dead which have not found rest, which is why they stay by the tombs. Could they have been fallen fighters who lost their lives in the resistance?" (*Miracle*) 255 n. 58.

16 See also *b. Giṭ* 69a; cf. T.W. Davies *Magic, Divination and Demonology Among the Hebrews and Their Neighbours* (London: Clarke and Leipzig: Spirgatis, 1897) 104.

17 Cf. Thompson *Devils* II, xxxv. In this connection it is worth quoting from Count d'Alviella's Hibbert lectures of 1892 where he says: "Sometimes it is deemed essential to make the spirit thus expelled pass into the body of a living being, a pebble, a scrap of wood, or some object which can be thrown away . . ." Count d'Alviella *Lectures on the Origin and Growth of the Conception of God* (London: Williams and Norgate, 1892) 88–9. G.R. Driver "Three Technical Terms in the Pentateuch" *JSS* 1 (1956) 98 says the Assyrian exorcists drove a goat into the wilderness and there slaughtered it, that it might take away a person's sickness.

18 J. Frazer, *The Golden Bough* Part 4, *The Scapegoat* (London: Macmillan, 1920) chap. I "The Transference of Evil", quotation from page 31. See also J.D.M. Derrett "Spirit-possession and the Gerasene Demoniac" *Man* (n.s.) 14 (1979) 268–93; Bultmann *History* 225 and Kee *Medicine* 86, citing Philostratus *Life* 3.38.

were once related to Jesus. (As we will see, the importance Jesus gave his exorcisms and the impression conveyed by the Synoptic Gospels show this.) Also, from different perspectives, each story can be seen to have its unique or uncharacteristic features. Mark 1.23—8 is set within a synagogue; Mark 7.24—30 is most probably a healing from a distance, and of a Gentile, and Mark 9.14—29 involves a sick boy as well as his father. So, perhaps it is unwise to begin by excluding uncharacteristic elements from the Jesus stories.

It is also to be pointed out that the early Church, in so far as it is represented by the Synoptic tradition, did not think this aspect of the Gadarene demoniac story as uncharacteristic of Jesus. It is notable that Matthew, who so often saw fit to cut and abbreviate stories of Jesus,[19] did not delete this motif as uncharacteristic or unworthy of Jesus. Further, that a variety of ancient cultures have left stories of demons proving their leaving people by acting on some third object, or, as in Mark 5, being transferred from the sufferer to another home tells in favour of the historicity of this aspect of the story. Yet, the Mark 5 story is still sufficiently different from any of the parallels to the pigs phenomenon that we do not suspect it to be written to suit an expected form.

Our discussion of the pigs episode in this story has led us into the question of historicity. We have seen that the pigs would have been understood as a temporary home for the demons on their way into the water. In the light of our discussion we can conclude that this element of the story probably belonged to the original tradition of the historical Jesus.

A second presupposition upon which the two-story hypothesis is based is that the exchange between Jesus and the demon, and particularly the use of the term λεγιών, are more likely to be Roman or Hellenistic in origin than Jewish or Palestinian.

The first part of this presupposition can be dispensed with more quickly than the second. It is enough to note that when we were examining the exchange between Jesus and the demoniac in Mark 1.21—8 a sufficient number of appropriate parallels were adduced to make it apparent that such exchanges were not out of place in a Jewish or Palestinian milieu. Regarding the second part of the presupposition, λεγιών is indeed a Latin loan word (*Legio*). However, it is found in Greek writings from the first century BC (cf. Diodorus Siculus 26.5) and there are many examples of its use in Greek papyri (e.g. P. Oxy. 1666.5f.[20]). Thus, there is good evidence for thinking that the word λεγιών was quite at home outside a strictly Roman milieu, especially as the Roman legions were an all too well

---

19   See Held in Bornkamm, Barth and Held *Tradition* 168–92.
20   See also MM 371; BAGD 467–8.

known fact of Jewish life in the New Testament period.[21] So, we conclude that the second presupposition is unsupported. The verbal exchange and the word λεγιών are not necessarily foreign to a Palestinian milieu but entirely appropriate in territory occupied by the Romans.

Another presupposition of those who argue for two stories being brought together here is that 5.1—20 does not fit the form of an exorcism story[22] and that a division of the material would bring one story into line with the form of other Gospel exorcism stories. But the use of form criticism to determine which stories do, and do not, belong to a particular tradition is a highly questionable methodology. Few stories, if any, show a pure "form". To set up one story against the others will always reveal differences, and arbitrarily to assign stories to a *Sitz im Leben* on "form" alone is for the historian to use "the wrong tool".[23]

It is further supposed that a different centre of interest and subject matter is added by the presence of the pigs. But, is it to be assumed that a story must have only one focal point? And, instead of introducing conflict, could not the pigs incident reflect upon, and heighten interest in the manifestly cured man? In other words, the fate of the pigs resulted in a crowd coming to see what had happened and they see a man clothed, seated and in his right mind.

Such a division of the story is also presumed to reduce difficulties in sorting out the start and end of the pericope. But the difficulties in the beginning of the pericope have been attributed to Mark by a two-story theory, and the difficulties of where the story ends remain in the first story.

Finally, it is supposed that the textual difficulties and inconsistencies in the extant story can be solved by dividing the story. However, the division of the story does not help explain the difficulty of the position of verse 8, nor does it explain variation in vocabulary, nor does it help in solving the problem of the end of the narrative. In fact, postulating the coalition of two stories creates at least one major difficulty: that of giving sufficient explanation as to why, in the first story, the crowd makes the

---

21 J.D.M. Derrett's suggestion that there are a number of military terms here ("Legend and Event: The Gerasene Demoniac: An Inquest into History and Liturgical Projection" in E.A. Livingstone [ed.] *StudBib 1978* II [Sheffield: JSOT, 1980] 63 and n. 4) is of little consequence for ἀποστέλλω, ἐπιτρέπω, ὁρμάω and ἀγέλη have wide varieties of meanings that do not, of themselves, suggest a military motif.

22 Bartlett *Exorcism* 139. See the criteria set out in Kertelge *Wunder* 52.

23 M.D. Hooker "On Using the Wrong Tool" *Theology* 75 (1972) 570–81; cf. G. Stanton "Form Criticism Revisited" in M. Hooker and C. Hickling (eds.) *What about the NT?* (London: SCM, 1975) 13–27. See also the discussion of form criticism in E. Güttgemanns *Candid Questions Concerning Gospel Form Criticism* (Pittsburgh: Pickwick, 1979).

radical demand for Jesus to depart from their region. From other exorcism stories of Jesus we might expect either fear or wonder, but not a request to leave the area.[24]

The result of this examination of the two-story hypothesis has cast considerable doubt on its usefulness in explaining either the origin of the suggested parts of the story or the difficulties in the story as it stands. We will have to see, as our own investigations of this passage proceed, if there are other explanations which could help explain the problems of the story.

Another major problem that has been tackled from time to time is the ending of the story. For example, R.H. Lightfoot said that the story could satisfactorily end at 5.15 for: "Evidence is given in this verse, first, of the reality and completeness of the cure ('clothed and in his right mind'), and, secondly, of the effect upon the witnesses ('they were afraid')."[25] Nevertheless, the obvious point to make is that while verse 15 could end the story it does not, and it must be shown, to support the view represented by Lightfoot, that verses 16—20 are an addition.

Verse 15 ends, καὶ ἐφοβήθησαν — "and they were afraid". This is possibly a Markan addition, for in the Markan framework the response to Jesus' miracle could be associated with 4.41.[26] However, such a response is to be expected.

Verse 16 (the witnesses reporting what had happened) has been thought to be out of place; not fitting well with verse 14 (the herdsmen running away to tell what had happened) and made redundant by verse 15 (people coming to see what had happened).[27] But, even though its "missionary" motif is in line with Mark's special interest, verse 16 is probably at least pre-Markan, for there is little evidence of Mark's hand, and the untidy state of the story is more likely to stem from Mark's tradition than his hand.

In verse 17 ἀπέρχεσθαι, ἄρχεσθαι and ὅριον may be evidence of Mark's creativity.[28] However, on the other hand, the request for Jesus to leave the region follows naturally from the people's fear of him and may be expected to be part of the original story. A decision is difficult but, on balance, I am inclined to conclude that verses 16 and 17 are part of Mark's tradition.

What then of verses 18—20, are they an addition to the original story? Wrede takes these verses as being composed in line with a "Messianic

---

24   Cf. J.F. Craghan "The Gerasene Demoniac" *CBQ* 30 (1968) 527.

25   R.H. Lightfoot *History and Interpretation in the Gospels* (London: Hodder and Stoughton, 1935) 88; see also Craghan *CBQ* 30 (1968) 527.

26   Pesch *Markus.* I, 292.

27   Anderson *Mark* 146.

28   See Pryke *Style* 141 and Neirynck *ETL* 57 (1981) 153; Neirynck *ETL* 63 (1987) 368.

Secret" theory; as being supplementary to the story, in the same category as 7.36 where Jesus is proclaimed against his will. For the view that it is a Markan supplement Wrede adduced a number of pieces of evidence. However, they are open to other interpretations. We can enumerate them.[29] (1) The contrast between verse 19 ("Go home...") and verse 20 ("he proclaimed in Decapolis") is not a formal one as verse 20 begins with καί and not δέ (cf. 1.45a; 7.36b).[30] Yet, we need to be aware that καί most probably reflects the Semitic adversative which is so common in Mark.[31] (2) οἶκος/οἰκία ("house") is not always a place of secrecy and retreat (cf. e.g. 2.1, 15; 3.30; 14.3). (3) The title ὁ κύριός ("the Lord") need not stand over against ὁ Ἰησοῦς ("Jesus") at any stage in the history of the story. (4) The man is not thought to be proclaiming Jesus' messiahship,[32] but simply "what Jesus had done". We could add that ὁ κύριός ("the Lord") may act as an assertion by Jesus that God has effected the cure, thus pointing away from himself. We are probably justified, therefore, in concluding that Mark did not compose these verses in line with any "Messianic Secret" theory.[33]

But, the question remains as to whether or not, for other reasons and in what way, Mark may have been responsible for verses 18—20. Verse 18a — "And as he was getting into the boat" — can most probably be attributed to at least the pre-Markan tradition which contributed the "boat" motif. However, it is noticeable that the man's request ἵνα μετ' αὐτοῦ ᾖ ("to be with him", 5.18) is virtually the same as the only other occurrence of the phrase in a similar form (ἵνα ὦσιν μετ' αὐτοῦ) in 3.14 as the purpose for which Jesus appointed the Twelve.[34] Thus, it is reasonable to suppose that Mark is responsible for verse 18b and therefore for καὶ οὐκ ἀφῆκεν αὐτόν ("and he would not let him") and probably for the ἀλλά ("but") of verse 19.

While there is not the contrast between verses 19 and 20 in the way Wrede thought, there is an obvious difference between them. The usual widest sense of οἶκος is "family" or "clan".[35] But, the healed man's "parish", Decapolis, while not conflicting with οἶκος, is certainly more extensive. "Decapolis" was most probably part of Mark's received tradition as it is unlikely that, probably writing in Rome, he would have had reason

29 From Burkill *Revelation* 92.

30 Cf. Taylor *Mark* 258. On the term Decapolis see S.T. Parker "The Decapolis Reviewed" *JBL* 94 (1975) 437–41.

31 See Taylor *Mark* 48–9, 57–8; C.F.D. Moule *An Idiom-Book of NT Greek* (Cambridge: Cambridge University Press, 1959) 178 and Black *Aramaic* 62–9.

32 Implied by Wrede *Secret* 141.

33 See also Burkill *Revelation* 92.

34 Taylor *Mark* 284 and K. Stock *Boten aus dem Mit-Ihm-Sein* (Rome: Biblical Institute, 1975).

35 See BAGD.

to add it if it was not already present. Yet, the vocabulary and style of verses 19 (ὑπάγειν, οἶκος) and 20 (ἀπέρχεσθαι,[36] ἄρχεσθαι,[37] κηρύσσειν[38]) are particularly Markan. Also, the contribution of ἵνα μετ' αὐτοῦ ᾖ and κηρύσσειν here further identify a probable Markan link between these verses and the theme of the call and mission of the disciples. We suspect, then, that Mark has rewritten and filled out a previously brief ending to highlight a latent missionary motif.[39]

Thus, in the pre-Markan tradition the end of this story probably extended beyond the reference to fear in the audience (verse 15). The pre-Markan ending probably included mention of the audience telling of what had happened (verse 16), and requesting Jesus to leave the region (verse 17). The request to be "with Jesus" (verse 18b) is probably Mark's addition to the mention of Jesus getting into the boat (verse 18a) and perhaps telling the man to go home (verse 19b). Mark probably filled out to highlight an ending (mentioning the man going home to Decapolis) which he recognized as containing a missionary motif useful to him.

We should now examine the central section of the pericope, noting any further significant Markan contributions, and noting also how far particular parts, or the story as a whole, relate to the historical Jesus.

In verses 2 and 6 Jesus twice meets the demoniac. Schweizer, for example, gives two possible explanations for this. His first solution is based on the possibility that the tradition has been altered so as to lose ἔδραμε from verse 2. Schweizer's second, attractively simple explanation is that verse 6 can reasonably be accounted for as a rather unskilful resumption of the story after the digression of verses 3—5.[40] And, we may note that Luke (8.29) has attempted to tidy up this point of the story.

For the variation in vocabulary between μνημεῖον (verse 2) and μνῆμα (verses 3 and 5) I can suggest no clear explanation, though μνῆμα could be a Markan word.[41] Even if μνῆμα is a Markan word — in that he introduced it into verses 3—5 — there seems to be no evidence to

---

36 On Mark's special interest in ὑπάγειν, οἶκος and ἀπέρχεσθαι see *HSE* 69, 78, 83; Pryke *Style* 141; Neirynck *ETL* 57 (1981) 153–6; Neirynck *ETL* 63 (1987) 369, 372.

37 This word has been the centre of some debate. See Taylor *Mark* 63f. It cannot be used as evidence for the Palestinian origin of this verse for the construction is good colloquial Greek (H. St. J. Thackeray "An Unrecorded 'Aramaism' in Josephus" *JTS* 30 (1929) 361–70, esp. 370; cf. Black *Aramaic* 125f.). In any case the locution is characteristic of Mark. See Pryke *Style* 79f.

38 Lightfoot *History*, extended note on 106ff.; Schweizer in *Neotestemantica et Patristica NovTSup* 6, 35f.; Neirynck *ETL* 57 (1981) 154; Neirynck *ETL* 63 (1987) 371.

39 Cf. Nineham *Mark* 155 and Schweizer *Mark* 113.

40 Schweizer *Mark* 112; cf. Taylor *Mark* 280. For parallels to the binding and shackling of the demonic see Geller *JJS* 28 (1977) 143–4. See also Derrett *Man* (n.s.) 14 (1979) 287.

41 In the NT Mark = 4; Luke = 2; Rev = 1.

suggest that either Mark has added, composed or significantly contributed to this section. In any case, nothing notable can be made of the distinction between the words.[42]

Verse 6 says that the demoniac ran from afar and fell down and worshipped (προσεκύνησεν) Jesus. At least such an interpretation of the action of the demoniac probably arose in the early Church, especially in the light of the supposed messianic confession which follows (verse 7). However, in the last section (§6) we saw that demoniacs were most probably extremely disturbed when they met Jesus, so προσεκύνησεν is probably a later interpretation of the falling down of the demoniac in front of Jesus.

What of the phrase φωνῇ μεγάλῃ ("a loud voice") in verse 7? We can probably draw the same conclusion about this as we did about ἀνακράζεν ("to cry out", 1.23). That is, since it is not used consistently in the exorcism stories, and since the phenomenon is known outside Christian tradition,[43] the phrase probably is an echo of a historical event.

We turn now to discussing the origin of the various elements of the conversation between Jesus and the demoniac (5.7—13).

1. τί ἐμοὶ καὶ σοί; ("What of me and you?", verse 7). This is the first of four phrases that constitute the demon's words to Jesus. In discussing Mark 1.24 (§6 above) it was established that the words of the demon there are to be understood as a defensive action designed to disarm the threatening exorcist. The context, structure and wording of this verse indicate that we should also understand this verse in the same way. That this first phrase is not dependent on 1.24 is suggested by the change in number from ἡμῖν ("we") to ἐμοί ("me").[44]

2. We have also previously argued that the *name* should be taken as part of the demon's address (see §6 above). We do not need to be detained by the name Ἰησοῦ in the address, but we should make mention of the important phrase υἱὲ τοῦ θεοῦ ("son of God", verse 7). There is no doubt that this appellation is of particular interest to Mark.[45] Yet, there is little other evidence of Mark's hand in this verse and this is the only time the phrase occurs in the vocative in Mark.

Even if Mark has not added the reference to Jesus as the "Son of God", it is possible that the Church before him felt it appropriate to introduce the title here. However, if we may anticipate some of the discussion in chapter IV we may note that the designation "Son of God" was entirely at

---

42 See O. Michel *TDNT* IV, 679 and C.J. Hemer *DNTT* I, 264.

43 E.g. Philostratus *Life* 4.20.

44 Bauernfeind *Worte* 24; cf. Burkill *Revelation* 88.

45 See [1.1]; 3.11; 8.38; 9.7; 12.6; 13.32; 14.36, 61; 15.39 and Dehn *Gottessohn* and Kee *Community* 121ff.

home in a Palestinian setting and that the designation was used to signify a close relationship to God. Furthermore, since demons were believed to include the character and origin of their opponents in their defence, it may be concluded that it is unlikely that the early Church needed to introduce "Son of God" here (cf. §17 below).

The last part of the titular address to Jesus is τοῦ ὑψίστου (*"The Most High [God]"*, verse 7). To begin with, we know from a Pseudo Danielic text among the Qumran Scrolls (4QpsDan Aᵃ [= 4Q243]) that in Palestine the title was used of figures probably other than the messiah or anointed one.[46] Though I can find no exact parallel to this title in the context of a demon's defence, the title is found in the magical-incantation literature and the appellation is not out of place here. PGM IV.1067f. calls a god "good and holy light of the most high god". In PGM V.46 an incantation's authority is "the name of the most high god".[47] In the New Testament this title is attested in two different traditions as part of a demon's defence against Christian exorcists: here and in Acts 16.17 — of Paul as a "servant of the Most High God". This, along with the fact that ὕψιστος, as a divine name, is on the margins of New Testament tradition,[48] points to the improbability that Mark or the early Church needed to introduce it into the demon's defence. Again, it seems that we can be reasonably confident that this title was included in the first report of this event.

Ὁρκίζω σε τὸν θεόν ("I adjure you by God", verse 7) is the third element in the demon's words of defence. Ὁρκίζω is entirely appropriate in this context.[49] That it would not need to have been added at any stage in the history of the transmission of this story is clear from later reactions to it. Matthew (8.29) omits it and Luke (8.28) softens it, suggesting that they object to the thought of a demon(iac) attempting to bind Jesus supernaturally. The form of the adjuration, ". . . by God", is entirely in keeping with the form found in the PGM. Two examples from PGM IV and one from a tablet can serve as examples. Lines 3019—20 of PGM IV read: "I adjure (ὁρκίζω) you by the God of the Hebrews . . .", and line 3046 reads: ". . . I adjure (ὁρκίζω) you by God the light bringer . . ."[50] A lead tablet from the large Necropolis of ancient Adrumetum, the capital of the region of Byzacium in the Roman province of Africa reads: "I bind (ὁρκίζω) you

46 J.A. Fitzmyer "The Contribution of Qumran Aramaic to the Study of the New Testament" *NTS* 20 (1973–4) 393; J.A. Fitzmyer *A Wandering Aramean* (Missoula: Scholars Press, 1979) 90–4. See also R.R. Trebilco "Paul and Silas – 'Servants of the Most High God' " *JSNT* 36 (1989) 51–73.

47 See also PGM XII.63f., 72; (cf. *T. Sol.* where the title is used); MM.

48 G. Bertram *TDNT* VIII, 620; see also Hahn *Titles* 291f.

49 See Twelftree *Christ* 43. See also Bruce *Acts* (1952) 358.

50 Cf. the use of Solomon's name in Josephus *Ant.* 8.45ff.

demoniac spirit, which lies here, by the holy names of Aoth . . ."[51] Thus, in
5.7, Mark probably understood the demon to be using God as his source of
power-authority to fetter Jesus.

The last part of the demon's words is, "Do not torment me" (μή με
βασανίσῃς, Mark 5.7). In Matthew 8.29 and Luke 8.28 we see the significance the early Church saw in the demon saying this. It is that the
term had clear eschatological signficance for the early Church. Have we
any confidence then in the historicity of this element of the defence? I
think, in view of what is said to happen to the demons (they are not
thought to be *finally* destroyed [see 5.10—13] and that Mark does not take
up the eschatological significance of 5.7), this phrase is probably original.

Understanding the position of verse 8 ("For he had said to him, 'Come
out of the man, you unclean spirit!' ") has long been a problem for inter-
preters of Mark. There are at least three possible solutions.[52] First, it could
be that verse 8 stood before verse 7 but the position was later changed
because the demon did not immediately obey the command. But, then we
ask, why was the command not simply omitted? Secondly, it could be that
verse 8 was not part of the original story but was added later by an
editor.[53] However, from what we have seen of other exorcism stories, it
would be surprising if such a command would need to have been added.
Thirdly, it could be that verse 8 is in its original position. Jesus is so
powerful that the demon at once senses it must leave its victim. An
explicit command is not readily necessary and it now comes as an after-
thought in a subordinate clause. Burkill prefers this alternative as the story
as a whole shows delight in the narration of subordinate details.[54] But,
verse 8 certainly reads like an explicit command. So, it seems that none of
these three solutions is adequate.

There is another possibility; one which permits verse 8 to remain in its
present position. In ἔλεγεν γὰρ αὐτῷ ("for he said to him" the original
narrator — Mark or, more likely, his predecessors — clearly intended the
following command to relate to what the demon had just said. Therefore,
perhaps as in Mark 1.24—5, on meeting Jesus, the demon cried out in his
defence. Then, perhaps simultaneously with the command of Jesus, the
demon further attempted to ward off Jesus' attack. So, in order to convey

---

51 See further: BAGD; cf. K.L. Schmidt *TDNT* V, 462f. and notes; cf. Josephus *Ant.*
    18.124); cf. P. Oxy 3275.40, 46; 3295.19, 24 where ὅρκος is an "oath". See also Bell (et
    al.) *Proceedings of the British Academy* 17 (1931) 251, lines 19f., cf. pp. 255, 266 and,
    e.g. PGM IV.3019, 3033, 3039, 3045, 3052, 3056; Deissmann *Studies* 274; cf. P. Oslo 1.153
    and pp. 72f.; (and though Christian, see *T. Sol.* passim); MM and LSJ.
52 See Burkill *Revelation* 89f.
53 Cf. Pryke *Style* 14.
54 Burkill *Revelation* 90.

this fast or overlapping dialogue, the narrator adopted the solution that we have in verse 8.[55] The advantage of this explanation is that it makes sense of verse 9 ("And Jesus asked him, 'What is your name? . . .' "). The possession of someone's name was widely held to be equivalent to having power over them.[56] If, as we shall show in a moment, this is how we are to understand verse 9, then it is redundant if the command of verse 8 was thought to be successful. If, however, the adjuration of the demon "by God", and the command to the demon "to come out" overlap in some way, perhaps cancelling each other out, so that Jesus is not at first successful, verse 9 becomes significant. That Jesus was not always thought to be initially and immediately successful in his healings is shown by the two-part cure of the blind man in Mark 8.22—6.[57] Also, Acts 19.13—19 is an example of an unsuccessful exorcism, in this instance, because the possessed man did not respect the exorcists.

But, are we justified in taking verse 9 as being Jesus' further attempt to gain ascendancy over the demon? We probably are for, as just noted, in the ancient world the possession of someone's name was thought to include power over that person. And, further, of the historicity of this notion in the context of a preternatural conflict we can be confident. On the one hand, we have no knowledge of any dogmatic reasons why the early Church would want to introduce this element into the tradition and, on the other hand, we have examples of exorcists' requests for names over that which they sought to exercise control. (E.g. note PGM IV.3039ff. as well as PGM XIII.242ff..[58]) When discussing Mark 1.25 we noted that other exorcists often seem to have had considerable difficulty in getting demons to speak or give their names. According to this story Jesus seems to have had no such difficulty, for the demon immediately supplies his name. But, has this success been attributed to Jesus? We cannot be certain. However, if our interpretation of the position and significance of verse 8 is correct then the early Church did not always seek to make Jesus instantly successful (cf. Mark 6.56; 8.22—6). So, on balance, it seems quite likely that

---

55 Cf. the *Good News Bible* translation which puts v. 8 in parenthesis. See also Derrett *Man* (n.s.) 14 (1979) 288 and his citations.

56 Green *ANRW* II.19.2 (1979) 635 and n.65. See also Langton *Essentials* 28f., 157; Weatherhead *Psychology* 65 and Aune *ANRW* II.23.2 (1980) 1546.

57 Loos *Miracles* 419ff.. E. Best "Discipleship in Mark: Mark 8.22–10.52" *SJT* 23 (1970) 325, calls this story a " 'botched' healing in which Jesus fails to give a blind man perfect sight at the first attempt, and only at the second fully restores his vision." However, in "The Miracles in Mark" *RevExp* 75 (1978) 539–54, reprinted in *Disciples and Discipleship* (Edinburgh: T & T Clark, 1986), Best says that "the two stages are not intended to imply that Jesus found the miracle difficult" (186 n. 22).

58 See also PGM I.162; IV.3037; cf. A. Deissmann *Light from the Ancient East* (London: Hodder and Stoughton, 1910) 257 and n. 8; Klostermann *Markusevangelium* 49; C. Bonner "The Technique of Exorcism" *HTR* 36 (1943) 44–5.

the demon's reported immediate reply accurately reflects a historical situation.

Paul Winter says that in the demon's reply — "My name is Legion; for we are many" (verse 9) — "an anti-Roman attitude definitely comes to the fore," discernible in the use of λεγιών.[59] Winter says that during the great revolt the *Legio Decima Fretensis* was stationed in Galilee near the place where this story has its *locale*,[60] and that the emblem of this legion was a boar. However, not only did Vespasian have the fifth, and fifteenth legions with him when he took Gamala (*War* 4.13), but the Roman legions were not restricted to any one area.

Jeremias also attempts to see the narrative as making a specific connection between the number of pigs and the number of soldiers in the Roman legion. However, the body of soldiers he cites is not a legion, which in the imperial period consisted of about 6,000 men, but a τέλος which had a strength of 2,048 men.[61] And, in any case, the lack of precision (ὡς, "about") in the use of δισχίλιοι indicates that no special significance was intended to be attached to the number of pigs in the herd. It is best then to see that no specific link was intended between the number of pigs and a Roman legion, nor that the early Christians were using this passage to express an anti-Roman sentiment.[62] Rather, in territory occupied by the Romans, "legion" was an appropriate term to express the great number of demons thought to be involved. Indeed, a Syriac incantation bowl is inscribed to protect a person "from all legions," which shows that such language is not out of place in this context.[63] And, such multiple possessions, usually successive and thought to be under a group leader, are well known in a variety of history of religions parallels.[64]

Mark 5.9 includes the phrase "because we are many" in the direct speech of the demon. Was this part of the original tradition? History of religions parallels show that it was important not only to know the name and how it related to the nature of the demon, but also the actual nature of the demon. A good example of this is PGM IV.1017—19 where a god reveals his name and nature: ". . . my name is Βαϊνχωωωχ. I am the one

---

59 P. Winter *On the Trial of Jesus* (Berlin: de Gruyter, 1961) 129. Cf. Theissen *Followers* 101–2 and K. Wengst *Pax Romana* (London: SCM, 1987) 65–8.

60 Winter *Trial* 129. He cites Josephus *War* 3.233, 289 and 458, 485. On the military background of 'legion' see J. Mateos "Tèrminos relacionados con 'Legión' en Mc 5,2–20" *Filologia Neotestamentaria* 1 (1988) 211–15.

61 Jeremias *Promise* 31 n. 5. Cf. H. Preisker *TDNT* IV, 68.

62 Contrast Wengst *Pax Romana* 66.

63 J.A. Montgomery *Aramaic Incantation Texts from Nippur* (Philadelphia: University Museum, 1913) 37.6–7; cf. 7.17. Also see *b. Ber.* 51a. On the appropriateness of a military term here see Derrett *Man* (n.s.) 14 (1979) 289.

64 See Derrett *Man* (n.s.) 14 (1979) 288. Note Luke 8.2.

who is from heaven; my name is Βαλcάμης." The phrase, "for we are many", fits this form of a demon's disclosing its nature. Luke's deleting this phrase from the demon's reply strongly suggests that the early Church did not seek to shape the demon's reply to fit the form.

A potential difficulty here is the constant change of numbers of demons, exemplified in the demon's reply to Jesus — "*My* name is Legion for *we* are many" (cf. 5.7f.). However, the change of numbers makes it obvious that the demon in mind here is multiform.[65]

In verses 10 and 12 the demon pleads for leniency. This component of the story was probably not introduced by the early Church for, as we have seen, other exorcism stories outside the New Testament contained this feature.[66] And, in view of the non-theological nature of the plea (contrast Matthew 8.29 and Luke 8.31), we can see no motivation for adding the element. It was held that demons were especially associated with particular areas from which they did not want to move.[67] In Matthew and Luke the "torment" which the demons seek to avoid is the eschatological punishment (Matthew 8.29; Luke 8.26 and 29). But in Mark that which the demons fear is simply being sent "out of the region". It seems then, at least in this story, that neither Mark nor his tradition associated this exorcism of Jesus with the final punishment or destruction of the demons.

The second part of the demon's request is that they should be allowed to enter into some pigs that were grazing on the side of the hill (verse 12). As we have argued already, this element of the story is probably part of the original Jesus tradition. In so far as water was understood as one of the appropriate havens of demons, the destruction of the pigs is the description of the demons plunging into a new home.[68] This uncharacteristic herd like behaviour of the pigs would certainly have caused the onlookers to conclude the pigs were "bewitched".[69]

Our survey of this Markan pericope leads us to support Bultmann's conclusion on this story. He says, "clearly this story is essentially intact in its original form."[70] We could also support Schweizer's suggestion that the inconsistencies and apparent redundancies in the text are probably due to the narrator's lack of skill[71] rather than the accumulation of material

---

65   A.R. Johnson *The One and the Many* (Cardiff: University of Wales Press Board, 1942) 29f. and notes; cf. Klostermann *Matthäusevangelium* 113; Hull *Magic* 103.

66   See also Klostermann *Markusevangelium* 49 and Twelftree *Christ* chap. II.

67   Taylor *Mark* 282; W. Foerster *TDNT* II, 6f.; O. Böcher *Christus Exorcista* (Stuttgart: Kohlhammer, 1972) 20ff.

68   On various interpretations of the stampede of the pigs see Loos *Miracles* 390ff.

69   See further on the behaviour of pigs Derrett *JSNT* 3 (1979) 5–6.

70   Bultmann *History* 210. Cf. Annen *Heil für die Heiden* 186.

71   Schweizer *Mark* 112, though he does not think that there are two stories here.

around an early story. We have also shown that much of this story most probably reflects tradition that rightly belongs to the original Jesus story.[72]

---

72 Cf. Latourelle *Miracles* 118–9.

§ 8 The Syrophoenician Woman's Daughter[1]
Mark 7.24—30 (/Matthew 15.21—8)

We are examining this pericope also in an attempt to identify and set aside Christian redaction in order to reconstruct the earliest form of the story.

> (24) And from there he arose and went away into the borders of Tyre. And entering into a house he did not wish any one to know it, and he was not able to be hidden; (25) but immediately a woman hearing about him, whose little daughter had an unclean spirit, came and fell down at his feet. (26) Now the woman was a Greek, a Syrophoenician by birth; and she asked him to cast the demon out of her daughter. (27) And he said to her; "Let the children first be fed, for it is not good to take the bread of the children and throw it to the dogs." (28) But she answered and said to him; "Lord; and the dogs under the table eat the crumbs of the children." (29) And he said to her; "For saying this go, the demon has gone out of your daughter." (30) And going away into her home she found the child lying on the bed and the demon gone.

Mark has this story in a section where Jesus is on a Gentile Mission (7.24—8.26).[2] Mark usually begins his pericopes with καί ("and"), but as δέ ("but") is used here we suspect he may wish to indicate a significant break in the story, since on the other times he uses δέ to start a paragraph they clearly imply a significant break in the story (1.14; 10.32 and 14.1).[3] While this pericope might belong primarily to the Gentile Mission in Mark, Jesus' freedom from the law, and the receptivity of the Gentiles are

---

1 Literature: A. Dermience "Tradition et rédaction dans la péricope de la Syro-phénicienne: Mark 7,24—30" *RTL* 8 (1977) 15–29; Pesch *Markus*. I, 391. Also, Gnilka *Markus* II, 43; G. Theissen "Lokal– und Sozialkolorit in der Geschichte von der syrophönikischen Frau (Mk 7.24—30)" *ZNW* 75 (1984) 202–25; B.C. Wee "The Syro-phoenician Woman – Mark 7.24–30; New Testament in the light of the Old" *Compass* 18 (1, 1984) 38–40; Latourelle *Miracles* 175–6; R.S. Sugirtharajah "The Syro-phoenician Woman" *ExpTim* 98 (1986) 13–15; Drewermann *Markus*. I, 472–92; A. Stock "Jesus and the Lady from Tyre. Encounter in the Border District" *Emmanuel* 93 (1987) 336–9, 358; Guelich *Mark* I, 381; G.R. O'Day "Surprised by Faith: Jesus and the Canaanite Woman" *Listening* 24 (1989) 290–301; Stock *Method* 209–15; F. Dufton "The Syrophoenician Woman and her Dogs" *ExpTim* 100 (1989) 417.
2 On the historicity of such a mission see Taylor *Mark* 633–6; Nineham *Mark* 197f.; Jeremias *Promise* 33.
3 C.H. Turner "A Textual Commentary on Mark 1" *JTS* 29 (1926–7) 152.

brought sharply into focus in this story, as it stands after the section on Jewish legalism (7.1—23).[4]

The evidence is not decisive but Mark may have reworking this introduction (verse 24).[5] However, whether or not the setting of the story in the region of Tyre and Sidon is Markan will depend to a large extent on the origin of verse 26, which says the woman was a Syrophoenician (see below).[6] The mention of going into a house as a retreat is probably Markan.[7] Although ἀλλά ("but", verse 25) is not a significant indicator of Mark's hand,[8] εὐθὺς ἀκούσασα ("immediately hearing") may be Markan redaction.[9] It is possible that θυγάτριον, the diminutive of daughter, is Mark's responsibility.[10] However, as this could be due to Semitic influence,[11] and since a phrase begun with a relative ἧς, "whose") and completed by a personal pronoun (αὐτῆς, "of her") is also probably due to Semitic influence,[12] this whole phrase is probably pre-Markan, including πνεῦμα ἀκάθαρτον ("unclean spirit").[13] There is nothing in the last part of verse 25 — the woman prostrating herself at the feet of Jesus — to intimate Markan editorial activity.

Verse 26a ("the woman was a Greek") may be from Mark's hand as it is one of his many parentheses.[14] This raises the question of the origin of the setting of this story. The question can be put thus: Would Mark or the early Church give a Gentile setting to the story?

Burkhill's view is that a story that had its origin in Syrophoenicia would not describe the woman as "a Syrophoenician by birth".[15] However, the description of the woman is for the hearers of the story. To describe the woman as a Greek may have led Jews to think she was a Hellenistic Jew. Adding "a Syrophoenician by birth" identifies the woman as a pagan

---

4 Anderson *Mark* 189f.; Schweizer *Mark* 151; T.A. Burkill "The Historical Development of the Story of the Syrophoenician Woman (Mark vii: 24–31)" *NovT* 9 (1967) 173; and "The Syrophoenician Woman: The Congruence of Mark 7.24–31" *ZNW* 57 (1966) 35.

5 See Bultmann *History* 38, 64; Best *Temptation* 79; Pesch *Markus.* I, 61; Kertelge *Wunder* 154,

6 See Marxsen *Mark* 69 and n.55. The point is not altered however, even if Burkill's criticism (*ZNW* 57 [1966] 35ff.) is correct of Marxsen's view that Mark takes up geographical data and refrains from supplementing it, for it is the internal evidence of this particular pericope that is important here.

7 See Stein *ZNW* 61 (1970) 78 and n. 29. Cf. Wrede *Secret* 36.

8 Neirynck *ETL* 57 (1981) 146.

9 On εὐθὺς see Kertelge *Wunder* 51 n. 58; cf. *HSE* 72; Neirynck *ETL* 57 (1981) 147.

10 Cf. Turner *Grammar* IV, 28.

11 BDF 111.3.

12 Black *Aramaic* 100f.; Turner *Grammar* IV, 21; cf. Taylor *Mark* 60.

13 See §6 n. 19 above.

14 Turner *Grammar* IV, 26 and those mentioned there.

15 Burkill *ZNW* 57 (1966) 23–37 and Burkill *NovT* 9 (1967) 161–77.

from the area.[16] Also, Mark shows an interest in the Gentiles and Jesus' Gentile Mission,[17] so he would hardly create this potentially offensive story. Thus, the traditional place reference can be retained as part of the original story.[18]

Verse 27a — "let the children first be fed" — is probably not a later addition to Mark.[19] Only πρῶτον ("first") might suggest Mark's hand, but the evidence is too slight to suggest that Mark is responsible for this phrase.[20] Again, in verses 27—8 (the conversation between Jesus and the woman) there is little evidence upon which to build a case for Markan redaction. The Jewish style of referring to Gentiles as "dogs"[21] tells against the Church ever creating this section of the pericope.[22] The closing two verses also show little of Mark's hand, save perhaps the reference to the woman going "home".[23]

Mark's interest in this pericope as an exorcism story seems slight. The centre of interest is on the woman, her origin, her faith or persistence, and upon Jesus' words. It seems that Mark found this story in his tradition much as we now have it, but he has reworked its introduction in order to fit it into his Gospel. In the next chapter we will discuss the historicity of a healing from a distance in the Jesus tradition.

---

16   Theissen *Miracle* 126. On the Aramaic behind "Syrophoenician/Canaanite" having both meanings see G. Schwarz "ΣΥΡΟΦΟΙΝΙΚΙΣΣΑ-ΧΑΝΑΝΑΙΑ (Markus 7.26/Matthäus 15.22)" *NTS* 30 (1984) 626–8.

17   Jeremias *Promise* 33; Taylor *Mark* (see index); Nineham *Mark* 197f.

18   To the contrary J.D.M. Derrett "Law in the NT: The Syrophoenician Woman and the Centurion of Capernaum" *NovT* 15 (1973) 161–86 reprinted with further annotations in his *Studies in the NT* I (Leiden: Brill, 1977) 145.

19   As suggested by Held in Bornkamm, Barth and Held *Tradition* 198, following Bultmann *History* 38.

20   Pryke cites πρῶτον as a Markan redactional word (*Style* 137) but *HSE* does not cite the word as significant of Mark's hand.

21   See also Jeremias *Promise* 29.

22   Cf. Taylor *Mark* 347. On Jewish attitudes to Phoenicians and Tyrians see Josephus *Ag. Ap.* 1.71.

23   See Stein *ZNW* 61 (1970) 78 and n. 29. Cf. Wrede *Secret* 36.

§ 9 The Epileptic Boy[1]
Mark 9.14—29 (/Matthew 17.14—21/Luke 9.37—43a)

Once again, we are attempting to isolate and set aside Christian redaction from this story in order to help trace elements in it that probably belong to the historical Jesus tradition.

> (14) And coming to the disciples they saw a great crowd around them and scribes arguing with them. (15) And immediately all the crowd when they saw him were greatly amazed and running to him greeted him. (16) And he asked them; "Why argue with them?" (17) And one of the crowd answered him; "Teacher, I brought my son to you, having a dumb spirit; (18) and wherever it seizes him it dashes him down, and he foams and grinds his teeth and becomes rigid; and I asked your disciples to cast it out, and they were not able." (19) But he answered them; "O faithless generation, how long am I to be with you? How long am I to endure you? Bring him to me." (20) And they brought him to him. And seeing him the spirit immediately it convulsed him, and falling on the ground he wallowed foaming. (21) And he asked his father; "How long has this been happening to him?" And he said; "From childhood; (22) and it has often thrown him into fire and into water to destroy him; but if you can do anything, help us having compassion on us." (23) But Jesus said to him; "If you can! All things are possible to him who believes." (24) Immediately the father of the child said crying out; "I believe; help my unbelief!" (25) But Jesus seeing that a crowd was running together, rebuked the unclean spirit saying to it; "Dumb and deaf spirit, I command you, come out of him and no longer enter him." (26) And crying out and greatly convulsing him it came out; and he became as dead, which caused most of them to say that he died. (27) But Jesus taking his hand raised him, and he arose.
>
> (28) And when he had entered the house his disciples asked him privately; "Why could we not cast it out?" (29) And he said to them; "This kind cannot come out by anything except by prayer."

It is Bultmann's opinion that, in this pericope, two miracle stories have been combined in the pre-Markan stage. Presumably they were brought together because of the similarity of the illness and healing.[2] Bultmann

---

1 Literature: Schürmann *Lukas*. I, 568; Kertelge *Wunder* 174-9; Pesch *Markus*. II, 97f.; Gnilka *Markus* II, 45; Best *Following* chap. 6; H. Achinger "Zur Traditionsgeschichte der Epileptiker–Perikope Mk.9, 14-29 par, Mt 17, 14-21 par, Lk 9, 37-43a" in A. Fuchs (ed.) *Probleme der Forschung* (Wien: Herold, 1978) 114-43; Latourelle *Miracles* 154; Drewermann *Markus*. II, 15-40.

2 Bultmann *History* 211. See also, e.g. Schweizer *Mark* 187; Anderson *Mark* 229; Nineham *Mark* 242; P.J. Achtemeier "Miracles and the Historical Jesus: A Study of Mark 9.14-29" *CBQ* 37 (1975) 476-7 and those mentioned by von W. Schenk "Tradition und Redaktion in der Epileptiker–Perikope Mark 9 14-29" *ZNW* 63 (1972) 76 n. 1; G.

admits that it is now difficult to make clear distinctions, but the first story may have occupied verses 14—20. This story would have had its point in the contrast between the Master and the magician's disciples, whose inability to heal provides the foil for the Master's power. Verses 21—7 are the scond story describing the paradox of unbelieving faith.

To support his theory Bultmann offers three pieces of evidence. 1. The disciples have a part to play in verses 14—19 only and, thereafter, pass from the scene, whereas in verses 21—2 the father takes the chief role, though he only has a minor one in verses 17—19. 2. The illness is described twice; in verses 18 and 21—2. 3. The crowd is already present in verse 14 yet, according to verse 25, comes on the scene for the first time.[3]

So, are there two stories here? 1. If we were to presume for the moment that the reference to the disciples in verses 28—9 is Markan then the disciples do indeed pass from the secne after verse 19a. However, this need not be an indication of there once being two stories for, in other stories, characters are introduced and withdrawn within a story. Mark 5.1—20, which we have argued to be a single story, has the herdsmen entering late in the story (§7 above).

2. Bultmann's second piece of evidence is that the illness is twice described. In fact it is probably described three times (verses 17c—18a, 20b, and 21c—22a). While this might indicate an amalgamation of stories there may be another explanation that would make these two or three "descriptions" inelligible as they stand.

The first description (17b—18a — "having a dumb spirit; and wherever it seizes him it dashes him down, and he foams and grinds his teeth and becomes rigid") comes at the very beginning of the story (after the introductory setting) as in Mark 5.2—5. It would conform to the first element in the form critics' analysis of miracle stories.[4]

In dealing with the other exorcism stories we have seen that a recurring element was the visible or audible consternation of the demon when confronted by the exorcist. That this second description of the illness (verse 20b) fits this category is clear from its opening phrase — "And seeing him . . ."

Also, in our examination of exorcism stories so far it has been apparent that an important part of the stories was the exorcist's knowing the demon by gaining knowledge of its name and thereby its character.[5] That

Petzke "Die historische Frage nach den Wundertaten Jesu, dargestellt am Beispiel des Exorzismus Mark. IX, 14—29 par" *NTS* 22 (1975–6) 186–8. To the contrary see Loos *Miracles* 401.

3   Bultmann *History* 211.

4   Kertelge *Wunder* 52.

5   See also Twelftree *Christ* chap. II.

the third description of the illness (verses 21—2) fits this category is manifest not only because it begins with a question — "How long has this been happening to him?", but also by the answer which mentions the demon's predilection for fire or water. Thus, the two or three descriptions of the illness do not require a two story hypothesis for their explanation.

3. Are there two crowds in this story — one in verse 14, and another in verse 25? Bultmann[6] takes ἐπισυντρέχει ("run together", verse 25) to refer to a second crowd coming to the area. No parallel to the word has been cited in classical Greek or in the papyri[7] and so its precise meaning is difficult to determine. Nevertheless, in this context, the meaning is probably that a crowd is converging on a single point.[8] In any case, the story does not require a two story theory to explain the mention of the crowd in verse 25 and it could be intended to be the same crowd as in verse 14.[9] It seems that we may conclude that the evidence from this story neither demands nor needs a two story hypothesis.[10] Now we need to discuss which parts of the story may, with reasonable probability, be attributed to redactors and which parts may be traced back to the first reports of Jesus' activity.

As might be expected, Mark's hand is particularly evident in the introduction. However, we do not need to discuss this for the story proper begins in verse 17 with the father saying that he had brought his demon-possessed son to the disciples who could not heal the boy.[11] In the *Acts of Thomas* (8.75—81) there is a story which has a similar chain of events but there is no indication that the story is in any way dependent on the account of the possessed boy in Mark 9.[12]

1. We have already offered an explanation for the three descriptions of the illness (verses 17b—18b, 20, 21b—22); that is, they fit the common "form" of an exorcism story. We should attribute these descriptions to the very earliest form of the story for they do not conform to the pattern of descriptions elsewhere in Mark (cf. 1.23, 26; 3.11; 5.2ff.; 7.25) nor does the vocabulary of the descriptions betray any particular early Church interests.

2. Does the rebuke by Jesus in 9.19 belong to the original story or is it from a Christian hand?

---

6 Bultmann *History* 211.
7 Cf. Taylor *Mark* 400; MM 247.
8 For its Aramaic background see Taylor *Mark* 400; Black *Aramaic* (1946) 85 n. 3.
9 See also M.–J. Lagrange *Evengile selon Saint Marc* (Paris: Gabalda, 1920) 241; A. Plummer *The Gospel According to St. Luke* (Edinburgh: T & T Clark, 1922) 220; Swete *Mark* 200.
10 So also Petzke *NTS* 22 (1975–6) 188.
11 On the Markan redaction of the introduction see Petzke *NTS* 22 (1975–6) 194–5.
12 Cf. Achtemeier *CBQ* 37 (1975) 473.

That Jesus is meant to be addressing the *disciples* in his rebuke to the "faithless generation" is clear from the use of αὐτοῖς ("them", cf. verse 20a). Being plural, this can only refer to the disciples or possibly the crowd. However, the crowd is not the focus of attention here. And, the conclusion of the pericope indicates that the disciples are firmly at the centre of interest.

A number of factors might indicate that it is Mark who is responsible for the reference to the disciples and their inability here. (a) Markan activity at each end of the pericope predisposes us towards suspecting Mark's hand in this reference to the disciples. (b) In view of the father's desperate cry, "I believe; help my unbelief!" (9.24), the rebuke may once have been directed towards the father. (c) Where faith is mentioned elsewhere in Mark as important in healing it is always that of those seeking the healing, either of the sick person (5.34; 10.52) or people acting on their behalf (2.5; 5.36). If 9.19 was intended to be directed towards the disciples it would be an exception to this pattern.

Thus, while Mark seems responsible for heightening the reference to the disciples' inability in verses 18b—19, the rebuke is so integral to this story that it was probably to be found in Mark's tradition. It is most likely that the early Church — as represented by Matthew and Luke — saw an echo of Deuteronomy 32.5 in this saying.[13] For some, such a conclusion casts doubt on the verse being in the earliest material.[14] However, the use of Deuteronomy 32.5 in Mark 9.19 is significantly different from the way the early Church generally used it. In the early Church Deuteronomy 32.5 seems to have been used to characterize the *pagan* world in contrast to the community of faith (see Matthew 12.39; Philippians 2.15 and Acts 2.40).[15]

3. As verse 24 deals with the faith of the father and not the disciples, it is probably part of the original tradition[16]. However, verses 22b—23 may have their origin in the post-Easter community; the father's cry for pity being a foil for Jesus' words on faith which are difficult to show as being pre-Easter in origin. On the other hand, the father's cry for help is consistent with Jesus' rebuke and does not show Jesus in a kindly light, in that he causes the father some grief, and so it is probably to be associated with the original story.

---

13 See, e.g. R.H. Gundry *The Use of the OT in Matthew's Gospel* (Leiden: Brill, 1967) 83–4; Schürmann *Lukas*. I, 570 n. 25; Beare *Matthew* 369.

14 See, e.g. H.E. Tödt *The Son of Man in the Synoptic Tradition* (London: SCM 1965) 224; Käsemann in *Essays* 40.

15 See H.E.W. Turner *Historicity and the Gospels* (London: Morbray, 1963) 73ff. cited §15 below.

16 Cf. Mark 1.40; 5.23, 28; Luke 5.5. Also Theissen *Miracle* 54f.

4. Verse 25 is the report of Jesus' exorcistic technique. "He rebuked" (ἐπετίμησεν) is used to describe Jesus' words which follow. The command of Jesus is said to be "Dumb and deaf spirit, I command you, come out of him and no longer enter into him."

(a) When dealing with Mark 5.8 we noted that there were no particular reasons why the early Church should have added the details of the address to the demon. And, on the other hand, the use of the demon's name in exorcistic incantations was a long and well established convention.[17] We conclude then that this element of the words of Jesus belongs to the historically authentic tradition.

(b) "I command you" (ἐγὼ ἐπιτάσσω σοι, cf. Mark 1.27). The phrase is also well known in the magical literature in the context of incantations seeking to control demons and gods. For example, PGM XIII.171 has "I command you, great one . . . demon of the great god . . ." and PGM VII.331 has ". . . Lord Anoubi, I command you; for I am . . ."[18] Even though the precise formula has not been found in the stories of other exorcists, [19] this is fitting vocabulary for an exorcist's command. Pesch suggests that ἐγώ has probably been introduced into the tradition in order to contrast the faith of Jesus with the powerless unbeliever.[20] However, as will be argued below (§18), this use of ἐγώ ("I") is most likely to be part of the authentic Jesus tradition (see §§10 and 18 below).

(c) ". . . And no longer enter into him" (καὶ μηκέτι εἰσέλθῃς εἰς αὐτόν). The Babylonian material illustrates the ancient belief in the re-entry of a demon into a person.

"Perform the incantation of Eridu . . .
That the evil Spirit, the evil Demon
    may stand aside,
And a kindly spirit, a kindly Genius be
    present."[21]

In PGM IV.3024f. there seems to be a provision to arrest a free-ranging demon to prevent it entering a person: "let thy angel descend . . . and let him draw into captivity the demon as he flies around this creature . . ."[22] Also, this apparent repetition in Mark 9.25 is a recognized routine in both Hellenistic and Jewish material. In PGM IV.1254 there is a Jewish prescription for the wearing of an amulet after a demon has been expelled.

---

17 Lucian *Philops.* 16; Philostratus *Life* 3.38; 4.20; (cf. *Acts Thom.* Act 3.31–3).
18 See Eitrem *Notes* 27.
19 Cf. Kee *NTS* 14 (1967–8) 240.
20 Pesch *Markus*. II, 94; cf. V. Howard *Das Ego Jesu in den synoptischen Evangelien* (Marburg: N.G, Elwert, 1975) 86–97.
21 Thompson *Devils* II, 85, cf. 8; I, 206, 207, (etc.).
22 See also Eitrem *Notes* 26; Luke 11.24–6; Deissmann *Light* 252 n. 2; Thompson *Devils* II, 59 and 85.

Eleazar is said to have "adjured the demon never to come back into him . . ." (Josephus *Ant.* 8.47). The demon with which Apollonius was dealing "swore that he would leave the young man alone and never take possession of any man again" (Philostratus *Life* 4.20). So the reported technique of Jesus accords well with the history of religions parallels. But, at this point, has the Synoptic tradition been shaped during its transmission in accordance with an accepted pattern of story telling technique? It is difficult to discover a precise literary convention that is being followed; Josephus has μηκέτ' εἰς αὐτὸν ἐπανήξειν (or, in some manuscripts, ἐπανελθεῖν, *Ant.* 8.47) but Mark 9.25 has μηκέτι εἰσέλθῃς εἰς αὐτόν. The whole of verse 25 is, to my knowledge, nowhere paralleled in its entirety. The last part of the formula in verse 25 is found in a story (Josephus *Ant.* 8.47), and in a prescriptive incantation in the magical papyri (see PGM IV.3024—25), as well as apparently on amulets (cf. PGM IV.1294). Further, Mark and his tradition show no desire to be thoroughly consistent in their representation of Jesus' exorcistic words. That is, they show no desire to adhere to a literary pattern. Finally, in view of the later Evangelists' hesitancy over this genre of Jesus' words in the tradition (cf. Matthew 17.18/Luke 9.42) it seems that we may be fairly confident that verse 25 is a genuine reflection of the words of Jesus the exorcist.

5. Verses 26—7 report the departure of the demon. Reports of the violent departure of demons were common in the ancient world (see §17 below) and it is found in other stories of Jesus (Mark 1.26; 5.13). Again, in view of Matthew's (17.18) and Luke's reticence here (4.35), this element in the story probably goes back to eyewitness accounts. Since the reference to Jesus taking the lad by the hand and raising him not only closely resembles 1.31 and 5.41 but also could hardly fail to remind the early Christians of Jesus' resurrection (see Acts 2.24, 32; 3.26; 13.33—4; 17.31) as well as power to awaken the dead, then the formulation — if not the content of this verse — may have originated after Easter. Over against these points it is necessary to note that the use of the hands in healing was so common in the Jewish world that it would in fact be surprising if Jesus did not use the technique.[23]

6. Finally, verses 28—9 relate the disciples' question to Jesus about their inability to cast out the demon. In view of the vocabulary, Mark may have given us this particular ending to the pericope.[24] Yet, the reference to

---

23 On the use of hands see D. Daube *The NT and Rabbinic Judaism* (Salem: Ayer, 1984) 224–46 and the bibliography in *DNTT* II, 152f..

24 Note, εἰς, οἶκος, μαθητής, ἴδιος, ἐπερωτᾶν, δύνασθαι (bis) and ἐξέρχεϲθαι and see *HSE* 19, 72–4, 76, 78.

this kind of demon only being able to be cast out "in prayer"[25] may not be Markan for he does not show prayer as an element in Jesus' technique or healing, or in anyone else's — notably the Strange Exorcist who is said simply to invoke a powerful name (Mark 9.38—41).[26] The reported technique of the disciples in 6.13 is anointing with oil not prayer.[27] Whether or not verses 28—9 were in this position in Mark's tradition is difficult to tell, though in view of the inconsistency between the motif of faith embedded in the pericope (verses 19, 23, 24) and prayer in this concluding sentence it may have been placed here by Mark. For, though it is possible that this inconsistency existed in Mark's tradition, inconsistencies would probably have been omitted or ironed out in the transmission of tradition.[28]

We began this section with the objective of setting aside Christian redaction in order to help trace elements in this story that probably belong to the historical Jesus tradition. In order to focus on Jesus' ability as an exorcist the disciples' inability is highlighted by redirecting Jesus' rebuke (verse 19) from the father to the disciples. Mark's special contribution to this story was probably in concluding it with an application appropriate for the Church. On the other hand, we have seen that there is probably a considerable amount of reliable historical recollection in this pericope, including the descriptions of the illness, the rebuke, Jesus' technique, and the violent departure of the demon.[29]

---

25 Some texts make reference to "fasting", see Taylor *Mark* 401 and Metzger *Commentary* 101.

26 Nineham (*Mark* 242) is incorrect in saying that the disciples were unable "to cast out an evil spirit *in his name* (v. 18)" (my emphasis). This form of exorcism is not in view here (v. 29).

27 On exorcism in the post–Apostolic Church see §16 n. 18 below.

28 On "inconsistency" as an indication of redaction see Stein *ZNW* 61 (1970) 78–9 and §5 above.

29 Cf. Achtemeier *CBQ* 37 (1975) 473 ". . .(there) is no indication that later interests in the story would have caused modifications in the story in the gospels, to make that story conform to later interests. We can, with some confidence, assume that the stories as now presented in the three synoptic gospels represent substantially the form given them by the respective evangelists." Cf. the reconstruction of Mark's tradition by Schenk *ZNW* 63 (1972) 93–4. See also Latourelle *Miracles* 152–4. To the contrary, arguing that the story reflects the early Church rather than an historical event, see Petzke *NTS* 22 (1976) 180–204.

§ 10 The Beelzebul Controversy[1]
Matthew 9.32—4; 12.22—30/Mark 3.22—7/Luke 11.14—23

This is one of the most important pieces of material in the Gospels relating to our theme. There is Q material here and we are presented with the possibility of Q containing a brief exorcism story. The charge against Jesus (Matthew 12.24/Luke 11.15/Mark 3.22, cf. 30) has been variously understood and so we must attempt to answer some questions. If the charge can be shown probably to be historically reliable, what would it have meant? What was meant by the term Beelzebul? From where did the term come? We should also ask what this passage tells us about Jesus' technique in exorcism and his impact on those around him. In turn, it will be necessary to take yet another look at the Spirit/finger saying of Matthew 12.28/Luke 11.20 to enquire about its historicity and meaning. In view of Best's treatment and understanding of the parable of the Strong Man (Mark 3.27), we will also need to ask how these verses may relate to Jesus' understanding of the fall of Satan.

---

1 Literature: Pesch *Markus*. I, 220f.. See also S. Aalen " 'Reign' and 'House' in the Kingdom of God in the Gospels" *NTS* 8 (1961-2) 215–40; E.C.B. MacLaurin "Beelzeboul" *NovT* 20 (1978) 156–60: Gnilka *Markus* I, 143; A.J. Hultgren *Jesus and His Adversaries* (Minneapolis: Augsburg, 1979); A. Fuchs *Die Entwicklung der Beelzebulkontroverse bei den Synoptikern. Traditionsgeschichtliche und redaktionsgeschichtliche Untersuchung von Mk 3,22-7 und Parallelen, verbunden mit der Rückfrage nach Jesus* (Linz: SNTU, 1980); B. Chilton "A Comparative Study of Synoptic Development: The Dispute between Cain and Abel in the Palestinian Targums and the Beelzebul Controversy in the Gospels" *JBL* 101 (1982) 553–62; J.-M. Van Cangh " 'Par l'esprit de Dieu – par le doigt'. Mt 12,28 par. Lc 11,20" in Delobel (ed.) *Logia* 337–42; R. Meynet "Qui donc est 'le plus fort'? analyse rhétorique de Mc 3, 22–30; Mt 12, 22–37; Luc 11, 14–26" *RB* 90 (1983) 334–50; F. Neirynck "Mt 12,25a/Lc 11,17a et la rédaction des évangiles" *ETL* 62 (1986) 122–33; Drewermann *Markus* I, 311–21; C. Mearns "Realized Eschatology in Q? A Consideration of the Sayings in Luke 7.22, 11.20 and 16.16" *SJT* 40 (1987) 189–210; L.M. White "Scaling the Strongman's 'Court' (Luke 11:21)" *Forum* 3 (1987) 3–28; B.J. Malina and J.H. Neyrey *Calling Jesus Names: The Social Value of Labels in Matthew* (Sonoma, CA: Polebridge, 1988) esp. 3–32; D.E. Oakman "Rulers' Houses, Thieves and Usurpers: The Beelzebul Pericope" *Forum* 4 (1988) 109–23; P. Sellew "Beelzebul in Mark 3: Dialogue, Story, or Sayings Cluster?" *Forum* 4 (1988) 93–108; M.D. Goulder *Luke. A New Paradigm* 2 vols. (Sheffield: JSOT, 1989) II, 502–9; Guelich *Mark* I, 166–86; A.O. Nkwoka "Mark 3:19b–21: A Study of the Charge of Fanaticism Against Jesus" *Biblebhashyam* 15 (1989) 205–21; Stock *Method* 129–38.

Matt. 12.22–30	Matt. 9.32–34	Mark 3.22–27	Luke 11.14–15, 17–23
(22) Then was brought to him a blind and dumb demoniac, and he healed him, so that the dumb man spoke and saw. (23) And all the crowds were amazed and said; "Is this the Son of David?" (24) But when the Pharisees heard it they said; "This man does not cast out the demons except by Beelzebul the prince of demons." (25) But knowing their thoughts he said to them; "Every kingdom divided against itself is laid waste and every city or house divided against itself will not stand. (26) And if Satan casts out Satan, he is divided against himself; how then will his kingdom stand? (27) But if I by Beelzebul cast out the demons, by whom do your sons cast them out? Therefore	(32) And as they were going away behold they brought to him a dumb demoniac man. (33) And when the demon had been cast out the dumb man spoke. And the crowds marvelled saying; "Never was anything seen like this in Israel." (34) But the Pharisees said; "By the prince of demons he casts out the demons."	(22) And the scribes who came down from Jerusalem said, "He has Beelzebul," and "by the prince of demons he casts out the demons." (23) And calling to them in parables he said to them; "How can Satan cast out Satan? (24) And if a kingdom is divided against itself, that kingdom cannot stand; (25) and if a house is divided against itself, that house will not be able to stand. (26) And if Satan has risen up against himself and is divided, he cannot stand but has an	(14) And he was casting out a demon [and it was] dumb; but when the demon had gone out the dumb man spoke, and the crowds marvelled. (15) But some of them said; "By Beelzebul the prince of demons he casts out demons." . . . (17) But he knowing their thoughts said to them; "Every kingdom divided against itself is laid waste and a house against itself falls. (18) And also if Satan is divided against himself, how will his kingdom stand? For you say by Beelzebul I cast out demons. (19) But if I by Beelzebul cast out the demons, by whom do your sons cast them out? Therefore they shall be your judges. (20) But if by the finger of God I cast out demons, then the kingdom of

Matt. 12.22–30	Matt. 9.32–34	Mark 3.22–27	Luke 11.14–15, 17–23
they shall be your judges. (28) But if by the Spirit of God that I cast out demons, then the kingdom of God has come upon you. (29) Or how can someone enter the house of a strong man and plunder his goods, except he first binds the strong man? Then indeed he may plunder his house. (30) The one who is not with me is against me, and the one who does not gather with me scatters.		end. (27) But no one can enter into the house of a strong man and plunder his goods, except he first binds the strong man, and then he plunders his house.	God has come upon you. (21) When the strong man fully armed guards his own palace, his goods are in peace; (22) but when one stronger assails him and overcomes him, his armour he takes away in which he trusted, and the spoils are distributed. (23) The one who is not with me is against me, and the one who does not gather with me scatters.

Mark introduces the pericope with a reference to the family[2] coming to seize Jesus because they said he was beside himself (3.19b—21). The authenticity of this is assured as it is unlikely to have been created by the early Church.[3] Further, the Johannine tradition also preserves a similar reference (e.g. John 10.20). In view of Mark's supplying verses 31—5 (Jesus' true family) to the present context[4] he may also have appended verses 19b—21 as the introduction to this particular pericope.[5]

---

2   That Mark intends οἱ παρ' αὐτοῦ to refer to Jesus' "family" rather than "friends" is evident from Mark's conclusion to the pericope where his mother and brothers are mentioned (3.31). See further, J.E. Steinmueller "Jesus and οἱ παρ' αὐτοῦ (Mark 3:21-21)" *CBQ* 4 (1942) 355–9; BAGD 610.

3   Taylor *Mark* 235.

4   That Mark is responsible for the position of vv.31–5 see, e.g. Schweizer *Mark* 83f.; Taylor *Mark* 245; J.D. Crossan "Mark and the Relatives of Jesus" *NovT* 15 (1973) 85ff., 96ff.; Stein *NovT* 13 (1971) 193f.; Mann *Mark* 251–2.

5   See Bultmann *History* 29f.; cf. Dibelius *Tradition* 47.

1. An Exorcism Story Matthew 12.22—3/Luke 11.14

It fairly clear that Matthew has entirely reworked these two verses. This is particularly obvious when we take into account the doublet in Matthew 9.32—3.

Matthew 12.22-3	Matthew 9.32-3	Luke 11.14
Then was brought to him a blind and *dumb, demon*iac and he healed him, so that *the dumb man spoke* and saw. (23) And all *the crowds* were amazed and said; "Is this the Son of David?"	And as they were going away behold they brought to him a *dumb demon*iac man. (33) And *when the demon* had been cast *out, the dumb man spoke. And the crowds marvelled* saying; "Never was anything seen like this in Israel."	And he was casting out *a demon* [and it was] *dumb*; and *when the demon had gone out the dumb man spoke, and the crowds marvelled.*

The material in either of the Matthean passages, which is paralleled in Luke, we may take to be from the Q tradition (in italics above).

Where Matthean passages agree against Luke in having προσφέρειν ("bring")[6] and δαιμονίζομαι ("demonized")[7] we are probably dealing with Matthean vocabulary rather than pointers to Lukan redaction.

In 12.22 Matthew's hand is evident in the demoniac being blind as well as dumb. The healed man is described as a dumb man who spoke *and saw.* However, καὶ βλέπειν seems to be an awkward addition. Further, of all the healings in the New Testament the only one not having a precursor in the Old Testament is the giving of sight to the blind. Accordingly, a fond hope for the Messianic Age was that the blind would receive their sight (Isaiah 29.18; [32.3]; 35.5; 42.7, 16, 18—20; 43.8; 61.1[8]). It is also pertinent to notice that the only time where the theme of the reception of speech occurs in the Old Testament it is twinned with the theme of the reception of sight (Isaiah 35.5 and 6). In 11.4—6, Matthew has already shown an interest in this Old Testament passage. And, one of the predominant themes Matthew continues to pursue is that of Jesus fulfilling the messianic hopes of the Old Testament.[9] Thus, in this eschatological and

---

6   Hawkins *Horae Synopticae* 7; Turner *Grammar* IV, 43.

7   Occurs as follows: John 10.21; Luke 8.36; Mark 1.32; 5.15, 16, 18; Matt 4.24; 8.16, 28, 33; 9.32; 12.22; 15.22.

8   LXX has "recovery of sight to the blind", cf. RSV note.

9   See also S. McConnell *Law and Prophecy in Matthew's Gospel* (Basel: Th.D. Thesis, 1969) 154f.; Gundry *OT in Matthew's Gospel* 208ff.

messianic context (Matthew 12.22—8) it is not surprising that Matthew would have wanted to heighten an already messianic healing and so alter Q in the way he has. It is consonant with this that among the Synoptics, τυφλός ("blind") has a relatively high frequency of occurrence in Matthew.[10] So, the version in Matthew 9.32—3 is most probably the earlier one.[11]

Regarding the verbalization of the crowd's amazement in Matthew 12.23, the evidence is in favour of a Matthean origin. That is, it seems to be a type of response to miracles that Matthew prefers.[12] Further, the response in Matthew 9.33 bears no resemblance to that in 12.23. Also, the title "Son of David", not found in Luke, is of particular interest to Matthew.[13] Thus, the actual words of the crowd in Matthew 12.23 cannot be traced back to Q.

From this exercise we can see that the common source material, Q, followed closely by Luke, involved a brief story of a dumb demoniac being healed so that he could talk, and the crowd was said to be amazed.[14]

R.H. Fuller, however, thinks that this miracle story is an editorial composition.[15] It is, he says, a story which is an "ideal scene" "deliberately created to carry the saying."[16] His support for this seems to be: 1. "After all, the church was interested in the saying, not in the setting," and 2. "the Beelzebul sayings (were) handed down without any setting by Mark and Q (Matt. 12.22 par.)."[17]

It is true that Mark does not use an exorcism story as a setting for the pericope, but to say that neither does Q is to beg the question, since both Matthew and Luke precede the controversy with an exorcism, and Fuller has not shown that this is not Q material. Fuller has also not shown that one Evangelist is dependent on the other.

The most important point for Fuller is that this exorcism was created because "the church was interested in the saying, not in the setting." But, at least Matthew and Luke have shown that they were interested in a

---

10   Matt = 17, Mark = 5 and Luke = 8.

11   So also C. Burger *Jesus als Davidssohn: Eine Traditionsgeschichtliche Untersuchung* (Göttingen: Vandenhoeck & Ruprecht, 1970) 77–9.

12   See 7.28; 9.8; cf. 15.31; 21.14. Luke has it only at 7.16 and 13.17. Cf. B. Gerhardsson *The Mighty Acts of Jesus According to Matthew* (Lund: CWK Gleerup, 1979) 74; Theissen *Miracle* 69.

13   Matt = 10, Mark = 4 and Luke = 5. See J.M. Gibbs "Purpose and Pattern in Matthew's Use of the Title 'Son of David' " *NTS* 10 (1963–4) 446–64; J.D. Kingsbury *Matthew: Structure, Christology, Kingdom* (London: SPCK, 1976) 99f. and notes.

14   Cf. J.S. Kloppenborg *The Formation of Q* (Philadelphia: Fortress, 1987) 121–2.

15   Fuller *Miracles* 25 n. 1. He feels the same about Matt 9.27-31, 32–34.

16   Fuller *Miracles* 32. Cf. Theissen *Miracle* 114, ". . . the miracle story is really (also) the introduction to an apophthegm."

17   Fuller *Miracles* 32.

setting for the material. And, how is it that they agree so closely on the setting? On Fuller's own evidence it is more reasonable to presume that the exorcism story is pre-Matthean and/or Lukan material. If it can be assumed that Luke had no knowledge of Matthew[18] then we are justified in thinking that the Q tradition contained a brief exorcism story at this point in which a dumb demoniac is healed, the man talks and the crowd is amazed.[19]

Luke describes the healing using ἐκβάλλων ("casting out", 11.14), while Matthew says ἐθεράπευσεν ("he healed") in 12.22, but uses ἐκβληθέν-τος ("cast out") in 9.33. This predisposes us towards thinking that Q used ἐκβάλλω ("cast out")[20] as the word to describe what Jesus was doing in his exorcisms. We will discuss this word a little more fully shortly.

The brevity of the account of the exorcism indicates that Q saw nothing special in Jesus' technique of exorcism and that it is primarily introductory in nature to what follows. That this introductory exorcism is of a *dumb* spirit is important. That exorcism had eschatological overtones for Q will become apparent later in the pericope. However, already in the introduction the eschatological dimension of exorcism is affirmed, since one of the hopes of the Messianic Age was that the dumb would sing for joy (Isaiah 35.5 and 6 and see above).

Even though Matthew in particular has drawn attention to this little story, its probable historical reliability is enhanced by its incidental trans-mission in Q. Further, the ensuing debate about exorcism presupposes that an exorcism first took place. And, to follow Bultmann, "no story original to the tradition would be likely to begin with a reference to some activity

---

18   For a test case in defence of this view see F.G. Downing "Towards the Rehabitation of Q" *NTS* 11 (1964–5) 169–87; also A.M. Honoré "A Statistical Study of the Synoptic Problem" *NovT* 10 (1968) 95–147, esp. 135. That Luke *did* use Matthew see, e.g. A.W. Argyle "Evidence for the View that St. Luke used St. Matthew's Gospel" *JBL* 83 (1964) 390–6 and R.T. Simpson "The Major Agreements of Matthew and Luke Against Mark" *NTS* 12 (1966–7) 273–84.

19   Cf. T.W. Manson *The Sayings of Jesus* (London: SCM, 1949) 82ff.; A. Polag *Fragmenta Q* (Neukirchen-Vluyn: Neukirchener Verlag, 1979) 50f. Q is sometimes said to contain *only* "sayings" material (see S. Petrie " 'Q' is Only What You Make It" *NovT* 3 [1959] 29) but apart from Luke 11.14, it may also have contained Luke 4.2–13; 7.1–10, 18–23; 11.29–32; see Kümmel *Introduction* 68. Kee, *Miracle* 205, says that the only miracle story deriving from the Q tradition is Luke 7.1–10.

20   In fact, Luke seems unlikely to have added the word for while it occurs 14 times in the material he takes up from Mark (Mark 1.12, 34, 39, 43; 3.15, 22, 23; 5.40; 6.13; 9.18, 28, 38; 11.15; 12.18) he only uses the word 5 times (from Mark 3.22; 9.18, 38; 11.15 and 12.8) and as far as we know he only once added the word to his tradition (Luke 20.21; cf. Mark 12.5). On the other hand, while Matthew only drops the word a few times (from Mark 1.12/Matt 4.1; Mark 1.39/Matt 4.23; Mark 1.43/Matt 8.4; Mark 7.26/Matt 15.25; Mark 9.18/Matt 17.16) he has a known predilection for θεραπεύω (see *HSE* 62).

of Jesus in quite general terms."[21] Thus, it seems probable that Mark (or his predecessors) has disposed of the exorcism story and inserted the remaining material about a debate on exorcism between 3.21 and 3.31—5 because it fitted well with the charge of Jesus' family that Jesus was mad (3.21).

2. *The Charge* Matthew 12.24/Mark 3.22/Luke 11.15[22]

Matthew and Luke agree (= Q) with Mark that an accusation was levelled at Jesus — but by whom? Matthew says it was the Pharisees and Mark says it was the scribes. Luke says that it was by some of the crowd. Each of the Evangelists is following his habit in this respect. Matthew seems concerned to make the Pharisees Jesus' opponents.[23] Mark's desire is to make the scribes Jesus' opponents.[24] This is in line with the tendency for tradition to take on proper names during its transmission.[25] However, Luke often drops such specific references from his sources.[26] Therefore, we can no longer know who directed the accusation against Jesus.

What was the nature of the accusation? Comparing Luke 11.15b (". . . he casts out demons by Beelzebul, the prince of demons") with Matthew 9.34b, Q appears to be better preserved in Luke 11.15b than in Matthew 12.24. In view of Matthew 12.27/Luke 11.19, "Beelzebul" was probably in Q here. There is no evidence for thinking that Q contained reference to Jesus "having" Beelzebul (cf. Mark 3.22). However, this is probably an omission for Mark has this much stronger accusation that Jesus was "possessed by Beelzebul" (Βεελζεβοὺλ ἔχει). This is most probably part of the authentic tradition for it is quite unlikely to be an invention of Mark or any other early Christian.

---

21 Bultmann *History* 13; so also J. Jeremias *NT Theology* (London: SCM, 1971) 91.

22 Luke 11.16 is similar to Mark 8.11 rather than any possible Q material (cf. Matt 16.1; 12.38) and so it probably does not belong to Q material. T. Schramm *Der Markus-Stoff bei Lukas* (Cambridge: Cambridge University Press, 1971) 46f.

23 Hill *Matthew* 215; cf. T.F. Glasson "Anti-Pharisaism in St. Matthew" *JQR* 51 (1960–1) 316–20; R. Hummel *Die Auseinandersetzung zwischen Kirche und Judentum im Matthäusevangelium* (Munich: Chr. Kaiser, 1966) 12–17; S. van Tilborg *The Jewish Leaders in Matthew* (Leiden: Brill, 1972).

24 See M.J. Cook *Mark's Treatment of the Jewish Leaders* (Leiden: Brill, 1978) 85ff. and J.C. Weber "Jesus' Opponents in the Gospel of Mark" *JBR* 34(1966) 214–22.

25 See E.P. Sanders *The Tendencies of the Synoptic Tradition* (Cambridge: Cambridge University Press, 1969) 188f. See also S. Schulz *Q: Die Spruchquelle Der Evangelisten* (Zürich: Theologischer Verlag, 1972) 204f. n .206; and B.M. Metzger "Names for the Nameless in the NT. A Study in the Growth of Christian Tradition" in P. Granfield and J.A. Jungmann (eds.) *Kyriakon: Festschrift Johannes Quasten* 2 vols. (Münster Westfalen: Aschendorff, 1970) I, 79–99.

26 At the following points Luke deletes references to the scribes from his Markan sources: Luke 4.32; 11.15, 37, 38; 9.37; 10.25, 27; 18.31; 20.41; 22.47, 54; 23.35. Though less often, Luke also deletes references to the Pharisees from his Markan sources: Luke 5.33; 11.16, 37; 22.20.

What did this two-part charge of being possessed and casting out demons by Beelzebul originally mean?[27] Did Jesus' audience think that he was using a particular foreign god to effect his exorcisms?[28] This idea involves the notion that "Beelzebul" is a Jewish distortion of "Baal-Zebub", the name of the god of Ekron in 2 Kings 1.2. But, (a) the connection of the name Beelzebul with the name of the Philistine god at Ekron seems quite late — no earlier than Jerome (c.AD 340—420).[29] (b) Outside the New Testament, Beelzebul is mentioned by Origen (CC VIII.25) and Hippolytus (Refutation 6.34), but they make no connection with the name of Ekron. (c) Josephus, who mentions the incident of Ahaziah (Ant. 9.19), has the phrase "the Fly-God of Akkron (Ekron)" using the same words as the Septuagint to render the latter part of the Hebrew Baal-Zebub traditionally supposed to mean "Fly-God".[30] Thus, even Josephus (c.37—100) does not seem to know a connection between Baalzebub of 2 Kings 1.2 and a term "Beelzebul".

A possible clue to the meaning of Beelzebul is in Matthew 10.25: "If they have called the master of the house Beelzebul, how much more will they malign those of his household."[31] Though it is rare in the Old Testament (1 Kings 8.13 = 2 Chronicles 6.2; Isaiah 63.15; Habakkuk 3.11), "Zebul" (זבל) can be used as a synonym for heaven and probably means "dwelling". A similar meaning is found in the Qumran scrolls.[32] In the Hellenistic period Baal was the chief cultic rival of the Yahwistic faith especially in the time of Antioches IV.[33] In later Old Testament writings the name "Lord of Heaven" was available only to Yahweh.[34] Now in Judaism and the New Testament pagan gods were said to be demons.[35]

"What better name then for Satan, the chief of the demons, than that of the chief of the heathen gods? He could not of course be called by his proper name — . . . this title is restricted to Yahweh — but this name 'Lord of Heaven' could be hinted at in a slight disquise."[36]

---

27 On it being a charge of magic see §24 below; J.H. Neyrey "Bewitched in Galatia: Paul and Cultural Anthropology" CBQ 50 (1988) 72-100 discusses Paul's accusation that the Galatians have been bewitched by teachers possessed and controlled by Satan (Gal. 3.1).
28 The view of W. Manson The Gospel of Luke (London: Hodder and Stoughton, 1930) 138; cf. BAGD.
29 Plummer Luke 301.
30 Ralph Marcus on Ant. 9.19 in St. J. Thackeray Josephus VI, 12 n.(a).
31 For most of what follows I am dependent on L. Gaston "Beelzebul" TZ 18 (1962) 247-55. Cf. E.C.B. MacLaurin "Beelzeboul" NovT 20 (1978) 156-60.
32 1QM 12.1, 2; 1QS 10.13; 1QH 3.34.
33 E. Bickermann Der Gott der Makkabäer (1937) esp. 50ff.; cited by Gaston TZ 18 (1962) 252 n. 21. Cf. Hengel Judaism and Hellenism I, 261; II, 172.
34 Ezra 1.2; ʹ5.11; 12; 6.9, 10; 7.12, 21, 23; Neh 1.4, 5; 2.4, 20; Ps 136.26; Dan 2.18, 19, 37, 44; 4.34; 5.23; Tob 13.11; 2 Macc 15.23.
35 LXX Ps 95.5; 1 Cor 10.20; cf. LXX Deut 32.17; Ps 105.37; Bar 4.7; Rev 9.20.
36 Gaston TZ 18 (1962) 253. Cf. W.E.M. Aitken "Beelzebul" JBL 31 (1912) 34-53.

We can conclude here that Jesus is accused of being inspired by Satan. The word used, Beelzebul = Baalshamaim = Satan, is transparent enough to be readily understood by Jesus and those around him.[37]

Thus, what the exorcism of Jesus leads the crowd to think is that he is evil and inspired not by God but by Satan (cf. Mark 3.22). As we have said, the historicity of such a charge can scarcely be doubted.

When we are drawing together conclusions in chapter IV from the examination of the data in this chapter we will be asking how such a charge could have arisen in the minds of those who observed Jesus as an exorcist (§§22 and 24).

3. Jesus' Reply Matthew 12.25—30/Mark 3.23—7/Luke 11.17—23

(a) The precise wording of the first part of the reply need not detain us and its meaning is clear: that is, it is impossible for Jesus to be casting out demons by Beelzebul/Satan for that would mean Satan was divided. Even if he were exorcising by Satan, even if Satan were divided against himself, Jesus' exorcisms would still mark the destruction of Satan and his kingdom.[38]

(b) The next argument — at least in Q — that is used to counter the charge is to point out the inconsistency of charging Jesus with being in league with Satan while not considering by whom their own people cast out demons.

It is apparent that Mark does not have this Q saying about the Jewish exorcists, nor those about Jesus' source of power-authority, and the kingdom of God (Matthew 12.27—8/Luke 11.19—20). In the light of Mark's evident interest in the relationship between the kingdom of God, the Holy Spirit and the exorcisms of Jesus, it is most unlikely that this saying we now have in Q was available to Mark or he would have most probably included it.

The question Jesus puts is, "by whom do your sons cast them out?"[39] The natural response to this of course would be "God", and the context supplies only two alternatives, Satan or God.[40] There is a problem here in the next verse (Matthew 12.28/Luke 11.20). Jesus is said to claim that

---

37 Cf. Gaston *TZ* 18 (1962) 253. Gaston goes on to suggest that *Zebul* was used, among the possible synonyms for heaven, probably because the Pharisees in the Beelzebul Controversy knew a certain claim made over the temple (254). See also Aitken *JBL* 31 (1912) 34—53.

38 The mention of Jesus calling to the disciples in parables is probably from Mark's hand; see Taylor *Mark* 239; Schweizer *Mark* 83f.; Dibelius *Tradition* 237; Kertelge *Wunder* 126 n. 505; Best *Temptation* 117; Schreiber *ZTK* 58 (1961) 16.

39 On οἱ υἱοί see C.E. Carlston *The Parables of the Triple Tradition* (Philadelphia: Fortress, 1975) 18 n. 11.

40 That Jewish exorcists did operate "by God" is clear from PGM IV.3019ff.

his exorcisms mark the arrival of the kingdom of God. What then is Q's understanding of Jesus' contemporary exorcists and their exorcisms? In Q's present arrangement, with Luke 11.19 and 20 juxtaposed, it has generally been thought that the obvious interpretation is that Q felt that the exorcisms of the Jews were related in some way to the coming of the kingdom of God. This interpretation has rightly been variously and vigorously avoided by New Testament critics.[41] Creed,[42] for example, resorts to Bultmann's hypothesis that verse 19 is a late insertion from the controversies of the early community with its Jewish opponents.[43] But, even if the reference to the Jewish exorcists is "late" it was still part of the Q material that Matthew and Luke used. Further, even to alter the present order of the material so that Luke 11.19 and 20 are no longer juxtaposed is of little help, for the problem of Q's understanding of the Jewish exorcists would still remain unanswered.

We cannot take up the suggestion of A.E. Harvey who supposes that Jesus' contemporaries were unsuccessful or only partially successful.[44] There is nothing in the text to support this and, in fact, the question about the Jewish exorcists' authority (Matthew 12.27/Luke 11.19) presupposes that they were successful. Nor, as our present study will show, is it possible to say, with C.C. Caragounis, that Jesus' exorcisms were of a different order because they lacked all *characteristica* of Jewish and Hellenistic exorcisms.[45]

There is, however, another alternative. The pericope up until Matthew 12.28/Luke 11.20 is *not* about the relationship between exorcism and the inbreaking of the kingdom of God. The Pharisees' accusation and Jesus' reply have, so far, *only* to do with Jesus' *source of power-authority*. Therefore, all that Q can possibly be saying about the Jewish exorcists is that they, in some way, share the same source of power-authority as Jesus. This notion of Jesus tolerating others as allies is made more plausible when we note Luke 11.23(/Matthew 12.30) and its positive doublet — "For whoever is not against us, is for us" (Luke 9.50/Mark 9.40). In both Luke and Mark this saying follows John's (the disciple's) report of a Strange Exorcist they tried to dissuade from operating because he was not

---

41 E.g. N. Perrin *Rediscovering the Teaching of Jesus* (New York: Harper & Row, 1976) 63; W.G. Kümmel *Promise and Fulfilment* (London: SCM, 1957) 105–6.

42 J.M. Creed *The Gospel According to St. Luke* (London: Macmillan, 1930) 160f.. Carlston *Parables* 18 also finds vv. 19 and 20 incompatible. See also Schweizer *Matthew* 284.

43 Bultmann *History* 14, followed by Kümmel *Promise* 105–6. Further on the origin of the connection between the two verses see G.R. Beasley-Murray "Jesus and the Spirit" in Descamps et de Halleux (eds.) *Mélanges Bibliques* 468 n. 1.

44 Harvey *Constraints* 109.

45 C.C. Caragounis "Kingdom of God, Son of Man and Jesus' Self-Understanding" *TynBul* 40 (1989) 230–1. Further, see chap. IV below.

following Jesus. Thus, Q is not alone in seeing Jesus being tolerant of other exorcists whom he is said to regard, at least to some extent, as allies. As the reply is entirely dependent upon the preceding charge, we can be assured of the probable historicity of the reply.

(c) The Spirit/Finger saying (Matthew 12.28/Luke 11.20) is one of the most significant verses with which we shall deal: "But if in a Spirit (Luke has "finger") of God I cast out demons, then the kingdom of God has come upon you." But, in understanding and interpreting this verse in the context of Q and perhaps the ministry of Jesus, we face a myriad of problems including: What was the wording of this verse in Q? Why, in Q, are the exorcisms of Jesus linked with the inbreaking of the kingdom of God? Can the saying be traced back to the historical Jesus? and, if so, What was its significance for Jesus?

(i) There is no need here to rehearse completely the debate about whether Q contained the word "Spirit" or "finger". There is good reason for taking "Spirit" as the original in Q.[46] In any case, the meanings of the variants are similar. In the Old Testament the term "finger of God" is used to identify the direct activity of God. So, in Exodus 31.18 it is the *finger* of God that wrote on the tablets of stone (see also Exodus 8.19; Deuteronomy 9.10 and Psalm 8.3). And, in the Qumran *War Scroll*, God is said to raise his *hand* against Satan (1QM 18.1—15). The activity of the *Spirit* of God also indicated the activity of God himself. In Ezekiel 11.5 the Spirit of the Lord falls on Ezekiel and he is addressed by the Lord. What is most interesting is that in Ezekiel 8.1 it is the *hand* of the Lord that falls on Ezekiel to produce a vision. Thus, here is an instance where "hand" and "spirit" are used synonymously. Further, in the Old Testament the "finger of God" is a variant of "the hand of God" with no alteration of meaning.[47]

(ii) Why are the exorcisms of Jesus linked with the inbreaking of the kingdom of God? This verse has three components, the exorcist ("*I*"),[48] the source of power-authority for the exorcism (*Spirit*), and the meaning attached to the combination of these two components — the inbreaking of the *kingdom of God*. So, are the exorcisms of Jesus linked with the coming of the kingdom because *Jesus* performs the exorcisms or because

---

46 For the literature see Dunn *Jesus* 44ff. and R.W. Wall " 'The Finger of God' Deuteronomy 9.10 and Luke 11.20" *NTS* 33 (1987) 144–50; van Cangh in Delobel (ed.) *Logia* 337–42 and Caragounis *TynBul* 40 (1989) 8–10.

47 See also 1 Chr 28.11–19. R.G. Hamamerton-Kelly "A Note on Matthew 12.28 par. Luke 11.20" *NTS* 11 (1964–5) 168; C.K. Barrett *The Holy Spirit and the Gospel Tradition* (London: SPCK, 1947) 144 and notes. On the finger of God as a symbol of power in the Greek world see Clement of Alexandria *Stromata* 6.16.133.

48 On the status of ἐγώ in Luke 11.20 see the apparatus in Nestle-Aland *NT Graece* ed. XXVI.

Jesus performs the exorcisms *in the Spirit of God*? Or, do we, in fact, have to choose between these two options?

It is generally recognized that the key element in this verse is "Spirit of God" by, or in, which Jesus operates.[49] However, from what we have just said about the previous verse (Matthew 12.27/Luke 11.19), where Q seems to accept that the Jews also operate on the same side as Jesus (cf. the Strange Exorcist — Mark 9.38—41/Luke 9.49—50), Jesus' source of power-authority may not be as unique as it has been claimed. Yet, on the other hand, while operating in the same sphere (of "God") as the Jewish exorcists, there is an aspect to Jesus' power-authority that was hitherto unknown. That is, in contrast to his contemporaries (note the adversative δέ), Jesus claimed it was the *Spirit* of God who provided him with his power-authority. The Spirit of God was not one of the Jewish rabbis' sources of power-authority.[50] In so far as we can tell, Q is making a unique claim for Jesus.

Although the use of ἐγώ is not everywhere in the New Testament to be taken as implying a contrast, or used for emphasis,[51] Stauffer is correct to say that "On the lips of the Synoptic Jesus the emphatic ἐγώ is relatively infrequent. It is found in warning, promises and commands uttered by Jesus with the sense of His divine power and authority."[52]

The only other time Q uses ἐγώ on the lips of Jesus it is to draw attention to the person of Jesus (Matthew 8.9/Luke 7.8). Hence, we can suggest that the breaking in of the kingdom is linked with Jesus' exorcisms in Q because *Jesus* in the *Spirit* casts out demons.

In Matthew 12.28/Luke 11.20 ἐκβάλλω is placed on the lips of Jesus in Q. How much is to be made of the use of this word is difficult to decide. So far as I know this is — along with Mark — the first time it is used in relationship to exorcism. In literature prior to the Gospels, for example in Tobit 6.17, the demons are not "cast out", but *flee* (φεύγω). When we take into account the two elements of Matthew 12.28/Luke 11.20 — casting out demons (that is, Satan [Matthew 12.26/Luke 11.18] — the enemy of God)

---

49 E.g. Dunn *Jesus* 44ff.

50 See also Str-B II, 526ff. Contrast Hengel *Charismatic Leader* 64 n. 102 who, speaking generally of Jesus' ministry, says: "It is quite likely that, by contrast with Jesus, contemporary apocalyptic-messianic prophets appealed freely to the 'Spirit'. According to the Easter texts and apocalyptic literature there was in Judaism nothing unusual in appealing to actual possession of the Spirit. . ." However, I have not been able to find any evidence to suggest that the "Spirit" was appealed to as a source of power-authority for exorcism.

51 BDF 227.1f.; cf. N. Turner *A Grammar of NT Greek* III (Edinburgh: T & T Clark, 1963) 37f.

52 E. Stauffer *TDNT* II, 348.

and the coming of the kingdom of God, the LXX's use of ἐκβάλλω may be useful in conjecturing the implication of its use in Q.

Most of the occurrences of ἐκβάλλω in the LXX are in contexts where an enemy, frustrating or standing in the way of God fulfilling his purpose for his chosen people of Israel, is cast out (ἐκβάλλω) *so that God's purpose can be fulfilled.* This purpose is most often the possession of the promised land. Two examples can illustrate this. First, "Little by little will I drive them out (ἐκβάλλω) before you, until you are increased and possess the land" (Exodus 23.30). Secondly, "The eternal God is your dwelling place, and underneath are the everlasting arms. And he thrust out (ἐκβάλλω) the enemy before you, and said, Destroy. So Israel dwelt in safety . . . in a land of grain and wine . . ." (Deuteronomy 33.27–8). In the light of the LXX's use of ἐκβάλλω, it may be that Q was implying that Jesus was casting out an enemy of God in order that God's purpose might be fulfilled — the coming of the kingdom of God.

(iii) What can we say about the historicity of the Spirit/finger saying? That the saying rightly belongs to the historical Jesus seems quite likely from the following: (1) The "kingdom" was a central theme of the public ministry of Jesus.[53] (2) The fact that the kingdom of God is said to have *already* come (ἔφθασεν),[54] which corresponds to מטא, suggests that the saying arose in Jesus' own ministry.[55] (3) Also, the verse is part of an antithetic parallelism — a characteristic of Jesus' speech.[56] (4) The early Church did not associate the dawning of salvation with Jesus' exorcisms (see also §29 below).[57] Together, these factors weigh in favour of the historical reliability of the Spirit/finger saying.[58] We will discuss the significance of this saying for Jesus in §29.

---

53 N. Perrin *The Kingdom of God in the Teaching of Jesus* (London: SCM, 1963) chap. 10; and *Rediscovering* chap. 1; Jeremias *Theology* par 11; R.H. Hiers *The Historical Jesus and the Kingdom of God* (Gainesville: University of Florida Press, 1973) chap. 2; J.R. Butts "Probing the Polling, Jesus Seminar Results on the Kingdom Sayings" *Forum* 3 (1987) 98–128.

54 On ἔφθασεν see Kümmel *Promise* 106–9. Cf. Jeremias *Theology* 34.

55 G. Dalman *The Words of Jesus* (Edinburgh: T & T Clark, 1902) 107. Jeremias *Theology* 103ff.; Barrett *Spirit* 140; D. Flusser *Jesus* (New York: Herder, 1969) 90; H. Baltensweiler "Wunder und Glaube im NT" *TZ* 23 (1967) 243–8.

56 Jeremias *Theology* 14. See also Dalman *Words* 202–3.

57 See Twelftree *Christ* chap. IV.

58 On the wide agreement of the historicity of this saying see Beasley–Murray in Descamps et de Halleux (eds.) *Mélanges Bibliques*, 468 and G.R. Beasley–Murray *Jesus and the Kingdom of God* (Grand Rapids: Eerdmans and Exeter: Paternoster, 1986) 356 n. 28, who cites Bultmann who affirmed that the saying can "claim the highest degree of authenticity which we can make for any saying of Jesus: it is full of that feeling of eschatological power which must have characterized the activity of Jesus" (Bultmann *History* 162). See also J.D.G. Dunn "Matthew 12:28/Luke 11:20 – A Word of

(d) In the Parable of the Strong Man (Matthew 12.29/Mark 3.27/Luke 11.21—2), is Luke following Q in the parable of the Strong Man (11.21—2), (while Matthew 12.29 follows Mark 3.27) or is he reworking Mark 3.27? Luke at least is following the *order* of Q here (cf. Matthew 12.28/Luke 11.20 and Matthew 12.30/Luke 11.23). That is, he has the same order as Matthew. It is uncharacteristic of Luke to rewrite Mark so extensively[59] and if he was, here, reliant on Mark it is surprising that he has only taken up ὁ ἰσχυρός ("the strong man") into the vocabulary. There is some evidence of Lukan activity in τὰ ὑπάρχοντα ("the goods"),[60] yet in the allusion here to τὰ σκῦλα αὐτοῦ διαδίδωσιν ("divides his spoil") of Isaiah 53.12a (τῶν ἰσχυρῶν μεριεῖ σκῦλα), Luke does not follow the Alexandrian text as usual.[61] Thus, it seems probable that Luke is following a tradition here other than Mark — probably Q.

That this parable was always in this context is not only suggested by the subject matter (see below) but because both Q and Mark agree on its context.[62] What can we say about this parable of the Strong Man reflecting words of Jesus? The comparison of a possessed person to a "house" is still common is the East.[63] Further, two Gospel traditons preserve this parable (Mark/Matthew and Luke) and the Gospel of Thomas (35) also has it. Thus, this parable most probably belongs to the authentic sayings of Jesus.

How did the Gospel writers understand the parable? The parable has two components; first, the Strong Man is bound (δήσῃ) or overpowered (νικήσῃ) and then, secondly, his house is plundered. It is a widely held view that the binding of Satan is to be seen as taking place at the Temptation (see §11 below). For example, Ernest Best takes it that the binding in the parable refers to a previous definite act — the Temptation — because δήσῃ is an aorist subjunctive.[64] However, an aorist subjunctive in a final clause does not only describe a single action but also expresses an action in which no particular stress is placed on the time of the action (see e.g. John 17.1, 21). And, with an aorist subjunctive following ἐὰν μή (Mark 3.27), a future, even uncertain, single act cannot be excluded.

Jesus?" in W.H. Gloer (ed.) *Eschatology and the New Testament* (Peabody: Hendrickson, 1988) 31–49; Caragounis *TynBul* 40 (1989) 8 n.39.

59 Marshall *Luke* 477.
60 Only once in Q (Matt 24.42/Luke 12.44) – following Edwards *Concordance*. Matt = 2 (excluding Matt 24.42), yet Luke = 14 (excluding Luke 12.44) and Acts = 25 and Paul = 12.
61 Lindars *Apologetic* 85; T. Holtz *Untersuchungen über die alttestamentlichen Zitate bei Lukas* (Berlin: Akademie–Verlag, 1968).
62 Taylor *Mark* 240; Crossan *NovT* 15 (1973) 92.
63 P. Joüon in J. Jeremias *The Parables of Jesus* (London: SCM, 1972) 197.
64 Best *Temptation* 13.

That the plundered "belongings" (τὰ σκεύη) is in the plural does not require the metaphor to refer to a plurality of exorcisms following a single binding (in the Temptations),[65] for "belongings" is probably a collective term, as Luke also understood it (Luke 11.21; cf. 8.3; 12.15, 33, 44; 14.33; 16.1; 19.8; Acts 4.32). Further, if Mark intended the binding to refer to a specific event in the past, like the Temptation story, then we might expect the subsequent plundering to be in the present rather than, as here, in the future (καὶ τότε . . . διαρπάσει, "and then he may plunder"). Also, we will find (see §11 below) little support for the notion of the defeat of Satan in any of the Temptation narratives. There is then nothing in this parable to point us to the Temptation traditions as the understood point of the defeat of Satan.

How would the parable have been understood by Jesus' and his audience? The Strong Man in verse 27 is obviously understood to be Satan. And, in verse 23 ("How can Satan cast out Satan?"), it is *Satan* who is being cast out *in exorcism*. Furthermore, the notions of binding (and loosing) are quite natural in the context of dealing with demons, exorcism and healing. For example, in Luke 13.16 the healing "looses" a woman whom Satan had "bound". In Mark 7.35 a "bound" tongue is healed (cf. Mark 5.3b; Luke 8.29). And, further, Deissmann has pointed out that running through antiquity is the idea that man can be bound or fettered by demonic influences.[66] Also, the progressive pattern of verse 27 — binding first and then plundering — fits the ancient method of dealing with demons. This is illustrated, for example, in the magical papyri. First, there was the adjuring to bind or restrict the demon, then the giving of directions to the demon — all in the same progressive act (see, e.g. PGM IV.3037ff.). If we note the metaphor of a house we gain further insight into the meaning of the parable for Jesus and his audience. In Luke 11.24—6 the metaphor of a house is used to describe the individual who is posssessed by a demon. What is at stake is the "house".[67] So also in Mark 3.27c it is the house that is taken from the Strong Man, the "Lord of the House" (3.22).

Thus, in conclusion, what we have here is a *parable of an exorcism*. Satan, the Strong Man, is bound and his house, the possessed person, is taken from him.[68] If, as we are suggesting, the binding was thought to

---

65 M.M.B. Turner "Prayer in the Gospels and Acts" in D.A. Carson (ed.) *Teach Us to Pray: Prayer in the Bible and the World* (Grand Rapids: Baker and Exeter: Paternoster, 1990) 320 n. 14.

66 Deissmann *Light* 306 and n. 5, see also 307ff.; and F. Büchsel *TDNT* II, 60 esp. n. 3.

67 Cf. Gospel of Thomas 35 which also takes the *house* rather than the contents to be at risk.

68 Cf. R. Otto "The Kingdom of God Expells the Kingdom of Satan" in B. Chilton (ed.)

refer to part of the role of exorcism then the tension Cranfield sees between verses 27 and 23b—26 is also resolved.[69]

To conclude this section we can note that the Beelzebul Controversy pericope contains probable reliable historical data in the brief exorcism story, the charge and reply, including the parable of the Strong Man which show that Jesus believed that in exorcism Satan was being cast out. We shall have more to say later in the light of this important pericope (see §§18 and 29 below).

The Kingdom of God (London: SPCK and Philadelphia: Fortress, 1984) 30. To the contrary see M. Limbeck "Jesus und die Dämonen. Der exegetische Befund" *BK* 30 (1975) 7–11. For a case that the 'Strong One' is the disciple in defence against Satan see Meynet *RB* 90 (1983) 334–50.

69 Cranfield *Mark* 138.

§11 The Temptations[1]
Mark 1.12, 13 and Matthew 4.1, 2, 11/Luke 4.1, 2, 13

The reason for drawing attention to this passage is that an examination of it may help towards answering the question, When for the Jesus of history is Satan defeated, in the Temptations, the exorcisms, the cross, at some future time, or a combination of these?

Matthew 4.1, 2, 11	Mark 1.12, 13	Luke 4.1, 2, 13
(1) Then Jesus was led up into the wilderness by the Spirit to be tempted by the devil. (2) And having fasted forty days and forty nights, afterward he was hungry. . . (11) Then the devil left him, and behold, angels came and ministered to him.	(12) And immediately the Spirit drove him out into the wilderness. (13) And he was in the wilderness forty days being tempted by Satan, and he was with the wild beasts, and the angels ministered to him.	(1) And Jesus full of the Holy Spirit returned from the Jordan and was led by the Spirit in the wilderness (2) for forty days being tempted by the devil. And he ate nothing in those days and when they were ended he was hungry. . . (13) And when the devil had ended every temptation he departed from him for a time.

1. For a start, it seems fairly clear that Luke does not intend to convey the idea that Satan was finally defeated in the Temptations, for he says that "the devil . . . departed from him for a time" (4.13). This is confirmed when we look at other references to Satan in Luke ([8.12]; 10.18; 11.18 and 13.16). Thus, we have an indication that Luke thought that Satan was

---

1 Literature: Jeremias *Theology* 68; Pesch *Markus.* I, 98–100; Fitzmyer *Luke* I, 519; F. Neugebauer *Jesu Versuchung: Wegentscheidung am Anfang* (Tübingen: Mohr, 1986); Kloppenborg *Formation of Q* 246–62; Guelich *Mark* I, 36; Drewermann *Markus.* I, 142–61; Stock *Method* 50–7; G.H. Twelftree "Temptation of Jesus" in J.B. Green and S. McKnight (eds.) *Dictionary of Jesus and the Gospels* (Downers Grove: IVP, 1992).

active throughout the ministry of Jesus. Conzelmann's contention that the period described between Luke 4.13 and 22.23 was "one free from the activity of Satan"[2] is thus hardly tenable.[3]

2. The relationship between the Temptations and the fall of Satan is less clear in Matthew. In 4.10 Satan is told to "go" (ὕπαγε) and in 4.11 he "leaves" Jesus (ἀφίησιν αὐτόν). However, in view of Matthew including the Beelzebul Controversy (12.22—32) and Jesus' rebuke to Peter, "Get behind me Satan" (16.23), it seems that Matthew also saw Satan's activity continuing in Jesus' ministry after the Temptations.

3. If neither Matthew nor Luke view the Temptations as the defeat of Satan, what can we say about Q? In fact, we are in much the same situation as we were with Matthew and Luke. Reference in Matthew 4.11a/Luke 4.13 to the devil leaving comes from Q.[4] However, the second part of the verse probably does not. Matthew's mention of the ministry of the angels comes from Mark (1.13), though ἰδού and προσῆλθον being typically Matthean are probably from his hand.[5] And, although Luke shows no particular interest in καιρός he does favour ἄχρι,[6] and only he uses the phrase ἄχρι καιροῦ (here and at Acts 13.11). So, it is most likely that it is Luke who adds the phrase at 4.13.[7]

If this is correct then the Q Temptations probably ended only with a simple reference to the devil leaving Jesus. From this we can hardly conclude that in the Q Temptations we have expressed the very important motif of the defeat of Satan. In fact, from other Q material, as with Matthew and Luke, we gain the distinct impression that Satan was not defeated at the Temptations. For, the Beelzebul Controversy (see §10 above) and — if it belongs to Q — the Return of the Seventy, portray not a defeated enemy but one *in the process* of being defeated.[8]

4. It is Ernest Best's view that in Mark the defeat of Satan is attached to the Temptation.[9] After an initial examination of the Markan Temptation pericope Best says that there is no overwhelmingly convincing theme in it, nor is there evidence to indicate in any clear way the result

2 H. Conzelmann *The Theology of St. Luke* (London: Faber and Faber, 1969) 170.

3 See further S. Brown *Apostasy and Perseverance in the Theology of Luke* (Rome: Pontifical Biblical Institute, 1969) 6ff. and Baumbach in J. Rohde *Rediscovering the Teaching of the Evangelists* (London: SCM, 1968) 243f.

4 Schulz *Q* 181.

5 Ἰδού, Matt = 62, Mark = 7, Luke = 57. Προσέρχεσθαι, Matt = 52, Mark = 5, Luke = 10; see also Schulz *Q* 181.

6 Hawkins *Horae Synopticae* 16; cf. Schürmann *Lukas.* I, 214 n. 198.

7 Cf. E. Klostermann *Das Lukasevangelium* (Tübingen: Mohr, 1929) 61.

8 See Twelftree *Christ* 109.

9 Best *Temptation* 15; cf. Carlston *Parables* 135 and n. 30; M.D. Hooker *The Message of Mark* (London: Epworth, 1983) 37; Kee *Medicine* 73; Beasley-Murray *Jesus and the Kingdom* 108–111, esp. 366 n. 4.

of the Temptation.[10] For this Best says we must look elsewhere in Mark — in the Beelzebul Controversy (3.19b—35). This we have done. Now we look at Mark's account of the Temptation and its immediate context.

Even if there is internal evidence suggesting that the Baptism and Temptation pericopes exhibit different strands of tradition,[11] Mark at least has them juxtaposed. (That the present literary relationship is at least earlier than the Synoptics is indicated by the same relationship between the two pericopes in Q.) Thus, in Mark we should understand these passages as contributing to the significance of each other and we might expect some consistency of understanding between them on the part of Mark.

The Temptation pericope is a mere two brief sentences in Mark so it is difficult to draw out directly what Mark has in mind here. When we observe the role of Satan in the rest of Mark there seems to be a consistency of use.[12] In 3.23 and 26 Jesus answers the Pharisees' charge that his ministry is authorized and empowered by Satan. In 8.33 Peter attempts to deflect Jesus from his intended mission and the retort is, "Get behind me, Satan . . ." These two references have to do with criticism of, and *deflection of Jesus from his ministry*. Into this pattern it is not difficult to fit 4.15 — where Satan is said to destroy the "mission" of the Sower. Turning to πειράζω we find that it is used on three other occasions (8.11; 10.2; 12.15) — all in the context of confrontations with the Pharisees. The reference in 8.11 is interesting. The Pharisees are asking Jesus for a sign to prove himself, with which we should compare the Q Temptation where Satan tempts Jesus to prove his sonship by throwing himself off the pinnacle of the Temple. So, perhaps, we have in 1.9—13 indications that Mark saw Satan's activity in the Temptation as having to do with *an attempt to deflect Jesus from his mission*.

Best says that on the basis of the Markan account alone we would be entirely ignorant of the outcome of the Temptation.[13] However, in view of the Old Testament background to the concept of the ministry of angels in the wilderness[14] where the purpose of the angels was to ensure the safety of "God's Chosen" in a trying period, we should be alert to the possibility that Mark is assuming a positive outcome, even though he does not specifically say so. If we examine the Old Testament background for light on Mark's reference to angels it is also possible that, although Mark may

---

10   Best *Temptation* 10.
11   Lohmeyer in Best *Temptation* 4 and n. 1.
12   1.13; 3.23, 26; 4.15; 8.33. Mark does not use διάβολος.
13   Best *Temptation* 10.
14   U.W. Mauser *Christ in the Wilderness* (London: SCM, 1963) 101; see 1 Kgs 19.5, 7; Ex 14.9; 23.20, 23; 32.34; 33.2.

have in mind the successful outcome of the Temptations, there need be no thought of *the* victory over Satan — simply the safe passage through a difficult period.

Hence the last part of 1.13 does not deflect us from our earlier suggestion and it confirms the idea that in Mark's Temptation it was Jesus' *mission* that was at stake. And, when we take into account the fact that immediately following the Baptism and Temptation Mark has Jesus embarking on mission (1.14—15) we are further justified in seeing Mark's Temptation narrative as relating to Jesus' mission.

So, there is a victory in Mark's Temptation, discernible from the pericope itself, but it is not *the* binding or overthrow of Satan:[15] *it is Jesus' overcoming Satan in relation to his mission*, the preaching of the Good News (1.14—15; cf. 1.1).[16]

None of the Synoptic traditions see *the* defeat of Satan being represented in the Temptation story. Therefore, on examination, none of the Gospel traditions is attempting to convey the notion that the Temptation story is to be associated with the idea of the final defeat of Satan. We have no reason to search behind the Temptation stories for an experience of the historical Jesus which he might have considered significant in the demise of Satan. We shall draw out further conclusions at an appropriate point in a later chapter.

---

15 Cf. R. Yates "Jesus and the Demonic in the Synoptic Gospels" *ITQ* 44 (1977) 39–42; Guelich *Mark* I, 38. Contrast Nineham *Mark* 63ff.; A. Jühlicher (*Die Gleichnisreden Jesu* 2 vols. [Tübingen: Mohr, 1910] II, 226) cautioned against associating the temptation narrative with the parable of the Strong Man for in the narrative Jesus successfully defends himself, whereas in the parable Satan is on the defensive so that "neither the Pharisees nor the evangelists, still less Jesus himself, will have read out of the temptation story a binding of Satan" (from Beasley–Murray *Jesus and the Kingdom* 109–10).

16 See also H.P. Thompson "Called–Proved–Obedient: A study in the Baptism and Temptation narratives of Matthew and Luke" *JTS* 11 (1960) 1–12.

§ 12 Jesus' Answer to John[1]
Matthew 11.2—6/Luke 7.18—23

We must at least briefly consider this pericope because healing from unclean spirits is mentioned in Luke 7.21. We need to discuss the origin of the reference. As this passage may have to do with Jesus' self-understanding in relation to his activities as an exorcist we need to consider the historicity of various elements of this passage. Matthew and Luke record the story as follows.

Matthew 11.2–6

(2) Now John hearing in prison the works of the Christ sending through his disciples (3) said to him; "Are you the coming one or do we look for someone different?"

(4) And answering Jesus said to them; "On going your way tell John what you hear and see; (5) the blind receive their sight and the lame walk, lepers are cleansed and the deaf hear, and the dead are raised up, and the poor have good news preached to them; (6) and blessed is he who is not offended by me."

Luke 7.18–23

(18) The disciples of John reported to him about all these things. And calling to him two of his disciples John (19) sent them to the Lord saying; "Are you the coming one or shall we look for another?" (20) And when they had come to him the men said; "John the Baptist sent us to you saying; 'Are you the coming one or shall we look for another?'" (21) *In that hour he cured many of diseases and plagues and evil spirits and to many blind he gave sight.* (22) And answering he said to them; "On going your way tell John what you saw and heard; the blind receive their sight, the lame walk, lepers are cleansed, and the deaf hear, the dead are raised up, the poor have good news preached to them; (23) and blessed is he who is not offended by me."

---

1 Literature: Jeremias *Theology* 43 and 103–5; Dunn *Jesus* 55–60; Marshall *Luke* 289; S. Sabugal *La Embajada mesiánica de Juan Bautista (Mt 11,2-6 = Lc 7,18-23)* (Madrid:

Our interest in this story is that Luke 7.20—1 does not appear in Matthew. That this material was originally part of Q could be indicated by Luke uncharacteristically leaving in a repetition[2] in 7.21, and by the fact that such repetitions (cf. Luke 15.21—2; 19.34) are to be attributed to a traditional biblical style.[3] On the other hand, the cumulative impact of a number of points leads to the conclusion that Luke is responsible for these two verses.

First, the vocabulary indicates Lukan redaction.[4] Secondly, 7.21 is an awkward addition into the context.[5] Thirdly, it is probably Luke who is responsible for the aorist, "you saw and heard" in 7.22 (εἴδετε καὶ ἠκούσατε, cf. Luke 10.23—4/Matthew 13.16—17), so that the disciples of John can indeed report specifically what they had *seen* and *heard*.[6] Our conclusion then is that the Q tradition is best preserved in Matthew, and that Luke is responsible for the reference to Jesus' healings "from . . . evil spirits" (Luke 7.21).[7] On this we shall comment further in a moment.

The introduction to this pericope[8] indicates that Q understood John's question as arising out of the activity of Jesus (τὰ ἔργα in Matthew 11.2 and περὶ πάντων τούτων in Luke 7.18). John the Baptist inquires: "Are you he who is to come, or shall we look for another?" (Matthew 11.4/Luke 7.19). In his reply Jesus directs attention to what can be seen and heard — including the healing miracles. But, it is not that Jesus is simply appealing to the miraculous to prove his status; he is helping John to see that the kingdom had come. Indeed the passage Jesus is said to echo (Isaiah 35.5 and 6a "then the eyes of the blind shall be opened, and the ears of the deaf unstopped; then shall the lame man leap like a hart") illustrates this very point. This passage makes no reference to a messianic figure[9] but only to the state of affairs in the New Age.

It is this state of affairs that Jesus is said to want John to notice. Even in the allusion to Isaiah 61.1 (Matthew 11.5/Luke 7.22, cf. also Isaiah

---

SYSTECO, 1980); Fitzmyer *Luke* I, 669; W. Wink "Jesus' Reply to John Matt 11:2–6/ Luke 7:18–23" *Forum* 5 (1989) 121–8.

2 On Luke's avoidance of repetition see H.J. Cadbury *The Style and Literary Method of Luke* (New York: Kraus, 1969) 83–90.

3 Schürmann *Lukas*. I, 410 n. 18.

4 Παραγίνομαι (*HSE* 79); δέ (Cadbury *Style* 142ff.); ἀνήρ (Hawkins *Horae Synopticae* 16); πρός (*HSE* 81; cf. Hawkins *Horae Synopticae* 21 and 45); perhaps ἐν ἐκείνῃ τῇ ὥρᾳ (cf. Black *Aramaic* 109); θεραπεύω ἀπό (Hawkins *Horae Synopticae* 19 and 41; Marshall *Luke* 291); πνευμάτων πονηρῶν (also at 8.2; 11.26 [par. Matt 12.45]; Acts 19.12, 13, 15, 16; Mark also does not use the phrase. Cf. Marshall *Luke* 291); χαρίζομαι (in the Gospels, Luke = 3, cf. Marshall *Luke* 291).

5 Cf. Marshall *Luke* 290; Stein *ZNW* 61 (1970) 78.

6 Cf. Creed *Luke* 106 and W. Manson *Luke* 78f.

7 Cf. Polag *Q* 40.

8 Discussed in more detail in Schulz *Q* 190f.

9 R.T. France *Jesus and the OT* (London: Tyndale, 1971) 96. Contrast Ps 146.7b–8a.

29.18—19) all reference to the One bringing the good news is dropped so that what is emphasized is not the messenger but the good news which is being preached to the poor.[10] But, as the climax of the core of the reply comes with a reference to Isaiah 61.1 there is the hint that Jesus is not without importance in the activities of the eschaton. For, as Stanton says, "it is not God himself but the one anointed with God's spirit who announces good tidings to the poor — Jesus."[11] This conclusion is enhanced by the climax of the pericope (Matthew 11.6/Luke 7.23) which appropriately refers to Jesus possibly hindering people perceiving the new state of affairs. Thus, for Q, the miracles and Jesus' preaching show that the kingdom has come and, in turn, this reflects on the identity of the One who performs the miracles and preaches to the poor.

Matthew and Luke take up this perspective, but with their own particular interests. While Q seems to have placed this pericope in a context that emphasized Jesus' person and authority,[12] Matthew has placed it in the context of the coming of the kingdom (chaps. 11—13) so that Jesus and the kingdom are twin themes and in turn Jesus is the Christ in word and deed.[13] Luke has made the significant addition of 7.21 — "In that hour he cured many of diseases and plagues and evil spirits and to many blind he gave sight."[14] This addition highlights Jesus' command to tell of what John's disciples had seen and heard. But, it also directs more attention to what Jesus was doing and turns the miracles into proofs of Jesus' status.[15] For our present study it is to be noted that Luke includes the cure of people from evil spirits as part of the evidence or proof that Jesus is the Coming One. If we note 10.18 (see §13 below, cf. 4.40) it may be that Luke wants to mark out exorcism as particularly important in his understanding of the kingdom. This relationship between exorcism, the person of Jesus, and the kingdom will be explored in chapter IV below.

---

10 Cf. Harvey *Trial* 9 and n. 21; also his *Contraints* 112. On the vexed question of the id-
    entity of the poor see, e.g. D.P. Seccombe *Possessions and the Poor in Luke-Acts* (Linz:
    SNTU, 1982).

11 G.N. Stanton "On the Christology of Q" in B. Lindars and S.S. Smalley (eds.) *Christ
    and Spirit in the NT* (Cambridge: Cambridge University Press, 1973) 30, cf. 32. Cf.
    Dunn *Jesus* 60f..

12 On the order of Q see V. Taylor "The Original Order of Q" in *NT Essays* (London:
    Epworth, 1970) 95—118.

13 Held in Bornkamm, Barth and Held *Tradition* 251.

14 Schürmann (*Lukas*. I, 410 n. 18) thinks that Matthew is following his custom of
    abbreviating his source so that Luke 7.21 would have been found in Q. But the signs
    of Lukan editing tip the balance in favour of this being a Lukan creation (cf.
    Marshall *Luke* 290f.).

15 Cf. Conzelmann *Luke* 191. This is the view which has dominated the understanding of
    Jesus' miracles. See John Locke *Works* (London: Tegg, Sharp and Son, 1823) "To
    convince men of this [his messiahship] he did his miracles: and their assent to, or not
    assenting to this, made them to be, or not to be, of his church" 7:7—18.

If Luke is responsible for 7.21 then this pericope can tell us very little about Jesus' understanding of his exorcisms. But, what of the historicity of the remainder of the passage? F.W. Beare says that "the words of Jesus are cast in a poetical structure, and may have originated as a Christian hymn of praise for the wonders of the Messianic age."[16] However, such structure may in fact be more indicative of the *ipsissima verba* of Jesus than the creativity of the early Christians.[17] Bultmann says that "in all probability the Baptist's question is a community product and belongs to those passages in which the Baptist is called as a witness to the Messiahship of Jesus."[18] However, it is very unlikely that the early Church would have created a tradition in which one of the major witnesses was seen, even as a foil, to doubt Jesus' mission. Further, Dunn has thoroughly explored the question of the historicity of this interchange and concludes that,

> "question and answer fit so neatly within the life–situation of Jesus and lack coherence if either or both were first prompted by a post–Easter situation, that the substance at least of the account must be regarded as historical. Jesus' words in [Matthew 11] vv.4—6 only really make sense as an answer to such a question posed by disciples of the Baptist."[19]

If this conclusion is correct, then it provides an important corrective or balance to the saying in Matthew 12.28/Luke 11.20. There his exorcisms are the focus of attention in relation to the kingdom. Here it is the healings, and particularly his preaching to the poor, in which God's eschatological reign is evident for Jesus.[20]

---

16 Beare *Matthew* 257.
17 Jeremias *Theology* 14–27, esp. 20–1.
18 Bultmann *History* 23. See also Fridrichsen *Miracle* 97–102.
19 Dunn *Jesus* 60.
20 Note Dunn *Jesus* 60ff. Cf. Bultmann *History* 126.

§ 13 The Disciples' Mission(s)[1]
Mark 6.7—12, 30/Matthew 10.1—15/Luke 9.1—6; 10.1—11, 17—20

It is beyond the scope of this present study to investigate the ministry of exorcism in the Christian community after Easter.[2] But, we need to include at least a brief examination of the mission charge for it may reflect something of the historical Jesus' understanding of his exorcisms, and the relationship between them and those of the disciples. Four different reports of the Disciples' Missions have come down to us. The key sections read:

Matthew 10.1	Mark 6.7	Luke 9.1
(1) And calling his twelve disciples he gave them authority over unclean spirits to cast them out and to heal every disease and every infirmity.	(7) And he called the twelve and began to send them out two by two and gave them authority over the unclean spirits.	(1) And calling the twelve together he gave them power and authority over all the demons and to heal diseases.

Luke 10.17–20

(17) The seventy [two] returned with joy saying; "Lord, even the demons are subject to us in your name." (18) And he said to them; "I saw Satan like lightning from heaven falling. (19) Behold I have given you authority to

---

1   Literature: Schürmann *Lukas*. I, 498f.; Jeremias *Theology* 231; Pesch *Markus*. I, 331f.; Gnilka *Markus* I, 236; J.D.M. Derrett "Peace, Sandals and Shirts (Mark 6:6b–13 *par*.)" HeyJ 24 (1983) 253–65; Fitzmyer *Luke* I, 755; Fitzmyer *Luke* II, 849–50, 864 and Fitzmyer *Luke the Theologian: Aspects of his Teaching* (New York: Paulist, 1989) 164–9; Drewermann *Markus*. I, 390–404; Guelich *Mark* I, 318–24; Stock *Method* 179–81. The brief nature of the following discussion does not warrant including the rather extensive texts.
2   See Twelftree *Christ* chap. IV.

Matthew 10.1   Mark 6.7   Luke 10.17–20

tread upon serpents
and scorpions, and
over all the power
of the enemy, and
nothing in any way
shall hurt you. (20)
Nevertheless do not
rejoice in this that
the spirits are
subject to you, but
rejoice that your
names are written in
heaven."

Hahn has convincingly shown that this variety of traditions arose from just two sources.[3] Mark 6.7—12 is one account followed by Luke in chapter 9, and the other is Luke 10, probably Q.[4] Matthew 10.1—14 is to be seen as a conflation of these two accounts.[5] The question arises: Do these two traditions represent one common mission discourse or two? From the pattern of the two traditions which are roughly paralleled in Mark and Luke it is probably best to see just one source behind these two traditions.[6] And when, in 22.35, Luke refers back to instructions given to the Twelve he alludes not to 9.11—12 but to 10.4,[7] the mission of the Seventy (Two).[8]

1. In view of the contributions on this material by F.W. Beare (see n. 5) above) it is pertinent that we should ask if Jesus ever sent his disciples out on mission before Easter. On the basis of the witness of more than one tradition, T.W. Manson said that "the mission of the disciples is one of the best attested facts in the life of Jesus."[9] But, as we have just noted, these traditions probably go back to a common source. And, on the other hand, Beare says, "that if such a mission took place, the Gospels tell us next to nothing about it. In Matthew especially, . . . the whole story (as apart from

---

3 F.C. Hahn *Mission in the NT* (London: SCM, 1965) 41–6 also Jeremias *Theology* 231.

4 Hahn *Mission* 41ff.; cf. D. Lührmann "The Gospel of Mark and the Sayings Collection Q" *JBL* 108 (1989) 62.

5 Schramm *Markus-Stoff* 26–9 and Hahn *Mission* 41; F.W. Beare "The Mission of the Disciples and the Mission Charge: Matthew 10 and Parallels" *JBL* 89 (1970) 2; Jeremias *Theology* 231.

6 Hahn *Mission* 42ff.

7 Marshall *Luke* 412; see also T.W. Manson *Sayings* 74.

8 On the reading of δύο see esp. Metzger *Commentary* 150f.; and "Seventy or Seventy-Two Disciples" *NTS* 5 (1958–9) 299–306; cf. also Beare *JBL* 89 (1970) 1 n. 1.

9 *Sayings* 73; cf. G.B. Caird "Uncomfortable Words II Shake off the Dust from your Feet (Mk. 6.11)" *ExpTim* 81 (1969–70) 41 – "The mission charge is better attested than any other part of the gospel record."

the charge) shrinks to the words: 'These twelve Jesus sent out' (10.5); and Mark and Luke add only that they come back and reported success."[10] Beare agrees with Bultmann that the missionary charge must, in the end, be included among the material produced by the Church.[11]

Yet there are clear hints in this material that it did not arise in the early Church.

(a) Of the two traditions (Mark 6.7–13 and Luke 10.1–11, [17–20]) the most primitive one is probably Luke's[12] and it is noticeable that Mark felt that the stringent requirements of the commission (as in Luke 10.4) were inappropriate for his church.[13] The wholly negative character of Luke 10.4 is particularly appropriate to the Palestinian *Sitz im Leben*.[14] The directive not to salute anyone on the road is so out of harmony with common courtesy in the East that its origin in the post-Easter community is unlikely.[15]

(b) What the disciples are to proclaim is the kingdom of God.[16] If the theme of the disciples' message had originated after Easter we might expect it to have been "Jesus" rather than the kingdom of God. The absence of any Christology in the disciples' message makes it probable that we have here a piece of pre-Easter tradition.[17]

(c) The Palestinian milieu of the personification of peace ("a son of peace" [18]) and shaking off the dust from their feet[19] also point to the pre-Easter origin of at least some of this material.[20] Thus, even if the framework of the mission charge has been supplied by the early Church,[21] we have here clear evidence that Jesus most probably sent disciples out on mission prior to Easter.[22]

2. The next question that requires our attention is, Did the disciples' mission charge contain specific instruction to cast out demons? The question arises because one of the sources (Mark 6.7) has Jesus giving the disciples authority over the unclean spirits (cf. Mark 3.15) while the other source (Q/Luke 10.9) has Jesus mentioning only healing the sick. Mark

10   Beare *JBL* 89 (1970) 12.
11   Beare *JBL* 89 (1970) 13. Bultmann *History* 145; contrast Jeremias *Theology* 133.
12   Hahn *Mission* 43; cf. Beare *JBL* 89 (1970) 10; Bultmann *History* 145.
13   Caird *ExpTim* 81 (1969–70) 41.
14   To the contrary see P. Hoffmann *Studien zur Theologie der Logionquelle* (Münster: Aschendorff, 1972) 312–31 and Schulz *Q* 415.
15   B.S. Easton *Luke* (Edinburgh: T & T Clark, 1926) 160.
16   Further see Kümmel *Promise* 22ff., 105ff.
17   Cf. Jeremias *Theology* 232.
18   See Str-B II, 166.
19   See Str-B I, 571; cf. Caird *ExpTim* 81 (1969–70) 41.
20   Cf. Jeremias *Theology* 232 and n. 1.
21   Marshall *Luke* 413.
22   Cf. Hengel *Charismatic Leader* 74.

may have added the reference to exorcism[23] for in view of Luke 10.17 where the returning disciples tell of their success in exorcism, Luke probably would not drop any such reference from his source. Thus, it appears that no such charge was given to the disciples. However, while it is difficult to show that a specific charge to exorcise was given to the disciples it is not difficult to show that the disciples probably involved themselves in exorcism.

First, we have seen that the pre-Markan and historical tradition in Mark 9.14—29 assumed the disciples' ability to cast out demons. Secondly, Mark himself believed the disciples to be exorcists (3.15; 6.7, 13). Thirdly, the Strange Exorcist pericope assumes that the followers of Jesus were exorcists (Mark 9.38/Luke 9.49). Fourthly, the return of the Seventy (Two) mentions the disciples being given "power over the enemy" which, as we will see, probably was at least of Palestinian origin (Luke 10.19). This variety of evidence is support for assuming that the disciples probably were involved in exorcism before Easter,[24] even though we cannot recover a specific charge of Jesus to do so. We could add, in view of Jesus' sending the disciples out to preach the kingdom of God, and the connection he made between the kingdom of God and the fall of Satan's kingdom and exorcism (see chaps. IV and VI below), that Jesus would have assumed that his command to preach the kingdom would have involved a ministry of exorcism.

3. What then of the disciples' return? Are there any historical reminiscences in the accounts of the disciples' return (Mark 6.30/Luke 10.17—20)? The Markan revision betrays the Evangelist's hand to such an extent that it appears to be predominantly redactional.[25] As Mark is not in the habit of inventing details for literary purposes,[26] we can perhaps say that at least a mention of the disciples' return was in Mark's tradition — but no more. Even the two-part report on what the disciples had done and taught may be from Mark's hand for, as we have seen (§6 above), he is intent on holding both aspects together, at least in Jesus' mission. We must then rely on Luke 10.17—20 to gain insight into the history of this tradition.

The case for recognizing this as coming from Luke's hand has not often been proposed,[27] nor is it generally thought to be from his source

---

23 Mark shows a distinct interest in exorcism. See Twelftree *Christ* 116–22.
24 Cf. Jeremias *Theology* 95; Hengel *Charismatic Leader* 73–4.
25 Cf. Taylor *Mark* 318.
26 Taylor *Mark* 318.
27 A relatively recent champion of this view has been Hoffmann *Logionquelle* 248ff. The key to this case is that Luke 10.1 is Lukan. But this being redaction may have no bearing on Luke 10.17–19 which Luke could have drawn from one of his sources. Hoffmann also says that 10.17–20 fits Luke's theology of mission. This argument however can show no more than that he has included material that is in line with

"L".[28] Rather it is more likely to be a compilation of material from tradition (verses 18 and 19) and Luke's hand.[29] The Palestinian elements in the pericope[30] suggest an early origin for this material, as especially does the connection between exorcism and the fall of Satan, a connection which the early Church did not maintain. It is quite likely, then, that this report is conveying historically reliable material.

Of particular interest is 10.18 — "I saw Satan like lightning from heaven falling." As this is an unusual report, in that Jesus is said to experience a vision,[31] and because of the strangeness of language, it is often taken to be a reliable reflection of Jesus' words.[32] This verse has been taken to refer to a number of different things.[33] For example, C.J. Cadoux says it is possible that we have here another allusion to the Temptations. But such a view is only possible if one begins with the assumption that the victory over Satan was represented in the Temptations.[34] Edward Langton says that it has been referred "to the original fall of the angels, to which so many references are made in Jewish apocalyptic literature."[35] Such a view is only possible if the verse is considered to be a saying detached from the present context.[36] However, authentic Jesus sayings in the Beelzebul Controversy (see §10 above) so relate exorcism and the fall of Satan that we would expect Luke 10.18 to be in its present context.

---

his theology of mission. S. Jellicoe ("St. Luke and the 'Seventy [–Two]' " *NTS* 8 [1960–1] 319–21) argues that it is Lukan in that Luke's love of the LXX led him to use the Letter of Aristeas – "Just as the seventy–two emissaries of Aristeas had, by their translation, brought the knowledge of the Law to the Greek–speaking world, so the seventy (–two) are divinely commissioned to proclaim its fulfilment in the Gospel message" (321). See also S. Jellicoe "St. Luke and the Letter of Aristeas" *JBL* 89 (1961) 149–55, followed by G. Sellin "Komposition, Quellen und Function des Lukanischen Reisebrichtes (Lk. 9.51–19.28)" *NovT* 20 (1978) 115.

28 T.W. Manson *Sayings* 73ff.; A.M. Hunter *The Work and Words of Jesus* revised edition (London: SCM, 1973) 203 and 208; G.B. Caird *The Gospel of St Luke* (Harmondsworth: Penguin, 1963) 144. That the passage comes from Q see B.H. Streeter *The Four Gospels: A Study of Origins* (London: Macmillan, 1924) 289f. and 291 and in W. Sanday (ed.) *Studies in the Synoptic Problem* (Oxford: Clarendon, 1911) 192 and J.C. Hawkins in Sanday (ed.) *Studies* 135. To the contrary see Kloppenborg *Formation of Q*.

29 Cf. Bultmann *History* 158 n. 1; Fitzmyer *Luke* II, 859.

30 A. Schlatter *Das Evengelium des Lukas* (Stuttgart: Calwer, 1960) 281. Note also Str–B II, 167f..

31 On the visions of Jesus see Kümmel *Promise* 133 and n. 27; cf. Fitzmyer *Luke the Theologian* 166–9.

32 Note Kümmel *Promise* 133f. and notes; J. Jeremias *Die Sprache des Lukasevangeliums* (Göttingen: Vandenhoeck & Ruprecht, 1980) 187–9.

33 Besides the two mentioned here see also, e.g. Jeremias *Parables* 122 n. 33.

34 C.J. Cadoux *The Historic Mission of Jesus* (London: Lutterworth, 1941) 66. Contrast W. Foerster *TDNT* VII, 157 and n. 28.

35 Langton *Essentials* 170.

36 As does Kümmel *Promise* 113.

On the face of it this verse seems to convey the idea that Jesus had seen Satan's speedy and complete defeat.[37] On closer investigation the verse probably tells a different story. To begin with, the modern eye regards the metaphor of lightning as conveying the idea of light, but above all speed. However, on the other occasions this word is used in the New Testament the accent is not on speed but on brightness (Matthew 24.27; 28.3; Luke 11.36; 17.24; Revelation 4.5; 8.5; 11.19 and 16.18). This is especially the case in Revelation where the term is used of the stunning and arresting brightness of God's activity with duration and speed being of no particular significance. Thus, for Satan to fall like lightning would not necessarily mean that his fall had been speedy or complete, but that it was both manifestly obvious and stunning. We should not make too much of the Greek tenses of this verse (ἐθεώρουν imperfect; πεσόντα aorist participle) but, in its being linked with exorcism, this obvious and stunning fall of Satan would seem to be considered an on-going process.[38] If this is correct then this pericope, particularly Luke 10.18, tells us that Jesus viewed even his disciples' exorcisms as linked with the fall of Satan. In turn, this reflects back on the Spirit/finger saying (Matthew 12.28/Luke 11.20) to confirm, indirectly, the notion that Jesus saw his exorcisms as having eschatological significance. Here is a view, expressed by Jesus, and without parallel in contemporary Judaism, that the vanquishing of Satan was taking place in the present,[39] rather than being complete.[40]

---

37 So Jeremias *Parables* 122 and E. Linnemann *Parables of Jesus* (London: SPCK, 1966) 102.
38 Cf. Moule *Idiom* 206.
39 See also Jeremias *Theology* 95.
40 As does S. Vollenweider " 'Ich sah den Satan wie einen Blitz vom Himmel fallen' (Lk 10:18)" *ZNW* 79 (1988) 187–203.

§ 14 The Brief Summary Reports

Apart from the longer stories we have been examining, there are also generalizing summaries of Jesus' ministry in the Gospels and Acts which mention exorcism and which we need to consider briefly. These summaries in the Gospels are at *Mark 1.32—4* (/Matthew 8.16—17/Luke 4.40—1); *Mark 1.39* (/Matthew 4.24/Luke 4.44) and *Mark 3.7—12* (/Matthew 4.24—5/12.15—16/Luke 6.17—19). In *Acts 10.38* Luke says Jesus "went about doing good and healing all who were under the power of the devil, because God was with him." If these brief statements are to contribute to our sketch of the historical Jesus then we must ask about the origin of this material.

1. *Mark 1.32—4*.[1] The objection of Vincent Taylor's that this pericope is not a summary statement such as 3.7—12 because it is connected with a particular time and place[2] need not detain us. It holds only in part, for the healing activity of Jesus is clearly summarized, introducing new information in a general and non-specific fashion. There is a mixture of redaction and pre-Markan tradition in this passage which may well reflect historical happenings.[3] However, the reference to demons and exoricsm ("the demon-possessed" [1.32]; "and he would not let the demons speak because they knew him" [1.34]) are generally agreed to be redactional rather than historical data.[4] It is best, then, for us to set this pericope aside in our search for authentic historical material.

2. *Mark 1.39*.[5] It is generally agreed that this verse comes from Mark's

---

1 Literature: Pesch *Markus*. I, 136; Gnilka *Markus* I, 85; Guelich *Mark* I, 63. On the sum- mary reports in Mark see W. Egger *Frohbotschaft und Lehre: Sammelberichte des Wirkens Jesu im Markusevangelium* (Frankfurt: Knecht, 1976); C.W. Hedrick "The Role of 'Summary Statements' in the Composition of the Gospel of Mark: A Dialogue with Karl Schmidt and Norman Perrin" *NovT* 26 (1984) 289–311 and notes.

2 Taylor *Mark* 180. On the nature of the summaries see Hedrick *NovT* 26 (1984) 293–4 and 311.

3 Gnilka *Markus* I, 85–6; Pesch *Markus*. I, 135; cf. Best *Disciples* 181.

4 E.g. Schweizer *Mark* 54; Gnilka *Markus* I, 86 and n. 1; Pesch *Markus*. I, 133–5. See also those mentioned in Pryke *Style* 11. Though, to the contrary see Guelich *Mark* I, 63–4.

5 Literature: Pesch *Markus*. I, 140; Gnilka *Markus* I, 87–9; Guelich *Mark* I, 67.

hand[6] so we must also put it aside in our search for material that can be traced back to the *Sitz im Leben* of Jesus' earthly ministry.

3. We are again in a similar position with *Mark 3.7—12*[7] as it is probably entirely redactional.[8] Nevertheless, Keck and Schweizer, for example, have argued for the details of the setting being a core of traditional material (3.7 and 8).[9] However, a *Sitz im Leben* for such material would be difficult to imagine.[10] In any case, these two verses tell us nothing about Jesus and exoricsm.

4. *Acts 10.38*. In discussing this verse we must take into account the fact that we are dealing with material that forms part of a speech in Acts; a subject on which there has been considerable debate.[11] In what has been called one of the most important and influential studies of the subject ever to have appeared,[12] Dibelius argued that Luke composed the speeches as well as provided their structure.[13] In particular, 10.38 is part of Peter's speech (10.34—43) which Dibelius argued to have been certainly contributed by Luke, on the grounds that it is unlikely that the early Church would have a place for a relatively long speech in a legend about the conversion of a centurion.[14] In any case, we do not need to pursue this debate, for the material certainly does not originate in the ministry of the earthly Jesus but in the life of the early Church.

This brief, cursory discussion of the summary reports in the Gospels and Acts establishes that none of the material relating to Jesus and exorcism can be shown to have most probably originated in the life of the historical Jesus. Therefore, we must leave it aside when we come to sketch our picture of the historical Jesus. Nevertheless, this data does show that the early Church remembered Jesus as an exorcist and that exorcism was a distinctive and important part of his ministry.[15]

---

6 Schweizer *Mark* 54; Gnilka *Markus* I, 88; Guelich *Mark* I, 70.

7 Literature: Pesch *Markus*. I, 202; Gnilka *Markus* I, 132; C.R. Kazmierski *Jesus, the Son of God* (Würzburg: Echter, 1979); Guelich *Mark* I, 141.

8 Best *Following* 36 and n. 55.

9 L.E. Keck "Mark 3.7-12 and Mark's Christology" *JBL* 84 (1965) 341-58; Schweizer *Mark* 79; and Pesch *Markus*. I, 198 who considers all of Mark 3.7-12 to be pre-Markan.

10 Best *Following* 36 and n. 55; Keck *JBL* 84 (1965) 341-58 whose critics are listed by Best in *Following* 49 n. 55. See also Nineham *Mark* 112.

11 Literature: F.F. Bruce "The Speeches in Acts – Thirty Years After" in R.J. Banks (ed.) *Reconciliation and Hope* (Exeter: Paternoster, 1974) 53–68 and G.H.R. Horsley "Speeches and Dialogue in Acts" *NTS* 32 (1986) 609-14. On the speech in particular see F Neirynck "Ac 10,36–43 et l'Evangile" *ETL* 60 (1984) 109–17.

12 Bruce in Banks (ed.) *Reconciliation* 56.

13 M. Dibelius "The Speeches in Acts and Ancient Historiography" (1949) in his *Studies in the Acts of the Apostles* (ed.) H. Greeven (London: SCM, 1956) 138–85.

14 Dibelius *Studies* 110.

15 See also Best *Disciples* 181.

IV
Jesus the Exorcist

§ 15 Historical Method

So far we have done two things. In chapter II we set out the background against which we can view the Gospel material relating to Jesus as an exorcist. Then, in the last chapter, we attempted to identify and set aside probable Christian redaction in the principal data relating to Jesus the exorcist. In turn, we were able to attempt to reconstruct the earliest recoverable reports of this aspect of the ministry of the historical Jesus. In order to do this we often had to address the inseparable question of historicity so that in some cases we have already drawn conclusions on the questions of historicity.

Nevertheless, our task now is to focus on the question of historicity. We need to subject these reconstructed reports to historical critical examination to see what data, not as yet discussed, may have originated from the earliest reports of those who witnessed the ministry of Jesus. So, an important question we must now discuss is, What criteria can we use to help identify probable authentic historical tradition in the Jesus stories?

There has been a great deal of discussion about the recovery of the sayings of the historical Jesus. This discussion has given rise to a series of well known, often discussed and variously modified, so-called "criteria" for identifying such sayings. Dennis Polkow has rightly suggested a hierarchy of criteria. (1) First, discounting redaction and (2) tradition. Secondly, authentic material must pass the test of the primary criteria: (3) dissimilarity,[1] (4) coherence and (5) multiple attestation. Then, the secondary criteria can be applied to material: (6) Palestinian context, (7) material

---

1 This criterion has been most widely used. See C.A. Evans "Authenticity Criteria in Life of Jesus Research" *Christian Scholar's Review* 19(1989) 6–31; C.A. Evans *Life of Jesus Research: An Annotated Bibliography* (Leiden: Brill, 1989) 107–8; Hollenbach *BTB* 19 (1989) 15–16. We can note a modification of the criterion of dissimilarity or discontinuity by Turner *Historicity* 74. He says:
"Where there is an overlap of interest between the Gospels and early Church, but a marked difference in the scale of treatment, we can be reasonably sure that we are on firm historical ground."
He goes on:
"Instances might be the Church, or the community of the disciples, and the passages which bear upon our Lord's Mission to the Gentiles."

consistent with the style, form, function and content of Jesus' ministry and (8) scholarly consensus.[2] These are so-called "criteria" for, as Ben F. Meyer pointed out to me in private correspondence, they are merely patterns of inference or indicators of historicity.

In the present study, our concern is not with the authenticity of the sayings of Jesus but with the historicity of narratives or reports of his activities. So far, little specific work has been done on tools for this task in the context of the search for the historical Jesus.[3]

In the search for and reconstruction of authentic sayings of Jesus it is, at least theoretically, possible to recover if not the *ipsissima verba* then at least the *ipsissimus sensus* of Jesus.[4] However, with narrative material we can never recover or recreate the underlying event in its complex entirely; that is lost to us in the irrecoverable past. In the stories we can never penetrate beyond the dimension and limits of interpretation and the selective reporting of those who first related an alleged event. We are restricted to judging whether or not, and in what way, the earliest reconstructable report, or event-description, might reflect an event in the life of historical Jesus.[5]

Nevertheless, taking into account the difference between sayings and narrative material and the varying value of the criterion, the same criteria can be used as tools to test the historical veracity of narrative material.

---

2 D. Polkow "Method and Criteria for Historical Jesus Research" in K.H. Richards (ed.) *SBLSP* (Atlanta: Scholars Press, 1987) 336–56. Cf. R. Latourelle "Authenticité historique des miracles de Jésus: Essai de criteriologie" *Gregorianum* 54 (1973) 225–62; R.H. Stein "The 'Criteria' for Authenticity" in R.T. France and D. Wenham (eds.) *Gospel Perspectives* I (Sheffield: JSOT, 1980) 225–63; M.E. Boring "Criteria of Authenticity. The Lucan Beatitudes As a Test Case" *Forum* 1 (1985) 3–38; revised as "The Historical-Critical Method's 'Criteria of Authenticity': The Beatitudes in Q and Thomas as a Test Case" in C.W. Hedrick (ed.) *The Historical Jesus and the Rejected Gospels* Semeia 44 (Atlanta: Scholars Press, 1988) 9–44; G.H. Twelftree "EI ΔE . . . EΓΩ EKBAΛΛΩ TA ΔAIMONIA. . ." in Wenham and Blomberg (eds.) *Gospel Perspectives* 6, 370 and Blomberg "Concluding Reflections on Miracles and *Gospel Perspectives*" in Wenham and Blomberg (eds.) *Gospel Perspectives* 6, 445–49; Evans *Jesus Research* 100–112. See the discussion "Objectivity and Subjectivity in Historical Criticism of the Gospels" by B.F. Meyer in his *Critical Realism and the NT* (Allison Park: Pickwick, 1989) 129–45.

3 Though see Mussner *Miracles* 27–39; R. Pesch *Jesu ureigene Taten? Ein Beitrag zur Wunderfrage* (Freiburg: Herder, 1970) and F. Mussner "Ipsissima facta Jesu?" *TRev* 68 (1972) cols. 177–85.

4 Cf. Vermes *Judaism* 81:
    "As for the famous *ipsissima verba*, a quest for these presupposes a degree of reliability in gospel tradition that modern research simply cannot justify. . . But is it not possible nevertheless to grasp at the very least something of a master's teaching? I would suggest that we can manage to perceive his ideas, the *ipsissimus sensus*, even without the actual words in which they were formulated".

5 Cf. H.D. Betz: "What then is the miracle story? The miracle story is neither the miracle itself nor talk about the miracle but a narrative with the special assignment

For example, the criterion of multiple attestation can be used.[6] If it can be shown that a type or genre of activity of Jesus — such as his reported association with women or his table fellowship with outcasts — is attested in more than one of the Gospel traditions then the probability that this kind of activity was part of the ministry of the historical Jesus is considerably enhanced (further, see 2 below). Of course, other criteria will need to be brought to bear on particular narratives, or parts thereof, to test their individual reliability. Apart from the careful use of these criteria I would suggest that there are others that we may use.

The place to begin is with Ernst Troeltsch, whose essay "Uber historische und dogmatische Methode in der Theologie" (1898) remains a starting point for a discussion of the problem of increasing our knowledge and understanding of the past.[7] In this piece Troeltsch set out three principles of historical method. First, the principle of criticism or methodological doubt (pp. 731—2) which means that the conclusions of a historian cannot be seen as absolute but are only, to a greater or lesser degree, probabilities, always open to further questioning and revision.[8] The second principle, which we will discuss in a moment, is that of analogy (p. 732). There is also, thirdly the principle of correlation or causation (p. 733) by which a historian supposes that every event has an identifiable cause or series causes.[9]

---

of serving as a kind of language envelope for the transmission and communication of the 'unspeakable' miracle event." "The Early Christian Miracle Story: Some Observations on the Form Critical Problem" in R.W. Funk (ed.) *Early Christian Miracle Stories* Semeia 11 (Missoula: Scholars Press, 1978) 70.

    Over against M. Mandelbaum, *The Anatomy of Historical Knowledge* (Baltimore and London: Johns Hopkins University Press, 1977) and, e.g. L.O. Mink "Narrative Form as a Cognitive Instrument" in R.H. Canary and H. Kozicki (eds.) *The Writing of History* (Madison: University of Wisconsin Press, 1978) 129–49, D. Carr "Narrative and the Real World: An Argument for Continuity" *History and Theory* 25 (1986) 117–31 and *Time, Narrative and History* (Bloomington: Indiana University Press, 1986) argues for the narrative character of human experience, both individual and social, so that a narrative account is not so utterly different in form from a series of events, nor is historical narrative condemned to misrepresent or transform events it depicts. Rather, narrative must be regarded as an extension of the primary features of events or event series. See also B. Hardy "Towards a Poetic of Fiction: An Approach through Narrative" *Novel* 2 (1968) 5–14; P. Munz *The Shapes of Time* (Middletown: Wesleyan University Press, 1977); F. Olafson *The Dialectic of Action* (Chicago and London: University of Chicago Press, 1979); J. Passmore "Narratives and Events" *History and Theory* 26 (1987) 68–74; A.P. Norman "Telling it like it was: Historical Narratives on their own Terms" *History and Theory* 30 (1991) 119–35.

6 See the list in Stein in France and Wenham (eds.) *Gospel Perspectives* I, 255 n. 13 for those who refer to this criterion.

7 E. Troeltsch *Gessammelte Schriften* 4 vols. (Tübingen: Mohr, 1913) II, 729–53.

8 Cf. Van A. Harvey *The Historian and the Believer* (London: SCM, 1967) 14.

9 Further see M. Bloch *The Historian's Craft* (Manchester: University of Manchester Press, 1954) chap. 5; E.H. Carr *What is History?* (London: Macmillan, 1961) chap. 4 and

1. It is to Troeltsch's second, and fundamental, canon of analogy that we turn to provide us with a valuable tool for our subsequent inquiries. Troeltsch explains:

> "Analogy with what happens before our eyes and what is given within ourselves is the key to criticism. Illusions, displacements, myth formation, fraud, and party spirit, as we see them before our own eyes, are the means whereby we can recognize similar things in what tradition hands down. Agreement with normal, ordinary, repeatedly attested modes of occurrence and conditions as we know them is the mark of probability for the occurrence that the critic can either acknowledge really to have happened or leave on one side. The observation of analogies between past occurrences of the same sort makes it possible to ascribe probability to them and to interpret the one that is unknown from what is known of the other."[10]

This principle has been taken up and restated by other historians. For example, Marc Bloch puts it: "In the last analysis, whether consciously or no, it is always by borrowing from our daily experiences and by shading them, where necessary, with new tints that we derive the elements which help us to restore the past."[11]

However, this principle has been severely criticized. As Troeltsch expounded it the principle of analogy required that there be a "fundamental homogeneity" (*Gleichartigkeit*) of all historical events (p. 732). Pannenberg has explained that, for Troeltsch this means that "all differences should be comprehended in a uniform, universal homogeneity."[12] However, this means that the historian's world-view dominates that of the past. Yet, it is most probable that no historical event can be contained, without remainder, by a contemporary or ancient analogue nor that a historian's knowledge and present experience contains all the possibilities of human existence.[13]

P. Gardiner *The Nature of Historical Explanation* (Oxford: Oxford University Press, 1961) Part III.

10 Troeltsch *Gesammelte Schriften* II, 732, quoted in W. Pannenberg *Basic Questions in Theology* I (London: SCM, 1970) 43–4.

11 Bloch *Craft* 44. Cf. D. Hume, "The maxim by which we commonly conduct ourselves in our reasonings is that the objects of which we have no experience resemble those of which we have. . ." *On Human Nature and the Understanding* ed. with a new introduction by A. Flew (London: Collier Macmillan, 1962) 121. Cf. also W. Dilthey,

> "If I am to see [a past human] . . as a person, to understand his mental life in its continuity and coherence, I must trace in his experience the lines of connection with which I am familiar in my own. I can do this in proportion as the consciousness of my own mental structure is present in and governs my understanding of his."

Gesammelte Schriften 12 vols. (Leipzig and Berlin: Teubner and Göttingen: Vandenhoeck & Ruprecht, 1958) VII, 214. From Harvey *Historian* 98.

12 Pannenberg *Questions* I, 46.

13 Cf. Pannenberg *Questions* I, 45–6. Cf. his *Jesus - God and Man* (London: SCM, 1968) 109, ". . . historical inquiry always takes place from an already given context of meaning, out of a preunderstanding of the object of inquiry, which, however, is modified and corrected in the process of research on the basis of the phenomena examined."

This brings us to the important point that a distinction is to be drawn between the positive and negative use of the principle of analogy.[14] A positive use of this tool means that if an analogue can be found for the historical event in question then the historian's verdict can be in favour of its historicity. On the other hand, however, if no contemporary analogue can be found, the strict or negative use of the principle of analogy means that the historian will reject the historicity of the reported event. But, this is illegitimate for it supposes that there is no variety in history; that analogous events must be precisely the same in all details.[15] This negative use of the tool is also illegitimate for, again, it supposes that the historian has at hand all possible and complete analogies and that the world-view of the historian is to determine the past and dominate his understanding of it.[16]

Rather, to rely on Pannenberg again, "to the extent that a datum of tradition bursts the known possibilities of comparison, it remains opaque even for the historian who, among all men, is equipped with extra-ordinary eyepieces for what has been."[17]

In other words, and in relation to our present enterprise, the canon of analogy is useful to us in establishing the probable historicity of a reported event in Jesus' ministry of exorcism only when we have an analogue at hand. If the analogue is not precise, and there are remainders, we shall be obliged to examine these further, but not to reject out of hand either the reported event or the remainders. Also, if no analogue — contemporary or ancient — can be found, judgement must be reserved and other canons of authenticity applied to the report. It is to these we now turn.

2. If an activity of Jesus which we are investigating is referred to, indirectly or incidentally, we may have a pointer to historical data. Arthur Marwich stated it in this way: "On the whole it can be said that a primary source is most valuable when the purpose for which it was compiled is at

---

14 On what follows see the discussion by T. Peters "The Use of Analogy in Historical Method" *CBQ* 35 (1973) 480 and Pannenberg *Questions* I, 44–50.

15 Cf. E. Meyer: "[History writing] is also engaged with typical forms, to be sure, but predominantly and in the first instance with the varieties" in Pannenberg *Questions* I, 46 n.87.

16 Cf. R.M. Frye "A Literary Perspective for the Criticism of the Gospels" in D.G. Miller and D.Y. Hadidian (eds.) *Jesus and Man's Hope* 2 vols. (Pittsburgh: Pittsburgh Theological Seminary, 1971) II, 199:
"The barbarian blindly asserts the primacy of his own temporal or cultural pro-vincialism in judging and understanding and interpreting all that occurs, and the learned barbarian does precisely the same thing, but adds footnotes."
See also H.G. Gadamer "The Continuity of History and the Existential Moment" *Philosophy Today* 16 (1972) 230–40, esp. 238.

17 Pannenberg *Questions* I, 50.

the furthest remove from the purpose of the historian."[18] That is, we have a *criterion of incidental transmission.*[19] Again, for example, if the parable of the Strong Man in the Beelzebul Controversy pericope can be shown to be authentic we have an incidental reference to Jesus being an exorcist.

3. From what we said above, if a class or category of sayings has been established as belonging to the bedrock of historical material then reported activities which cohere with this (while not automatically, without further discussion, thereby established as authentic) can at least be given the benefit of the doubt in relation to historicity. For example, in relation to our theme, if some or all of the sayings that are now found in the Beelzebul Controversy pericope can be shown, most probably, to have come from the authentic Jesus tradition then we are predisposed to consider more favourably the historicity of an exorcism story in the Gospel tradition than if we were unable to find an authentic saying of Jesus that assumed that he was an exorcist.[20] So, we have the criterion of *coherence with reliable sayings material.*

4. The witness of extra-canonical material can, with care, be used to help test the historicity of events behind Gospel narratives. Thus, for example, Jesus' choosing disciples is supported by Jewish traditions (*b. Sanh.* 43a).[21]

5. Finally, we can take as historically reliable those reports, like the baptism of Jesus and the crucifixion of Jesus which, at least in the early stages of the transmission of the tradition, would have been embarrassing for the early Church to transmit.

It is with these principles of historical method in mind that we set out now to sketch a picture of the historical Jesus the exorcist.

---

18 A. Marwick *The Nature of History* (London: Macmillan, 1970) 136.

19 Marwick *History* 136, draws attention to Henry Guerlac's distinction between the "intentional record" and the "unwitting testimony" of official records and private correspondence. (See H. Guerlac "Some Historical Assumptions of the History of Science" in A.C. Crombie (ed.) *Scientific Change* (London: Heinemann, 1963). See also J.D. Milligan "The Treatment of an Historical Source" in *History and Theory* 18 (1979) 184.

20 Cf. Pesch *Jesu ureigene Taten?* 25, 147, 151, 153–4. Matt 12.43/Luke 11.24–6 assumes the notion of exorcism but not that Jesus was an exorcist.

21 See G.H. Twelftree "Jesus in Jewish Traditions" in D. Wenham (ed.) *Gospel Perspectives* 5 (Sheffield: JSOT, 1984) 289–341.

§ 16 Was Jesus an Exorcist?

The fundamental question which we have so far left in abeyance, but which only now we have sufficient evidence to answer, is whether or not the historical Jesus was in fact an exorcist.[1]

To the extent that exorcism is the expelling of evil spiritual beings from people and, therefore, for some, an incredible form of healing, an answer to this question will depend on the predisposition of the twentieth century reader towards accepting reports of miracles as part of the tradition of the historical Jesus. We need to discuss this issue briefly, for a number of contemporary and older students of the historical Jesus wish to delete reports of the supernatural from the Jesus tradition.[2] In countering this view, and so being open to permitting reports of miracles to be part of the Jesus tradition, we need to question two views in particular.

First, we must call into question the view expressed by Hume. He said that miracles "are observed chiefly to abound among ignorant and barbarous nations . . ."[3] There is plenty of evidence, to which I have drawn attention elsewhere that, in antiquity, the miraculous was by no means unquestionably accepted.[4] Yet, R.M. Grant has argued that the first century AD was a period in which credulity increased. However, some of Grant's evidence is questionable.[5] For example, in *Antiquities* 2.167—70, Josephus says that the miraclulous promises made by messianic prophets shortly before the Jewish revolt were surely not characteristic of the age as a whole. Also, as A.E. Harvey mentions, the note by Pliny in *Natural*

---

1 On what follows see also Dunn and Twelftree in *Churchman* 94 ·(1980) 211–15, and an earlier version of some of the material in this section in Twelftree in Wenham and Blomberg (eds.) *Gospel Perspectives* 6, 361–400.

2 E.g. W. Bousset *Kyrios Christos* (New York and Nashville: Abingdon, 1970) 100; M. Grant *Jesus* (London: Weidenfeld and Nicholson, 1977) 39. See the discussion in J. Engelbrecht "Trends in Miracle Research" *Neotestamentica* 22 (1988) 139–61.

3 Hume *On Human Nature* (ed.) Flew 123. Cf. R.J. Sider "The Historian, The Miraculous and Post–Newtonian Man" *SJT* 25 (1972) 309–19; M. Maher "Recent Writings on the Miracles" *New Blackfriars* 56 (658, 1975) 165–74; R. Young "Miracles and Credulity" *RelS* 16 (1980) 465–8; D. Odegard "Miracles and Good Evidence" *RelS* 18 (1982) 37–46.

4 See Twelftree *Christ* chap. V. Cf. Harvey *Constraints* 101–2 who draws attention to other primary evidence. Contrast Best *Disciples* 179.

5 See Harvey *Constraints* 102 n. 21.

History 31.18—24 ("in Judaea rivus sabbatis omnibus siccatus"), "is probably no more than a slightly fanciful report of the well-known phenomenon of an intermittent spring, of which Jerusalem afforded a notable example."[6] Thus, the miracle stories cannot be dismissed simply because they are viewed as arising in a more credulous world than our own.

Secondly, we must call into question the general point that because of the milieu of the origin of the Jesus tradition it was inevitable that legendary stories would adhere to the Jesus tradition.[7] It is noticeable that although Jesus lived among contemporaries who were credited with miraculous powers, the tradition of miracles surrounding Jesus is of a different order from other ancient miracle traditions. For example, in contrast to the Gospel traditions, in Jewish traditions miracle workers were not credited with curing lameness or paralysis.[8] Also, the Jewish traditions know nothing of a rabbi raising the dead.[9] Having discussed points like these Harvey is justified in concluding that, ". . . the tradition of Jesus' miracles has too many unusual features to be conveniently ascribed to conventional legend-mongering. Moreover, many of them contain details of precise reporting which is quite unlike the usual run of legends and is difficult to explain unless it derives from some historical recollection; and the Gospels themselves . . . show a remarkable restraint in their narratives which contrasts strangely with the delight in the miraculous for its own sake which normally characterizes the growth of legend."[10]

So, we return to the question: was Jesus an exorcist? From the sayings and narrative material in the Synoptic Gospels I have surveyed it would seem that we could only conclude that exorcism was a part of the ministry of the historical Jesus. I can now proceed to draw together evidence that suggests that Jesus was most probably an exorcist, even though ἐξορκιστής is never used of him (cf. Acts 19.13).

1. As it is easier to establish the historicity of the sayings material in the Gospels, we shall begin with the sayings of Jesus in the Synoptic traditions which presume his ability as an exorcist. In the Beelzebul Controversy pericope (Mark 3.22—7 and Matthew 12.22—30/Luke 11.14—23, see §10 above), Q and the Evangelists have brought together two sayings on exorcism. They are, the saying that Jesus exorcised by the Spirit of God (Matthew 12.28/Luke 11.20) and the parable of the Strong

---

6 Harvey *Constraints* 102 n. 21.
7 I have taken up this point from Harvey *Constraints* 99f.
8 Harvey *Constraints* 100; cf. Smith *Parallels* 81–4.
9 Cf. Bultmann *History* 233.
10 Harvey *Constraints* 100. Cf. W. Kirchschläger "Wie über Wunder reden?" *BLit* 51 (1978) 252–4.

Man (Mark 3.27/Matthew 12.29; and Luke 11.21f. [?Q]). Luke 13.22 has the warning to Herod, "Go tell that fox, 'Behold, I cast out demons and perform cures today and tomorrow, and the third day I finish my course . . .'"[11] These sayings and the Beelzebul charge, which must be posited among the indisputably historical elements of the Jesus tradition, only make sense in the light of Jesus being an exorcist; they presuppose a ministry of exorcism.[12]

2. In chapter III we have been able to show that in the Synoptic traditions there are exorcism stories legitimately associated with the historical Jesus (Mark 1.21—8, the demoniac in the Capernaum synagogue; 5.1—20, the Syrophoenician woman's daughter; 9.14—29, the epileptic boy and Matthew 9.32—3/12.22/12.22/Luke 11.14, the dumb demoniac).

But what about Luke's story of the healing of Simon's mother-in-law in Luke 4.38—9? Luke says that Jesus "rebuked the fever and it left her" (ἐπετίμησεν τῷ πυρετῷ καὶ ἀφῆκεν αὐτήν, 4.39).[13] Yet, a glance at a Synopsis reveals that Luke's source for this story, Mark 1.29—31,[14] has only "he came and took her by the hand and lifted her up, and the fever left her." In other words, Luke's "exorcism" story at 4.38—9 has its origin only in his own editorial work.

As we said in §5 above, we must also leave aside from consideration the story in Luke 13.10—17 of the "woman who had a spirit of infirmity" (γυνὴ πνεῦμα ἔχουσα ἀσθενείας). Although some kind of "evil" spirit is considered to be the cause of the illness, the features of the story are so different from the. traditional exorcism stories that Luke is unlikely to regard this as an exorcism story.[15] We are left, then, with four major stories and the brief one associated with the Beelzebul Controversy which have the origin of at least their core in the ministry of the historical Jesus.

3. In the Synoptics and Acts there are also brief generalizing summaries of Jesus' ministry which show that the early Church assumed that he was an exorcist (Mark 1.32—4/Matthew 8.16—17/Luke 4.40—1; Mark 1.39/Matthew 4.24/Luke 4.44; Mark 3.7—12/Matthew 4.24—5; 12.15—16/Luke 6.16—19; 4.41; see §14 above). In Acts 10.38 Luke mentions Jesus "healing

---

11 Further, and on the historical reliability of these sayings, see §10 above and Twelftree in Wenham and Blomberg (eds.) *Gospel Perspectives* 6, 364—5. Cf. Dunn *Jesus* 44 and H. Koester *Introduction to the NT* 2 vols. (Philadelphia: Fortress and Berlin and New York: de Gruyter, 1982) II, 79.

12 Cf. Latourelle *Miracles* 167—8.

13 On Jesus standing over the woman see Twelftree in Wenham and Blomberg (eds.) *Gospel Perspectives* 6, 394 n. 17.

14 Schramm *Markus-Stoff* 85—91. On Luke's intention in this pericope see Twelftree *Christ* 104.

15 See Twelftree in Wenham and Blomberg (eds.) *Gospel Perspectives* 6, 394 ns. 11 and 18.

everyone under the power of the deviL" However, the result of our
investigation was that none of this material can be shown to have most
probably originated in the life of the historical Jesus. What these particular
data show is that at least the early Church believed Jesus to have been an
exorcist.

4. Looking outside the New Testament there is further evidence to be
noted which assumes that Jesus was an exorcist.

(a) *Names,* often of those considered to have been or be powerful
exorcists, were used by other exorcists in their incantations.[16] In the New
Testament era the name of Solomon was probably that most widely used
by exorcists (see Pseudo-Philo *LAB* 60; Josephus *Ant.* 8.46—9). In *Antiquities* 8.42—9, Josephus illustrates the important implication of using the
"name" of another exorcist. He begins this story by considering Solomon's
prowess in wisdom, cleverness, musical compositions and ability to compose incantations and forms of exorcism. So, to prove Solomon's ability in
"the art used against demons" (*Ant.* 8.45) Josephus goes on to tell the story
of Eleazar using Solomon's name in an exorcism.

Extra biblical material also shows that Jesus' name was thought to be a
powerful element in incantations for exorcisms. In *Contra Celsum,* Origen
says of the Christians: ". . . they do not get the power which they seem to
possess by any incantation but by the name of Jesus . . ." (I.6; cf. I.67). The
magical papyri also make use of Jesus' name in its formulae: "I adjure you
by the god of the Hebrews Jesu, . . ." (PGM IV.3019f.; cf. IV.1227). To a
lead tablet from Megara R. Wünsch supplies a lacuna to restore the name
of "Jesus".[17] Also, Jewish healers took up Jesus' name into their incantational repertoire. This is plainly evident in that the rabbis prohibited
healing by Jesus' name.[18]

Even in the New Testament there is evidence of such practices. In
Mark 9.38 (/Luke 9.49) John comes to Jesus and says, "Teacher, we saw a
man casting out demons in your name . . ." In Acts 19.13 the sons of Sceva
attempt to perform an exorcism with the incantation, "I adjure you by the
Jesus whom Paul preaches." We could perhaps add Matthew's characterization of false prophets who say, "Lord, Lord, did we not . . . cast out

16 More widely on the use of Jesus' name in ancient magic see Aune *ANRW* II.23.2
    (1980) 1545–9. See also S.V. McCasland *By the Finger of God* (New York: Macmillan,
    1951) 110–11.

17 See Eitrem *Notes* 9 and notes.

18 Cf. *t. Hul.* 2.22f.; *j. Šabb.* 14.4.14d; *j. 'Abod. Zar.* 2.2; *b. 'Abod. Zar.* 27b. On the use of
    Jesus' name by Jewish exorcists see D. Chowlson "Das letzte Passahmahl, Christi"
    Mémoires de l'acad. imp. des sciences de S. Pétersbourg VII, 41, 1, Petersburg, 1882,
    100–107, cited by Fridrichsen *Miracle* 170 n. 29. On the use of Jesus' name in magic
    bowls see Geller *JJS* 28 (1977) 149–55.

demons in your name, and do many might works in your name?"
(Matthew 7.22).

The New Testament also shows the Christian community using Jesus'
name in its exorcisms. The Seventy (Two) return with joy saying, "Lord,
even the demons are subject to us in your name!" (Luke 10.17). Acts 16.18
portrays Paul casting out a spirit with the words, "I charge you in the
name of Jesus Christ to come out . . ." And, though later, the longer
ending of Mark is also evidence that the early Church used Jesus' name in
its exorcisms: "And these signs will accompany those who believe: in my
name they will cast out demons . . ." (16.17).

And, finally, on the use of the "name" of Jesus, we can note that later
in the post-apostolic Church Jesus' name was still being used as an
effective means of casting out demons. For example, Arnobius says that
Jesus' name "when heard puts to flight evil spirits" (*Adv. Gent.* 1.46).[19]

Therefore, probably one of the strongest pieces of evidence that the
historical Jesus was thought to be an exorcist is the variety of material
showing that Jesus' name was being used by other exorcists.

(b) Apart from mentioning the use of Jesus' name in incantations there
are instances where Jesus is referred to which might betray a tradition
relating to Jesus as an exorcist. The rabbis preserve such a tradition in
b. Sanhedrin 43a: "Jesus was hanged on Passover Eve. Forty days previously the herald had cried, 'He is being led out for stoning because he
has practised sorcery . . .'"

As I have argued elsewhere, this tradition need not have originally
referred to Jesus of Nazareth.[20] Nevertheless, as we have just noted, in that
Jesus' name was forbidden by the Jews to be used in healing it is possible
evidence that Jesus was considered to be a powerful healer and exorcist
(*t. Ḥul.* 2.22—3; *j. Šabb.* 14.4; *j. 'Abod. Zar.* 2.2; *b. 'Abod. Zar.* 27b).

Also, Origen quotes a saying of Celsus which may betray a tradition
that Jesus was thought to be an exorcist: "He was brought up in secret and
hired himself out as a workman in Egypt, and after having tried his hand

---

19 Cf. Justin *Dial*. 30.3; 76.6; 85.2; *Apology* 2.6. The topic of exorcism in the post–
    apostolic period is beyond the scope of this present study. See W.M. Alexander
    Demonic Possession in the NT (Edinburgh: T & T Clark, 1902) 129–233; A. Harnack
    The Mission and Expansion of Christianity I (London: Williams and Norgate, 1908)
    126–46; Wm.W. Everts "Jesus Christ, No Exorcist" *BS* 81 (1924) 355–62; J.S. McEwin
    "The Ministry of Healing" *SJT* 7 (1954) 133–52; W. Michaelis "Exorzismus" *RGG* II,
    833–4.

20 Twelftree in Wenham and Blomberg (eds.) *Gospel Perspectives* 5, 319–21. I no longer
    think that *b. Sanh.* 43a "is probably an echo of the charge laid against Jesus by the
    Pharisees (sic.) preserved in Mark 3.22" Dunn and Twelftree *Churchman* 94 (1980) 213.

at certain magical powers he returned from there, and on account of those powers gave himself the title of God" (*CC* I.38; cf. I.60).[21]

Even though these pieces of evidence from *b. Sanhedrin* 43a and Origen are too late to be of direct value to us they indicate a continuing tradition that Jesus was thought of as having had considerable success in the control of demons. This tradition was fostered by the ongoing debate between Jews and Christians.

So far I have ignored the testimony of the Johannine material. The Fourth Gospel, epistles and Apocalypse of John say nothing about exorcism nor of Jesus being an exorcist. In a moment we will draw together what is an impressive amount and range of kinds of evidence that shows Jesus was most probably an exorcist. In the light of this evidence it does not seem reasonable to suggest that the author(s) of the Johannine material knew nothing of the tradition that Jesus was an exorcist. Rather, the Johannine literature probably suppresses or ignores this tradition. Can this be explained?

It cannot be that John was embarrassed about portraying Jesus as a man of his time, using the healing techniques of his contemporaries.[22] For John is happy to include other techniques familiar to other healers: healing from a distance (4.46—54) and the use of spittle (9.1—7).[23]

On the other hand, a number of aspects of Johannine theology have probably contributed to the suppression of Jesus' association with exorcism. First is the Johannine notion of the function of Jesus' miracles. The end of an earlier addition of the Gospel than we now have spelt out the Johannine understanding of the role of the miracles of Jesus as follows. "Jesus did many other signs in the presence of the disciples, which are not written in this book; but these are written that you may believe that Jesus is the Christ, the Son of God, and that believing you may have life in his name" (20.30—1). In other words, for John, the miracles are considered so to reveal the identity of Jesus that the readers would conclude that he was the Christ. So, not only did John choose spectacular miracles, but miracles — like the turning of water into wine — which were thought to be the work of God. By contrast, to associate Jesus with the relatively common healing of exorcism performed by many other healers would have appeared banal.

A second factor which may have contributed to the Johannine material not mentioning Jesus being an exorcist may be linked with the playing

---

21 See also *Pistis Sophia* 102.255, 258; 130.332—5; Hippolytus *Refutatio* 7.15, 20 and K. Berger "Die königlichen Messiastraditionen des Neuen Testaments" *NTS* 20 (1974) 10 n. 38.
22 So Taylor *Mark* 171.
23 See §17 below and Twelftree *Christ* chap. II. On what follows also see Twelftree *Christ* 88—90. Cf. Kee *Miracle* 231.

down of the theme of the kingdom of God. In the Synoptic Gospels, exorcism and the kingdom of God are so closely associated that for John to exclude one probably meant that he felt it necessary to exclude the other.

Thirdly, in the Synoptic Gospels the defeat of Satan is linked with Jesus' exorcisms. In John the defeat of Satan is linked with the cross (cf. John 14.30; 16.11). This shift in Johannine theology probably carried with it the need to remove reference to exorcisms, which other Christians had associated the defeat of Satan. Probably for these reasons the Johannine material suppresses the tradition that Jesus was an exorcist.

The evidence we have been looking at in this section, which suggests that Jesus was an exorcist, supports our conclusions throughout chapter III that we are obliged to place the stories of Jesus as an exorcist within the traditions of his earthly life. In other words, we are required to agree with the consensus of scholarly opinion that the historical Jesus was an exorcist,[24] but, also, that "any historical picture of Jesus that does not include his activity as exorcist will be a distortion."[25]

---

24 E.g. Strauss *Life* 415–37, esp. 436; Richardson *Miracle* 68–74; Käsemann in *Essays* 39–40; Robinson *New Quest* chap. VI; Fuller *Miracles* chap. 2; Perrin *Rediscovering* 65; O. Betz *What Do We Know about Jesus?* (London: SCM, 1968) 58; Hahn *Titles* 292; Jeremias *Theology* 86–92; Böcher *Christus* 166–70; G. Vermes *Jesus the Jew* (Glasgow: Fontana, 1976) 58–65; Dunn *Jesus* 44; Koester *Introduction* II, 78–9; Best *Disciples* 181. Eitrem *Notes* 20, cf. 57, who, in defining an exorcist on the basis of the use of ὁρκίζω σε, suggests that as Jesus does not use the term he was not an exorcist. This, however, is far too narrow a definition of an exorcist (see chap. II above).

25 Achtemeier *CBQ* 37 (1975) 491. Contrast Pesch, *Jesu ureigene Taten?* 17–34, who argues that while Jesus' own words and Jewish literature testify to Jesus being an exorcist, the Gospel exorcism stories are so influenced by early Church interests that they cannot be used to prove that Jesus was an exorcist.

§ 17 Jesus as an Exorcist[1]

In this study we are trying to make a contribution to our understanding of the historical Jesus; to sketch a picture of the historical Jesus as an exorcist. As a first step we have been able to establish that the early Church maintained a tradition of Jesus being an exorcist. An examination of the data also shows that the historical Jesus was an exorcist with a high reputation.

In the light of the preceding chapter we can now draw together those elements in relation to Jesus and exorcism in the Gospel traditions which we found to be probably historically reliable and rightly belong to the tradition of the historical Jesus. We are now in a position to answer the principal motivating question of this book: *If Jesus was an exorcist what did those who saw him at work report of his techniques as an exorcist?*

1. The Demoniacs

To begin with, the reported identity of the demoniacs with whom Jesus came into contact may help us see how Jesus might have been viewed by his contemporaries. Also, knowing the identity of the demoniacs will contribute to our understanding of the focus of Jesus' ministry.

It is currently popular to argue that possession and mental illness was "caused, or at least exacerbated by social tension" and was "a socially acceptable form of oblique protest against, or escape from, oppression."[2] Thus, demoniacs are seen to be socially rootless people, driven to the margins of society by the social and economic crises in Palestine.[3] However, an examination of the Gospel data modifies this view of

---

1 Cf. Twelftree in Wenham and Blomberg (eds.) *Gospel Perspectives* 6, 368–83.
2 Derrett *Man* (n.s.) 14 (1979) 288, citing H. Bietenhard "Die Dekapolis von Pompeius bis Traian: ein Kapitel aus der neutestamentlicher Zeitgeschichte" *ZDPV* 79 (1963) 24–58 and S.T. Parker "The Decapolis Reviewed" *JBL* 94 (1975) 437–41; P.W. Hollenbach "Jesus, Demoniacs, and Public Authorities" *JAAR* 49 (1981) 575; Theissen *Followers* Part Two. Cf. R. Otto *The Kingdom of God and the Son of Man* (London: Lutterworth, 1943) 43, "a particularly strong wave of demonism had overflowed the world of Palestine" quoted with approval but with no evidence by Theissen *Miracle* 250.
3 Cf. Theissen *Followers* 36 and also previous note.

the demoniacs with whom Jesus dealt. This data, being transmitted quite incidentally (see §15 above), provides us with reliable historical material.

The demoniac in the Capernaum synagogue (Mark ·1.21—8) is described as having an unclean spirit. We suggested above (§6) that the chaotic and unpredictable character of demoniacs could mean that at times the man showed no adverse symptoms of his condition. Or, the demon only revealed itself when confronted by a spiritual enemy. In any case, the Gospel tradition portrays a man, with no previous symptoms of having an unclean spirit, in the mainstream of Jewish society and participating in the religious life of his community.

The story of the Gadarene demoniac (Mark 5.1—20) reveals a different picture; he lived on the margins of society among the tombs, perhaps living in the burial caves (see Numbers 19.11, 16; 11QTemple 48.11—13; 49.5—21; 50.3—8 and *Acts of Andrew* 6; Jerome Letter 108.13). To be "unclean" meant he would have been thought to be rejected by God (cf. *m. Kelim*; Isaiah 35.8), unable to enter the Temple or participate in worship or religious meals.

The crying out and bruising himself with stones may have originated in a mourning ritual which had got out of hand.[4] This is a distinct possibility in that the story has its setting among burial tombs. That there had been unsuccessful attempts to restrain the Gadarene demoniac (Mark 5.3—4) shows that one way violent demoniacs were dealt with was by chaining them. This may also be a reference to previous unsuccessful attempts by other exorcists, for this shackling or hobbling has parallels in the magic bowls.[5]

Not all demoniacs were cut off from society. The epileptic boy (Mark 9.14—29) appears to have remained with his family. He also appears to have been sufficiently controllable for him to accompany his father to see the disciples of Jesus.

The Syrophoenician woman's demonized daughter also remained in a family situation. However, the woman does not bring her daughter out of the home. Can we speculate that the girl was a danger to the public, or too sick to move or terrified of leaving home? The woman, being Hellenized, may have been from the leading stratum of society[6] — probably by no means on the margins of society — and found her daughter's sickness an embarrassment, for the demon-possessed were the focus of ridicule (cf. Philo *In Flaccum* 36, 40). And, if being cared for at home is a

---

4 See Derrett *Man* (n.s.) 14 (1979) 287.
5 See the references in M.J. Geller "Jesus' Theurgie Powers: Parallels in the Talmud and Incantation Bowls" *JJS* 28 (1977) 141–55.
6 Cf. Theissen *ZNW* 75 (1984) 202–25.

sign of wealth,[7] we perhaps have here, as in the story of the epileptic boy, evidence that these families may have had financial means above the average.

From this cursory investigation, we can see that the demoniacs with whom Jesus came in contact cannot all be said to have come from the margins of Palestinian society. There was a man, normally showing no symptoms of his condition, living in the mainstream of his society and taking part in the religious affairs of his community; a girl and a boy, living with their, perhaps, wealthy parents, as well as the preternaturally powerful man abandoned to the tombs on the edge of his community. With this range of sufferers it is unlikely that Jesus' contemporaries would have seen any special focus in this part of his ministry.

From our examination of the Jesus stories we can see that the reports of observers contained a number of features of his techniques as an exorcist.

2. Exorcism at a Distance

What can we say about the historicity of the story of the Syrophoenician woman's daughter (Mark 7.24–30), an exorcism from a distance? First, there is nothing in the pericope that necessitates a healing from a distance — the dauther could have accompanied the woman, perhaps on a stretcher (cf. Mark 2.3 and 9.14–29). Secondly, there is nothing in the pericope that dictates the need for a particular type of healing — in this case an exorcism. However, verse 30, which mentions the demon having gone, is not generally thought to be the product of Christian redaction[8] and we suggested that verse 25, which sets the scene, is probably authentic. Thirdly, other stories of this kind can be cited. One in particular is from the Talmud. It is similar to the healing of the Centurion's boy (Matthew 8.5–13/Luke 7.1–10).

> "It happened that when Rabban Gamaliel's son fell ill, he sent two of his pupils to R. Hanina ben Dosa that he might pray for him. When he saw them, he went to the upper room and prayed. When he came down, he said to them,
> 'Go, for the fever has left him.'
> They said to him,
> 'Are you a prophet?'
> He said to them,
> 'I am no prophet, neither am I a prophet's son, but this is how I am blessed: if my prayer is fluent in my mouth, I know that the sick man is favoured; if not, I know that the disease is fatal.'

---

7 Hollenbach *JAAR* 49 (1981) 571, citing G. Rosen *Madness in Soceity: Chapters in the Historical Sociology of Mental Illness* (Chicago: University of Chicago Press, 1968, reprinted 1969) 64, 69, 125–35.

8 Cf. Pryke *Style* 16, 143.

They sat down, wrote and noted the hour. When they came to Rabban Gamaliel, he said to them,

'By heaven! You have neither detracted from it, nor added to it, but this is how it happened. It was at that hour that the fever left him and he asked us for water to drink' " (b. Ber. 34b).[9]

This story from the Talmud and Mark 7.24—30 are clearly independent,[10] yet come from the same milieu. In this connection van der Loos cites a story of a woman who dreamed that her daughter had been healed in the temple of Aesculapius at Epidaurus.[11] However, this story has few contacts with the New Testament story. Another story that does have closer links with the Mark 7 story is one from Philostratus' *Life of Apollonius* 3.38. No literary links are to be found between this and the Jesus story, but they do both have in common the motif of healing at a distance. We can conclude that the phenomenon was clearly at home in both a Greek and a Jewish milieu and therefore this technique of Jesus' does not place him specifically against either background. We can be reasonably confident then that Jesus, like other exorcists of his period, was known as an exorcist able to heal from a distance.[12]

3. Initial Dramatic Confrontation

In the very brief story associated with the Beelzebul Controversy there is no mention of any confrontation between Jesus and the dumb demoniac (Matthew 9.32—3/12.22/Luke 11.14). However, the other four major exorcism stories relate an initial dramatic confrontation between Jesus and the demoniac, or, in the case of Mark 7.25, between Jesus and the sufferer's mother.

In Mark 1.23 the man screams out (ἀνέκραξεν) when he meets Jesus in the Capernaum synagogue so that it is suddenly obvious that he is a demoniac. And, in Mark 9.20, on seeing Jesus, the demon threw a boy into a convulsion, so that "he fell on the ground and rolled about, foaming at the mouth." In Mark 5.6—7, the Gadarene demoniac ran, fell on his knees in front of Jesus (προσεκύνησεν αὐτῷ) and shouted out when he saw Jesus. In the fourth story it is the sufferer's mother who encountered Jesus. According to Mark, she came and fell at Jesus' feet (προσέπεσεν πρὸς τοὺς πόδας αὐτοῦ, 7.25).

---

9 From Vermes *Judaism* 8.

10 Cf. Fiebig *Jüdische Wundergeschichten* 22.

11 R. Herzog *Die Wunderheilungen von Epidauros* (Leipzig: Deitrich, 1931) 17 in Loos *Miracles* 330. Cf. Kee *Miracle* chap. 3.

12 On the probable historicity of the story of the Synophoenician woman's daughter see also S. Légasse "L'épisode de la Cananéenne d'après Mt 15,21-28" *BLE* 73 (1972) 21-4; Mann *Mark* 319; cf. Drewermann *Markus*. I, 483-92.

We are suspicious at least of the Christian interpretation of the actions of these two characters.

In relation to ἀνακράζειν (Mark 5.7) we can note that the word has a religious significance in the Greek world,[13] but only in relation to the demonic. The Greeks and the Romans generally felt it barbaric and unworthy of the gods.[14] So, we can infer nothing in the use of the word itself in Mark save that, as far as Mark is concerned, we are dealing with the demonic. In the LXX ἀνακράζειν is used especially in the context of crying or calling on God in some individual or national emergency.[15] In contrast, the New Testament does not use ἀνακράζειν in this sense, save, it might be argued, in Mark 1.23/Luke 4.33. So we can detect no religious motif in its use in Mark 5.7.

However, the situation is different with προσκυνεῖν. Προσκυνεῖν, to fall on one's knees or to worship, is used of the mocking worship of Jesus by the soldiers (Mark 15.19).[16] Προσπίπτειν, to fall down at another's feet, is also used to denote worship. For example, in Luke 5.8, Simon Peter's confession of Jesus as Lord is accompanied by a falling at Jesus' feet. Mark only uses the word here in 7.25, at 3.11, where demons fall down or worship Jesus the Son of God, and in 5.33, of the woman who touched the hem of Jesus' garment coming in fear and trembling and falling at Jesus' feet. These latter two verses are often considered to be redactional.[17] Thus, it is possible that either Mark or his predecessors introduced the "worship" interpretation into what might have happened in the dramatic confrontation between Jesus and the demoniacs.

Nevertheless, we still have to examine the possibility that on meeting Jesus the demoniacs cried out and fell (i.e. πίπτειν) to the ground.

Not surprisingly, each of the verses mentioning the dramatic confrontation, bears the stamp of Mark's authorship. However, the evidence is probably not sufficient to indicate that the material came entirely from his hand.[18]

In fact, there are reasons for thinking that the early Church did not need to introduce the element of an initial dramatic confrontation into the stories of Jesus. On the one hand, when examining the story of the demoniac in the synagogue (Mark 1.21—8, see §6 above) we were able to conclude — in so far as the first three Evangelists represent the interests

---

13 Grundmann *TDNT* III, 898.
14 Grundmann *TDNT* III, 899.
15 Grundmann *TDNT* III, 899.
16 Cf. H. Greeven *TDNT* VI, 763.
17 See those listed by Pryke *Style* 14.
18 In more detail see Twelftree in Wenham and Blomberg (eds.) *Gospel Perspectives* 6, 371.

of the early Church — that it is quite unlikely that the early Church introduced the consternation of the demoniacs into the form of the stories
of Jesus.

On the other hand, the historical reliability of this feature in the story
is greatly enhanced by the existence of ancient as well as twentieth
century analogues. From Philostratus' *Life of Apollonius* 4.20 we have a
report of a youth who exhibits symptoms of demon-possession when in
the presence of Apollonius.[19] There are also contemporary examples of the
so-called demonic presence or activity in a person only becoming evident
when confronted by the name of Jesus. One story of a woman with falling
spells has the line ". . . when the name of Jesus or Christ were mentioned
she would immediately go into a trance." Then, in another modern report,
it is said that ". . . the moment the name of Jesus was mentioned, he went
into another coma, his legs shot from under him, and he lay spread-eagled
and inert on the floor."[20]

Finally, here, we can make the point that the case for inauthenticity of
the initial dramatic confrontation rests on literary or oral dependence on
an established form,[21] but evidence is against precisely such a verbal dependence.

So, to return to our question, Does the reported consternation go back
to the accounts of those who witnessed the historical Jesus the exorcist at
work? From the evidence we have examined it is probable that, like his
contemporaries, Jesus the exorcist was seen to evoke a disturbance in the
demon(iac)s who confronted him.

4. The Words of the Demon(iac)s

In Mark 5.20 the initial confrontation between Jesus and the demoniac is
not accompanied by any speaking on the part of the demoniac. In the
brief story associated with the Beelzebul Controversy (Matthew 9.32—3/
12.22/Luke 11.14) we know nothing of any exchange between Jesus and the
demoniac. In Mark 7.25—6 the woman falls at Jesus' feet and begs Jesus to
heal her daughter. And, in the remaining two stories the distress felt by
the demon(iac) in the initial dramatic confrontation is the vocalized:
"What have we to do with you, Jesus of Nazareth? Have you come to
destroy us? I know who you are, the Holy One of God!" (Mark 1.24) and

---

19 See also Lucian *Philops.* 16; (cf. 31); Philostratus *Life* 3.38; 4.20; (cf. *Acts of Peter* 2.4.11;
    Acts of Andrew 13 [Hennecke II, 403] *Acts of Thomas,* 5.44f.; *Acts of John* "The
    Destruction of the Temple of Artemis" 40); see also Lucian *Disowned* 6; *b. Pesaḥ*
    112b–113a.

20 Quoted respectively in more detail in G.H. Twelftree "The Place of Exorcism in
    Contemporary Exorcism" *St. Mark's Review* 127 (1986) 25 and Twelftree *Christ* 11.

21 Kertelge *Wunder* 52.

"What have I to do with you, Jesus, son of the Most High God? I adjure you by God not to torment me" (Mark 5.7).

In dealing with the first of these passages we dismantled the hypothesis that these exclamations were attributed to the demons in an attempt to defend Jesus from the accusation of being in alliance with Beelzebul (§10 above). We need to ask, What was the content of the utterances of the demon(iac)s?

In the last chapter we established the historicity of Jesus being addressed by the demons as *Jesus of Nazareth* (Mark 1.24), Son of *the Most High (God)* (Mark 5.7), *The Holy One of God* (Mark 1.24), and that the demons used the *"I know"* (Mark 1.24), *"I adjure"* (Mark 5.7) and *"What have I to do with you"* (Mark 1.24; 5.7) formulae.

It remains for us to examine the demoniacs' use of the phrase *Son of God* (Mark 3.11 and 5.7).[22] We must all but ignore Mark 3.11 (and parallels) for it comes from what is generally recognized to be an editorial summary (see §14 above).[23] What we need to note is that at least the Evangelists thought that the demons addressed Jesus as "the Son of God". However, we must examine Mark 5.7 more closely and ask the question, did the demons address Jesus the exorcist as Son of God?

Because it was not a Jewish designation for the hoped-for bearer of salvation, Kümmel says that it is "historically extremely unlikely that Jesus was addressed by demon-possessed men as 'Son of God'."[24] Kümmel assumes that the title has an Hellenistic origin.[25] But, can we assume that the title in Mark 5.7 originally had deliberate messianic connotations, and is the title Hellenistic in origin?

Recent New Testament researsch[26] clearly shows that the father-son language and the term "son of God" are quite at home in a Palestinian setting.[27] In fact, Hengel concludes his survey of Hellenisitc material, in relation to the search for the origin of the title "Son of God" in New

---

22 The volume of literature on "Son of God" is overwhelming. Much of the material is collected in the following: *TDNT* VIII, 334; *ThWNT* X/2, 1282f.; *DNTT* III, 665f.; see also "Sohn Gottes" in *RGG* (3rd. ed.) VI, 118–20 and M. Hengel *The Son of God* (London: SCM, 1976); Harvey *Trial* 39–44 and J.D.G. Dunn *Christology in the Making* (London: SCM, 1980).

23 E.g. see Taylor *Mark* 225; Nineham *Mark* 112; Schweizer *Mark* 78ff.; Guelich *Mark* I, 142.

24 W.G. Kümmel *Theology of the NT* (London: SCM, 1974) 74.

25 Kümmel *Theology* 76.

26 Notably K. Berger "Zum traditionsgeschichtlichen Hintergrund Christologischer Hoheitstitel" *NTS* 17 (1970–1) 422–4; Vermes *Jesus* 206–10. See also Vermes *Judaism* 72.

27 Vermes *Jesus* 205–10; *JJS* 23 (1972) 28–50 and 24 (1973) 51–64; cf. Flusser *Jesus* 98ff.; Hengel *Son* 42 n.85; J.D.G. Dunn *Unity and Diversity* (London: SCM, 1977) 45 and notes.

Testament Christology, by saying that the results are entirely unsatis-factory.[28]

If we survey the use of the term "*Son* (of God)" in the Old Testament and Judaism an important dimension of this word (בר/בן) emerges.[29] To quote Hengel,

> "In contrast to '*huios*' it not only (or even primarily) designates physical descent and relationship, but is a widespread expression of subordination, which could describe younger companions, pupils and members of a group, membership of a people or profession, or a characteristic. In this extended sense it was also used in a number of ways in the Old Testament to *express belonging to God.*"[30]

Hengel has in mind three ways. First, there were the members of the heavenly court. In Daniel 3.25, Nebuchadnezzar sees a figure "whose appearance is like a son of the gods" in the fiery furnace.[31] Secondly, as in Exodus 4.22—3, God's people Israel is addressed as "Son of God". Thirdly, the Davidic King, after Egyptian models, was called "Son of God" (cf. 2 Samuel 7.12—14).[32]

Moving to the rabbinic literature we find material that relates to a particular group of men ("Men of Deed") which shows that some of the holy men were understood to be designated "son" by God and addressed as such by him. This evidence has been collected by Vermes (see notes 26 and 27 above) and can be summarized as follows.

Ḥanina ben Dosa, for example, was designated or proclaimed "son of God" by a heavenly voice. And, Rabbi Meir is actually called "Meir my son" by the Holy One himself (*b. Ḥag.* 15b). Further, according to Rab, the great Babylonian teacher and collector of Galilean traditions, the following comment was heard day after day during the life of Ḥanina ben Dosa: "The whole world draws its sustenance because [of the merit] of Ḥanina my son and Ḥanina my son suffices himself with a *kab* of carobs from one Sabbath eve to another" (*b. Ta'an.* 24b; *b. Ber.* 17b; *b. Ḥul.* 86a).

A prayer of Honi the Circle-Drawer also shows that the title "son" characterized the holy individual's relationship with God. "O Lord of the world, your children have turned their faces to me, for that I am like a son of the house before you" (*m. Ta'an.* 3.8).

In the context of this present study it is important to note that this kind of divine communication was also heard by the demons: "They hear (God's voice) from behind the curtain . . ." (*b. Ḥag.* 16a). So we hear of

---

28 Hengel *Son* 41.
29 Such a survey has been done before on more than one occasion; e.g. E. Schweizer (et al.) *TDNT* VIII, 340–55; and recently Hengel *Son* and Dunn *Christology* chap. II.
30 Hengel *Son* 21, his emphasis.
31 Hengel *Son* 21f.; G. Fohrer *TDNT* VIII, 347f.
32 Hengel *Son* 22–3.

Satan or Agrath, the Queen of the demons, saying to Ḥanina, "Had there been no commendation from heaven, 'Take heed of Ḥanina and his teaching!' I would have harmed you" (*b. Pesaḥ.* 112a, quoted §3 above). Thus, although in the rabbinic material the demons do not actually refer to rabbis as "Son of God", what evidence there is in this literature indicates that it was a ḥasid's standing with God, characterized as sonship, that particularly concerned the demons.

The use of "Son of God" in association with a person's standing with God is clear in the *Wisdom of Solomon.*

> "(The righteous man) professes to have knowledge of God,
> and calls himself a child of the Lord . . .
> and boasts that God is his father.
> Let us see if his words are true,
> and let us test what will happen at the end
>   of his life;
> for if the righteous man is God's son, he
>   will help him . . ." (2.13, 16b–18a).[33]

Thus, again "Son of God" is connected with, or even denotes, a special relationship with God.

This same motif is clear in a fragment from the Qumran material. The pertinent lines of 4QPsDan Aᵃ read as follows.

> "[But your son] shall be great upon the earth, [O King! All (men) shall make [peace], and all shall serve [him. He shall be called son of] the [G]reat [God], . . . He shall be hailed (as) the Son of God, and they shall call him Son of the Most High . . ."[34]

As this fragment is poorly preserved it is not possible to say to whom the third person singular masculine refers.[35] Nevertheless, these lines are examples of "Son of God" being used to denote a character having a special relationship with God. We can also note that "Son of God" appears as synonymous or at least a parallel designation to "the Most High" (cf. Mark 5.7).

What this evidence shows is, first, that so far as the geo-cultural categories are valid, the designation "Son of God" seems to have been at home in Hellenistic-Judaism as well as Palestinian-Judaism. Secondly, we see that one of the important functions of the title was to signify the close relationship of the righteous man to God. It could also, denote a person

---

33 RSV translation. Cf. Matt 4.6/Luke 4.10–11.

34 Tentative translation by J.A. Fitzmyer "The Contribution of Qumran Aramaic to the Study of the NT" *NTS* 20 (1973–4) 393.

35 See the discussion in Fitzmyer *NTS* 20 (1973–4) 392. Dunn *Christology* 47 places Mark 3.11 and 5.7 together as demonic confessions. However, we have seen 3.11 is probably entirely rewritten by Mark so that only 5.7 can be said to be a *demonic* confession. Nevertheless, Dunn is right to say that it "would seem to imply recognition simply of one specially commissioned or favoured by God without necessarily evoking the idea of a divine being sent from heaven."

considered to be operating in the sphere of God, particularly in relationship to his dealings with evil spirits.[36] Thirdly, in the light of the
evidence from Qumran it may well have been a Jewish messianic title.

This last point would suggest that the very early Church may have
thought it appropriate to introduce this "messianic" title into the words of
the demons. However, the early churches do not seem to have made much
use of the title "Son of God" as a confession.[37] Hebrews 1.5 suggests that
the early Church took over the association of Psalm 2.7 and 2 Samuel 7.14
in reference to the exalted Jesus[38] — rather than the pre-Easter Jesus. That
is, it denotes an "adoptionist" Christology[39] rather than a birth or incar-
nation Christology. The second point that Dunn makes is that, "If the
confession of Jesus as Son of God plays little role in the witness of the
earliest Christians it certainly *came to full flower within the widening
mission of Hellenisic Jewish Christianity.*"[40]

These two points — that the use of the title was relatively late, and that
it was of particular interest to the Hellenists, suggest that the title may not
have been added to the words of the demons by the earliest Church. But
when used by the demoniacs it characterized Jesus' standing with God, not
his messiahship or ontological sonship.[41]

On the other hand, it is more than likely that the earliest Church did
not need to introduce the appellation into the tradition. If we keep in
mind that the words of the demons in Mark are defensive words that
include the name, character and origin of the opponent, then, along with
what we have just said about the "Son of God", it is particularly
appropriate in designating the sphere in which Jesus operated as an exorcist. That is, the demons did not supernaturally recognize Jesus.[42] Rather,
he was seen to be an exorcist in the Jewish tradition where healers such
as Jesus often relied on "God" as a source of power-authority. So, in turn,
the demons attempted to disarm Jesus by exposing his allegiance to God.
We can conclude that the words "Son of God", in all probability, belong to
the reliable historical tradition of Mark 5.7.

---

36   Vermes *Jesus* 206–10.
37   Dunn *Unity* 45.
38   Dunn *Unity* 45.
39   Dunn *Unity* 45.
40   Dunn *Unity* 46, his emphasis.
41   Cf. the statement by Harvey ". . . the phrase 'Son of God' probably meant no more
     than a righteous and innocent man who had perhaps achieved an unusual degree of
     piety, and there is no convincing evidence that it had come to have any further
     meaning by the time of Christ" (*Constraints* 163). See also Dunn in n. 27 above.
42   E.g. L. Morris *The Gospel According to St. Luke* (London: IVP, 1974) 109 and 156;
     Maynard *NTS* 31 (1985) 584 *"every synoptic use* of this idiom ["Τί ἐμοὶ καὶ σοί"]
     involves the recognition of the divine nature of Jesus by demon or by persons
     possessed by demons" (his emphasis).

5. Jesus' Words of Exorcism[43]

From the discussions in the last chapter we were able to establish that the words of Jesus the exorcist to the demons included, "Come out . . ." (Mark 1.25; 5.8; 9.25); "Be quiet" (Mark 1.25); "What is your name?" (Mark 5.9); "(I) command you . . ." (Mark 9.25); ". . . and no longer enter into him" (Mark 9.25). On these words of Jesus a number of points emerge.

First, it is generally held that Jesus used no formulae to effect his exorcisms. For example, E. Stauffer put it; "There are no magic formulae in the Gospels. The most common means of healing is Jesus' word of power."[44] If what we have been arguing is correct then this view is incorrect. We have seen that Jesus did use words and phrases or parts of incantations or formulae which would have been used, at least in situations requiring preternatural control and would have been readily recognized by his contemporaries as such. To quote David Aune: "The great gulf which some New Testament scholars would place between 'the powerful word of the Son' and 'magical incantations' is simply non-existent.[45] The short authoritative commands of Jesus to demons in the Gospel narratives are formulas of magical adjuration."[46] Whether or not it is correct to call these words or incantations "magical" we shall have to inquire in the next chapter. For the moment we can note that it is plain, from the evidence, that Jesus was a man of his time in at least using recognizable formulae or incantations in his commands to the demons.[47]

---

43 In more detail see Twelftree in Wenham and Blomberg (eds.) *Gospel Perspectives* 6, 378–81.

44 E. Stauffer *TDNT* III, 210; see also, e.g. W. Grundmann *TDNT* II, 302; McCasland *Finger* 110–15: ". . . he cast out demons by his personal command, not by means of any kind of formulae, incantations, ritual or magical objects" (112); Taylor *Mark* 176; E. Fascher *Die formgeschichtliche Methode* (Giessen: Töpelmann, 1924) 127f.; S.E. Johnson *The Gospel According to St. Mark* (London: Black, 1960) 48; Latourelle *Miracles* 167.

45 Aune *ANRW* II.23.2 (1980) 1532 here cites E. Stauffer in *TDNT* II, 626 as an example.

46 Aune *ANRW* II.23.2 (1980) 1532. In a note at this point Aune mentiones O. Böcher *Das Neue Testament und die dämonischen Mächte* (Stuttgart: Katholisches Bibelwerk, 1972) 33ff. appropriately describing Jesus' commands to demons as *Wortzauber*. See also H. Remus " 'Magic or Miracle'? Some Second-Century Instances" *SecCent* 2 (1982) 138: "To say that the Jesus of the Synoptics worked his wonders simply by a word is erroneous. Many of them simply happen, and in others he employs manipulations and material objects."

47 On Jesus' wider healing technique and its relation to so called "magic" see Hull *Magic* and Aune *ANRW* II.23.2 (1980) 1537 who, rightly, says in his conclusion: "Unfortunately, the term 'magic' itself has been a red herring in a great deal of the scholarly discussion." He goes on to say of his own work, "We have used the term without any pejorative connotations, referring only to the pragmatic and religiously deviant features of magic as a necessary and universally present substructure of religious systems" (p. 1557).

Secondly, associated with this is the question of the extent to which Jesus' words as an exorcist are parallaled in other literature. Barrett says that the charge to silence in Mark 1.23 seems to have no parallel.[48] Indeed, in lines that were quoted in chapter II above, some ancient exorcists clearly had great difficulty in getting the demons to speak (PGM XIII.242ff.). Yet, Jesus seems to have experienced no such difficulty; in the earliest recollections of Jesus' exorcistic ministry demoniacs were particularly vocal in his presence (Mark 1.23—5; 5.7—9; [cf. 3.11]).

However, although Jesus' charge to "silence" involves an element of the sense "be silent/keep quiet," the implications involved in the use of the word are clearly much stronger and broader than this, and best understood in Mark 1.25 as *"be bound"* or *"be muzzled"* (see §6 above). Thus, Barrett is incorrect to say that Jesus' charge in Mark 1.23 is unparalleled (see n. 48 above).

Thirdly, it is clear from our interpretation in the light of the context of Jesus' words "What is your name?" (Mark 5.9) that, although it may have unpalatable christological implications for some, Jesus was not initially successful in all his healings. We have the two-part cure of the blind man in Mark 8.22—6 as supporting evidence for our case. Thus, as I have suggested before, by the time Jesus had asked the question in Mark 5.9, he had already commanded the demon to come out of the man. But in response the demon had, rather than submitting, tried to fend off Jesus' attack. So apparently, being initially unsuccessful, Jesus attempts another way of overcoming the demon; asking its name.[49]

6. The Demons' Plea for Leniency

In Mark 5.10—12 the demons plead for leniency when it is reported that they have been overpowered by Jesus. "And he begged him greatly not to send them out of the country. Now there was there on the mountain a great herd of pigs feeding, and they begged him saying, 'Send us into the pigs so that we can enter into them.'"

In extra biblical material, the earliest extant example of this feature of an exorcism story is in *1 Enoch* 12—14. Azazel and his cohorts are seized with fear and trembling on hearing of their impending doom. Azazel asks Enoch to plead their case before the Lord of heaven. However, the petition is not granted. Another example is in *Jubilees* 10 where Mastema, the chief of the evil spirits, makes a plea for mercy. This time the request is granted. In the light of these examples, and there being no theological interest in the motif in Mark (contrast Matthew 8.9; Luke 8.31), we have

---

48 Barrett *Spirit* 57.
49 See further, Twelftree in Wenham and Blomberg (eds.) *Gospel Perspectives* 6, 379.

already suggested (§7 above) that this plea for leniency was part of the original report of Jesus' exorcism.

7. Transfering Demons

We noted in §7 that it is sometimes said that the pigs episode was the proof offered by Jesus for the success of his exorcism.[50] However, arguing' against this view I have suggested that the following three points need to be considered. First, the demons were probably thought to have been transferred from the man to the pigs and then to the sea. Secondly, it was sometimes thought appropriate to transfer the demons from the sufferer to some object like a pebble or piece of wood or a pot or some water in order to effect a cure. These objects, thought to contain the demons, were thrown away or destroyed to effect and perhaps signify the demon's departure from the situation.[51] Then, thirdly, the proof of the cure in the story in Mark 5 is not the destruction of the pigs but the people seeing the cured man "sitting there, clothed and in his right mind" (verse 15b). Thus, rather than as a proof of cure, the pigs episode was probably understood as an integral part of the cure.[52]

8. The Violence of Jesus' Exorcisms[53]

Despite the gentleness with which the life of Jesus is often characterized, we have considerable violence mentioned in the reports of Jesus as an exorcist. The drowning of the pigs in Mark 5.11—13 is perhaps the best example. In Mark 1.26 the demon is said to convulse the man and in Mark 9.26 the demon also apparently convulsed the boy and left him as dead.

We can give two reasons why this aspect of the reports of Jesus' exorcisms is most probably historically reliable. First, there are stories outside the New Testament showing similar violence, yet they are sufficiently different to show that there is no dependence on them by the New Testament writers. For example, the demon cast out by Eleazar upset a bowl of water:

> "Then wishing to convince the bystanders and prove to them that he had this power
> [of exorcism], Eleazar placed a cup or foot basin full of water a little way off and
> commanded the demon, as it went out of the man, to overturn it and make known to
> the spectators that he had left the man" (*Ant.* 8.49).

---

50 See, e.g. Bultmann *History* 225; Dibelius *Tradition* 87–8.
51 Twelftree in Wenham and Blomberg (eds.) *Gospel Perspectives* 6, 399 n. 80 and §7 above.
52 Twelftree in Wenham and Blomberg (eds.) *Gospel Perspectives* 6, 382 and §7 above.
53 Bonner *HTR* 36 (1943) 47–9 and "The Violence of Departing Demons" *HTR* 37 (1944) 334–6. In the second article Bonner cites a modern example. See also Twelftree *Christ* 11–12.

Also, the demon Apollonius exorcised departed with violence.

> "Now when Apollonius gazed on him, the ghost in him began to utter cries of fear and rage, such as one hears from people who are being branded or racked; . . . Apollonius addressed him with anger, as a master might a shifty, rascally, and shameless slave and so on, and he ordered him to quit the young man and show by a visible sign that he had done so. 'I will throw down yonder statue,' said the devil . . . But when the statue began by moving gently, and then fell down, it would defy anyone to describe the hubbub which arose thereat . . ." (*Life* 4.20).

The other reason we can give for this part of the reports of Jesus' exorcisms being most probably historically reliable is that Mark shows no consistent use of, nor interest in, this violence. Thus, in 1.26 the convulsion occurs as the demon leaves; in the story of the Gadarene demoniac the story begins with the description of violent symptoms of the sickness but the later violence is not related to the sufferer but the drowning of the pigs. The story of the Syrophoenician woman's daughter contains no element of violence; in chapter 9 the whole story of the possessed boy is couched in violence; violence in the encounter as well as in the healing.

Conculsions. In this section we have begun to gather together what can be gleaned from the Gospel traditions about the historical Jesus as an exorcist. We can see that the demoniacs he healed were not all from the perimeter of society. Like other exorcists of his time Jesus healed at a distance, there was an initial dramatic confrontation between Jesus and the demoniac which gave rise to a conversation in which the demons tried to defend themselves and Jesus commanded the demon to leave the sufferer. We noted that it cannot be said that Jesus did not use so-called "magical" incantations but that his words of command were recognizable formulae or incantations. We also noted, despite possible unpalatable christological implications for some, that Jesus was not always initially successful. During the exchange between the demon(iac)s and Jesus the demon(iac)s were said to plead for leniency. We cannot escape the fact that some of Jesus' exorcisms were characterized by violence. We turn now to discuss features of the reported technique of Jesus that were distinctive.

§ 18 Distinctive and Unique Features of Jesus' Methods

In the light of the material presented in chapter II there seem to be some aspects of the contemporary exorcistic technique that Jesus did *not* use.

1. Absence of Mechanical Devices

A feature common to many other exorcist's technique was the aid of some apparatus, device, or feature of speech. In the ancient Babylonian texts hair, knots, water, branches of tamarisk, meteorites and pottery were used in association with the healing rite to expel demons. In the ancient Egyptian papyri human milk and fragrant gum, for example, were said to be used. In Tobit 8.3 burning incense caused the demon to flee. In *Jubilees* 10.10 and 12 "medicines" are used, and in *Genesis Apocryphon* 20 Abraham lays hands on Pharaoh. In Josephus' writing, Eleazar uses a finger ring containing a pungent root, and a bowl of water. In another story, Josephus tells of David using music to charm away an evil spirit. In the rabbinic literature there is evidence that material aids were particularly abundant in Jewish exorcisms — amulets, palm tree prickles, wood chips, ashes, earth, pitch, cumin, dog's hair, thread, and trumpets. Lucian of Samosata tells of exorcists' threatening the demons and using iron rings. The magical papyri also witness to the use of a wide variety of technical aids in expelling demons. For example, amulets, olive branches, oil from unripe olives, mastiga plants, lotus pith, marjoram, and special sounds produced by the exorcist are mentioned.

All this seems extremely remote from "Be bound, and come out of him" (Mark 1.25) or "Dumb and deaf spirit, I command you, come out of him and no longer enter him" (Mark 9.25).[1] We have argued that the destruction of the pigs properly belongs to the authentic tradition of the historical Jesus. However, the pigs are not used to expel the demons, but to provide somewhere for the demons to go after they had been expelled.

Although the use of technical devices of one kind or another seem to be the most prominent method of exorcism in the ancient world — even

---

1 Cf. Hull *Magic* 68.

among the rabbis — Jesus cannot be said to be alone in his simple verbal
technique. Although the tone of his voice and the gaze of his eyes was
important to Apollonius' success, he did use only words to effect the
exorcism in *Life* 4.20. A more important parallel which does not permit
us to see Jesus' verbal technique as unique is from a Jewish milieu. As we
noted above, Rabbi Simeon is said to have cast out a demon from a girl
simply by calling out — "Ben Temalion, get out! Ben Temalion, get out!"

Nevertheless, despite these two parallels, the impression remains that
even if it was not unique, Jesus' simple unaided words of command to the
demons stand out as particularly characteristic and distinctive of his reported method.[2]

But could this characteristic of Jesus' method be a construct of the early
Church in that it sought to set Jesus over against the techniques that
pervaded the era? Probably not. In other healings Jesus is said to have utilized means other than mere words.

To heal the deaf mute (Mark 7.33), the blind man near Bethsaida (Mark
8.23) and the man born blind (John 9.6) Jesus is said to use spittle as part
of his healing procedure. There is ample evidence showing that the use of
spittle was part of the healing technique of the ancient world. It is used,
for example, in the Babylonian texts,[3] in the magical papyri[4] and in
Pliny.[5] And, importantly, the rabbis prohibit its use.[6] Thus, so far as I can
see, against Calvin, Fenner, Strack and Billerbeck and van der Loos,[7] there
is nothing to separate Jesus' use of spittle from its use in the ancient
world, or that he or the Gospel writers thought he was using it any
differently from anyone else. So, in this aspect of his healing technique,
the earliest Church was clearly not endeavouring to remove or isolate
Jesus from his milieu.

The use of his hands and the laying on of hands were clearly
characteristics of Jesus' healing ministry.[8] This also was part of the healing
technique of the Jews as, for example, the story of Abraham's cure of
Pharaoh in the *Genesis Apocryphon* 20 illustrates. This healing story is an

---

2 Cf. R. Latourelle "Originalité et Fonctions des miracles de Jésus" *Gregorianum* 66
   (1985) 641–53.

3 F.W. Nicholson "The Saliva Superstition in Classical Literature" *Harvard Studies in
   Classical Philology* 8 (1897) 23–40 and n. 1; also Hull *Magic* 76–8; Loos *Miracles* 306–13.
   On the Babylonian texts in particular see A. Jeremias *Babylonisches im NT* (Leipzig:
   Hinrichs, 1905) 108; Eitrem *Notes* 46.

4 E.g. PGM III.420.

5 Pliny Nat. Hist. 28.37.

6 See *b. Šeb.* 15b (cf. L.B. Blau *Das altjüdische Zauberwesen* [Strasbourg: Trübner, 1898]
   68). The Essenes did not permit spitting, Josephus *War* 2.8.

7 See Loos *Miracles* 310 and notes.

8 See E. Lohse *TDNT* IX, 431–2; Aune *ANRW* II.23.2 (1980) 1533.

exorcism, yet the early Church did not introduce the method into the exorcism stories of Jesus.[9] In the light of this it is hard to see why the early Church would want to delete it if it was already part of the technique of the historical Jesus the exorcist.[10]

In the Gospels we have very few examples of Jesus' ministry of exorcism so we may not be able to draw an absolute conclusion. Nevertheless, from the evidence we have, Jesus does not seem to have used mechanical aids. So, the characteristically simple, unaided, verbal technique Jesus is said to use in his exorcisms is probably not a construct of the early Church,[11] and should be posited among the authentic reflections of the historical Jesus.

If we note which healings in our period rely on "aids" and which do not, it is immediately obvious that the cultic or incantational tradition is saturated with aids, medicines, and devices whereby the generally unknown exorcist appeals to sources of power-authority beyond himself. What Jesus, Apollonius and some of the rabbis have in common, besides their reputed ability to heal without tangible aids, is that their power-authority base does not appear to be other than their own personal force (see §3 above). It is to this that we now turn.

2. No Explicit Prayers or Power-Authority Invoked

One of the pervading characteristics of the exorcisms which we surveyed in chapter II above was the exorcist's making plain, in the preliminaries of the exorcism rite, by what authority he operated. That is, the exorcist either invoked the aid of a source of power-authority or aligned himself with some higher power in order to effect the submission of the demon.

In the Ebers Papyrus from ancient Egypt the healer or magician began with the announcement of his source of power-authority by declaring the origin of himself and his technique and accompanying remedies. The

---

9 Jongeling (et al.) (*Aramaic Texts* I. 99 n.22) are incorrect when they say "the practice of laying on of hands as an act of exorcism is well attested in the New Testament, cf. especially Mark V.23. . ." because Mark 5.23 is *not* treated as an exorcism and 1QapGen is our only other piece of evidence. Cf. Aune *ANRW* II.23.2 (1980) 1533, "In Hellenistic traditions, touch as a healing rite is used by the gods in legends and stories, but only very rarely by human miracles workers." Aune notes that the few examples O. Weinreich cites are not earlier than the third century AD. O. Weinreich *Antike Heilungswunder* (Giessen: Töpelmann, 1909) 45–8.

10 On Jesus "sighing" see Loos *Miracles* 325.

11 Some of the Apologists tried to make a case for the authenticity of Jesus' miracles on the grounds that he used *no* aids or medicines at all; see the literature cited by Fridrichsen *Miracle* 89ff. and Loos *Miracles* 305f. The suggestion by E.R. Micklem in *Miracles and the New Psychology* (Oxford: Oxford University Press, 1922) 105, that Jesus sometimes used oil in his healing is without foundation.

Babylonian texts also show that the exorcist began by announcing himself as the agent of a god.

"I am the sorcerer – priest of Ea,
I am the messenger of Marduk;
To revive the (?) sick man
The great lord Ea hath sent me."[12]

The persistence of this practice is demonstrated by its occurrence in the magical papyri (e.g. PGM IV.3019).

It has also become clear that a frequent source of power-authority was sought in the use of powerful names. For example, as we have noted, one of the most commonly used names in this period seems to have been "Solomon".

Not only was the origin of the exorcist's powers and the names invoked of significance but, as we have noted in chapter II, the essence of the power-authority was to be found in the spells or incantations and medicines themselves. This is the case in the Babylonian, ancient Egyptian, magical papyri, Tobit, *Jubilees* and rabbinic material.

Sometimes where there is no evidence of a power-authority being located in a higher power upon which the exorcist called, in the use of a strong name, or in a particular incantation, the exorcist is said to *pray* as part of the healing technique. The Qumran scrolls portray Abraham as praying for the Pharaoh in order to expel the evil spirit (1QapGen 20). Ḥanina ben Dosa, though using no incantations, prays (*b. Ber.* 34b; cf. *b. Taʿan.* 24b).[13] A striking exception to this is the story we related above of Rabbi Simeon exorcising a demon from the Roman Emperor's daughter with a simple command. Another exception to this pattern is the tradition about Apollonius who neither prays nor exhibits any reliance upon an exterior power-authority, but is an effective exorcist by reason of his personal force alone (*Life* 4.20). But, the general picture remains: exorcists of the period conducted their healing using a conspicuous or recognizable power-authority, incantations or prayers.

With this in mind we can look at the words and techniques of Jesus as an exorcist (Mark 1.25; 5.8ff.; [7.29]; 9.25).

(a) *Jesus does not appear to call on any source of power-authority.*[14] This is more than likely a clear reflection of Jesus' actual practice. First, in view of Matthew 12.28/Luke 11.20 — where Jesus confesses to operate by

---

12 Thompson *Devils* I, 13, Cf. XXV.
13 Cf. Honi and Nakdimon in relation to rain making. See Fiebig *Jüdische Wundergeschichten* 16ff.
14 Cf. Aune ". . . there is no evidence to suggest that Jesus himself invoked the name of God or any other powerful names in the rituals which he used to effect exorcisms and healings" *ANRW* II.23.2 (1980) 1545 who also cites Eitrem *Notes* 10f.

power-authority of the Spirit of God, and Mark 3.28 — where the saying about the Holy Spirit is linked with the question of Jesus' source of power-authority — it is indeed surprising that those responsible for the transmission of the Jesus material did not reflect this in the exorcistic words of Jesus. That is, if the early Church was attempting to accommodate Jesus to the techniques of other exorcists, we might have expected Jesus to be depicted as saying something like, "I adjure you by God (or the Spirit of God) . . ." But we do not.[15] Second, we have already established the probable historicity of the Beelzebul charge (Matthew 12.24/ Luke 11.15/Mark 3.22 see §10 above). This charge is more readily understood if, in fact, Jesus did not make clear his source of power-authority.[16] So, the evidence suggests that, as part of his technique, Jesus did not intimate that he relied on any outside power-authority — not even on the Spirit of God.

(b) A coordinate of this point is that Jesus did not use any "powerful name" as a power-authority or component of his technique. That is, for example, he does not use the name of God as other Jews did (cf. PGM IV.3019) or the Spirit of God as we might have expected if the tradition was seeking to conform Jesus' technique to the saying in Matthew 12.28/ Luke 11.20. It cannot be argued that the early Church was attempting to distance Jesus from his contemporary healers for they have retained his exorcistic words which were formulae familiar in the world of incantations (see §17 above).

(c) Thus, as we have seen, Jesus used words or incantations which were of a piece with his environment. To this extent we should ask if it was in these incantational words and phrases that the early Church or Jesus thought was the locus of the effect of his exorcisms.

With respect to the early Church it seems plain that it did not see Jesus' words themselves as holding the key to his successful healings. If they did see Jesus' words as the significant factor in his exorcisms then it is sur-prising that they did not emulate them in their own healing ministry. What the early Church does, as is illustrated by Acts 16.18, is use quite different wording (παραγγέλλω σοι rather than say ἐπιτάσσω σοι as in Mark 9.25) and take up using a "powerful name" — "Jesus Christ". The most important indication that the early Church did not place any particular significance on Jesus' actual exorcistic words, and that it did not see Jesus placing any special emphasis on them, is to be found in the brief

---

15 Dunn and Twelftree *Churchman* 94 (1980) 214–15.
16 Cf. Vermes *Jesus* 64. We cannot agree with Vermes that Jesus was accused *be-cause* he never invoked any human source for, even as Vermes notes (p. 66), some rabbis exorcised demons without invoking an authority.

allusions to Jesus' exorcisms where no "words" are recorded. It is simply stated that he cast out a demon (e.g. Matthew 12.22/Luke 11.14). Though the number of examples is not great, this conclusion is further confirmed in that, though the Synoptic tradition preserves special words of Jesus in relation to other healings — ταλιθα κουμ[17] (Mark 5.41) and εφφα-θα[18] (Mark 7.34), perhaps for the purpose of guiding Christian healers[19] — it does not seek to do so in relation to the exorcism stories.

If Jesus felt he was relying on the force of his incantations to bring about the subjugation of the demons, that is, if the particular form and content of the words was of vital importance, it is surprising that the formulae display such divergence of form and content. This is noticeable when we set out Jesus' exorcistic words.

"Be muzzled and come out of him" (Mark 1.25).

"Come out unclean spirit from the man!" . . . "What is your name?" (Mark 5.8–9).

"Dumb and deaf spirit, I command you, come out of him and no longer enter him" (Mark 9.25).

We do not need to include Mark 7.29 in this list, for it is not a command to the demon. The form of the first command (1.25) is a binding followed by a direction; the second (5.8—9) has a direction, an address, and then a subjugating question; and the third (9.25) has an address, a binding, and two directions. Thus, there is no consistency in representing any form, save that each has the minimal command involving some kind of subjugating word — different in each case, and the directive — which is consistently represented as "Come out!" This variety does not seem to indicate any particular interest in using a correct formula save that in so far as an exorcism is involved, the words obviously require that the demon is overpowered and expelled.

(d) It has just been noted how important *prayer* was in some traditions of exorcism — notably the Jewish milieu. Others have shown how important prayer was for Jesus.[20] A considerable amount of this importance has probably to be attributed to the early Church. Luke in particular seems intent on enhancing Jesus' prayer life.[21] Regardless of the extent of the historical core here it is significant to notice that at no point does the

---

17 Str–B II, 10.

18 Str–B II, 17f.. See also M. Black "ΕΦΦΑΘΑ. . ." in Descamps et de Halleux (eds.) *Mélanges Bibliques* 57–60.

19 Aune *ANRW* II.23.2 (1980) 1534–5 and n. 126. Though against Aune, it is to be noted that the tradition has not preserved formulae in the "original" language for exorcism.

20 See, e.g. Fiebig *Jüdische Wundergeschichten* 72; J. Jeremias *The Prayers of Jesus* (London: SCM, 1967) 72–8; Dunn *Jesus* 15–21 (and notes).

21 P.T. O'Brien "Prayer in Luke–Acts" *TynBul* 24 (1973) 111–27; S.S. Smalley "Spirit, Kingdom and Prayer in Luke–Acts" *NovT* 15 (1973) 59–71; cf. also Dunn *Jesus* 17 and n. 23; A.A. Trites "Some Aspects of Prayer in Luke–Acts" in P.J. Acthemeier (ed.) *SBLSP*

tradition seek to attribute or report the practice of prayer to any part of Jesus' exorcistic technique even though prayer was apparently used in early Christian healing (James 5.14—15; cf. Mark 9.29).[22] The only occasion when prayer is attributed to Jesus as part of, or associated with his "healing" techniques, is in the raising of Lazarus in John 11.41—2. But, the prayer is not really part of the healing for Jesus utters no request; he gives thanks for already being heard.[23] Jesus is portrayed as not needing to make a request in prayer.[24] Rather, the prayer is for the bystanders, so that they may see the glory of God in the miracle.[25] So, in view of the importance of prayer in contemporary Jewish healings and the Gospel traditions' agreed importance of prayer for Jesus, the technique of exorcism — unaccompanied by prayer — is best taken as faithfully reflecting Jesus' healing procedure.

To conclude this point; one of the outstanding characteristics — though we cannot claim it to be entirely unique — is that Jesus invoked no power-authority, and neither saw any particular significance in his incantations nor used prayer as part of the healing of demoniacs.

3. Ὁκίζω

A third element of contemporary exorcistic technique that Jesus did not use was the word ὁρκίζω (Aramaic = שׁבע). The use of this word could have been treated under the last section, but its reported absence from Jesus' words addressed to the demons is potentially of such significance that it deserves separate treatment. So far as I can see from our discussion above (§7), in connection with incantations or spells, ὁρκίζω means "to charge", "adjure", or *"bind someone by another being"*. This meaning is clear in Mark 5.7: *"I adjure by* God, do not torment me,"* and in Acts 19.13: *"I adjure* you *by* the Jesus whom Paul preaches"* (cf. 1 Thessalonians 5.27).[26]

In the light of this it is indeed surprising that, in the transmission of the Jesus stories, ὁρκίζω did not find its way into the material on the lips of Jesus. The use of a form of ὁρκίζω in 1 Thessalonians 5.27 shows that the early Church did not totally object to its use. Ὁρκίζω is used in relation to

---

(Missoula: SBL, 1977) 59—77 and A.A. Trites "The Prayer-Motif in Luke–Acts" in C.H. Talbert (ed.) *Perspectives on Luke-Acts* (Danville: Association of Baptist Professors of Religion and Edinburgh: T & T Clark, 1978) 168—86.

22 Cf. Aune *ANRW* II.23.2 (1980) 1533.
23 Bultmann *John* 407–8.
24 Cf. C.K. Barrett: "In view of the complete unity between the Father and the Son there is no need for uttered prayer at all" *John* 402.
25 B. Lindars *The Gospel of John* (London: Marshall, Morgan and Scott, 1972) 401.
26 See §7 n. 51 above.

an invoked power-authority, and the Synoptic tradition has it in Matthew 12.28/Luke 11.20 that such an invoked power for Jesus' technique was the Spirit of God. That the tradition did not translate this across into the incantations used by Jesus would seem to be an indication, again, of the reliability of our knowledge of the incantations used by Jesus.

The use of ὁρκίζω in exorcistic formulae is part of the practice of invoking a superior power to carry out the wishes of the exorcist. Jesus apparently neither acknowledged the use of a source of power-authority nor used the accompanying ὁρκίζω or its equivalent. Instead, and in line with this convention of Jesus' is the congruous appearance of ἐγώ/יִנֲא in his incantation at Mark 9.25. The emphatic ἐγώ/יִנֲא [27] is relatively infrequent on the lips of Jesus in the Synoptics,[28] and it is not consistently used in the words of Jesus to the demons (only at Mark 9.25). This suggests that the early Church is not responsible for it in Mark 9.25. The use of ἐγώ was not a feature of the contemporary incantations of adjuration [29] and so it is possible that its use by Jesus is of some significance in understanding him as an exorcist (see §29 below).

4. No Proofs

The question of whether or not Jesus the exorcist's technique involved seeking proof of success hinges on the nature of the "pigs episode" in Mark 5. In discussing that passage it was argued that the destruction of the pigs was to be seen not as proof of success, but as an integral part of the cure. The seeking of a proof would decidedly enhance the reputation of Jesus and it is perhaps surprising that the tradition did not either maintain this element in the stories of Jesus, or add it if it was not already there. Since the tradition shows no interest in so doing and since Mark 5.11ff. is not a "proof" we shall take it that this element was not part of Jesus' technique.

So, in contrast to his contemporary exorcists, Jesus used no mechanical devices (apart from the pigs in Mark 5), no explicit prayers or invoked power-authority, no powerful name, and no proofs.

There are two natural conclusions that we should draw from these last three sections. That is, first, in declaring no reliance on a power-authority, and not using ὁρκίζω or proofs, but in simply ordering the demon out

---

27   On which see E. Schweizer *Ego Eimi* (Göttingen: Vandenhoeck & Ruprecht, 1965) 18f.; Jeremias *Theology* 250–5.

28   Stauffer *TDNT* II, 348 (quoted §10 above). On ἐγώ in the Synoptics see Howard *Das 'Ego'*.

29   In fact, so far, I have been unable to find any examples that parallel its use in Mark 9.25.

(once using the emphatic "I"), and then in saying that his power-authority was the Spirit/finger of God, *Jesus' technique of exorcism*, if not innovative, *would have at least been very conspicuous.* Secondly, *Jesus believed that while he was operating out of his own resources, at the same time, he believed that it was God who was to be seen as operative in his activity.*

§ 19 Miracle and Message in Jesus' Ministry

Our task here is to analyse the relationship between the exorcisms and preaching ministry of Jesus.

In the Gospels there is an intimate relationship between the activities of Jesus and his preaching. There is no doubt that much of this picture is the result of the activity of the Evangelists and their predecessors. This relationship is apparent in the work of the Evangelists on a number of levels. On a very basic level, miracles and message are said to be conducted in association with each other. For example, Matthew says, "And he went about all Galilee, teaching in their synagogues and preaching the Gospel of the kingdom and healing every disease and every infirmity among the people" (Matthew 4.23/Mark 1.39).[1] On another level the material is actually grouped so that the teaching and miracles are associated. For example, in the two cycles, Mark 4.35—6.44 and 6.45—8.26, there are included, in rough parallel, sea miracle, preaching, healings, and a feeding.[2] And, the first part of Mark's Gospel is so structured that Jesus' proclamation of the kingdom (1.14—15) is followed and elaborated by a healing (1.21—8).[3] On yet another level the miracles are related in order that a particular point can be made either by, or in relation to, Jesus. Thus, in Mark 4.41 the miracle is related primarily so that the point can be made, "Who then is this . . .?" And, in Mark 9.28—9 (the disciples' question about their failure as exorcists), it is clear that one of the reasons why the preceding miracle story has been related is so that the Evangelist can incorporate some teaching of Jesus on prayer. Finally, we can note another level of this relationship: on occasions miracle and message are so woven together that they form a single fabric as in Mark 2.1—12 and 3.1—6, but especially in the Fourth Gospel (e.g. John 9.1—41).[4]

---

1 See also Mark 1.21-2/Luke 4.31-2; Mark 6.1-6/Matt 13.53-8/Luke 4.16-30.
2 See Achtemeier *JBL* 89 (1970) 265.
3 X. Léon-Dufour *The Gospels and the Jesus of History* (London: Collins, 1968) 123.
4 Further on miracle and message in Mark see R.T. France "Mark and the Teaching of Jesus" in France and Wenham (eds.) *Gospels Perspectives* I, 109-11. Cf. also Mark 8.14-21.

This intimate relationship between miracle and message portrayed in Jesus' ministry is also found reproduced in the mission of the disciples. In Mark 3.14—15 the disciples are "sent out to preach and have authority to cast out demons" (cf. 6.12). In Luke 10.9 the command to the disciples is, ". . . heal the sick . . . and say to them, 'The kingdom of God has come upon you . . .' " (cf. Matthew 10.1, 7/Luke 9.2).

In spite of all this, it is important to inquire whether this relationship between "word and action" is to be traced back to the historical Jesus, or whether it is a conception which has its origin in the early Christian community. Our most productive way forward is to note some sayings of Jesus where his proclamation and activity are presumed or related, and also to notice those stories where miracle and message are interwoven in the very structure of the story.

There are four *sayings* in particular that merit attention; the Spirit/ finger saying (Matthew 12.28/Luke 11.20), the parable of the Strong Man (Mark 3.27/Matthew 12.29/Luke 11.21—2), the reply to John the Baptist (Matthew 11.5/Luke 7.22), and the judgement on Chorazin and Bethsaida (Matthew 11.21—3/Luke 10.13—15).

We have already discussed and upheld the authenticity of the first three logia. On the third, the judgement saying of Matthew 11.21—3/Luke 10.13—15,[5] Bultmann says that it is a product of the community since it looks back on Jesus' activity as something already completed and pre-supposes the failure of the Christian mission in Capernaum.[6] Also, Käsemann says that the Revelation of John demonstrates that these kind of curse and blessings are among early Christian forms of prophetic proclamation and that this particular passage is one of them, and it recalls the Christian formulation of Matthew 7.22—3.[7] However, there is a minimal link with Matthew 7.22—3 ("mighty works"), and the "curse and blessing" form in Revelation does not have the pairing of "curse and blessing" (cf. Revelation 8.13) nor the parallelism evident in Matthew 11.21—3. The passage does presuppose the failure of mission, but the towns mentioned are not determinative of the tradition, and the post-Easter Church, at least as reflected in documents produced in the second half of the first century, show no interest in Chorazin.[8] And, notably, this form is

---

5 Apart from the literature cited below see Fridrichsen *Miracle* 75f.
6 Bultmann *History* 112, though, in contrast, see his *Jesus and the Word* 124.
7 Käsemann in *NT Questions* 100.
8 W. Grundmann *Das Evangelium nach Lukas* (Berlin: Evangelische Verlagsanstalt, 1963) 211; cf. E. Neuhausler *Anspruch und Antwort Gottes* (Düsseldorf: Patmos, 1962) 200f.

to be found in the Wisdom material.[9] Finally, there is evidence in the passage that the tradition comes from an early Aramaic source.[10]

It seems best to suppose that the tradition behind Matthew 11.21—3/ Luke 10.13—15 is to be traced back to the historical Jesus. Mussner goes so far as to say that, "If there is one pre-Easter logion, then it is the lament of Jesus over these three cities of his native Galilee!"[11]

These four sayings that originate from the ministry of the historical Jesus associate miracle and mission. In Matthew 12.28/Luke 11.20 Jesus makes a direct connection between his exorcisms and the coming of the kingdom of God — the essence of his proclaimed message (cf. Mark 1.14— 15)[12]. Mark 3.27/Matthew 12.29/Luke 11.21—2 gives the exorcisms of Jesus a wider significance than the mere casting out of unclean spirits, viz. the very downfall or destruction of Satan and his kingdom. And we have seen (§10 above) that the establishment of the kingdom of God is directly related to the downfall of the kingdom of Satan. And, Matthew 11.21— 3/Luke 10.13—15 links the mighty miracles with a characteristic of Jesus' proclamation — that men should repent (cf. Mark 1.14—15).[13] Matthew 11.4/Luke 7.22 brings the words and deeds of Jesus together as aspects or characteristics of the eschatological age.

Two miracle *stories* in particular are interwoven with Jesus' teaching and preaching.

First, Mark 2.1—12 (/Matthew 9.1—8/Luke 5.17—26), the story of the paralytic and his four friends. Here the combination of teaching and miracle may be the result of the amalgamation of what were once separate traditions.[14] Thus, all we can confidently conclude is that the early Church saw an indivisible link between what Jesus was doing and what he was saying.

Secondly, Mark 3.1—6 (/Matthew 12.9—14/Luke 6.6—11), the story of the man with a withered hand. This narrative is the last of a block of three conflict stories (Mark 2.18—3.6). Bultmann thinks that the origin of the controversies over the Sabbath usually cannot be put any earlier than the debates in the early Church.[15] On the other hand, the early Church did not

---

9   K. Berger *NTS* 17 (1970–1) 10–40; cf. D. Hill "On the Evidence from the Creative Role of Christian Prophets" *NTS* 20 (1973–4) 271–4 and J.D.G. Dunn "Prophetic 'I' – Sayings and the Jesus Tradition: The Importance of Testing Prophetic Utterances Within Early Christianity" *NTS* 24 (1977–8) 181f.

10   Jeremias *Promise* 50 n. 1; see also Jeremias *Theology* 10f., 15f., and 19.

11   Mussner *Miracles* 21.

12   Cf. Perrin *Kingdom* and Jeremias *Theology* 31–5.

13   Jeremias *Theology* 152–6.

14   Taylor *Mark* 191f.; Schweizer *Mark* 60; Anderson *Mark* 98f.

15   Bultmann *Jesus* 14; cf. *History* 12 and notes.

face conflict with the Jews about Sabbath healings.[16] The saying of Jesus in verse 4 is the centre of the story. As it is both harsh and not decisive for the early Church's abandonment of the seventh day observance it is probably an authentic saying of Jesus.[17] And, as the saying presupposes a specific act like the one described,[18] we will take the saying and its present setting as authentic.

What does this story tell us about Jesus' link between his miracles and preaching? In short, the healing and the teaching are of a piece in Jesus' radical rejection of the rabbinic Halakah on the Sabbath which prevented people from fulfilling God's commandment to love (cf. Mark 2.27).[19] And, we may go on to conclude that the integral relationship between "word and action" can be traced to the ministry of the historical Jesus.

Having established that a relationship between miracle and message goes back to the historical Jesus we can now focus attention on the *nature* of that relationship with respect to the *exorcisms* of Jesus.

The relationship has often been characterized by the word "sign". That is, the miracles have little or no intrinsic significance but point beyond themselves to something more important — the message of the coming of the kingdom.[20] We need only mention two examples of this view.[21] Ridderbos says that Jesus' miracles serve only as *proofs* of Jesus' power, a view that Luke took up.[22] Fridrichsen gives pride of place to Jesus' message, with the miracles accompanying and confirming the proclamation.[23] Bultmann also sees the miracles, especially the exorcisms, as signs of the dawning of the coming kingdom.[24] There is no doubt that this view was held by at least some sectors of the early Church represented in the New Testament, the most important being John's Gospel which understands Jesus' miracles as authenticating Jesus and his message. For example, ". . . even though you do not believe me, believe the works, that you may know that the Father is in me and I am in the Father" (10.38; cf.

---

16   Schürmann *Lukas*. I, 309f.; cf. Marshall *Luke* 234.

17   Anderson *Mark* 111f.; W. Scott in *DNTT* III, 408. Cf. Jeremias *Theology* 6 and 208ff.

18   Anderson *Mark* 112.

19   See Jeremias *Theology* 208ff.

20   Cf. Sevenster cited by Loos *Miracles* 281; Kallas *Significance* 77.

21   For other examples see Loos *Miracles* 280–6. Also E. Schweizer *Jesus* (London: SCM, 1971) 43; M. Grant *Jesus* 33 and n. 18; Aune *ANRW* II.23.2 (1980) 1533.

22   Ridderbos cited in Loos *Miracles* 282.

23   In Loos *Miracles* 282.

24   Bultmann *Jesus Christ and Mythology* 12f.; also cited by Hiers *SJT* 27 (1974) 37, see 38 for mention of others who hold these views; also Kee *Origins* 62; Koester *Introduction* II, 79; R. Leivestad *Jesus in His Own Perspective* (Minneapolis: Augsburg, 1987) 125; H.K. Nielsen *Heilung und Verkündigung* (Leiden and New York: Brill, 1987).

2.23; 4.54; 12.18; 20.30).[25] In Acts the miracles of Jesus are mentioned only twice (2.22 and 10.38), and in each case the miracles are seen as signs authenticating Jesus' mission.

When we examine the four sayings of Jesus which we have mentioned above, the picture is significantly different. In the judgement saying (Matthew 11.21—3/Luke 10.13—15) the relationship between miracle and message is not clear; all that is said is that the miracles are expected to bring about repentance. This could be construed to mean that Jesus saw his miracles as authenticating his mission. But, over against this we should set three traditions that relate Jesus' refusal to give a sign; Mark 8.11 (Matthew 16.1—4), Q (Matthew 12.39/Luke 11.29) and the Gospel of Thomas 91.[26] This is strong evidence against the view that Jesus used his miracles to authenticate his mission (cf. Matthew 4.3/Luke 4.3). In reply to John the Baptist (Matthew 11.5/Luke 7.22) the miracles and the message are equated, they are equally part of a whole; they are both events of the New Age. In the parable of the Strong Man (Mark 3.27/Matthew 12.29/ Luke 11.21—2; see §10 above), *the exorcisms* do not illustrate the message of the downfall of the kingdom of Satan, but *themselves constitute that very downfall.* And, in the Spirit/finger saying (Matthew 12.28/Luke 11.20), Jesus says that the exorcisms themselves are the coming of the kingdom.[27] Therefore, the exorcisms are not, as Otto Betz thinks, preparatory to the coming of the kingdom.[28] They do not illustrate, extend, or even confirm Jesus' preaching. In the casting out of demons, the mission of Jesus itself is taking place, being actualized or fulfilled. In short, *in themselves the exorcisms of Jesus are the kingdom of God in operation.*[29]

---

25 Cf. Hiers *SJT* 27 (1974) 37f., and note Fridrichsen *Miracle* 63–72.

26 I take it that the Gospel of Thomas is independent of the synoptic tradition. See the discussion in, e.g. B. Chilton "The Gospel According to Thomas as a Source of Jesus' Teaching" in Wenham (ed.) *Gospel Perspectives* 5, 155–75. It is interesting to note that in *b.B. Mes.* 59b there is a legendary account of a doctrinal argument around the end of the first century AD between Rabbi Eliezer ben Hyrcanus and his colleagues which Vermes relates as follows.

"Having exhausted his arsenal of reasoning and still not convinced them, he performed a miracle, only to be told that there is no room for miracles in a legal debate. In exasperation he then exclaimed: 'If my teaching is correct, may it be proved by Heaven!' Whereupon a celestial voice declared: 'What have you against Rabbi Eliezer, for his teaching is correct?' But this intervention was ruled out of order because in the Bible it is written that decisions are to be reached by majority vote" (Vermes *Jesus* 81–2).

27 R.H. Hiers *The Kingdom of God in the Synoptic Tradition* (Gainesville: Florida Univesity Press, 1970) 63. Cf. Borg *Conflict*: ". . . Jesus' exorcisms were the Kingdom of God manifested within the world of history" (253).

28 O. Betz "Jesu Heiliger Krieg" *NovT* 2 (1958) 128–9. Cf. Hiers *SJT* 27 (1974) 35–47.

29 Cf. Yates *ITQ* 44 (1977) 44 and Leivestad *Jesus* 106–7. See also Hunter *Work* 83;

It is this conclusion and this dimension to Jesus' exorcisms, more than anything else, which sets him out over against his background and environment. Even if every other aspect of Jesus' technique may have had at least a faint echo in other material, it is this indivisibility of miracle and message which reveals the exorcisms of Jesus to be especially unique. Jesus' exorcisms were not simply "healings" but were the coming of the kingdom of God.[30] We will take up this point in chapter VI when we discuss Jesus' self-understanding in relation to his exorcisms.

Kee *Medicine* 73. Cf. G.N. Stanton *Jesus of Nazareth in NT Preaching* (Cambridge: Cambridge University Press, 1974):

> "Jesus' proclamation and his actions and conduct were linked inseparably; his teaching was not merely a series of prophetic propositions illustrated by his actions and conduct, for the latter were as much 'message' as his words. Similarly, as has been emphasised recently, Jesus' parables were intended neither to convey timeless truths, nor to illustrate the proclamation of Jesus; they themselves were 'message' " (175).

Cf. Borg *Conflict* 253.

30 On the "sign" value of miracles in Plutarch see Kee *Medicine* 88–94 and in the pharisaic traditions, Kee *Miracle* 70–3, 155.

§ 20 Conclusions

The whole of this chapter has been a gathering of results from the previous two chapters. We have tried to draw a picture of Jesus as an exorcist.

From this chapter we are left in no doubt that the historical Jesus was an exorcist. Even with the case in Mark 5, where Jesus was not immediately successful, the biblical and extra-biblical material leaves us in no doubt that Jesus was an extraordinarily powerful and successful exorcist. We are left in no doubt that he was a "man of his time". We can see that the twentieth century notion that Jesus healed with a "mere word" is an oversimplification, even misrepresentation, of Jesus' healing procedure. He was an exorcist who used words or incantations, all of which would have been readily recognized by those around him. On one occasion Jesus even used a herd of pigs as part of his technique.

In his treatment of "The Form and History of Miracle Stories," Bultmann dealt with the ancient material that bears a resemblance to elements in the Synoptic miracle stories.[1] What Bultmann was attempting to show through these "parallels" was that the early Christian oral tradition was dependent on Jewish and Hellenistic folk traditions for its stories and miracle motifs.[2] While such a situation may, for some, reduce the "culture-shock" between first and twentieth century Christianity, this historical and hermeneutical contortion is unacceptable for it needs to be stated categorically that Bultmann's is an unproved case. The most important factor which Bultmann failed to take into account was that evidence which he produced to show that folk stories and miracle motifs had come into the oral tradition on the exorcism of demons is later than the formation of the Synoptic tradition. So, over against Bultmann, it is just as likely and reasonable to suppose that folk traditions and miracle motifs have made their way from the early Christian tradition to these traditions.

---

1   Bultmann *History* 218ff.; Dibelius *Tradition* 133ff.
2   Bultmann *History* 240.

This was one of the results, in part, of Goodenough's majestial work.[3]. In this and the last chapter, our study militates against the notion of an accretion of elements of miracle traditions onto the Synoptic tradition from outside.

In many ways, Jesus as an exorcist was a very ordinary exorcist; demons were distressed and threatened by his presence, there was a struggle between demon and exorcist, there were familiar incantational exchanges between Jesus and the demon(iac)s, and we know of one occasion when Jesus healed a demoniac from a distance. On the other hand, there were aspects of Jesus' exorcism which, although not unique, stand out as particularly characteristic of his procedure. Unlike probably most exorcisms of the era, no mechanical aids were used, such as special artifacts or the laying on of hands. Jesus neither used nor offered proof of his cures — save the evidence of the healed demoniacs (Mark 5.15). In contrast to others, he did not even declare the source of his power-authority; not even that he was dependent upon the Spirit of God.

Thus, what begins to mark out Jesus' exorcistic ministry from the technique of his fellows is that not only did he claim no outside aid for his success, but, also, he seems to have consciously emphasized that his resources were none other than his own person ("I . . ."). We can agree with Hengel where he says:

> ". . . where the problem of the small significance which attaches to the Spirit in the case of Jesus is concerned, we should have to consider whether the reason for its rare appearances in the original tradition is that Jesus did not need to have to resort to the Spirit as an intermediary, given his unique claim to authority, drawn as it was from the immediacy of his relation to God."[4]

Although in historical investigation it is hazardous to claim something as unique, it appears that Jesus' giving his exorcisms a dimension of significance beyond the mere healing of demented individuals was just that. Jesus was the first one to link the relatively common phenomenon of exorcism with eschatology. Though Jesus is not unique in combining the role of teacher and exorcist.[5] Jesus stands out in his era as one who not only relied on his own resources for success in exoricsm, but at the same time claimed that in them God himself was in action and that that action was the coming of God's eschatological kingdom.

---

3 Goodenough *Symbols* II, 173ff. and 191.

4 Hengel *Charismatic Leader* 63; cf. R. Pesch "Zur theologischen Bedeutung der 'Macht-taten' Jesu. Reflexionen eines Exegeten" *TQ* 152 (1972) 203–13. See also E. Fuchs, "Jesus dares to make God's will effective as if he himself stood in God's stead." Quoted by Hengel *Charismatic Leader* 68; see also 87.

5 Contra R. Kampling "Jesus von Nazaret – Lehrer und Exorzist" *BZ* 30 (1986) 237–48.

The historical Jesus the exorcist does indeed come to us as One unknown, as a stranger to our time.[6] But, we must not excise that strangeness from the historical Jesus. How important it is then, that we should go on to discover how his contemporaries assessed him and interpreted this dimension of their Jesus. For thereby we twentieth century Christians may understand him better and find a way to begin to understand and interpret Jesus the exorcist for our time.

---

6 Cf. Schweitzer *Quest* 399 and 401.

V
As Others Saw Him

§ 21 Introduction

We are now in a position to explore the ways in which people in the first century responded to Jesus the exorcist. This is, in a sense, secondary to our purpose of recovering the historical Jesus the exorcist. However, if we can gain at least some impression of the early responses to and assessments of this aspect of Jesus' ministry it will, in turn, help to fill out our picture of Jesus the exorcist.

The most readily available materials to recover possible responses to Jesus are the writings of the early Church. From these we are able to realize not only the responses to Jesus by the early Church, but behind these interpretations and responses, we may also be able to recover some of the initial responses to Jesus' exorcisms by the original audiences. Apart from the New Testament, there is other literature which acknowledges Jesus to be an exorcist and we will not ignore this in an attempt at salvaging early responses to Jesus' exorcistic ministry.

It needs to be stressed that, in the first place, we are conducting a historical inquiry and so we are not asking how we in the twentieth century should understand or categorize Jesus the exorcist but how those of his era responded to, and understood him.

In order to do this we shall, first, analyse the Gospel material relating to Jesus' exorcisms to see what it can tell us about his audience's response to him. Secondly, with the aid of extra-biblical material, we will critically examine some of the suggestions as to how people in the first and second centuries assessed or categorized Jesus the exorcist.[1]

---

1 Cf. Borg *Theology Today* 45 (1988) 280–92 and B.J. Lee *The Galilean Jewishness of Jesus* (New York: Paulist, 1988).

§ 22 Jesus' Audience

If we scrutinize the Gospel material relating to Jesus the exorcist four broad categories of response are preserved. (1) It is often said that Jesus' exorcisms moved the observers to *fear and amazement* (Mark 1.27/Luke 4.36; Mark 5.14/Matthew 8.33/Luke 8.34; Matthew 12.23/Luke 11.14). (2) On occasions the tradition proposes that, as a result of Jesus' exorcisms, some bystanders declared him to be *mad and demon-possessed* (Mark 3.21, 30; [John 7.20; 8.48; 10.20]). (3) Some said that it was *by Beelzebul* that he cast out demons (Mark 3.22/Matthew 12.24/Luke 11.15) and (4) others are said to conclude that Jesus the exorcist was *the Messiah* (Matthew 12.23). Our task now is to assess the historicity and meaning of the Gospel records at these points. We will deal with the first two points here and, because of their significance, the other two points we will take up in separable sections below.

1. *Fear and amazement* as a response to Jesus' exorcisms (Mark 1.27/Luke 4.36; Mark 5.14/Matthew 8.33/Luke 8.34; Matthew 12.23/Luke 11.14). This is sometimes thought to be a stereotyped closing motif in the miracle stories.[1] When we were dealing with Mark 1.27 in chapter III we were able to cast some considerable doubt on this assumption, but we were unable to decide on the historicity of this element in the Gospel stories.

A way forward in approaching this problem is to ask if there could have been anything in Jesus' exorcisms that might have created fear or amazement in the bystanders.

(a) In relation to Mark 1.27 — "And they were all amazed" — Taylor admits that θαμβέω is remarkable since the Jews were not unfamiliar with exorcism. But, Taylor goes on to suggest that, "the astonishment is due to the fact that Jesus casts out the unclean spirits with a word, without the use of magical formulae . . ."[2] Taylor's idea that Jesus' technique consisted of a mere word may come from Matthew 8.8/Luke 7.7 where the centurion asks Jesus to "say a word" so his boy will be healed (cf. Matthew

---

1   See those cited in Loos *Miracles* 131ff. and Theissen *Miracle* 69–71.
2   Taylor *Mark* 176. Taylor also quotes Fascher *Die formgeschichtliche Methode* 127f.

8.16 and Luke 4.36). But, in the last chapter, we have already shown that Jesus did use "magical formulae" or "incantations" in his exorcisms.

(b) We have also shown (chap. IV) that Jesus' virtual lack of the use of mechanical aids in his exorcisms was not a feature deleted from the tradition. We have seen that although healing by words alone was most probably not unique to Jesus, it seems to have been sufficiently extra-ordinary that it may have been the cause of some amazement to those who witnessed his exorcisms. The same could also be said on the brevity of his healing technique.

(c) In Mark 5.14 the drowning of the herd of pigs is said to cause the herdsmen to flee. As the pigs episode properly belongs to this exorcism story it is not surprising that this exorcism should produce such a response. However, the mention of fear at this point may, as we saw (§7 above), be redactional.

(d) Though Jesus' methods have parallels, we have seen in the last chapter that there are very few reports in the literature of similar healings. It could be, then, that the crowd had not seen such an exorcist or one with such success.

In conclusion, we can see that like any exorcism, those of Jesus would have caused fear and amazement in the observers not least because, at times, they had extraordinary features.

2. *Mad and demon-possessed* (Mark 3.21, 30; [John 7.20; 8.48; 10.20]). As his introduction to the Beelzebul Controversy Mark has "those with him" (οἱ παρ' αὐτοῦ) say that Jesus was "beside himself" (ἐξέστη).[3] Whether "those with him" were the friends or family of Jesus need not detain us, though Mark clearly intended the phrase to mean "family" (see 3.31).[4] That this charge goes back to the life situation of Jesus is quite probable for it is hardly a charge that the Church would introduce into the tradition. In fact, Matthew (12.22; cf. 46ff.) and Luke (11.14; cf. 8.19ff.) suppress the incident (see §10 above). Our confidence in the historicity of the charge is further increased when we take into account the independent tradition of John 10.20 where Jews are said to charge Jesus with being mad (μαίνεται).

But, did this charge in Mark 3.21 originally have any connection with Jesus' activity as an exorcist? The Fourth Gospel, though containing no exorcism narratives, preserves the charge of madness. However, John con-

---

3 H. Wansbrough suggests that it was the *crowd* that was "out of control" ("Mark 3.21 – Was Jesus out of his Mind?" *NTS* 18 [1972] 133f.). But κρατῆσαι can hardly mean "calm down". Cf. Dunn *Jesus* 384 n. 115; D. Wenham "The Meaning of Mark 3.21" *NTS* 21 (1974–5) 295f.; Nkwoka *Biblebhashyam* 15 (1989) 205–21, considers this passage to contain a misplaced charge of fanaticism.

4 E. Best "Mark 3.20, 21, 31–35" *NTS* 22 (1975–6) 309–19; Guelich *Mark* I, 172.

sistently shifts all criticism away from the activity of Jesus to his teaching and so we cannot be sure of the value of his testimony on this point.

We are left with Mark. The Beelzebul Controversy is obviously related to Jesus as an exorcist. It is fairly certain that the accusations in 3.19b—21 were in the position Mark now has them. In the first place, although these verses display a Markan hand,[5] Q (Matthew 12.22—3/Luke 11.14) has a miracle as the introduction to the Beelzebul Controversy. Second, when we note that the Markan account of the Beelzebul charge (3.22) is one of *demon-possession* (see §10 above) — so severe that it is most probably authentic — and that demon-possession was thought to be equivalent to being mad[6] we can see why 3.21, 22 (and 30) were brought together even if they were not originally part of the same report.

We need to consider why Jesus' observers charged him with being possessed and, in his exorcisms, acting as a tool of Satan (Mark 3.22/ Matthew 12.24/Luke 11.15).

It cannot be that Jesus was accused of being in league with Satan because he did not reveal his source of power-authority or be exorcising "in the name of" say, "God". From rabbinic traditions we know of another Jewish exorcist who did not declare his source of power-authority yet was not ousted from the community (Rabbi Simeon in *b. Me'il.* 17b).

An answer to our question may come if we look more widely across Jesus' ministry to indications of difficulties Jesus may have had with the religious authorities.

(a) Later we will be suggesting that Jesus may have been considered as something similar to one of the ḥasidic charismatics (see §26 below). In the past it has been argued that these charismatics were strict Pharisees.[7] More recently it is being recognized that the ḥasidim were highly individual and sometimes, indeed, opposed to that generally prevailing and not to be identified with the Pharisees.[8] Vermes says that there are two reasons for this tension between the charismatics and institutional Judaism.

First, the ḥasidim refused to conform in matters of behaviour and religious observance.[9] From what we know of Jesus from the Gospels his behaviour and religious observance were not entirely conventional. For

5 See Pryke *Style* 12. Cf. Best *NTS* 22 (1975–6) 309f..

6 Anderson *Mark* 121; John 10.20; (Acts 12.15f.). In Josephus *Ant.* 6.168 Saul, who had had a demon which was charmed away, is said to have been "restored to himself". See also Vermes *Jesus* 64–5.

7 E.g. A. Büchler *Types of Jewish-Palestinian Piety* (London: Jews College, 1922) 264.

8 S. Safrai "Teaching of Piestists in Mishnaic Literature" *JJS* 16 (1 and 2, 1965) 15–33. Cf. Flusser *Jesus* 56; Neusner *Traditions* III, 314, also cited with approval by Vermes *Jesus* 80 and nn.109, 110.

9 Vermes *Jesus* 80; cf. Green *ANRW* II.19.2 (1979) 625, 646–7 and see Jeremias *Theology* 226.

example, Jesus is shown to be in the company of women of ill-repute (e.g. Luke 7.36—50). Also, Jesus is shown as disregarding Sabbath laws (e.g. Mark 3.1—5) and standing over against the Mosaic law (e.g. Matthew 5.38—9). In Mark 7.1—23, Jesus is shown to be attacking Pharisaic rules concerning ritual purity.

Second, the charismatics caused tension because of their sense of un-restrained authority. To quote Vermes: "The charismatics' informal famil-iarity with God and confidence in the efficacy of their words was . . . disliked by those whose authority was derived from established channels."[10] As examples of this in Jesus' ministry we can cite the story of the paralytic being forgiven (Mark 2.1—12) and the story of the cleansing of the Temple (Mark 11.15—19/Mathew 21.12—17/Luke 19.45—8 and John 2.13—25). Also, in the face of popular expectation, Jesus is said to refuse to perform miracles to authenticate his status before God (Matthew 12.38—42/Luke 11.29—32).[11]

(b) Further, those who responded to Jesus' unauthenticated, or perhaps self-authenticating call were not even his family but sometimes the religious, political and social outcasts. Thus, we find part of the back-ground to the charge in what Kee says: "This prophet, lacking human credentials or the support of the established structures of society, is a radical threat to both the religious and social institutions of his culture."[12]

(c) Jesus was a Galilean. Galileans were an independent, aggressive and militant people. Josephus said they had "always resisted any hostile

---

10 Vermes *Jesus* 80. Cf. Hollenbach *JAAR* 49 (1981) 577, relying on A. Kiev (ed.) *Magic, Faith, and Healing: Studies in Primitive Psychiatry Today* (New York: Free, 1964) 460-2,
    ". . . while most healers are regarded, and see themselves as servants of their society, a few overstep the bounds of this intergration and become threats to the stability of their society."

11 It is not that the Messiah was expected to be a wonder—worker or charismatic. (See Schürer *History* II, 525 n. 42 "This view [that the Messiah will prove his identity by means of miracles] is absent from the rabbinic texts. '. . . *the Messiah. . . is never mentioned anywhere in the Tannaitic literature as a wonder-worker* per se' " (J. Klausner *The Messianic Idea in Israel* [1904, New York: Macmillan, 1955] 506). Rather, it was probably expected that claims of a special relationship with God required an authenticating sign. See *b. Sanh.* 98a where R. Jose b. Kisma, a Babylonian Amora, and his disciples, discuss the sign attending the coming Messiah and *b. B. Meṣ.* 59b where Rabbi Eliezar's teaching is authenticated by a voice from heaven (quoted §19 n. 26 above). Cf. Matt 11.2–6/Luke 7.18–23; Josephus *Ant.* 20.97 (where Theudas the false prophet "stated that he was a prophet and that at his command the river would be parted"); *b. Sanh.* 93b on Bar Koziba's claim to be the Messiah failing on the grounds that he could not "judge by the scent". See also A.B. Kolenkow "Relationships between Miracle and Prophecy in the Greco–Roman World and Early Christianity" in *ANRW* II.23.2 (1980) 1482–91.

12 Kee *Miracle* 158.

invasion, for the inhabitants are from infancy inured to war" (*War* 3.41).[13]
Vermes tells us that in Jerusalem, in Judaean circles, the Galileans had the
reputation of being unsophisticated. "In rabbinic parlance, a Galilean is
usually referred to as *Gelili shoteh*, a stupid Galilean. He is presented as a
typical 'peasant', a boor, a *'am ha-arez*, a religiously uneducated person."[14]
In line with this we note that in Mark 3.22 the critics of Jesus are said to
be scribes from Jerusalem.

Further to this we may note what Josephus says about the Jesus
movement. In Acts 5.34—9 Jesus and his followers are compared to the
popular messianic movements of Theudas and Judas the Galilean.[15] In
Josephus, Judas and a Theudas (identified with the Theudas of Acts by
most, though not all scholars[16]) are roundly condemned. Josephus says that
Theudas is a γόης (cheat, rogue or imposter) and he is said to have
deceived (ἀπατάω) people (*Ant.* 20.97—9). In a section on these subversive
leaders and movements Josephus says of Jesus and his followers: "About
this time there lived (a certain) Jesus, a wise man . . . For he wrought
surprising feats and was a teacher of such people as accept the (unusual)
gladly" (*Ant.* 18.63f.). And Josephus, reflecting Jewish as well as Roman
establishment views, would most probably have had the Jesus movement
in mind when he says, ". . . I cannot conceal my private sentiments, nor
refuse to give my personal sympathies scope to bewail my country's
misfortunes. For that it owed its ruin to civil srtife, and that it was the
Jewish tyrants (τύραννοι) who drew down upon the holy temple the un-
willing hordes of the Romans . . ." (*War* 1.10).[17]

In the light of his being considered a social and religious deviant, and
leading a potentially subversive movement, Jesus would have been seen as
a radical threat to the establishment. Thus, it is not surprising that Jesus
was alienated by the religious establishment and condemned with the most

---

13 Note S. Freyne "The Galileans in the Light of Josephus' *Vita*" *NTS* 26 (1980) 397–413
    correcting the view that Galilee was the home of *militant revolutionaries* in the first
    century. He argues that Josephus depicts the Galileans as his aggressive militant
    supporters whose mission it was to preserve peace in Galilee. Here we can note
    Bultmann's conclusion that Jesus was finally crucified as a messianic agitator, *Jesus
    and the Word* 29.

14 Vermes *Judaism* 5. On the *'am ha-aretz* see A. Oppenheimer *The 'Am Ha-aretz: A
    Study in the Social History of the Jewish People in the Hellenistic-Roman Period*
    (Leiden: Brill, 1977).

15 On the question of "How Revolutionary Was Galilee?" see the chapter of that title in
    S. Freyne *Galilee From Alexander the Great to Hadrian* (Wilmington: Glazier and
    Notre Dame: University of Notre Dame Press, 1980) 208–55.

16 See Bruce *Acts* (1952) 147 and Haenchen *Acts* 252.

17 Further on these passages and their reconstruction see Twelftree in Wenham (ed.)
    Gospel Perspectives 5, 289–308.

cutting criticism: he was not from God but, in his exorcisms, was acting as an agent of Beelzebul or Satan.[18]

In conclusion, the original observers most probably accused Jesus the exorcist of being a religious deviant: demon-possessed and motivated by Satan.[19] Although the charge of being a religious deviant is equivalent to being motivated by Satan we cannot be sure that, as an exorcist, Jesus was considered mad. We have also seen that his exorcisms caused his audience to experience fear and amazement.

---

18 Cf. Vermes *Jesus* 82: "Since *halakhah* became the corner–stone of rabbinic Judaism, it is not surprising that, despite their popular religious appeal, Jesus, Hanina, and the others, were slowly but surely squeezed out beyond the pale of true respectability." Also, Green *ANRW* II.19.2 (1979) 646, "The bulk of the evidence from the first two centuries shows that charismatic types who claimed miraculous powers were anti- thetical to and played little role in early rabbinism. God might work miracles, but early rabbis could not."

19 This conclusion is in line with J.Z. Smith's research in *ANRW* II.16.1 (1978) 429:
    "I shall propose as an initial interpretation of the demonic the sort of model raised to recent prominence by Mary Douglas and others concerned with issues of taxonomy: that negative valence is attached to things which escape place (the chaotic, the rebellious, the distant) or things found just outside the place where they properly belong (the hybrid, the deviant, the adjacent)."
    Here Smith cites M. Douglas *Purity and Danger: An Analysis of Concepts of Pollution and Taboo* (Harmondsworth: Penguin, 1970) and among others, R. Bulmer "Why is the Casswary not a Bird?" *Man* (n.s.) 2 (1967) 5–25.

§ 23 Messiah?

Did the exorcisms of Jesus lead his observers to conclude that he was the Messiah?[1] Although this question really belongs in the previous section, because of its importance for Christology and Christian theology we will treat it separately. Old Testament passages such as Isaiah 32.1—20 can hardly be thought to raise the expectation that the Messiah would be an exorcist. However, the question of whether or not Jesus' exorcisms were proofs of his messiahship is brought into focus by Matthew 12.23 which specifies the crowd's response to Jesus' healing a demoniac as, "Can this be the Son of David?"[2]

However, when we examined the Beelzebul Controversy pericope, (§10 above) we concluded that this acclamation by the crowd had its origin in Matthew's redactional activity. Therefore, it would be natural to conclude that Jesus' exorcisms did not, at least for the crowd, demonstrate or prove his messiahship. However, the matter cannot be left there for Matthew might be reflecting an earlier tradition about such a response to Jesus. Also, the work of a number of scholars suggests that the messianic hopes of the time involved an expectation that the Messiah would cast out demons.[3] So, the question remains open, Did his exorcisms lead Jesus' audience to conclude that he was the Messiah?

A possitive reply to this question could be based on two points.

First, it is suggested that there was a hope that the Messiah would deal with evil spirits and it is assumed that Jesus' exorcisms would be seen as

---

1 For discussion of messianic expectations in the first century AD see Leivestad *Jesus* chap. 5; J. Neusner, W.S. Green and E.S. Frerichs (eds.) *Judaism and their Messiahs at the Turn of the Christian Era* (Cambridge, UK and New York: Cambridge University Press, 1987); I.M. Zeitlin *Jesus and the Judaism of His Time* (Cambridge, UK: Polity, 1988) 38–44.

2 On the equation of "Messiah" and "Son of David" in the Gospels see G.F. Moore *Judaism in the First Centuries of the Christian Era* 2 vols. (Cambridge, MA: Harvard University Press, 1946) II, 329 and notes; R.H. Fuller *The Foundations of NT Christology* (London and Glasgow: Collins/Fontana, 1969) 111f. See also Mark 3.11.

3 Str–B IV, 534f.; Russell *Method* 287; Barrett *Spirit* 57ff.; P. Volz *Die Eschatologie der jüdischen Gemeinde im neutestamentlichen Zeitalter* (Hildesheim: Olms, 1966) §31; Schürer *History* II, 526–9; Sanders *Jesus* 161.

the fulfilment of that hope (see n. 2 above). The evidence that can be cited is Testamentt of Levi 18.11f.; Testament of Judah 25.3; Testament of Zebulon 9.8; Testament of Dan 5.10f.; Testament of Reuben 6.10—12; *Assumption of Moses* 10.1, 3; *Sifra Leviticus* 26.6; *Pesiqta Rabbati* 36; *1 Enoch* 10.4 and 55.4.

Secondly, with Matthew 12.23 in mind — "Can this be the Son of David?" — and in view of the tradition of Solomon's expertise in combating demons, it can be seen how "Son of David" might have been thought a particularly appropriate title for the Coming One in this context. To this we can add that the title "Son of David" comes from the very earliest traditions and was little used outside Palestine.[4] And, despite the uncertain history of the title prior to the Christian era,[5] there is some evidence that it was in use among the rabbis in the late first century.[6]

What are we to make of this evidence? Did his exorcisms show that Jesus was the Messiah?

First, we can consider the use of "Son of David" in connection with exorcism. To our knowledge, the title "Son of David" occurs for the first and only time in pre-Christian literature in Psalms of Solomon 17.21(23): "raise up for them their king, the son of David."[7] In the passage 17.21(23)—46, which is based on 2 Samuel 7,[8] the hope is expressed that God will raise up a king who will, for example, throw off alien domination, recapture Jerusalem and purify it of the heathen, and rule in purity and righteousness. But, no mention is made of exorcism or even dealing with demons. The Dead Sea document 4 QFlorilegium (4Q174), a collection of midrashim on some eschatological texts from the Old Testament, mentions the "shoot of David" (1.11). However, neither exorcism nor the defeat of evil spiritual beings are mentioned as a role for this figure. There may be a slight association seen between this figure and the destruction of evil for in 1.7—9, 2 Samuel 7.11b ("And I shall give you rest

---

4 Burger *Davidssohn* 41. On Matthew's use of the title see J.D. Kingsbury *Structure* 99–103 and literature cited. See also B.M. Nolan "The Figure of David as a Focus for the Christology of Matthew" *Scripture Bulletin* 12 (1981) 46–9 and W.R.G. Loader "Son of Daivd, Blindness, Possession, and Duality in Matthew" *CBQ* 44 (1982) 570–85; D.J. Verseput "The Role and Meaning of the 'Son of God' Title in Matthew's Gospel" *NTS* 33 (1987) 532–56; J. Bowman "David, Jesus the Son of David and Son of Man" *Abr-Nahrain* 27 (1989) 1–22.

5 D.C. Duling "The Promises to David and their Entrance into Christianity – Nailing Down a Likely Hypothesis" *NTS* 20 (1973–4) 68f.

6 Klausner *The Messianic Idea* 392.

7 Dalman *Words* 317; Fuller *Christology* 33; Str-B I, 525. The *Pss. Sol.* are to be dated mid first century BC; O. Eissfeldt *The OT: An Introduction* (Oxford: Blackwell, 1965) 613 and R.B. Wright in *OTP* 2, 640–1.

8 Dalman (*Words* 317) says that the actual designation is probably dependent upon such passages as Isa 9.5 (LXX); 11.10; Jer 23.5; 33.15.

from your enemies") is interpreted as the Lord, who in the eschaton, gives rest from all the sons of Belial.[9] The rabbinic material[10] also does not link the often mentioned figure, Son of David, with exorcism or dealing with Satan and the demons.

If we look at this from the other side we see that the expectation that the Messiah would do battle with evil spirits does not involve the term or title "Son of David". The title is used in conjunction with the control of demons in the Testament of Solomon (e.g. 1.5—7). However, this has been so thoroughly reworked by a Christian hand that it cannot be used to establish the nature of the pre-Christian messianic hope. Thus, the certain pre-Christian use of the title in a messianic context is not related to exorcism nor dealing with demons.

It should not surprise us that in the Jewish literature of the New Testament era the "Son of David" figure was not expected either to be an exorcist or at all directly involved in the defeat of evil. For, at least in rabbinic Judaism, interest was directed not so much on the person and the tasks of the eschatological figure as on the fact that the eschaton comes in and through him.[11]

As we have noted, the title is used frequently in Jewish literature from the Psalms of Solomon on, so it cannot be seen as a peculiarly Christian designation.[12] But, the association of the title with a therapeutic Messiah does seem to be a Christian innovation preserved in the Matthean tradition (Matthew 9.27; 12.23; 15.22; 20.30, 31). The innovative association of "Son of David" with exorcism probably came about because, as *LAB* 60 adumbrates and the whole of the Testament of Solomon makes explicit, the title "Son of David" was the one available messianic title that had strong healing connotations.[13] So, in short, prior to its use in Christian circles "Son of David" was not connected with the Coming One's expected dealings with Satan and the demons and, thus, evidence in this area does not support the possibility that Jesus' observers would have immediately responded to his exorcisms with the acclamation of Matthew 12.23.

Second, in trying to discover whether or not Jesus' exorcisms showed his audience he was the Messiah, we should examine the literature which has been cited as evidence that the expected Messiah would deal with

---

9 For a detailed treatment of this text see G.J. Brooke *Exegesis at Qumran: 4QFlorilegium in its Jewish Context* (Sheffield: JSOT, 1985).
10 Cited by Dalman *Words* 317; Str–B I, 525 and Bousset and Gressmann *Die Religion* 226–7.
11 Cf. Lohse *TDNT* VIII, 481.
12 *Pss. Sol.* 17 (cf. Sir 47.11; 1 Macc 2.57); Dalman *Words* 317; Fuller *Christology* 33 and see n. 8 above.
13 Cf. Duling *HTR* 68 (1975) 235–52.

Satan and his minions to see if it involved an expectation that the Messiah would be an exorcist.

1. It is to be noted that much of the evidence comes from the *Testaments of the Twelve Patriarchs.* In using this material as part of the background of Christian origins, some care must be exercised for it has long been accepted that the Testaments have undergone Christian interpolations.[14] There is at present considerable debate over the origins of the Testaments which was inaugurated primarily by de Jonge's work.[15] This debate need detain us only in so far as it alerts us to the necessity of examining each of the passages from the Testaments, cited early in this section, to see whether or not the pertinent lines have a Christian origin.

> *Testament of Reuben* 6.10–12.
> "Draw near to Levi in humility of your hearts in order that you may receive blessing from his mouth. For he will bless Israel and Judah, since it is through him that the Lord has chosen to reign in the presence of all the people. Prostrate yourselves before his posterity, because (his offspring) will die in your behalf in wars visible and invisible. And he shall be among you an eternal king."

We should exclude this passage from the evidence, for its reference to dealing with Satan and the demons is not plain. In any case, the section 6.5—12 looks like a later addition[16] and the awkward reference in verse 12 to an eternal king dying in wars visible and invisible quite probably refers to Jesus.

> *Testament of Levi* 18.11b—12.
> "The spirit of holiness shall be upon them.
> And Beliar shall be bound by him.
> And he shall grant to his children the authority to trample on wicked spirits."

The whole of this chapter, which has some agreements with the Testament of Judah 24, is probably a hymn which glorifies Christ.[17] Also, verses 6—7 appear like a description of Jesus' baptism.

---

14 See references given by H.F.D. Sparks' review of M. de Jonge *The Testaments of the Twelve Patriarchs: A Study of Their Texts, Compositon and Origin* (Assen: Van Gorcum, 1953) in *JTS* 6 (1955) 287. Quotations from the Testaments are from *OTP* 1.

15 de Jonge *Testaments*. On the present debate see J. Becker *Untersuchungen zur Entstehungsgeschichte der Testamente der zwölf Patriarchen* (Leiden: Brill, 1970); M. de Jonge "The Interpretation of the Testaments of the Twelve Patriarchs in Recent Years" in M. de Jonge *Studies on the Testaments of the Twelve Pariarchs: Text and Interpretation* (Leiden: Brill, 1975) 183–92; H.D. Slingerland *The Testaments of the Twelve Patriarchs: A Critical History of Research* (Missoula: Scholars Press, 1977) esp. chap. VI; M. de Jonge "The Main Issues in the Study of the Testaments of the Twelve Patriarchs" *NTS* 26 (1980) 508–24; H.W. Hollander and M. de Jonge *The Testaments of the Twelve Patriarchs: A Commentary*.(Leiden: Brill, 1985); M. de Jonge "The Testaments of the Twelve Patriarchs: Christian and Jewish. A Hundred Years After Friedrich Schnapp" *NedTTs* 39 (1985) 265–75.

16 de Jonge *Testaments* 37.

17 de Jonge *Testaments* 89; cf. M. Black "Messiah in the Testament of Levi xviii" *ExpTim* 60 (1948–9) 322.

"The heavens will be opened,
and from the temple of glory sanctification will come upon him,
with a fatherly voice, as from Abraham to Isaac.
And the glory of the Most High shall burst forth upon him.
And the spirit of understanding and sanctification shall rest upon him <in the water>"
(cf. Mark 1.10–11).

Verse 3 — "And his star shall rise in heaven like a King" — is probably a reflection of Matthew 2.2. Verse 12b — "And he shall give
authority to his children to tread upon evil spirits" — can be compared
with Luke 10.19. The origin of verse 12a — "And Beliar shall be bound by
him" — is dificult to judge. If it is compared with Matthew 12.29/Luke
11.21, where Jesus binds the Strong Man, then perhaps verse 12a could well
have a Christian origin. However, although Beliar is a relatively late title
for Satan,[18] it does have a brief pre-Christian history (e.g. *Jubilees* 16.33).[19]
On balance, I think that it is difficult to see the passage as certainly being
pre-Christian, even though it contains an older term.

Testament of Judah 25.3b.
"There shall no more be Beliar's spirit of error, because he will be thrown into eternal
fire."

The reference to a spirit of deceit or error (πνεῦμα πλάνης) is reminiscent of 1 Timothy 4.1 and 1 John 4.6. The idea of the destruction of
Satan by casting him into the fire forever may reflect Matthew 8.29 (cf.
Luke 12.5). Thus, we have little confidence in the pre-Christian origin of
these notions here. In any case, there is no reference to a specific individual being involved nor that exorcism was thought to be the way in
which Beliar would be defeated.

Testament of Zebulon 9.8.
"And thereafter the Lord himself will arise upon you, the light of righteousness with
healing and compassion in his wings. He will liberate every captive of the sons of men
from Beliar, and every spirit of error will be trampled down. He will turn all nations
to being zealous for him. And you shall see <God in human form>,[20] he whom the
Lord will choose: Jerusalem is his name."

The treading upon spirits of deceit probably reflects Luke 10.19—20 (cf.
Mark 16.18; see also on Testament of Judah 25.3b above). That God will be
seen in the fashion of a man probably comes from a Christian hand
(though see Erza 1.26). That the reference to the defeat of Beliar is in the

---

18 The earliest occurrences being *Sib. Or.* 3.63, 73, about mid–second century BC. (J.J.
    Collins "The Provenance and Date of the Third Sibyl" *Bulletin of the Institute of
    Jewish Studies* 2(1974) 1–18. Cf. G.A. Barton *ERE* II, 459. W. Bousset *ERE* I, 587ff.;
    R.H. Charles *The Revelation of St. John* 2 vols. (Edinburgh: T & T Clark, 1920) II,
    71ff.; K. Galling *RGG* (3rd ed.) I, 1025f.; W. Foerster *TDNT* I, 607.

19 See previous note and Eissfeldt *The OT* 615ff. and literature cited.

20 εν σχηματι ανθρωπου is found in only one manuscript (M. de Jonge *Testamenta XII
    Patriarcharum* [Leiden: Brill, 1964] 46).

context of probable Christian material reduces our confidence in its pre-Christian origin.

Testament of Dan 5.10–11a.

"And there shall arise for you from the tribe of Judah and (the tribe of) Levi the Lord's salvation.

He will make war against Beliar;

he will grant the vengeance of victory as our goal.

And he shall take from Beliar the captives, the souls of the saints; . . . "

Once again we should probably attribute the second and succeeding lines of verses 10f. to a Christian writer. For, as de Jonge says:

". . . after the usual 'and for you the salvation of the Lord will arise from the tribes of Judah and Levi', there follows immediately: 'and *he* will wage war against Beliar. . .' This is the beginning of a Christian passage dealing with the Messiah."[21]

Thus, in conclusion, little confidence can be placed in any of the references from the Testaments of the Twelve Patriarchs for portraying pre-Christian messianic hopes. Nor is there always an understanding that an individual would be responsible for the destruction of Beliar.

2. *1 Enoch* 55.4, part of the Similitudes of Enoch, contains a reference to the final judgement.

"You would have to see my Elect One, how he sits in the throne of glory and judges Azaz'el and all his company, and his army, in the name of the Lord of the Spirits."

Since none of chapters 37—71 were found at Qumran there has been, until recently, some doubt about the early date of this material. However, the consensus of opinion now is that the Similitudes are Jewish and date from the first century AD.[22]

In the final judgement the Elect One or Messiah sits in judgement of Azazel and the fallen angels. However, again, there is no suggestion that exorcism would be involved. Therefore, we could not conclude from this text that the Messiah was expected to be an exorcist.

3. We need also to consider Strack and Billerbeck's citation of *Sifra Leviticus* 26.6 and *Pesiqta Rabbati* 36[23] in relation to the pre-Christian messianic hope entailing the defeat of Satan and his demons.

"R. Shim'on said: When is God honoured? At the time when there are no Mazziqin [demons] at all, or at the time when there are Mazziqin but they can no longer do any harm? So says Ps. 92.1: A Psalm, a song for the Sabbath day, that is for the day that brings the Mazziqin in the world to rest so that they do no more harm" (*Sifra Leviticus* 26.6).

---

21 de Jonge *Testaments* 87, his emphasis; cf. 92.

22 J.T. Milik (ed.) *The Books of Enoch* (Oxford: Clarendon, 1976) 91; M.A. Knibb "The Date of the Parables of Enoch: A Critical Review" *NTS* 25 (1979) 345–9; cf. C.L. Mearns "The Parables of Enoch – Origin and Date" *ExpTim* 89 (1977–8) 118f.; E. Isaac in *OTP* 1, 7 and Charlesworth in *Princeton Seminary Bulletin* 6 (1985) 102.

23 Str–B IV, 527, followed by Barrett *Spirit* 59 from where the quotations below have been taken.

> "When he [Śatan] saw him [the Messiah], he trembled and fell on his face and said: Truly this is the Messiah, who one day will hurl into Gehinnom me and all the angel princes of the peoples of the world . . ." (*Pesiqta Rabbati* 36).

However, neither of these references can be admitted as evidence of the nature of the pre-Christian hope. The former reference can come from no earlier than the middle of the second century AD[24] and the *Pesiqta Rabbati* is dated between the fourth and ninth centuries.[25]

4. We are left then with only the *Assumption of Moses* 10.1, 3 as a possible useful reference.

> "Then his kingdom will appear throughout his whole creation.
> Then the devil will have an end.
> Yea, sorrow will be led away with him . . .
> For the Heavenly One will arise from his kingly throne.
> Yea, he will go forth from his holy habitation with indignation and wrath on behalf of his sons."

However, we must also discount this passage. In verse 1 the hope — "And then Satan shall be no more" — is related not to the work of any individual messianic figure but states what will happen when the Lord's kingdom shall appear. Verse 3 does mention an individual ("the Heavenly One") but he is not related to the destruction of Satan and he is not a human figure but God himself (cf. 10.7). In 9.1 there is a hero, Taxo, who seems to precede the appearance of the kingdom, but his task is not part of either the establishment of the kingdom or related to the destruction of Satan. His task is simply to exhort his hearers to good works; perhaps a preliminary to the coming of the kingdom (9.7; 10.1). Thus, as far as we can see, the author of the *Assumption of Moses* would certainly not be looking for a Messianic figure who would do battle with Satan, let alone be an exorcist.[26]

5. Finally, we can consider *1 Enoch* 10.4 where Rapheal is told to

> "Bind Azaz'el hand and foot (and) cast him into the darkness!"

Here God's representative is involved, but exorcism is not mentioned. This is an example from the literature of the period in which the "Messiah" was not indispensable to the eschatological kingdom, and "Messiah" and "Messianic concepts" are not always found together.[27]

The *conclusion* we should draw from our examination of this material is that in pre-Christian literature there seems to be no connection between

---

24 The rabbi mentioned (Simeon) is from the second century as Barrett (*Spirit* 59) notes.

25 See Schürer *History* I, 97; cf. *EncJud* 13, 335.

26 In this category we should include *T. Jud* 25.3 and 4QFlor 1.7 which also see the demise of Satan as part of the *new state of affairs* rather than the work of a particular individual.

27 See Russell *Method* 309 and 285.

a messianic individual and his specific battle with Satan and the demons through the ordinary act of exorcism. So, it is difficult to see Jesus' observers connecting what was a common occurrence in their day with Jesus being self-evidently the Messiah.

I am not concluding that, in general, it was not possible for Jesus' audience to come to the conclusion that he was the Messiah. That is a different question. But, I am concluding that for the observers of Jesus as an exorcist there is little to suggest that they would have so assessed him and his significance. They had no immediately adequate frames of reference from which to draw such a conclusion.[28] When Barrett says: "The argument of Jesus, . . . that his exorcisms were a sign of the proximity of the kingdom of God, would be perfectly comprehensible even to those who disagreed with its assumption,"[29] he is correct in so far as such an explanation of the significance of exorcism may have been *comprehensible*. For, as we saw in §3 above, the Qumran community associated David with the dealing with demons. But, we must dissent from his view that Jesus' exorcisms were a *sign* (see §19 above) and the implication that such an interpretation of the exorcisms was self-evident.[30] Indeed, if Jesus was, in his exorcisms, self-evidently the Messiah then it is difficult to explain why the Fourth Evangelist does not make use of what would potentially be a useful component in his Gospel.[31]

---

28 Sanders *Jesus* 170, ". . . the miracles themselves, . . . do not push us further towards the view that Jesus was an eschatological prophet. There is nothing about miracles which would trigger, in the first–century Jewish world, the expectation that the end was at hand."

29 Barrett *Spirit* 59.

30 Cf. Leivestad *Jesus* 74–5.

31 Contrast Harvery *Constraints*: ". . . we may say that such was the sense of enslavement to the spirit–world felt by so many of his contemporaries that Jesus could hardly have been acknowledged as their saviour had he not seemed to have struck a decisive blow against this redoubtable enemy" (118).

§ 24 Magician?

In this section we will discuss a presentation of the view that Jesus was seen as a magician.

We do not need to enter the full debate on the definition of magic and the relationship between miracle and magic.[1] It will sufffice to note, for the moment, that the difficulty in defining magic and its relation to miracle is that views and definitions are almost as various as the cultures which have faced the problem. For example. Lucian of Samosata attacks Peregrinus and Alexander of Abonuteichos as false prophets, for they are accepted by the unlearned yet are, in his opinion, really charlatans and sorcerers (γόης καὶ τεχνίτης, *Peregrinus* 13; cf. *Alexander* 1, 2). This· shows, at least, the similarity of message and technique between those considered "magicians" and those considered to be representing true religion.

Further, it is recognized, by Lucy Mair for example, that an absolute distinction between magic and miracle is difficult to draw.[2] As an example, she notes that Durkheim wants to draw a distinction between magic and religion on the grounds that magic has no Church and is practiced by individuals for the benefit of other individuals. But, this definition takes no account of beneficent magic performed on behalf of the community.[3] In the light of her discussion, Mair says that, as a general rule, "The efficacy of magic may be thought to depend essentially upon the correct treatment of substances used (including words spoken over

---

1   See the summary discussion by Aune *ANRW* II.23.2 (1980) 1510–16 and Garrett *Demise* 11–36. See also M. Marwick *Witchcraft and Sorcery: Selected Readings* (Harmondsworth: Penguin, 1970). Cf. the amusing story of a Ju–Ju man of Kumamu in West Africa explaining the difference to Gregory Dix, in his *Jew and Greek: A Study in the Primitive Church* (Westminster: Dacre, 1953) 93.

2   L. Mair *An Introduction to Social Anthropology* (Oxford: Clarendon, 1972) 225. See also G.P. Corrington "Power and the Man of Power in the Context of Hellenistic Popular Belief" in Richards (ed.) *SBLSP* (1984) 259–60; E.V. Gallagher *Divine Man or Magician? Celsus and Origen on Jesus* (Chico: Scholars Press, 1982) 48–9.

3   Mair *Anthropology* 225. Cf. E. Durkheim *The Elementary Forms of Religious Life* (London: Allen and Unwin, 1976) 42–7.

them) independently of assistance from any supernatural being."[4] However, this is far too simplistic and does not stand in the face of evidence.

We are better served by David Aune's research. At the conclusion of his discussions he sets out four interrelated propositions which can provide background to our study.

"(1) Magic and religion are so closely intertwined that it is virtually impossible to regard them as discrete socio–cultural categories. (2) The structural–functional analysis of magico–religious phenomena forbids a negative attitude towards magic. (3) Magic is a phenomenon which exists only within the matrix of particular religious traditions; magic is not religion only in the sense that the species is not the genus. A particular magical system coheres within a religious structure in the sense that it shares the fundamental religious reality construction of the contextual religion. (4) Magic appears to be as universal a feature of religion as devian behavior is of human societies."[5]

It is Professor Morton Smith's belief that " 'Jesus the magician' was the figure seen by most ancient opponents of Jesus" and that this picture was destroyed in antiquity after Christians got control of the Roman empire.[6]

The most important implication of Smith's book is that he considers this view of Jesus to be correct, so that not only was Jesus considered to be a magician, but Jesus actually was a magician in terms of the first century understandings of that category (p. 59).[7] As Smith's work cuts so directly across the path of our study we must engage in debate with it.

To support his theory Morton Smith first surveys the reports about Jesus in the Gospels. Then he looks at the Jewish and pagan material. These two areas are assessed before returning to the Gospels to see how the evidence accords with the picture that had emerged so far — that Jesus was a magician.

---

4 Mair *Anthropology* 225. Cf. G. van der Leeuw *Religion in Essence and Manifestation* (London: Allen and Unwin, 1938) 423.

5 Aune *ANRW* II.23.2 (1980) 1516. See also A.B. Kolenkow "A Problem of Power: How Miracle Doers Counter Charges of Magic in the Hellenistic World" in G. MacRae (ed.) *SBLSP* (Missoula: Scholars Press, 1976) 105–10; J.Z. Smith in *ANRW* II.16.1 (1978) 425–39; Remus in *SecCent* 2 (1982) 127–56; H. Remus "Does Terminology Distinguish Early Christian from Pagan Miracles? *JBL* 101 (1982) 531–51; H. Remus *Pagan-Christian Conflict Over Miracle in the Second Century* (Cambridge, MA: Philadelphia Patristic Foundation, 1983); G. Luck *Arcana Mundi. Magic and the Occult in the Greek and Roman Worlds* (Baltimore and London: Johns Hopkins University Press, 1985) chaps. I and II; D.E. Aune "The Apocalypse of John and Graeco–Roman Revelatory Magic" *NTS* 33 (1987) 481–501; Garrett *Demise* 4 and note also Herzog *Epidauros*; "magic is always other people's faith" (140). Cf. Malina and Neyrey *Calling Jesus Names* chaps. 2 and 3.

6 M. Smith *Jesus the Magician* (London: Victor Gollancz, 1978) vii, followed recently by Sanders *Jesus* 165–9. Cf. Geller *JJS* 28 (1977) 141–55. In *Die Versuchung Christi* (Oslo: Gröndahl, 1924), S. Eitrem proposed that in the Temptation Jesus was being induced to become a magician. Contrast the critique by H.J. Rose's review of Eitrem in *Classical Review* 38 (1924) 213.

7 Pages in parentheses refer to Smith's *Magician*.

I

The first explicit references to Jesus being a magician are found in later Christian, Jewish, and pagan material. We shall begin by taking up points from this material as it is the most important in Smith's case.

1. Two of the early corner-stones in chapter 4 ("What the Outsiders Said — Evidence Outside the Gospels") of *Jesus the Magician* are that *Pantera*, and its variants, is the "name generally given by Jewish tradition to Jesus' father,"[8] and that *Ben Stada*, the son of Pantera, is to be identified as Jesus (p. 47). The key passage, at one time censored from the Talmud, is *b. Sanhedrin* 67a.[9] Smith gives no evidence as to why any of these names should be identified with Jesus and his family. However, R. Travers Herford, on this particular point a precursor of Smith, rests the case on a passage from *t. Ḥullin* 2.22—3 which mentions healing "in the name of Jesus ben Panthera." He says that in the light of these two passages "it is impossible to doubt that the reference is to Jesus of Nazareth."[10] The considerable evidence against this slim argument is, first, that the title *Jesus ben Panthera* is not uncommon in the Talmud,[11] and, second, that Ben Stada lived a century after Jesus.[12] Smith, then, has no good reason for identifying the names of *b. Sanhedrin* 67a and *t. Ḥullin* 2.22—3 with Jesus and his family. Ben Stada can probably be regarded simply as a false prophet executed during the second century at Lydda.[13]

The reason why Professor Smith wishes to make these connections is that the following passage, from *b. Šabbat* 104b, could then be made to refer to Jesus: "But did not Ben Stada bring forth witchcraft from Egypt by means of scratches (in the form of charms) upon his flesh?" Smith says that this tattooing almost certainly refers to Jesus.[14] Then, a little later, Smith says, "Moreover, Paul claimed to be tattooed or branded with 'the marks of Jesus,' Gal. 6.17 — most likely, the same marks that Jesus had carried" (p. 48).

---

8 Smith *Magician* 46. Cf. R.T. Herford *Christianity in the Talmud and Midrash* (Clifton, NJ: Reference Book Publishers, 1966) 35ff.
9 See *b. Sanh.* 67a (London: Soncino, 1935) 456 n. 5.
10 Herford *Christianity* 38.
11 H.L. Strack *Jesus die Häretiker* (Leipzig: Hinrichs, 1910) chap. IV.
12 *b. Giṭ.* 90a. Epstein's note to *b. Sanh.* 67a (London: Soncino, 1935) 457.
13 See the previous note. J. Derenbourg *Essai sur l'histoire et la géographie de la Palestine* (Paris: Impériale, 1867) 468–71 n. 9; J. Klausner *Jesus of Nazareth* (New York: Macmillan, 1927) 21 and notes; cf. esp. Herford *Christianity* 344ff. and notes and J.Z. Lauterbach "Jesus in the Talmud" in his *Rabbinic Essays* (New York: KTAV, 1973) 477. Further see Twelftree in Wenham (ed.) *Gospel Perspectives* 5, 318–9.
14 Smith *Magician* 47. His evidence for this is the unsupported statement – "because the same charges are specified by second century pagan and Christian writers as elements in the Jewish account of him" (47).

For evidence he relies on Lietzmann's note on Galatians 6.17 ("Henceforth let no man trouble me; for I bear on my body the marks of Jesus"). In turn, Lietzmann is dependent upon Deissmann's use of the Demotic and Greek Papyrus J.383. The spell reads:

"Do not persecute me, you there! – I am
ΠΑΠΙΠΕΤ... ΜΕΤΟΥΒΑΝΕΣ
I carry the corpse
of Osiris and I go
to convey it to
Abydos, to carry it to
its resting–place, and to place it
in the everlasting chambers. Should anyone trouble me,
I shall use it against him."[15]

In the light of the spell Deissmann says, "One can hardly resist the impression that the obscure metaphor all at once becomes more intelligible: *Let no man venture* κόπους παρέχειν *for me, for in the* βαστάζειν *of the marks of Jesus I possess a talisman against all such things.*"[16]

Whatever we make of Deissmann here, we need to note that he sees it as a *metaphor — and no more.*[17] There is no evidence that disposes us to do otherwise. And, Smith produces no evidence that would suggest Paul thought he was tattooed after the fashion of a magician.

2. Further, in his effort to make Jesus a magician Smith summons Suetonius and Tacitus to his aid. *First* he quotes Suetonius' *Life of Nero* 16.2 — "Penalities were imposed on the Christians, a kind of man (holding) a new superstition (that involves the practice) of magic." On the use of *maleficus*, which Smith here translates as *magic*, we shall have more to say in a moment. It is sufficient to note here that this translation is by no means certain.

Secondly, Professor Smith quotes Tacitus (*Annals* 15.44.3—8) on the persecution by Nero. In this passage Tacitus says that the Christians were convicted, not so much on the count of arson as for "hatred (*odium*) of the human race." Of the last phrase Smith says that it "is most plausibly understood as referring to magic" (p. 15). But, this could only be the case if one's mind was predisposed to so seeing it. Smith contends that the usual explanation is inadequate. He says the usual view is,

"that it is an application to the Christians, who were still a Jewish group, of the Roman belief about Jews in general, is derived from Tacitus' comment on the Jews in *Histories* V.5, 'among themselves they scrupulously keep their promises, and are quick to pity and help [each other], but they hate all outsiders as enemies' " (p. 51).

---

15 Cf. Deissmann *Studies* 354; H. Lietzmann *An die Galater* (Tübingen: Mohr, 1971) 45f.
16 Deissmann *Studies* 358, his emphasis.
17 Lietzmann (*Galater* 45) more reasonably says that 6.17 is undoubtedly related to 2 Cor 4.10; Rom 8.17; Phil 3.10 and Col 1.24.

This, he argues, is inadequate because, when speaking of the Jewish hatred of others, he does not consider it as grounds for total extermination of them as he does for the Christians. Hence, the Romans' attitude to Christians must be distinguished from their general view of Jews (p. 51).

Against this we can note two things. *First,* in the *Annals,* Tacitus is not levelling *charges* against the Christians. He is attempting to give reasons why Nero should have persecuted the Christians. And, further, it does not seem that *odium* was a legal charge.[18] *Secondly,* Smith fails to note that the term "hatred of the human races" certainly is used in antiquity as grounds for *Jewish* persecution.[19] There is, then, no reason at all why we should assume that in the use of the phrase, "hatred of the human race", Tacitus thought that the Christians were guilty of anything different from the Jews.

But, we need to question Smith's statement that "hatred of the human race" is a charge appropriate to magicians as popular imagination conceived them (p. 52). It is not absolutely clear, but it seems that Smith wishes to equate "hatred of the human race" with cannibalism, which he adequately shows was thought in antiquity to be associated with magic, magicians and witches. However, Smith has offered no evidence that we should make the prior connection between "hatred of the human race" and cannibalism. Thus, there is no need to see more in the phrase than Frend's definition: "It involved not so much the desire to do personal damage but to turn one's back on obligations to one's fellow men, and it was regarded as a characteristic Jewish fault."[20]

3. Next among Smith's witnesses is Pliny the Younger and his letter to Trajan.[21] The section of the letter that is of interest here is Pliny's hearing of Christian apostates: "that it was their habit on a fixed day to assemble before daylight and sing by turns a hymn (*carmen*) to Christ as a god." The operative word here is *carmen.* Sherwin-White has reviewed the possible interpretations and he says,

"The short answer is that *carmen dicere* is ordinary Latin for to sing a song or to intone verses . . . It is true that *carmen* may mean the set formula of, for example, an oath, . . . and *carmen dicere* might mean an invocation as in a magical rite. But the normality of the phrase from the pen of a literary man, the contrast with *maledicerent christo* in S.5, and the conjunction of *quasi deo,* all favour the original interpretation as a hymn of praise."[22]

---

18   W.H.C. Frend *Martyrdom and Persecution in the Early Church* (Oxford: Blackwell, 1965) 174 n. 51.
19   Frend *Martyrdom* 162 and footnotes.
20   Frend *Martyrdom* 162.
21   Pliny *Letters* X.96.
22   A.N. Sherwin-White *Letters of Pliny: A Historical and Social Commentary* (Oxford: Clarendon, 1966) 704f. Sherwin-White is interacting principally with C. Mohlberg, C.C. Coulton and H. Lietzmann with regard to early Christian liturgical practices.

Smith calls Sherwin-White's treatment a "whitewash" (p. 180). However, as he offers no evidence to counter Sherwin-White's conclusions it seems reasonable to conclude that Pliny is not here referring to magical incantations or spells, but to the Christians' hymns.

4. With the *Dialogue with Trypho*, by Justin Martyr, reference to a charge of magic is at last clear. Smith (pp. 55 and 81) focuses his argument on the word πλάνος (pp. 55 and 81). This, as we shall see, is indefensible, for πλάνος was by no means a synonym for "magician" (see section III.2 below). This is clear in *Dialogue* 69 where Justin distinguishes between the terms — "For they dared call him a magician and a deceiver of the people." Strangely, Smith relegates reference to his potentially important passage to a footnote.[23] Justin is noting that a *Jewish* opinion of Jesus was that he was a μάγος. Two important points need to be mentioned. First, that this charge of magic is from those who wish to discredit the reputation of Jesus, and second, that Justin is at pains to refute the charge as being false. Here we see that the charge of being a magician is a social classifier so that "your magic is my miracle, and vice versa."[24]

5. Smith is also correct in seeing a contrast between the work of Jesus and the work of magicians as lying behind a fragment of an otherwise unknown Apologist *Quadratus* which is preserved by Eusebius.[25] The fragment reads,

> "But the works of our Saviour were always present, for they were true, those who were cured, those who rose from the dead, who not merely appeared as cured and risen, but were constantly present, not only while the Saviour was living, but even for some time (ἐπὶ χρόνον ἱκανόν) after he had gone, so that some of them survived even till our own time" (*HE* 4.3.2; cf. Irenaeus *Adversus Haereses* 2.32.3–4 and Smith p. 55).

However, we can go beyond Smith's "contrast" and see here a *refutation* by Quadratus of a charge of magic against Jesus. The two comments made on the last point apply: the charge of magic is being made by opponents of mainstream Christianity, and the charge is roundly refuted.

6. The next major witness for Professor Smith's case is *Celsus* (*CC* I.6, 28, [cf. 38], 68). Again, the evidence is clear that Celsus did consider Jesus to be one who practised magic (γοητεία). For example, Celsus says, ". . . it was by magic that he was able to do the miracles which he appeared to have done . . ." (*CC* I.6). And, ". . . because he was poor he hired himself out as a workman in Egypt, and there tried his hand at certain magical

---

23   Smith *Magician* 180 and see below where Justin is quoted more fully.

24   R.M. Grant *Gnosticism and Early Christianity* (New York: Harper & Row, 1964) 93. Cf. A.F. Segal "Hellenistic Magic: Some Questions of Definition" in R. Van den Broek and M.J. Vermaseren (eds.) *Studies in Gnosticism and Hellenistic Religions* (Leiden: Brill, 1981) 349–75; Remus *SecCent* 2 (1982) 148–50.

25   See R.M. Grant "Quadratus, The First Christian Apologist" in R.H. Fischer (ed.) *A Tribute to Arthur Vöörbus* (Chicago: Lutheran School of Theology, 1977) 177–83.

powers on which the Egyptians pride themselves . . ." (*CC* I.28; cf. 38 and 68).

Smith rightly recognizes the obvious import of these passages; that Celsus thought that Jesus was one who practised magic. But, where Smith goes beyond his evidence is where he suggests that the picture Celsus gives us may be correct (p. 59).[26]

Summary. In chapter 4 of his book Professor Smith has been trying to do two things. Principally he wants to show that Jesus' contemporaries outside the Gospels thought that he was a magician (pp. 67, 68, cf. 53f.). The second objective of Smith, which we will leave for the moment, is that this notion of Jesus being a magician may be the correct view of him, though Smith gives no evidence.

On Smith's principal objective a number of things should be said. *First,* Smith gives the misleading impression that he has reviewed all of the non-Gospel evidence for the outsiders' image of Jesus (p. 64). But, there is at least one snippet of information from Suetonius' *Claudius* 25.4 that shows that not all references to Jesus can be construed to refer to Jesus being a magician. Suetonius says of Claudius; "He expelled the Jews from Rome, on account of the riots in which they were constantly indulging, at the instigation of Chrestus." This reference to Christ — "Chrestus" being a popular mis-spelling of the name "Christ"[27] — is by no means complimentary. However, Suetonius seems to have no wish to give any idea that Chrestus was a magician.[28]

Secondly, Professor Smith's case fails to convince us that the Jewish writers he cites, or Suetonius, Tacitus, or Pliny, thought that Jesus was a magician.

---

26 See also S. Benko "Early Christian Magical Practices" in K.H. Richards (ed.) *SBLSP* (Chico: Scholars Press, 1982) 9–14. Kee, *Miracle* 268, goes beyond the evidence in *CC* in suggesting that the charge of Celsus is close to that of the opponents in the Gospel tradition in the story of the Beelzebul Controversy (Mark 3.22–3) for Celsus does not suggest that Jesus is in league with the evil powers. Kee, himself, admits later that there were not just two but a number of alternative categories in which miracle—workers could be put.

  "In this epoch, both champions and critics of miracle—workers are agreed as to what the basic issues are: are miracles evidence of divine wisdom and power, of demonic power and wizardry, or fraud and chicanery?" (*Miracle* 273).

  Further on the second century debate on Jesus see G.N. Stanton "Aspects of Early Christian–Jewish Polemic and Apologetic" *NTS* 31 (1985) 377–92, esp. 379–85.

27 See F.F. Bruce *Jesus and Christian Origins Outside the New Testament* (London: Hodder and Stoughton, 1974) 21 and M.J. Harris "References to Jesus in Early Classical Authors" in Wenham (ed.) *Gospel Perspectives* 5, 353–4.

28 Although Smith has not adequately dealt with Josephus, the problems of the authenticity of *Ant.* 18.63–4 make a discussion of the use of the passage here virtually impossible. P. Winter "Josephus on Jesus" *Journal of Historical Studies* 1 (1968) 289–302 and in a revised form in Schürer *History* I, 428–41. See also Twelftree in Wenham (ed.) *Gospel Perspectives* 5, 301–8.

Thirdly, Smith seems to assume that he is dealing with the views of Jesus' contemporaries. However, he does not show that the views held by those he cites were the views of the contemporaries of Jesus. In other words, charges that phenomena or persons were considered as magical or magicians need to be historically assayed in relation to their own life-situation, not evaluated by looking back from later times, as Smith does.[29]

Fourthly, the material cited from Justin, Quadratus and Origen clearly shows that there were those who said that Jesus was a magician and that his miracles were performed by magic. But, of course, each of these charges is forcefully rebutted. And it is untenable, in the face of this, and without other evidence, to say this picture of Jesus was correct. At best, we are dealing with a second century social classification. To determine the correctness or relevance of the charge there is no alternative but to return to the New Testament to see if, from the meagre evidence, we can come to some conclusion. This we shall do later.

II

Having attempted to show that Jesus' "contemporaries" thought him to be a magician, Smith goes on, in chapter 5 ("What the Outsiders Meant") to spell out what these "contemporaries" meant when they con- sidered Jesus to be a magician. Smith recognizes the difficulty of this task (pp. 68f.) and acknowledges the need for defining magic in a first century con- text.[30] However, although Smith gives an adequate general picture of the various notions of what a first century magician was, he fails to relate these notions to his evidence in the previous chapter. The result is that, of the whole spectrum of possible choices (p. 80), we do not know, from Smith, which one, or more, of these definitions might have been appro- priate or understood by, say, Celsus or Quadratus' opponents. This also we shall have to investigate later.

---

29 Kee *Miracle* 211 n. 60, makes the same criticism of Smith as well as Hull *Magic* However, on pp. 213–5 Kee comes close to, if not actually making the same mistake. Segal, in Van den Broek and Vermaseren (eds.) *Gnosticism* "Its [magic] meaning changes as the context in which it is used changes" (351).

30 On the other hand, it seems to me that Aune *ANRW* II.23.2 (1980) makes a mistake when he says that
   "The wonders performed by Jesus are magical because they occur within a context of social deviance in which widely accepted but generally unattainable goals highly valued in Judaism are thought to be accomplished for particular individuals through the application of generally successful management techniques" (1539).
   For, what Aune has not shown is that Jesus' contemporaries had this view of his deviance.

III

We can now return to the Gospel material and see what Smith makes of it. First, in dealing with the Gospels he considers "What the Outsiders Said."[31] He deals with the opinions of various relevant sectors of first century society; for example, "Common Opinion" (pp. 21ff.) and "Family and Towns-people" (pp. 28ff.). What Professor Smith does is to catalogue the opinions of these groups, almost invariably adverse. For example, he notes the charge of casting out demons by Beelzebul (Mark 3.22/Matthew 12.24/Luke 11.15; p. 81), and that Jesus was said to be a Samaritan (John 8.48; p. 21), and that he had a demon (John 8.48). We now take up these key items in Smith's argument.

1. Smith contends that John 8.48 — "You are a Samaritan and have a demon"[32] — means that the accusers thought that Jesus was a magician.[33] His reason for arguing this is that " 'had' a demon seemed sometimes to mean that he was himself possessed, sometimes that he had control of a demon and could make it do miracles" (p. 77). Smith (pp. 31–2) is correct in noting that ἔχειν ("to have"), does, in some cases, mean to have something under control.[34] But, it is doubtful if this meaning is intended in the New Testament.[35] In Greek philosophy and religion, there are two meanings of "to have". If the demon is for *good*, it is the *person* who possesses it, but in relation to *evil spirits* it is the person who is *passive* in the spirit's possession of him. Turning to the New Testament, "to have" (ἔχειν) does not mean "to have in one's power" or "to possess". Rather, it expresses a spatial relationship and means "to bear in oneself."[36]

In the light of this, the accusation that Jesus performed miracles "because he has Beelzebul" (ὅτι Βεελζεβοὺλ ἔχει, Mark 3.22) may seem a difficulty. On the other hand, first, although the concept of the demonic "to have" is extended, Beelzebul is still no more than the chief demon.[37] Secondly, the reply of Jesus in Mark 3.23, "How can Satan cast out Satan?" implies not that Jesus is using or manipulating the possessing power, *but the reverse*. And, thirdly, in 3.30 Mark ends the section with the comment — "for they had said 'He has an unclean spirit'." We can

31 Smith *Magician* 21 (chap. 3).
32 This verse, in a Homily by Abraham, Bishop of Ephesus in the sixth century, is cited with the addition καὶ ἐκ πορνείας γεγέννησαι. J. Mehlmann "John 8.48 in Some Patristic Quotations" *Biblica* 44 (1963) 206; cf. 8.41.
33 Smith *Magician* 32, 47f.; (n. p. 179), 77, cf. 96f.
34 E.g. Demonsthenes *Orations* 47.45.
35 To the contrary, without evidence, C.H. Kraeling "Was Jesus Accused of Necromancy?" *JBL* 59 (1940) 154.
36 H. Hanse *TDNT* II, 816–32, esp. 821ff.
37 Hanse *TDNT* II, 822.

conclude by repeating that in the Gospels ἔχειν does not mean "to have in one's power" but "to be controlled by", in this case by an evil spirit.

Nevertheless, it is clear that two of the Evangelists feel that Jesus' contemporaries charged him with having a demon. In the New Testament world Satan and magic could be associated (e.g. *Jubilees* 48.9—11; *Martyrdom of Isaiah* 2.4—5; CD 5.17b—19).[38] However, what we must decide here is what δαιμόνιον ἔχειν ("to have a demon") would have meant for the Evangelists in particular, and why Matthew and Luke do not agree here with John and Mark.

(i) The point at which to begin is by noting that Matthew and Luke do not take up Mark's phrases ἔλεγον πνεῦμα ἀκάθαρτον ἔχει ("they said he has an unclean spirit" 3.30) and Βεελζεβοὺλ ἔχει ("he has Beelzebul" 3.22). They alter Mark so that Jesus acts *by* or *in* the power of Beelzebul rather than say Jesus "has" a demon or Beelzebul. We have seen (§10 above) that Beelzebul was most probably a pseudonym for Satan. Mark is transmitting the accusation that Jesus was possessed or controlled by Satan and performed his exorcism under his aegis. Such a notion was clearly unacceptable to Matthew and Luke.

(ii) In John's Gospel there has been no attempt to hide the accusation that Jesus had a demon (7.20; 8.48—52; 10.20).

John 8.48 — "The Jews answered him, 'Are we not right in saying that you are a Samaritan and have a demon?' " (cf. 7.20; 8.52 and 10.20). The accusation has two elements; first that Jesus is a Samaritan, and then second, that he has a demon. The first element — "You are a Samaritan" — has been variously interpreted.[39] The best way forward is to note that John 8.48 supplies only a single reply to the accusation — "I have not a demon". Consequently, even if the two elements are not exactly synonymous, an understanding of the second element of the accusation — "You have a demon" — may clarify the meaning of being called a Samaritan.

In *John 10.20* δαιμόνιον ἔχει is immediately followed by μαίνεται ("he is mad"). There is no reason to see the latter phrase as more than supplementing the first so that the two phrases are synonyms.[40] Besides this verse there are four other occurrences of μαίνομαι in the New Testament. In each of the cases it characterizes *a disbelieved message of good news*.

---

38 Garrett *Demise*, chap. 1, assumes that an accusation of being in league with Satan is a charge of being a magician.

39 As a Samaritan, Goet or Gnostic; Bultmann *John* 299 n. 4; see also J. Bowman "Samaritan Studies I" *BJRL* 40 (1957-8) 298-308.

40 So, e.g. R.E. Brown *The Gospel According to John* 2 vols. (London: Chapman, 1971) I, 387; Lindars *John* 365; Barrett *John* (1967) 314.

First, in Acts 12.15 Rhoda is disbelieved (μαίνῃ) when she relates the good news that Peter is standing at the door. Second, in response to Paul's defence, Felix says that Paul is mad (μαίνῃ) to which Paul replies that he is not mad but speaking the sober truth (Acts 26.24—5). Then, third, in 1 Corinthians 14.23 Paul says that when outsiders hear an assembled Church speaking in tongues will they not say they are mad (μαίνεσθε)? This is not strictly or directly good news but is inspired by God and its interpretation may bring good news (1 Corinthians 14.5c, 13—19). Finally, the verse in which we are presently interested is a response by some of the Jews, placed at the end of the Good Shepherd discourse. It is not a response to Jesus' miracles or activities but to his words, and in particular (as in the other references to δαιμόνιον ἔχεις — 7.20; 8.48—9; note 10.20b), a response to words of Jesus *pertaining to his own status and his relationship to God.* As the two parts of the accusation in John 10.20 appear to be synonymous we can conclude that *for John some of the Jews were characterizing what was for them an unbelievable message.*[41]

The phrase in 8.48 is the same and the situation is similar to that in 10.20. We can then approach 8.48 assuming that δαιμόνιον ἔχεις could well have a similar meaning for John. To confirm this we see that the first element of the 8.48 accusation — "You are a Samaritan" — agrees with this interpretation. After noting the points of contact and the points of contrast between Samaritan theology and the Fourth Gospel Bowman says,

"As to John 8.48 there is sufficient in the Johannine picture of Jesus which would suggest to Jews that Jesus was not as the scribes and Pharisees if we can judge these by later Rabbinic writings. His emphasis on faith, on belief instead of fulfilment of ritual religious acts would seem strange. If there is any historical foundation for the speeches in John 8 it is not surprising that the Jews regarded him as a Samaritan."[42]

Bowman is aware that the Jews would not have meant their accusation literally; it was as if Jesus were acting the Samaritan by putting forth such unbelievable opinions.[43]

In Mark, the term "to have a demon" is used in the context of a debate over Jesus' source of power-authority for his miracles. To his accusers his miracles appear to be authorized and enabled by Beelzebul. Similarly, in Matthew 11.18 and Luke 7.33, the term is used in an accusation directed against the *activity* of John the Baptist.[44] But, in John the charge of having

---

41 Cf. Preisker *TDNT* IV, 361. See also S. Pancaro *The Law in the Fourth Gospel* (Leiden: Brill, 1975) 87—101.

42 Bowman *BJRL* 40 (1957-8) 306.

43 Bowman *BJRL* 40 (1957-8) 307-8.

44 The phrase δαιμόνιον ἔχειν is used by Matthew and Luke only in relation to John the Baptist's asceticism (Matt 11.18/Luke 7.33) and the Gadarene demoniac (Matt 8.28/Luke 8.27).

a demon has been removed from the context of Jesus' *activity* and is now to be found in relation to the *teaching* of Jesus.

We have been trying to show that Smith is mistaken in thinking that John 8.48 is to be taken as an accusation of magic against Jesus. We have shown that the charge that he was a Samaritan and demon-possessed expressed the judgement that Jesus' message was unbelievable.

2. Vital to Smith's programme of trying to show that Jesus was a magician is his interpretation of a πλάνος as a "magician".[45] The mainstay of Smith's case is an article by Father J. Samain who Smith says has persuasively argued that in the Gospels πλάνος means "magician". But, in fact, what Samain has shown is that although outside the New Testament πλάνος can mean magician, one has to determine from the context how to translate it. Only after this does Samain go on to suggest that the context, particularly of Matthew 27.63, invites the translation "magician".[46] However, Samain says that Jesus was never expressly changed with practising magic nor being a magician.[47]

In Greek, an early meaning of πλανάω was to "lead astray". The active sense of "deceit" is late and rare[48] — with a shift to its negative aspect.[49] It is this aspect of the word that was taken up into the LXX. This group of words is used mainly for sins against God and more specifically for idolatry. And, interestingly, sin is caused not by ungodly metaphysical forces such as the devil, but by humans, or even by God. Also, the word group is used in the rejection of false prophecy.[50] This glance at the pre-New Testament use of the πλανάω word group illustrates that there is neither a direct use of the word in connection with magic, nor is it used as a synonym for magic.

We can return to Smith and Samain who suppose that the term was either equivalent to a direct accusation of magic or that it actually means "magician".[51] Their evidence fits into three broad categories. *First*, there is the evidence which illustrates the use of the word in the context of early Christian apologetics in defence of Jesus. *Secondly*, there is the related used of the word in pagan condemnation of Jesus. *Thirdly*, Smith and Samain have drawn on the use of the word outside the debate about Christ.

---

45 Smith *Magician*, e.g. 33, 54, 181.
46 J. Samain "L'accusation de magie contre le Christ dans les Evangiles" *ETL* 15 (1938) 449–90.
47 Samain *ETL* 15 (1938) 454.
48 H. Braun *TDNT* VI, 229; Didorus Siculus *Hist.* 2.18 (P. London II.483.19).
49 Plato *Republic* 444b; *Phaedo* 81a.
50 Braun *TDNT* VI, 233.
51 Samain *ETL* 15 (1938) 456; Smith *Magician* 33, 174.

It is the latter category of the use of the word that is most useful in discovering its relationship to such words as γόης and φαρμακός. But, at this point Samain has very little evidence. He relies on Josephus' use of πλάνος. Samain says that Josephus puts messianic pretenders among γόητες and οἱ πλάνοι.[52] In fact, what Josephus does in using πλάνος is to use it in parallel with, and as a synonym for ὁ ἀπατῶν (cheat, rogue, imposter). He says: "Deceivers and imposters, under the pretence of divine inspiration ·fostering revolutionary changes, they persuaded the multitude to act like madmen, and led them out into the desert under the belief that God would there give them tokens of deliverance" (*War* 2.259). This is of little help to Samain as Josephus mentions nothing about these people that would suggest that they were magicians. There is, in Josephus, no need to translate πλάνος other than by "imposter" or "deceiver". Even γόης is best translated "charlatan" rather than "magician".[53]

As we have noted above, the πλανάω word group, in the transferred sense in the pre-New Testament period, is used primarily in relation to erring from right teaching or correct doctrine. It is not, so far as I can tell, used on its own to described the work of a magician (γόης). It has this meaning where it is linked, as it is in relation to the later debate concerning Jesus, with miracles.

When we turn to examine the use of πλανάω, πλάνη and πλάνος in the New Testament, by or in relation to Jesus, it is never related to miracles or to the work of Jesus. The πλανάω group of words always has to do with being deceived in relation to the truth of the Christian message. (The one possible exception to this is Matthew 24.24 — "For false Christs and false prophets will arise and show great signs and wonders, so as to lead astray . . ." But, even here, it is not the signs and wonders that are themselves in question but the false Christs and prophets who will do the leading astray by means of signs and wonders.) I would propose then that, for the Evangelists, the use of πλάνος was not understood as a direct comment on the way Jesus performed his miracles but reflected what Jesus' accusers felt: that, in general, Jesus was leading people astray, that he was socially and religiously unacceptable.

It is only when we move into the second and following centuries that πλάνος was linked with the miracles of Jesus in such a way that makes it clear that those attacking and rejecting Christianity were rejecting the validity of the miracles of Jesus. Thus, in talking of the miracles, Eusebius says he has been

---

52   Samain *ETL* 15 (1938) 462.

53   We cannot, then, agree with Aune, *ANRW* II.23.2 (1980) 1540, that "Samain presents an iron–clad case for understanding the charge of imposter [Matt 27.63] as an accusation that Jesus performed miracles by trickery or magical techniques."

"arguing with those who do not accept what we have said, and either completely dis-
believe in it, and deny that such things were done by him at all, or hold that if they
were done, they were done by wizardry (γόητεία) for the leading astray (πλάνη) of
the spectators, as deceivers (πλάνοι) often do" (*Proof of the Gospel* 3.4.31).

And, earlier, Eusebius sets the accusation of ὁ πλάνος over against the
character and teaching of Jesus in such a way as to give the distinct
impression that those with whom Eusebius was arguing were, in using
πλάνος, referring to Jesus' miracles.[54]

Thus, it is necessary to conclude that ὁ πλάνος, by itself, cannot be
equated with "magician" and that neither Jesus' contemporaries nor the
Evangelists understood ὁ πλάνος to designate Jesus as "magician". It was
only later, in the second and following centuries, that this word was linked
with the accusation that Jesus was a "magician".

3. Yet another item in Smith's agenda is to equate κακοποιός and κακὸν ποιῶν with "magician", so that the accusation by the Jews in John
18.30 — "If this man were not κακὸν ποιῶν, we would not have handed
him over" — becomes a charge of magic.[55]

This can be dealt with relatively quickly. In citing 1 Peter 4.15,
Tertullian and Cyprian use *maleficus* for κακοποιός ("evil doer").[56] Smith
then says that *maleficus* is equivalent to "magician".[57] However, as shown
by 1 Peter 2.12 and 14, the normal meaning of κακοποιός is "evil doer"
and there is no evidence for the use of κακοποιός in the sense of
"magician" in Greek legal terminology.[58] Also, when *maleficus* is used,
even if not synonymously, at least in a context where the term ‹ *might*
carry the idea of "magician" or "sorcerer", its magical connotations are
made *explicit* in the context by the use of some related or qualifying
word(s). So, for example, in *Codex Justinianus*, Smith's principal witness,
maleficus is qualified so that it *might* take the meaning of "magician".

"No person shall consult a soothsayer (*haruspex*), or an astrologer (*mathematicus*) or
diviner (*horiolis*). The wicked doctrines of augurs (*vates*) shall become silent. The
Chaldeans and wizards (*magi*) and all the rest whom the common people call magicians
(*malefici*), because of the magnitude of their crimes, shall not attempt anything in this
direction" (*Codex Justinianus* IX.18.7).

But, against Smith, it could quite readily be argued that, even in this passage, *maleficus* is not a synonym for *magic* but a generic term used
simply to describe any evil activity.

---

54 Eusebius *Proof* 3.2 and 3.
55 Smith *Magician* 33 and note p. 174.
56 Tertullian *Scorpiace* 12.3; Cyprian *Testimonia* 3.37.
57 Smith *Magician* 174 citing *Codex Theodosianus* IX.16.4; *Codex Justinianus* IX.18.7.
58 F.W. Beare *First Epistle of Peter* (Oxford: Blackwell, 1961) 167; J. Ramsey Michaels *1 Peter* (Waco, TX: Word, 1988) 266–7.

Even if Smith's evidence were granted, there is still no evidence to show that in using *maleficus* for κακοποιός, Tertullian and Cyprian (see above) understood 1 Peter 4.15 as being a reference to "magician" or "sorcerer". For, in every other case where I have seen *maleficus* used, it demands no other translation than "evil doer". That the sense of "evil doer" is too vague to be a legal accusation under Roman law is an unsupportable notion.[59] For, apart from the major crimes condemned by Roman statutes for Italy, governors elsewhere were very largely left to their own discretion in recognizing crimes and determining their sentences.[60]

At this point we conclude, in the first instance, that *maleficus* is a general term for "evil doer", save where it is qualified to take on a specific meaning. Thus, in the second instance, we conclude that the use of *maleficus* for κακοποιός by early Christian writers is not to be taken to mean that they thought the later term was equivalent to "magic".[61] Therefore, finally, the Jews' charge in the Gospels that Jesus is a κακὸν ποιῶν cannot be taken as being understood by the Evangelists as a charge of magic.

IV

There are clear charges of magic in some later literature which we should examine.[62]

First, *the opponents of Quadratus*. In *The History of the Church* 4.3.2 (quoted above) Eusebius mentions Quadratus, an Apologist during the time of Hadrian. Quadratus is quoted as saying that the Saviour's works were always present because they were true (ἀληθής). That is, those who were healed were not only seen being healed, or raised from the dead, but remained present during Jesus' ministry as well as after his departure. The charge of magic that Quadratus is countering has nothing to do with methods or motives for healing but with performing acts which give the impression or appearance of being miracles while in fact they are mere tricks.

---

59 Cf. Smith *Magician* 33.
60 Sherwin-White *Letters* 699, 782; cf. Pliny *Letters* X.96.3; Tacitus *Annals* 15.44; C. Bigg *Epistles of St. Peter and St. Jude* (Edinburgh: T & T Clark, 1902) 137. See also A.N. Sherwin-White *Roman Society and Roman Law in the NT* (Oxford: Oxford University Press, 1963).
61 Cf. the review of Smith by Frank Kermode in *The New York Review of Books* XXV (20, Dec 21st, 1978, p. 58); "It is perfectly plausible that magicians might be referred to as evil doers. It does not follow that one could not accuse somebody of doing evil without claiming that he was a magician."
62 For further discussion of anti-magic passages see Fridrichsen *Miracle* 85–102; Remus *Pagan-Christian Conflict*; Gallagher *Divine Man*.

Secondly, *the opponents of Justin Martyr.* In the *Dialogue with Try-pho* Justin quotes Isaiah 35.1—7 and says how Christ fulfils this prophecy. He

> "healed those who were maimed, and deaf, and lame in body from their birth . . . raised the dead, and cause(d) them to live . . . But though they saw such works they asserted it was magical art. For they dared to call him a magician, and a deceiver of the people" (*Dial.* 69).

This passage is set in the context of a discussion of counterfeit miracles by the devil. It is over against this that Justin sets the reality of the miracles of Christ which are, in turn, said to be magical (φαντασία) and deceptive. In this connection Justin is clearly thinking of the questions of the authenticity or materiality of Jesus' miracles rather than the means by which they were performed. In any case, more importantly, Trypho's assessment is of limited value for a study of the historical Jesus, for it comes a century after the time of Jesus and tells us nothing of the view of Jesus' contemporaries.

Thirdly, *Celsus*. The charge of Celsus is that Jesus was the same as those sorcerers who were trained by the Egyptians. What, says Celsus, characterized the activity of these people was their "displaying expensive banquets and dining-tables and cakes and dishes which are non-existent, and who make things move as though they were alive although they are not really so, but only appear as such in the imagination" (*CC* I.68).

Celsus has in mind the stories of few loaves feeding many people, as well as Jesus raising the dead. Again, the essence of the charge is that Jesus' miracles were magical in that they only appeared to take place. And, indeed, Origen answers the charge along these lines by trying to show that Jesus used no tricks. In essence, Origen's reply is: Would one whose moral character was above reproach fabricate his miracles and by these fabrications call people to holy lives?[63]

V

Summary and Conclusions. It is often thought that if an exorcism does not involve the use of physical or mechanical aids or incantations then the healing is not magical. Thus, it is said "the NT miracles of Jesus have no connexion with magic, or with magic means and processes . . ."[64] There is

---

63 Gallagher *Divine Man* 172, "The criteria ultimately rests on the shared assumption that 'a god ought to do good for men' ". Kee, *Miracle* 273, comes to a similar conclusion. Cf. Eusebius *Proof* 3.3
64 Grundmann *TDNT* II, 302. Cf. e.g. W. Kirchschläger "Exorcismus in Qumran?" *Kairos* 18 (1976) 52.

a note of desperation here.[65] The abhorrence of magic in the Bible is noted and so, at all cost, Jesus must be absolved from any charge of magic — magic defined in terms of technique.[66] There are two problems or errors here.

First, there is a problem of definition. We have seen that, in relation to miracles and exorcism, the bald categories of "magical" (= evil)/"non-magical" (= good), when defined in terms of technique, are not helpful in understanding the exorcisms in the New Testament era.[67]

The second problem in the attempt to absolve Jesus from the charge of magic is one relating to historical method. If we define magic in terms of technique — physical aids or incantations — it is an error of historical judgement to say that the techniques of Jesus, in exorcism for example, have nothing to do with magical processes or that in this way he is quite unique and separate from his contemporaries.[68] We saw in chapters III and IV above that there is good evidence to say that Jesus' technique as an exorcist had clear parallels in this so-called "magical" or incantational world.

In our response to Smith we have tried to show that his programme has failed on at least three counts.

1. Smith has not been able to show that Tacitus, Suetonius or Pliny thought that Jesus was a magician in any sense.

2. Where the charge of magic is clear — in Justin Martyr, Quadratus and Celsus — Smith has not taken into account that these opinions are not from contemporaries of Jesus. He also misunderstands the particular notions of magic involved in these accusations. That is, the substance of the charge against Jesus did not relate to his having used incantations or particular methods. This charge comes sometime later, as in Arnobius *Adversus Gentes* 1.43. In relation to performing miracles the charge of "magic" here revolved around two important factors.

First, the *life-style of the individual*. If as a miracle-worker, the person was a cheat, liar or murderer (etc.), he was considered to be a magician.[69] We can illustrate this further. In Acts 13.10 Elymas the sorcerer (ὁ μάγος) is attacked by Paul because he is full of deceit and trickery. Also, Lucian attacks those who took advantage of the πολλοί by offering false wares (*Philosophies for Sale* 2.11—12; see also Philostratus *Life* 7.39).[70] Therefore,

---

65 See the editorial review of Hull *Magic* in *ExpTim* 85 (1973–4) 355f.

66 Cf. Mendelsohn *IDB* III, 223ff.; Hull *IDBSup* 312ff. Further see Remus *JBL* 101 (1982) 531–51.

67 Contrast Hull *Magic* chap. IV.

68 E.g. L. Morris *The Cross in the NT* (Exeter: Paternoster, 1976) 56f. and notes.

69 Cf. the categories in Acts 13.10 and see above on Tertullian; also Fridrichsen *Miracle* 91f.

70 See also Corrington in Richards (ed.) *SBLSP* (1984) 258–9 and Garrett *Demise* 4–5.

magic is not simply deviant behaviour, as Aune argues, but deviant behaviour associated with working miracles which are considered to be empowered by spiritual forces.[71] *Secondly*, of singular importance was the *authenticity and longevity of the "magician's" results* (cf. Quadratus above and Philostratus *Life* 8.7). That is, if his work proved to be a fraud he was deemed a magician.[72]

3. Smith has also failed to show that charges laid against Jesus in the New Testament relate to a charge of magic.[73] What we have shown is that what Jesus' contemporary critics were concerned about was not his allegiance to any realm of "magic", but that he must have been demon-possessed, by Satan himself.[74] Even though a definition of magic is best generally approached through the notion of deviance, and Jesus' religious inclinations were considered deviant, the evidence does not support the view that Jesus' critics considered this deviance in terms of him being a magician.

As the second and third century charges against Jesus are quite different from those reflected in the Synoptics, they are of little value in understanding how Jesus' contemporaries assessed him as an exorcist. And, as the Jesus tradition itself cannot support the view that Jesus was charged with magic, we can take it that *it is false to think that Jesus' contemporaries considered him to be a magician*[75] or that the charge that Jesus practised magic is a motif permeating the Jesus tradition.[76] In fact, if the charge of magic had been known by the Gospel writers we would have expected them to take the opportunity to spell it out and reject it as they did with other criticisms of Jesus.

Gallagher *Divine Man* notes that Celsus contends "that magic is only effective with uneducated people with those of depraved moral character, which those who have studied philosophy are impervious to its power since they are careful to lead a healthy life" (45), cf. *CC* VI.41.

71 Cf. Aune *ANRW* II.23.2 (1980) 1515.

72 Fridrichsen *Miracle* 89f.

73 In *Strange Tales About Jesus* (Philadelphia: Fortress, 1983) P. Beskow, commenting on Smith's *Secret Gospel of Mark*, says that it is a riddle

"... how Morton Smith has been able to derive so many strange ideas from this brief and not very disturbing text. He proclaims four theses based on the support of this fragment: 1. that Jesus appeared as a magician. . . The odd thing about Morton Smith's theses is that none of them have (sic) any worthwhile support in the fragment. Jesus does name a miracle, but there is nothing more magical about this one than miracles described elsewhere in the Gospels" (103).

74 Cf. Kee *Medicine* 73, "The Jewish religious leaders, observing his exorcisms, do not dismiss him as a trickster or as a fake, but infer that he is able to control the demons because he is in league with their leader".

75 Cf. Winter *Trial* 144 and especially see the critical review of Smith by J.-A. Bühner "Jesus und die antike Magie. Bemerkungen zu M. Smith, Jesus der Magier" *EvT* 43 (1983) 156–75. Cf. W. Wink "Jesus as a Magician" *USQR* 30 (1974) 3–14.

76 Samain *ETL* 15 (1938) 490.

§ 25 Necromancer?

"Was Jesus accused of Necromancy?" asks C.H. Kraeling.[1] His answer is "Yes". Kraeling's case centres around his understanding of Mark 6.14—16 — Herod's view of Jesus: "John, whom I beheaded, has been raised." His argument is, briefly, as follows.

Herod has heard a report of Jesus, most likely of Jesus' mighty works. But, John did no miracles (John 10.41). What then is the connection that Herod is making between Jesus and John? It cannot be that Jesus is John *redevivus* for the ministries of Jesus and John overlap (Matthew 11.2—6/ Luke 7.18—23). So Kraeling suggests that the connection is necromancy.[2]

The backbone of Kraeling's case is that, apart from the sayings relating to Jesus in John (7.20; 8.48, 49, 52; 10.20), and the reference in Luke 8.29 to the Gadarene demoniac, the locution ἔχειν δαιμόνιον means "to have a demon under one's control and to make him do one's bidding."[3] Kraeling gives the impression that this phrase is used on a number of other occasions. In fact, it appears only in Matthew 11.18/Luke 7.33, and Kraeling gives us no evidence for thinking that this verse was intended to convey the notion of John having a demon under his control. Kraeling also mentions the Beelzebul charge in this connection (Mark 3.22). However, we have just seen that this interpretation of the charge is improbable. This severely undermines if not destroys Kraeling's case.

---

1 Kraeling *JBL* 59 (1940) 147–57.
2 Kraeling *JBL* 59 (1940) 153.
3 Kraeling *JBL* 59 (1940) 154.

§ 26 Hasid?

Would Jesus' audience have seen him as one of their charismatic rabbis? In *Jesus the Jew* Geza Vermes considers that Jesus is represented in the Gospels "as a man whose supernatural abilities derived, not from secret powers, but from immediate contact with God, (which) proves him to be a genuine charismatic."[1] This conclusion may adequately define Jesus' activity and character in terms of *our* understanding of a charismatic. But, can we go so far as to say "that the person of Jesus is to be seen as part of the first-century charismatic Judaism and as the paramount example of the early Hasidim or Devout"?[2] In other words, would Jesus' contemporaries have considered him one of their charismatic rababis? Yes, says Vermes.[3]

Vermes places Jesus among the charismatic rabbis as a result of an examination of Jesus as a healer, particularly as an exorcist, and by comparing him with Honi and Hanina ben Dosa. In relation to exorcism, the material Vermes produces to set up the background for Jesus is from Tobit, *Jubilees*, Josephus, Qumran and the rabbinic literature.

Our first task here is to note that there are some general objections to the view that Jesus was a rabbi. In contrast to Jesus, the rabbis seemed to have little interest in eschatology, nor did they speak in a prophetic manner.[4] And, in the conclusion to his chapter on "The Constraints of the Law", Harvey says:

> "We have tried, so far as our knowledge permits us, to lay out the options which would have been open to anyone who acquired the reputation, as Jesus undoubtedly did, of being a teacher. The evidence of the gospels - taken . . . as a whole, and

---

1 Vermes *Jesus* 79, cf. Dunn *Jesus* 88; Barrett *Spirit* 57 and Borg *Conflict* Preface, 73, 230-1.
2 Vermes *Jesus* 79.
3 Vermes *Jesus* 79. Cf. Bühner *EvT* 43 (1983) 156–75; Borg *Conflict* 230-1; E. Rivkin *What Crucified Jesus?* (Nashville: Abingdon, 1984) chaps. 4 and 5. For a critique of the *hasid* as a 'type' see D. Bermann "*Hasidim* in Rabbinic Tradition" in P.J. Achtemeier (ed.) *SBLSP* 2 vols. (Missoula: Scholars Press, 1979) 2, 15–33 and Freyne in Nickelburg and Collins (eds.) *Ideal Figures* 223–58.
4 Neusner *Traditions* I, 395; Harvey *Constraints* 93 n. 88.

therefore less vulnerable to the suspicion of fabrication by the early church – tells strongly against Jesus having adopted any of these options as he found them. Rather, his activity had features drawn from several of them, and indeed his record stands out from that of any other figure of his time and culture (with the possible exception of John the Baptist) in that he combined learning and expertise of the scribes with the freedom and directness of a prophet. Moreover, unlike the sages of the Pharisaic schools, his teaching was inseparable from the particular circumstances which he invited people to believe now prevailed."[5]

Secondly, over against Vermes, particularly in relation to Jesus as an exorcist, we are able to set out some evidence that provides a corrective to Vermes' position. I say "corrective" for, as we have seen in the last three chapters, Jesus was indeed an exorcist at one with his Jewish milieu. But, I also say "corrective" because we have produced evidence to show that Jesus' audience may not have classed him simply as one of their rabbis.

1. Most importantly, the rabbis were most probably not the only exorcists in Palestine in Jesus' time. There were probably exorcists like Eleazar, like the Abraham of the *Genesis Apocryphon*, the exorcists represented in the magical papyri, the sons of Sceva, the Strange Exorcist, perhaps travelling Cynics, as well as rabbis like Honi and Hanina ben Dosa (see the conclusion to chapter II above). This great variety of traditions means that Jesus' audience was probably aware of a great range of exorcists and their methods, with the rabbis representing only one aspect of that variety.

2. Although, of all the exorcists in first century Palestine, Jesus was probably most like the charismatic rabbis there are some important differences between him and the rabbis.

(a) Although, on one occasion, we see the report of a rabbi using no technique, save the command to the demon to get out (§7 above), Jesus is almost (cf. Mark 5.10ff.) consistently simple in his exorcistic technique. Even Vermes recognizes this difference between Jesus and many of his contemporary exorcists when he says that "no rite is mentioned in connection with these achievements. In fact, compared with the esotericism of other methods, his own, as depicted in the Gospels, is simplcity itself."[6]

(b) In the last chapter we spent some time examining the relationship between miracle and message in the Gospels. One of the conclusions of that discussion was that this unique relationship is to be traced back to the historical Jesus. So far as I know none of the hasidim made any connection between their miracles and a message.[7]

---

5 Harvey *Constraints* 65.

6 Vermes *Jesus* 65 and n. 31.

7 On the theological intention of the rabbinic miracle stories see K. Schubert "Wunderberichte und ihr Kerygma in der rabbinischen Tradition" *Kairos* 24 (1982) 31-7.

(c) Closely related to this point is the specific significance that the historical Jesus gave to his miracles. That is, in the last chapter we saw that Jesus understood his exorcisms in particular to be the kingdom of God in action. Not only is Jesus' general preoccupation with the kingdom unique, but so also is the significance he attributed to his exorcisms. This preoccupation with the kingdom of God and its relationship to exorcism is not something found in Judaism's charismatics.[8]

(d) We noted above (§18) that although prayer was probably important for the historical Jesus, and the early Church enhanced this importance, prayer was never part of Jesus' technique of exorcism. There are examples (e.g. *b. Me'il.* 17b) of rabbis healing without prayer, but with a simple command. However, this seems to be the exception (see *m. Ber.* 5.5; *b. Ber.* 34b). Primarily on the basis of this point Harvey says:

> "All the conditions are there: Jesus both shows extraordinary powers of prolonged concentration and adopts an intimate (though not, in his case, bartering or bantering) style of address to God; and he instructs his followers in both the necessity and the power of prayer for performing miracles; but few of his mighty works are explicitly attributed to prayer."

Harvey concludes that "the style of the 'Charismatic' is not the one chosen by Jesus."[9]

If our argument is correct Vermes' view needs at least some correction. Although the nearest parallel to Jesus of Nazareth and his disciples are the rabbis and their pupils, and although Jesus the exorcist was at one with his Jewish environment, a significant aspect of his ministry that seems to mark off Jesus over against the rabbis is his healing and exorcistic ministry.[10] So, would Jesus' audience have viewed him as another ḥasid? If they did, is it not probable that, as an exorcist, Jesus would have been seen as displaying characteristics that meant that he did not fit entirely into their understanding of a wandering charismatic?[11]

---

8 See also A.R.C. Leaney's review of Vermes in *JTS* 25 (1974) 490.

9 Harvey *Constraints* 107.

10 B. Lindars "Jesus and the Pharisees" in C.K. Barrett, E. Bammel and W.D. Davies (eds.) *Donum Gentiticum: NT Studies in honour of David Daube* (Oxford: Clarendon, 1978) 51–63 sounds a warning against too ready an assumption that the gap can be closed between Jesus and the Pharisees or Galilean teachers of the period.

11 Cf. Freyne in Nickelburg and Collins (eds.) *Ideal Figures* 223–58, who criticizes Vermes on the grounds that "when all the material that might conceivably be included in the production of a suitable profile has been considered, it seems that we would still have to query the possibility of the charismatic being in itself a viable type within the overall religious context of Palestinian life in the early centuries of our era" (247). The limits set on the scope of our study preclude the need to enter into the debate as to whether or not Jesus, as an itinerant preacher, was more like a Cynic philosopher than a rabbi. See Hengel *Charismatic Leader*; Theissen *Radical Religion* 2 (1975) 84–93; Kee *Origins* 68.

We have, in the second part of this chapter, examined three possible ways in which it has been suggested Jesus' contemporaries would have assessed him. Our discussions have shown how unlikely it is that the categories of "magician" or "necromancer" would have been used. While Jesus' overall ministry may have caused him to be seen as a hasid, as an exorcist it is doubtful if those who witnessed him at work would have considered him just another of their charismatic rabbis. In the conclusions to this chapter we will make our own suggestions in this connection.

§ 27 Conclusions

In this chapter we have been considering some of the suggestions as to how Jesus the exorcist might have been understood or categorized by his contemporaries. We have cast doubt on the proposals that have so far been offered. It is unlikely that, in observing his exorcisms, bystanders would have deemed Jesus to be either a (or the) Messiah, or a magician, or a necromancer. Further, we have suggested correctives to the notion that Jesus the exorcist would have been viewed as a charismatic rabbi.[1]

How then might Jesus have been understood or assessed by his contemporaries?

Our answer needs to take account of the following points. *First*, even though we have suggested the need for correctives to the notion that Jesus the exorcist would have been viewed as a charismatic rabbi, viewed over all, his life-style and ministry most nearly matches that of such figures. Apart from the individuals mentioned above in §26 there is evidence, particularly from Josephus,[2] but also from the New Testament, that Palestine was particularly fertile soil for fostering peripatetic charismatics and rabbis.[3]

Secondly, our inquiry into the background of Jesus' ministry of exorcism highlighted a tradition of wandering charismatic healers in first century Palestine.

Before the first World War Bousset called Jesus a "wandering preacher" and more recently Theissen has characterized him as a "wandering cha-

---

1 In view of the present position of the "divine–man" debate – in which it is now generally doubted that it is a useful category to use in relation to Jesus – it is unnecessary for us to consider it in our discussion. See J.D. Kingsbury "The 'Divine Man' as the key to Mark's Christology – The End of an Era?" *Int* 35 (1981) 143–57; Dunn *Jesus* 69 and notes; C.R. Holladay *Theios Aner in Hellenistic-Judaism* (Missoula: Scholars Press, 1977); (cf. the review of Holladay by W. Telford in *JTS* 30 [1979] 246–52); Gallagher *Divine Man* chap. VI; Blackburn *Theios Anēr* 263–6.

2 Josephus *War* 2.117–9, 259, 261–3, 433; 7.253, 437–41; *Ant.* 18.2–10, 23–5, 85–7; 20.97–8, 102, 167, 169–72, 188.

3 Cf. Hengel *Charismatic Leader* 201 and Twelftree in Wenham (ed.) *Gospel Perspectives* 5, 289–310.

rismatic".[4] There are sayings in the Gospels which reflect weak ties with his family (e.g. Mark 3.21; Luke 8.19—21; 11.27—8) and home (e.g. Matthew 8.20; Mark 10.28—30) as well as a low view of material .possessions (e.g. Matthew 6.25—32; Mark 10.21; Luke 10.1—7). The stories also carry a variety of place names where Jesus is found — Jerusalem, Bethany, Galilee, Nain, Nazareth, Cana, Capernaum, Chorazin, Bethsaida and Gergesa, for example — which support the many generalizing statements in the Gospels such as "as he was going away".

On the other hand, Jesus seems to have worked from a home he had in Capernaum (Matthew 4.13; Mark 2.1; John 2.12)[5] and some of the Galilean towns mentioned are within easy walking distance of Capernaum. While it is not possible to characterize Jesus the exorcist as a homeless charismatic preacher on the margins of society, he seems to have been sufficiently mobile for it to be probable that his audience viewed him, in part, in the light of what they would have known of wandering Cynic healers.

Thirdly, in chapter II above, we have seen that there was a great variety of methods and types of exorcisms and exorcists in the traditions. There were traditions such as those in the magical papyri which primarily preserved the techniques of exorcists. There were stories of healings in which, like that of Eleazar by Josephus, the exorcist was of little significance. There were stories, like those of Abraham in the *Genesis Apocryphon*, where the healer was of central importance. There was material, both Hellenistic and Jewish, which contained stories of men who were exorcists as well as prophets or philosophers. There were traditions in which exorcisms relied on special techniques and others which relied on the personal force of the exorcist, and others which relied on a combination of these extreme alternatives.

With regard to this variety we concluded that the most reasonable categories applicable to the material are that the success of some exorcisms depended on the *performance* of special traditions, while others depended on the *person* of the exorcist himself for their effectiveness.

Fourthly, apart from the Synoptic tradition's objective to portray Jesus as the Messiah and later generations' accusation of magic, the earliest layers of the Jesus tradition give no hint of an attempt to categorize Jesus along any of the lines reviewed earlier in this chapter. In fact, the only clear category brought to bear on Jesus' activity was one of "good", that is, from God, or "evil", that is, from Satan (Matthew 12.24ff./Luke 11.15ff.).

---

4 Bousset *Kyrios Christos* 117 and Theissen *Followers* chap. 2 and also F.H. Borsch "Jesus, the Wandering Preacher?" in Hooker and Hickling (eds.) *What about the NT?* 45–63.

5 Further see E.F.F. Bishop "Jesus and Capernaum" *CBQ* 15 (1953) 427–37.

Fifthly, it cannot even be maintained that the exorcisms of Jesus would have suggested the divine origin of Jesus[6] for, as the stories of Abraham in the *Genesis Apocryphon* and of Noah in *Jubilees* indicate, such stories could simply be used to reflect the upright character of the exorcist.[7]

Therefore, it is appropriate that we should conclude this discussion with the suggestion, *not* that *as an exorcist* Jesus "transcended" the categories of the first century.[8] Rather *it is improbable that his contemporaries saw him as either, (a) fitting or could have fitted him into any categories* or, (b) *attached any "labels" to him that were available to them.* We can agree with Hengel when he says:

"Even within the characterization we have preferred, of an 'eschatological charismatic', he remains in the last resort incommensuarble, and so basically confounds every attempt to fit him into the categories suggested by the phenomenology or sociology of religion."[9]

It is not surprising then that his audience is said to have probably reflected on whether or not he was a "good" or "evil" healer (cf. Matthew 12.24ff./Luke 11.15ff.; Acts 10.38). We can also concur with a conclusion of Harvey's.

"Jesus evidently opted for a type of miraculous healing which was bound to be dangerously ambiguous; but, at least according to the records, he carried it out with the absolute minimum of those technical procedures which would most surely have aroused suspicion about his true credentials and motives."[10]

For the early Church the exorcisms of Jesus were seen as yet another aspect of his ministry, albeit a very important aspect. Perhaps for Mark, in particular, it was seen as the most important part of Jesus' ministry, which was conscripted into the programme of showing that Jesus was the Messiah.[11]

---

6   Cf. Tiede *Charismatic* chap. 3.

7   See Twelftree *Christ* 30–1.

8   Cf. Morris *Cross* 56f.

9   Hengel *Charismatic Leader* 69. In the context of a discussion of Jesus as a teacher Hengel also says that ". . . Jesus stood *outside any discoverable uniform teaching tradition of Judaism.* It is not possible to assign him a place within the development of contemporary Jewish traditions" (his emphasis, 49). See also Koester *Introduction* II, 77–8 and Bühner in *EvT* 43 (1983) 156–75, esp. 174–5.

10   Harvey *Constraints* 109.

11   Further see Twelftree *Christ*.

VI
Jesus The Exorcist: His Self-Understanding

§ 28 Introduction

The historian's picture of Jesus as an exorcist involves not only the recovery of the outward features of this aspect of his ministry but, also, so far as it is possible, some idea of Jesus' self-understanding. This task is also of interest to modern theology and the present day debate on exorcism.[1]

However, in the wake of Schweitzer's exposure, much of the nineteenth century reconstruction of Jesus' self-understanding has been shown to tell us more about nineteenth century theology than about the Jesus of the first century. One result of this has been the denial that it is possible to know much or anything about the mind of the historical Jesus. For example, in 1926 Fridrichsen wrote; "What took place in the depths of Jesus' soul will always remain a mystery no source will be able to uncover ... "[2]

Nevertheless, as James Dunn says,

"While a biography of Jesus is indeed impossible, particularly a biography in the modern sense which traces out the hero's growth in self-awareness and in understanding of himself and his world, that does not mean that we can say nothing at all about Jesus' self–consciousness and spiritual experience at *some* points in his ministry."[3]

So, what we will do in this brief chapter is test this last statement and see if it is possible to say something about Jesus' understanding of his exorcisms, viz. — How did Jesus view himself as an exorcist? and, What did he think he was doing?

---

1 See particularly Dunn *Jesus* 13. Following Charlesworth *Jesus Within Judaism* 131, I have avoided the term "self–consciousness" as "it might be misunderstood as reminiscent of nineteenth–century romanticism and the pursuit of a biography on Jesus." The self–understanding of Jesus in his ministry is also seen in his teaching, see Lindars in Barrett, Bammel and Davies (eds.) *Donum Gentilicum* 51–63. For literature on Jesus' self–understanding see Evans *Jesus Research* 128–38.

2 Fridrichsen *Miracle* 72. Cf. Bultmann *Jesus and the Word* 14; D. Nineham "Epilogue" in J. Hick (ed.) *The Myth of God Incarnate* (London: SCM, 1977) 188.

3 Dunn *Jesus* 12–13, his emphasis. Cf. Charlesworth *Jesus Within Judaism* 131–64; Leivestad *Jesus* 12.

§ 29 Exorcism and Eschatology

Jesus was well aware that he was not the only exorcist in the community. In a debate with some of his opponents he asks rhetorically about the methods of some other Jewish exorcists (Matthew 12.27/Luke 11.19). On another occasion John reports to Jesus that the disciples had seen someone using his name to cast out demons. Also, from the use of his name in incantations, Jesus would have been able to conclude that he was considered a successful and powerful exorcist.

In chapter III we saw that it is the collection of sayings now found in the Beelzebul Controversy pericope which has the greatest potential in telling us about Jesus' views of his exorcisms (see §10 above). Arguably the most important saying in the Beelzebul Controversy pericope is the Spirit/finger saying (Matthew 12.28/Luke 11.20). We have already arued for its authenticity (§10 above). We can now ask, what does it tell us about Jesus' understanding of his exorcisms?

In *Jesus and the Spirit* James Dunn has addressed this question and one of his answers is that "Jesus believed that he cast out demons by the power of God" (p. 47). However, it is probably better to say that it was by the *Spirit* of God that Jesus cast out demons for, it is the *Spirit* that is mentioned in the tradition here. Jesus was quite conscious that the source of his power-authority for exorcism was in the wholly new eschatological Spirit of God, and not simply in himself or his techniques.

It is misleadning to say, as does James Dunn, that in this verse we can see that Jesus is aware of an "otherly" power as if this was particularly significant here, for such experience was common to holy men.[1] Some of the exoricsts mentioned in chapter II were aware of, and relied upon, just this kind of power; a power-authority outside themselves.

But, we have also argued that not only is "Spirit" significant in this verse but so also is the "I" (§10 above). Thus, Jesus was not simply claiming that the exorcisms performed by or through the eschatological *Spirit* of God meant that the kingdom of God had come, but that those

---

1 Dunn *Jesus* 47, though see his point (b) there. See Borg *Conflict* 253.

exorcisms which *he* performed — by or through the eschatological Spirit of God — meant that the kingdom of God had come. In other words, we can say that the awareness of the presence and empowering of the eschatological Holy Spirit had so given him a consciousness of his messianic identity that for Jesus the hoped-for kingdom had arrived, not only because of the activity of the Holy Spirit, but also because it was *he* who, in the Spirit, was casting out demons. Therefore, it is only half correct to say "Where the *Spirit* is there is the kingdom."[2] Jesus' understanding is better reflected by saying that where the *Spirit* is operative in *Jesus* there is the kingdom.[3]

From what has been said so far, for Jesus, the exorcisms were not preparatory for the coming of the kingdom,[4] but were themselves the kingdom of God in operation. This conclusion depends, to some extent, on ἔφθασεν ("has come") in Matthew 12.28/Luke 11.20. However, Sanders says that in interpreting this verse: ". . . it seems to me obviously dubious to lean so heavily on the meaning of the verb ἔφθασεν." And, he continues, "How can we know that the Greek accurately captures not only something Jesus said but also the nuance which he intended to convey?" Sanders' reply is that "clearly we cannot."[5] Of course, in the nature of historical enquiry, we cannot finally know whether or not the Greek ἔφθασεν reflects what Jesus said, or a nuance he intended. However, ἔφθασεν (and probably ἤγγικεν as well, Mark 1.15) is most likely to be a translation of קרב which means "to come" or "to arrive".[6] So, despite Sanders' hesitation, at the very least, on the basis of this verse, we can say that Jesus understood his exorcisms as having something to do with the coming of the kingdom of God, whether or not that "coming" was imminent, taking place or realized. In turn, we can agree with Dunn when he says, "So far as Jesus was concerned, the exercise of this power [in exorcism] was *evidence that the longed-for kingdom of God had already come upon his hearers*; his exorcisms demonstrated that the last days were already present."[7] In the light of Matthew 12.28/Luke 11.20, we can go

---

2 Dunn *Jesus* 49 and his "Spirit and Kingdom" *ExpTim* 82 (1970–1) 39, his emphasis.

3 Dunn almost says this in *ExpTim* 82 (1970–1) 39. Cf. Dunn *Jesus* 47f. Leivestad *Jesus* 106 says that the "I" of this saying must be emphasized. Bultmann, *History* 239, says Jesus "concludes from his success that the Kingdom of God has come." This can hardly be, for, there is no question that other exorcists were successful – even in Jesus' eyes. Cf. Mark 9.38/Luke 9.49f.; Matt 12.27/Luke 11.19.

4 As Betz *NovT* 2 (1958) 116–37. Further, see the discussion in Beasley–Murray *Jesus and the Kingdom* 75–80.

5 Sanders *Jesus* 134.

6 Cf. Kümmel *Promise* 106 n. 6; Dalman *Words* 107 and Caragounis *TynBul* 40 (1989) 12–23.

7 Dunn *Jesus* 47 (his emphasis). He goes on to say,

further and suggest that Jesus believed that *where the Spirit was operating in him there was the coming of the kingdom of God.*[8] This self-understanding of Jesus is well expressed in the Gospel of Thomas: "Jesus said, he who is near me is near the fire, and he who is far from me is far from the kingdom" (82). That is, the coming of the kingdom is not only linked to Jesus' message nor even his words and actions but with the person of Jesus.[9]

Another authentic saying in the Beelzebul Controversy pericope, to which we need draw attention, is the parable of the Strong Man (Mark 3.27/Matthew 12.29 and Luke 11.21f., see §10 above). We have shown there that in this parable Jesus takes his exorcisms to be the casting out or defeat of Satan.

According to literature reflecting thinking of the New Testament period, the binding of the powers of evil or the demise of Satan was expected in the Messianic Age (e.g. Isaiah 24.21f.; *1 Enoch* 10.4ff.; 11ff.; 1QS 4.18f.).[10] When we were reviewing the way others assessed Jesus the exorcist we saw that the consensus of scholarly opinion is that in the first century it was *expected* that the Messiah would defeat Satan by casting out demons (see §23 above). This suggestion is represented in Matthew

---

"We should not permit our familiarity with this aspect of Jesus' preaching to dull the edge of this assertion. For this was an astonishing and audacious claim. The *eschatological* kingdom was *already present!*" (his emphasis).

See also Dunn and Twelftree *Churchman* 94 (1980) 220. While this claim that the kingdom had already dawned is unique to Jesus we should not over emphasize the difference between Jesus and the thinking of his contemporaries who saw the present as the last moments of this world. See 2 Bar 85.10 (early second century AD); 4 Ezra 5.50–5; 14.10 (late first century AD); J.H. Charlesworth "The Historical Jesus in the Light of Writings Contemporaneous with Him" *ANRW* II.25.1 (1982) 460–9.

8 Cf. Twelftree in Wenham and Blomberg (eds.) *Gospel Perspectives* 6. Cf. R. Bultmann *Theology of the NT* 2 vols. (London: SCM, 1952 and 1955) I, 7 ". . .what are the signs of the time? He himself! *His presence, his deeds, his message!*" (his emphasis); Borg *Conflict* 73, 253. Further on Jesus' self-understanding ("if *I* cast out demons") see Leivestad *Jesus* 106. In a review article of G. Theissen's *Urchristliche Wundergeschichten*, Achtemeier notes that Theissen thinks that:

"Because the present calamitous times have been broken by Jesus' miracles, episodic salvation could occur. Because such episodic salvation/healing could occur, one could announce that future salvation was already at hand in the present."

But, says Achtemeier: ". . . what of the miracle stories themselves? Where in them is a word about this eschatological dimension of the miracles?" ("An Imperfect Union. Reflections on Gerd Theissen, *Urchristliche Wundergeschichten*" in Funk [ed.] *Early Christian Miracle Stories* 65). Surely Matt 12.28/Luke 11.20 supplies the eschatological framework for, at the least, the exorcisms of Jesus (cf. Jesus' answer to John the Baptist Matt 11.2–6/Luke 7.18–23).

9 See also R.B. Gärtner "The Person of Jesus and the Kingdom of God" *Today* 27 (1970) 32–43, esp. 37 and 43. On Q's caution in relation to this understanding of exorcism in its tradition see Mearns *SJT* 40 (1987) 189–210.

10 See Dunn and Twelftree in *Churchman* 94 (1980) 220 and n. 31.

where, on seeing Jesus cast out a demon, an amazed crowd asks "can this be the Son of David?" (12.23). But, in examining the evidence that speaks of the Coming One's involvement in exorcism and the defeat of Satan two things emerged. *First*, all connections between a Messianic individual, exorcism and the defeat of Satan were found in material that had been either written or redacted by Christians. *Second*, the *Assumption of Moses* 10.1 and 3, which is potentially useful in understanding first century Messianic expectation, simply anticipates the demise of Satan in the New Age (see §23 above). Thus — as we concluded at the end of §23 above — prior to the New Testament even though the end of Satan was expected in the eschaton,[11] there is no specific connection made between exorcism and eschatology. That the connection is found in authentic words of Jesus but not found before Jesus, it appears that *it was Jesus himself who made this connection between exorcism and eschatology.*[12]

But, what was the nature of the defeat of Satan that Jesus had in mind? Were the exorcisms the final and complete defeat, or perhaps the beginning of the defeat of Satan? Or what? These questions arise because quite different notions of the defeat of Satan can be detected in the Gospel traditions.

Matthew has the Beelzebul sayings about the defeat of Satan tied to Jesus' exorcisms (12.25—9). But, alongside this we need to place a number of other passages from Matthew which exhibit a different view. The first passage is 8.29b where Matthew adds (see §7 above) to the demon's question "What do you want with us . . .?" — the notion of them being tormented *before their time*. The implication of this is that it is Matthew who thought that the torment of the demons lay in the future beyond Jesus' exorcisms. With this future element, the two passages we are about to mention, and the use of "torment" in Revelation of the last time (14.11; 20.10; cf. 9.5; 18.7, 10, 15) it seems likely that Matthew places the final torment of the demons in the last time.

The second pericope to consider is the parable of the Wheat and the Tares (Matthew 13.24—30). I have argued elsewhere that the main features of this parable are probably to be traced back to the historical Jesus, including the reference to the destruction of the enemy's work in the eschaton.[13]

---

11 Cf. O. Böcher "Exorzismus" in *Theologische Realenzyklopädie* 10 (Berlin and New York: de Gruyter, 1982) 749.

12 In contrast to this, having surveyed the cult of Asclepius Kee says that "there is no suggestion that the healing had any meaning outside of itself; it is not a pointer to a spiritual transformation or a promise of anything transcendent" (*Miracle* 87). On miracles in early Judaism see A. Guttmann "The Significance of Miracles for Talmudic Judaism" *HUCA* 20 (1947) 363–406.

13 Twelftree *Christ* 80–1.

The third passage to be noted is 13.36—43 — the interpretation of the parable of the Wheat and the Tares — which Jeremias has convincingly shown to be the work of Matthew.[14] Here the devil is at work *until the final judgement* when all causes of sin and all evil doers will be thrown into the fire.

The fourth and perhaps clearest expression of when Matthew thinks Satán will finally be defeated is 25.41, "Depart from me, you cursed, into the *eternal fire* prepared for the devil and his angels." This verse comes in a unit on the Last Judgement (25.31—46) that is so thoroughly Matthean that it may all be his own work.[15] In this verse, and the previous two, the end of Satan for Matthew is at the end of time, the last judgement.

From this investigation of the view of the end of Satan in Matthew we see that he has picked up the view from a tradition which has its origin in the life of the historical Jesus — at least in the instance of the parable of Wheat and the Tares — that Satan is to be finally defeated in the last judgement. But, along side this tradition is the view (compare, e.g. Matthew 12.29), which also most probably has its origin in the life of the historical Jesus, that the defeat of Satan was taking place in the exorcistic ministry of Jesus.

Mark's view is less clear. However, in so far as the disciples are paradigms of the post-Easter Church and they have been given the task of casting out demons (6.7—12; [cf. 16.12]) he does not see Satan as finally or completely defeated in the exorcistic ministry of Jesus. Yet, again, we see that Jesus' exorcisms are also associated with the defeat of Satan (3.27).

Like the other two Synoptic Evangelists, Luke has the Beelzebul sayings relating the exorcisms of Jesus and the casting out of Satan. Further, in 10.18 he records that Jesus says he saw Satan falling while the disciples were away on a mission that included casting out demons. But, he still sees Satan active after the end of Jesus' healing ministry in Satan's inspiration of Judas' betrayal (22.3, cf. 31). Notably, Luke has Paul performing an exorcism (Acts 16.16—18). Thus, for Luke, Satan was not finally nor completely defeated in Jesus' exorcisms nor any other part of his ministry.

---

14 Jeremias *Parables* 224–5.
15 Cf. R.H. Stein *An Introduction to the Parables of Jesus* (Philadelphia: Westminster, 1981) 143, "The great majority of scholars argue for the view that the interpretation is essentially a Matthean creation, and for many Jeremias' analysis of this passage makes it 'impossible to avoid the conclusion that the interpretation of the parable of the Tares is the work of Matthew himself [quoting Jeremias *Parables* 84–5]' Others have attempted to find in the interpretation a pre–Matthean layer of the tradition [citing J.D. Crossan "The Seed Parables of Jesus" *JBL* 92 (1973) 260–1], but in essence the interpretation is still seen as being primarily the work of Matthew."

John's Gospel has a number of verses that let us see what he thought of the defeat of Satan. The absence of exorcism in the Fourth Gospel means that the defeat of Satan could hardly be linked to them. Particularly important is 12.31. Jesus is talking about his death and says "now shall the ruler of this world be cast out." It is unlikely that we could trace this back to the historical Jesus.[16] Here the defeat of Satan, the ruler of this world, is directly linked with the death of Jesus (cf. 14.30 and 16.11). Yet, over against this we must put Jesus' prayer "that you should keep them from the evil one" (17.15).[17] So, even if John saw Satan as being defeated in the death of Jesus he was certainly not saying Satan was finally destroyed for the early community felt that it still had to deal with him.

The question that arises out of this discussion is, What is the origin of these views, and, importantly for our purposes, which view or views can be traced back to the historical Jesus?

We have argued that the Spirit/finger saying of Matthew 12.28/Luke 11.20 is a faithful reflection of the intention of the historical Jesus in relation to his exorcisms. That is, Jesus saw his exorcisms as having something to do with the defeat of Satan. Yet, we see that there is material in the Jesus tradition that assumes the continuing reality and activity of Satan until the end of the age. The amount of material is not great; it includes the commission in Mark 16.17, the parable of the Wheat and the Tares (Matthew 13.24—30), the explanation of the parable of the Wheat and the Tares (Matthew 13.36—43), the parable of the Net and its explanation (Matthew 13.47—50), and the parable of the Sheep and Goats (Matthew 25.1—46). Although only the parable of the Wheat and the Tares stands up to historical scrutiny we have in this parable evidence that the historical Jesus associated the defeat of Satan and evil with the last judgement.[18]

Therefore, on the one hand, Jesus associates his exorcism with the defeat of Satan, yet, on the other hand, he sees the defeat of Satan as taking place in the last judgement. How are we to resolve this apparent tension? The view of C.K. Barrett probably reflects that of most scholars, even though he is not talking about the historical Jesus: "The devil is defeated, but he is not destroyed. The Church was too well acquainted with his devices to suppose that Satan had died."[19] Is this view correct?

---

16 "The Ruler of this World" occurs in the NT only in John. Cf. R. Schnackenburgh *The Gospel According to St. John* 2 vols. (London: Burns and Oates, 1968 and 1980) II, 390ff. and Bultmann *John* 431.

17 Bultmann *John* 508 and n. 1.

18 Twelftree *Christ* 80–1.

19 Barrett *Spirit* 52.

For a resolution of the problem we need to turn to literature reflecting views of the period in which the defeat of Satan is pictured with the same tension.[20] The earliest reference that is of value to us is in the so-called *Isaiah Apocalyse* (Isaiah 24—27). Isaiah 24.22 reads:

"They [the host of heaven] will be gathered
  together as prisoners in a pit;
they will be shut up in a prison,
  and after many days they will be punished."

The identity of the "host of heaven" is not clear but they are probably the rebellious powers in heaven thought to be controlling or manipulating the heathen nations (cf. Deuteronomy 32.8 and Daniel 10.13). In the Isaiah passage the defeat of the rebellious powers of heaven is pictured as taking place in two distinct stages. *I Enoch* develops this simple picture, clarifying how the first century mind probably understood the nature of the two stages of the defeat.

"And . . . the Lord said to Raphael, 'Bind Azaz'el hand and foot (and) throw him into the darkness!' And he made a hole in the desert which was in Duda'el and cast him there; he threw on top of him rugged sharp rocks. And he covered his face in order that he may not see the light; and in order that he may be sent into the fire on the great day of judgment" (*I Enoch* 10.4–6).

The first stage, depicted in the picture of covering Azazel with rugged sharp rocks, is described as a "binding"; a preparation for the final and complete destruction of the leader of the evil minions.[21] A little further on in *I Enoch* 10.11—13 the initial stage of the defeat is also described as one of binding. The second stage is said to take place at the great day of judgement and the picture is one of fire (cf. 19.1). A few lines further on in chapter 10 the same is said of the minions of Semyaza, another representation of Satan.

". . . bind them for seventy generations underneath the rocks of the ground until the day of their judgment and of their consummation, until the eternal judgment is concluded" (10.12; cf. 18.14–9.2; 21.6–10; 90.23–7 and also *Jubilees* 5.6–10; 10.5–9.

This two stage notion of the defeat of Satan and his angels fits well with what we saw reflected of the view of the historical Jesus. However, we need to note that, while the imagery of the material we have just cited mentioned nothing about how the leader of the evil minions was to be bound, Jesus clearly equates the first or preliminary stage of the defeat of Satan with his exorcisms (Matthew 12.28/Luke 11.20). As the parable of the

---

20 Isa 24.21f.; *1 Enoch* 10.4–6, 12f.; 18.14–19.2; 21.6f.; 90.23–4; *Jub.* 5.5–10; 10.4–9. See also 2 Pet 2.4; Jude 6; Rev 20.1–3. Cf. Moore *Judaism* II, 338–45.

21 The place "Dudael" is a puzzle. It could derive from "the jagged mountains of God" (<'A>δουδαήλ) though see M.A. Knibb (ed.) *The Ethiopic Book of Enoch* in consultation with E. Ullendorff 2 vols. (Oxford: Clarendon, 1978) 2, 87 n. and M. Black *The Book of Enoch or 1 Enoch* (Leiden: Brill, 1985) 133–5.

Wheat and the Tares shows (Matthew 13.24—30), Jesus maintained the view, prevalent in the period, that the second and final stage of the defeat was to take place in the last judgement.

Exorcism was then probably of great importance, even of central importance to Jesus in the conception of his ministry. But, his reply to John the Baptist warns us against thinking that Jesus saw his exorcisms as of exclusive importance. In our discussion of Jesus' answer to John the Baptist (§12 above) we concluded that Jesus probably did not mention his exorcisms when he was describing the "signs of the times" to John's disciples (contrast Luke 7.21). Thus, for Jesus, the kingdom was present because of his exorcisms, and also because of the preaching to the poor and other miracles.[22]

We saw in chapter II that names of exorcists with powerful reputations were used by others as power-authorities for their exorcisms. We also saw that Jesus was aware that others were using his name in their exorcisms (Mark 9.38f./Luke 9.49f.; Luke 10.17—20). Might we not then presume that this would have been reflected in his own self-understanding — that he was indeed a powerful exorcist?

We have seen in the last few pages that it is possible to say something about Jesus' self-understanding in relation to his exorcisms. In the words of Dunn (referring particularly to the claims in Matthew 12.28/Luke 11.20 and Luke 10.18): "These claims imply *a clear sense of the eschatological distinctiveness of his power*: Jesus' mighty acts were in his own eyes as epochal as the miracles of the Exodus and likewise heralded a new age."[23]

In this section we have been able to show that *Jesus was the first to make the connection between exorcism and eschatology. For him, his exorcisms were the first or preliminary binding of Satan who would finally be destroyed in the eschaton.*

---

22 Luke, in particular, picks up and develops this theme. See further §5 n. 7 above.
23 Dunn *Jesus* 48, his emphasis.

VII

§ 30 Conclusions

This study has been an attempt to contribute to our knowledge of the historical Jesus. Such an enterprise is important because of the presupposition that the life, ministry and passion of the earthly Jesus were important to the early Church and remain of key significance for the contemporary Church. The particular focus of this study has been the reported ministry of exorcism of Jesus. The set of three inter-related questions motivating this book has been: If Jesus was an exorcist, (a) What did the first reports of his activities as an exorcist contain? (b) How would he have been viewed by those who saw him at work? and (c) How did Jesus understand his ministry of exorcism? This study is potentially profitable because of the contrast between the relative lack of interest in Jesus' ministry of exorcism shown in modern "lives" of Jesus, and the Synoptic Gospels' great interest in Jesus as an exorcist.

1. The first result we can record from our study is that we are able unhesitatingly to support the view that Jesus was an exorcist. And, we need to carry this conclusion forward in two directions. First, Gospel traditions, other New Testament writings and extra canonical data are agreed that Jesus was a particularly successful and powerful exorcist. This is evidenced, for example, by his name soon being taken up as a power-authority by his contemporary or near contemporary exorcists. Second, it is mistaken for modern "lives" of Jesus virtually to ignore this aspect of the ministry of the historical Jesus or to relegate it to a subsection of a small section on his reported miracles. Such an approach may make the picture of a "life" of Jesus more palatable to twentieth century Christians but the result is a distorted picture of the historical Jesus. The picture of the Jesus we have sketched may well be strange to our "enlightened" eyes.

The nature of the Gospel traditions means it is no longer possible to determine how much of Jesus' time was taken with performing exorcisms. Yet, as our study has shown, exorcism was one of the most obvious and important aspects of his ministry, both from the perspective of Jesus and the later Gospel writers. Therefore, to sketch a picture of the historical Jesus without significant reference to his ministry of exorcism is to produce a distortion of the evidence.

2. The first century Palestinian background against which we should place Jesus the exorcist seems to have been rich in variety of notions available on exorcism and exorcists. The intellectual currency of the time was wider than that represented by the Jewish charismatics and their healing methods. First century Palestinians were most probably well aware of, and practised forms of exorcism that are represented in the ancient Babylonian and Egyptian texts and papyri as well as the later magical papyri. Tobit, *Jubilees*, the Dead Sea Scrolls, *LAB*, the New Testament itself, Josephus, rabbinic literature, Lucian and Philostratus, most probably represent the kinds of exorcists that would have been familiar to Jesus' observers. However, it seems mistaken to rely on the New Testament Apocrypha and the Testament of Solomon to give us independent information on first century ideas.

In first century Palestine there were most probably exorcists like the Eleazar of Josephus' story, like the Abraham of the *Genesis Apocryphon*, like those reflected in the magical papyri, like the Strange Exorcist, the Jewish exorcists of the Beelzebul Controversy, the sons of Sceva, the wandering Cynic healer-philosophers, as well as the Jewish charismatics.

Moreover, if this if right, then there were exorcisms that ranged between those which were thought to be successful because of what was said in the incantations, and done in the rituals, and on the other hand there were those that were thought to be successful because of who performed the healing. The individuals of this later category with powers of exorcism are found both as legendary figures in literature as well as figures in history. These individuals, including Jesus of Nazareth, indigenous to first century Palestine, were men whose reputable character and wisdom were thought to be reflected in miracles done either in their name or actually by them. When, in the light of this, we examine the principal data on Jesus and exorcism a number of points emerge.

3. Exorcism stories have neither been appended to the Gospel tradition from other traditions nor rewritten in the light of other traditions. The Jesus behind the Gospels is at one within his environment not because the early Church adjusted the tradition but because Jesus the exorcist was a man of his time.

4. Virtually all of the techniques of Jesus the exorcist would have been familiar to those who observed him. The exorcism from a distance, the initial dramatic confrontation between Jesus and the demoniacs which gave rise to verbal exchanges in which the demon(iac) sought defence and leniency, Jesus' commanding words or incantations to the demon, the use of objects (pigs!) to provide an alternative habitat for the evicted demons and the violence associated with his exorcisms all cause Jesus to appear at one with his fellow exorcists.

5. Yet, we cannot ignore some quite significant factors that, to varying degrees, most probably set Jesus apart from his contemporary exorcists. Some exorcisms of the period, like those performed by rabbi Simeon and Apollonius, were effective without mechanical aids. These, and those performed by Jesus, would probably have been marked as relatively distinctive. Also, like few of his contemporaries Jesus appeared to use no prayers, as some of the rabbis may have, nor was he reported as invoking any power-authority or as using a powerful name. That is, Jesus never adjures or binds a demon *by* an outside authority.

6. So far as we can see from this study, those who observed Jesus as an exorcist did not accuse him of being a magician. In fact, as we concluded at the end of §25 above, it is reasonable to suppose that if the Gospel writers or their traditions knew of any charge of magic they would have taken the opportunity to spell it out and refute it as they had done with other criticisms of Jesus. The criticism, a most horrific criticism of Jesus in relation to his exorcism, was that he was evil rather than good; operating under the aegis of Satan rather than God. The charge that Jesus was a magician is evidenced only from second and third century literature onwards.

The evidence, as we saw it, also does not allow us to conclude that Jesus' observers thought him a necromancer or even simply another of their charismatics. Rather, there seems to have been such a variety of notions of exorcism and exorcists available in first century Palestine that Jesus was probably not categorized by his contemporaries beyond being good or evil.

7. Matthew 12.23 alleges that the crowd responded to an exorcism by acclaiming Jesus to be the Messiah; "Can this be the Son of David?" However, we concluded that this verse has a history no earlier than Matthew's redaction. That the crowd might have thought Jesus' exorcism marked him as the Messiah assumes that, in the first century, people expected the Messiah to be an exorcist. Up to the present this has been an assumption of scholarship. However, no certainly pre-Christian literature anticipates a messianic figure doing battle with Satan through the relatively ordinary healing of exorcism. In turn, we conclude that it was Jesus who first made the connection between exorcism and eschatology. It was he who associated the notion of the cosmic, supernatural battle against the kingdom of Satan in the eschaton with the very act of an ordinary exorcism. Satan was being defeated and the coming of the kingdom of the God was taking place in his exorcisms (cf. the parable of the Strong Man).

8. First century Palestinians believed — and Jesus shared the view — that Satan's defeat would take place in two stages. In the beginning of the

eschaton Satan would be bound so that, in the end, he could be finally destroyed. It seems that Jesus saw his, and the exorcisms of his disciples, as the first stage of the defeat of Satan.

9. For Jesus, an exorcism was a confrontation between himself and the demonic in which the demonic was defeated. Here, as in his belief that he was undertaking the first stage of the defeat of Satan, we touch on a most unique feature of Jesus' understanding of his exorcisms. He is seen to rely on his own power-authority by saying "I command . . ." Yet, in a round-about way, he informs his critics that he is operating by the eschatological Spirit of God (Matthew 12.28/Luke 11.20). The unique and unprecedented aspect of Jesus' exorcisms is that he gave profound meaning to the relatively ordinary event of an exorcism.

Part of the significance Jesus attributed to his exorcism is apparent in the Spirit/finger saying (Matthew 12.28/Luke 11.20) where he assigns a connection between exorcism and eschatology. Lest it be thought we are resting too much on this one verse it is worth recalling that, indirectly, the saying in Luke 10.18 shows the eschatological significance Jesus attributed to exorcism as does the parable of the Strong Man. That, in general, Jesus saw eschatological significance in his ministry is seen by his choice of twelve disciples and his "cleansing" of the Temple.

Over against the idea that Jesus considered that Satan was defeated and that the kingdom had come because of the coming of the eschatological Spirit, it is probably a more faithful representation of Jesus' understanding of his exoricisms to say that where *the Spirit was operating in him there was the focus of the coming of the kingdom.* This means that we can probably say that Jesus would have been aware of considerable uniqueness in his relation to God and to what he thought God was doing around him (cf. Matthew 11.2—6/Luke 7.18—23).

Jesus the exorcist was a man of his time, performing exorcisms in much the same way as some of his wandering exorcist contemporaries. However, while exorcism was by no means the only aspect of his ministry, particularly in his exorcisms (carried out by the power-authority of the eschatological Spirit) he believed the first stage in the defeat of Satan and his kingdom was taking place in order that the kingdom of God could come.

Bibliography

I. Primary Texts and Sources

Allegro, J.M. and Anderson, A.A. *Discoveries in the Judaean Desert of Jordan V:1 (4Q-158-4Q186)* (Oxford: Clarendon, 1968).

Allison, F.G. *Menander: The Principal Fragments* LCL (London: Heinemann and New York: Putnam, 1921).

Audollent, A. (ed.) *Defixionum Tabellae* (Frankfurt Main: Minerva GmbH, Unveränderter Nachdruck, 1967).

Avigad, N. and Yadin, Y. *A Genesis Apocryphon: A Scroll from the Wilderness of Judea* (Jerusalem: Hebrew University and Magnes Press, 1956).

Barthélemy, D. and Milik, J.T. *Discoveries in the Judaean Desert I: Qumran Cave I* (Oxford: Clarendon, 1955).

Baillet, M. *Discoveries in the Judaean Desert VII: Qumran Grotte 4 III (4Q482-4Q-520)* (Oxford: Clarendon, 1982).

Baillet, M., Milik, J.T. and de Vaux, R. *Discoveries in the Judaean Desert of Jordan III: Les petites grottes de Qumrân* (Oxford: Clarendon, 1962).

Bell, H.I., Nock, A.D. and Thompson, H. "Magical Texts from a Bilingual Papyrus in the British Museum" *Proceedings of the British Association* 17 (1931) 235-87.

Betz, H.D. (ed.) *The Greek Magical Papyri in Translation* (Chicago: University of Chicago Press, 1986).

Blau, L.B. *Das altjüdische Zauberwesen* (Strasbourg: Trübner, 1898).

Bourghouts, J.F. (ed.) *Ancient Egyptian Magical Texts, Nisaba 9* (Leiden: Brill, 1978).

-- *The Magical Texts of Papyrus Leiden I, 348* (Leiden: Brill, 1971).

Braude, W.G. *Pesikta rabbati* 2 vols. (New Haven: Yale University Press, 1968).

Bryce, H. *The Seven Books of Arnobius Adversus Gentes* ANCL vol. 19 (Edinburgh: T & T Clark, 1871).

Burrows, M. (et al.) (eds.) *The Dead Sea Scrolls of St. Mark's Monastry* I The Isaiah[a] Manuscript and Habakkuk Commentary (New Haven: American Schools of Oriental Research, 1950).

-- *The Dead Sea Scrolls of St. Mark's Monastery* II/2 The Manual of Disciple (New Haven: American Schools of Oriental Research, 1951).

Chadwick, H. (ed.) *Origen: Contra Celsum* (Cambridge: Cambridge University Press, 1980).

Charles, R.H. (ed.) *The Apocrypha and Pseudepigrapha of the Old Testament* 2 vols. (Oxford: Clarendon, 1913).

-- *The Ascension of Isaiah* (London: Black, 1900).

-- *The Assumption of Moses* (London: Black, 1897).

Charlesworth, J.H. (ed.) *The Discovery of a Dead Sea Scroll (4Q Therapeia): Its Importance in the History of Medicine and Jesus Research* (Lubbock, TX: Texas Tech University Press, 1985).

-- *The Old Testament Pseudepigrapha* 2 vols. (Garden City, NY: Doubleday & Co., 1983 and 1985).

Cohoon, J.W. and Crosby, H.L. *Dio Chrysostom* LCL, 5 vols. (London: Heinemann and Cambridge, MA: Harvard University Press, 1932–51).

Colson, F.H. and Whittaker, G.H. (et al.) (eds.) *Philo* LCL, 12 vols. (Cambridge, MA: Harvard University Press and London: Heinemann, 1929–53).

Conybeare, F.C. (ed.) *Philostratus: The Life of Apollonius* LCL, 2 vols. (Cambridge, MA: Harvard University Press and London: Heinemann, 1948).

Cross, F.M. "Fragments of the Prayer of Nabonidus" *IEJ* 34 (1984) 260–4.

Danby, H. *The Mishnah* (Oxford: Oxford University Press, 1933).

Delling, G. (ed.) *Antike Wundertexte*. KIT, 79^2 (Berlin: de Gruyter, 1960).

Denis, A.-M. (ed.) *Fragmenta Pseudepigraphorum Quae Supersunt Graeca* PVTG, 3 (Leiden: Brill, 1970).

Diehl, E. (ed.) *Anthologia Lyrica Graeca* BSGRT, 3 vols. (Leipzig: Teubner, 1925).

Dods, M. Reith, G. and Pratten, B.P. *The Writings of Justin Martyr and Athenagoras* AN-CL vol. 2 (Edinburgh: T & T Clark, 1867).

Downing, F.G. (ed.) *The Christ and the Cynics* (Sheffield: JSOT, 1988).

Dupont-Sommer, A. *The Essene Writings from Qumran* (Oxford: Blackwell, 1961).

Epstein, I. (ed.) *The Babylonian Talmud* 34 vols. (London: Soncino, 1935–48).

Fiebig, P. (ed.) *Antike Wundergeschichten zum Studium der Wunder des Neuen Testamentes* (Bonn: Marcus und Weber, 1911).

—— *Jüdische Wundergeschichten des neutestamentlichen Zeitalters* (Tübingen: Mohr, 1911).

—— *Rabbinische Wundergeschichten des neutestamentlichen Zeitalters* KIT, 78 (Berlin: de Gruyter, 1933).

Finkelstein, L. *Sifre on Deuteronomy* (New York: Jewish Theological Seminary of America, 1989).

Fitzmyer, J.A. "The Contribution of Qumran Aramaic to the Study of the NT" *NTS* 20 (1974) 393. 4QpsDan A².

—— (ed.) *The Genesis Apocryphon of Qumran Cave I* (Rome: Pontifical Biblical Institute, 1966).

—— and Harrington, D.J. (eds.) *A Manual of Palestinian Aramaic Texts* (Rome: Biblical Institute, 1978).

Foerster, W. *Gnosis: A Selection of Gnostic Texts* 2 vols. (Oxford: Oxford University Press, 1972 and 1974).

Fowler, H.N. *Plato: Euthyphro, Apology, Crito, Phaedo, Phaedrus* LCL (London: Heinemann and Cambridge, MA: Harvard University Press, 1966).

Freedman, H. and Simon, M. (eds.) *Midrash Rabbah* 10 vols. (London: Soncino, 1939).

Gaster, T.H. *The Scriptures of the Dead Sea Sect* (London: Secker & Warburg, 1957).

Gifford, E.H. *Eusebii Pamphili Evangelicae Praeparationis* 4 vols. (Oxford: Oxford University Press, 1903).

Ginzberg, L. *The Legends of the Jews* 7 vols. (Philadelphia: Jewish Publication Society, 1909–38).

Goodwin, C.W. *Fragment of a Graeco-Egyptian Work Upon Magic* (Cambridge: Deighton, 1852).

Grant, R.M. (eds.) *Gnosticism: An Anthology* (London: Collins, 1961).

Grenfell, B.P. and Hunt, A.S. (eds.) *The Oxyrhynchus Papyri* (London: Egypt Exploration Fund, 1898–).

Griffith, F.L. and Thompson, H. (eds.) *The Demotic Magical Papyrus of London and Leiden* 3 vols. (London: Grevel, 1904–9).

Gulick, C.B. *Athenaeus: The Deipnosophists* LCL, 7 vols. (London: Heinemann and New York: Putnam and Cambridge, MA: Harvard University Press, 1927–41).

Gummere, R.M. *Seneca and Lucilium Spistulae Morales* LCL, 3 vols. (London: Heinemann and New York: Putnam, 1917–25).

Harmon, A.M., Kilburn, K. and Macleod, M.D. *Lucian* 8 vols. (London: Heinemann, New York: Macmillan and Putnam and Cambridge, MA: Harvard University Press, 1913–67).

Harrington, D.J. (et al.) *Pseudo-Philon, Les antiquités bibliques* 2 vols. (Paris: Cerf, 1976).

Hartel, G.S. *Thasci Caecili Cypriani* CSEL vol. 3 (New York and London: Johnson Reprint, 1965).

Heikel, I.A. *Eusebius Werke* GCS vol. 23 (Leipzig: Hinrichs, 1913).

Hennecke, E. *New Testament Apocrypha* 2 vols. (London: SCM, 1963 and 1965).

Herford, R.T. *Pirke Aboth* (New York: Schocken, 1962).

Hicks, R.D. *Diogenes Laertius: Lives of Eminent Philosophers* LCL, 2 vols. (London: Heinemann and Cambridge, MA: Harvard University Press, 1925).

Holladay, C. (ed.) *Fragments from Hellenistic Jewish Authors* vol. 1 *Historians* Texts and Translations, 20; Pseudepigrapha Series, 10 (Chico: Scholars Press, 1983).

Horner, G. *Pistis Sophia* (London: SPCK, 1924).

Horseley, G.H.R. (ed.) *New Documents Illustrating Early Christianity* 5 vols. (Sydney: The Ancient History Documentary Research Centre, Macquarie University, 1981–89).

James, M.R. (ed.) *The Apocryphal New Testament* (Oxford: Clarendon, 1924).

— *The Biblical Antiquities of Philo* (New York: KTAV, 1971).

Jonge, M. de, (et al.) *The Testaments of the Twelve Patriarchs. A Critical Edition of the Greek Text* (Leiden: Brill, 1978).

Jongeling, B. Labuschagne, C. and van der Woude, A.S. (eds.) *Aramaic Texts from Qumran* vol. 1 (Leiden: Brill, 1976).

Kee, H.C. (ed.) *Medicine, Miracle and Magic in NT Times* (Cambridge: Cambridge University Press, 1986) Appendix, 4Q Therapeia.

Kittel, R. (ed.) *Biblia Hebraica* (7th ed. Stuttgart: Württembergische Bibelanstalt, 1951).

Knibb, M.A. (ed.) *The Ethiopic Book of Enoch* in consultation with E. Ullendorff 2 vols. (Oxford: Clarendon, 1978).

Koetschau, P. *Origenes Werke* GCS. vols. 2 and 3 (Leipzig: Hinrichs, 1899).

Lauterbach, J.Z. (ed.) *Mekilta de-Rabbi Ishmael* 3 vols. (Philadelphia: The Jewish Publication Society of America, 1933–35).

Lake, K. (ed.) *The Apostolic Fathers* LCL, 2 vols. (Cambridge, MA: Harvard University Press and London: Heinemann, 1912 and 1913).

— Lawlor, H.J. and Oulton, J.E.L. (eds.) *Eusebius: The Ecclesiastical History* LCL, 2 vols. (Cambridge, MA: Harvard University Press and London: Heinemann, 1926, 1932).

Lightfoot, J.B. (ed.) *The Apostolic Fathers* (London: Macmillan, 1891).

Lipsius, R.A. and Bonnet, M. (ed.) *Acta Apostolorum apocrypha* I (Lipsiae: Mendelssohn, 1891–).

Lohse, E. (ed.) *Die Texte aus Qumran. Hebräisch und deutsch* (München: Kösel, 1971).

Luck, G. *Arcana Mundi. Magic and the Occult in the Greek and Roman Worlds. A Collection of Ancient Texts Translated, Annotated, and Introduced* (Baltimore and London: Johns Hopkins University Press, 1985).

MacMahon, J.H. *The Refutation of all Heresies by Hipploytus* ANCL vol. 6 (Edinburgh: T & T Clark, 1868).

Malherbe, A.J. (ed.) *The Cynic Epistles* (Atlanta: Scholars Press, 1977).

Marcus, R. (ed.) *Philo Supplement* LCL, 2 vols. (Cambridge, MA: Harvard University Press and London: Heinemann, 1953).

McCown, C.C. (ed.). *The Testament of Solomon* (Leipzig: Hinrichs, 1922).

Milik, J.T. (ed.) *The Books of Enoch: Aramaic Fragments of Qumran Cave 4* (Oxford: Clarendon, 1976).

Montefiore, C.G. and Loewe, H. *A Rabbinic Anthology* (New York: Schocken, 1974).

Montgomery, J.A. *Aramaic Incantation Texts from Nippur* (Philadelphia: University Museum, 1913).

Moore, C.H. and Jackson, J. *Tacitus: The Histories: The Annals* LCL, 4 vols. (London: Heinemann and Cambridge, MA: Harvard University Press, 1925–37).

Murray, A.T. *Demosthenes Private Orations* LCL, 3 vols. (London: Heinemann and Cambridge, MA: Harvard University Press, 1936–9).

Naveh, J. "A Medical Document or a Writing Exercise? The So-called 4Q Therapeia" *IEJ* 36 (1986) 52–5.

Nestle, E. and Aland, K. (eds.) *Novum Testamentum Graece* (26th ed.; Stuttgart: Deutsche Bibelstiftung, 1979).

Neusner, J. (ed.) *The Tosefta* 6 vols. (New York: KTAV, 1977–81).

— *The Mishnah* (New Haven and London: Yale University Press, 1988).

Oldfather, C.H. (et al.) *Diodorus of Sicily* LCL, 12 vols. (London: Heinemann and New York: Putnam's Sons and Cambridge, MA: Harvard University Press, 1933–67).

Oldfather, W.A. *Epictetus* LCL, 2 vols. (London: Heinemann and New York: Putnam's Sons, 1926–8).

Ploeg, J.P.M. van der "Un petit rouleau de psaumes apocryphes (11 QPsAp^a)" in G. Jeremias (et al.) (eds.) *Tradition und Glaube: Das frühe Christentum in seiner Umwelt* (Göttingen: Vandenhoeck & Ruprecht, 1971) 128–39 (+ pls. II–VII).

— "Le psaume XCI dans une recension de Qumrân" *RB* 72 (1965) 210–17 (+ pls. VIII–IX).

Preisendanz, K. (ed.) *Papyri Graecae Magicae. Die griechischen Zauberpapyri* 3 vols. (Leipzig: Teubner, 1928, 1931, 1941).

— and Henrichs, A. (eds.) *Papyri Graecae Magicae* 2 vols. (2nd ed. Stuttgart: Teubner, 1973–74).

Pritchard, J. (ed.) *Ancient Near-Eastern Texts* (3rd ed. Princeton: Princeton University Press, 1969).

Puech, É. "*11QPsAp^a*: Un rituel d'exorcismes. Essai de reconstruction" *RevQ* 14 (1990) 377–408.

Rackham, H. *Pliny: Natural History* LCL, 10 vols. (London: Heinemann and Cambridge, MA: Harvard University Press, 1938–63).

Radice, B. *Pliny: Letters and Panegyricus* LCL, 2 vols. (London: Heinemann and Cambridge, MA: Harvard University Press, 1969).

Rahlfs, A. (ed.) *Septuaginta* 2 vols. (Stuttgart: Deutsche Bibelstiftung, 1935).

Reifferscheid, A. and Wissowa, G. *Tertulliani opera* CCL vol. 2, (Turnhout: Brepols, 1954).

Roberts, A. and Rambaut, W.H. *The Writings of Irenaeus* ANCL vols. 5 and 9 (Edinburgh: T & T Clark, 1868).

Robinson, J.M. (ed.) *The Nag Hammadi Library in English* (San Francisco: Harper & Row, 1988).

Rodkinson, M.L. (ed.) *New Edition of The Babylonian Talmud* 15 vols. (New York: New Amsterdam Book Company, 1896–1903).

Rolfe, J.C. *Suetonius* LCL, 2 vols. (London: Heinemann and Cambridge, MA: Harvard University Press, 1913–14).

Sanders J.A. *Discoveries in the Judaean Desert of Jordan IV: The Psalm Scroll of Qumran Cave 11 (11QPs^a)* (Oxford: Clarendon, 1965).

Schmidt, C. *Die alten Petrusakten* (Leipzig: Hinrichs, 1903).

— *Pistis Sophia* (Copenhagen: Nordisk, 1925).

Schuller, E.M. *Non-Canonical Psalms from Qumran: A Pseudepigraphic Collection* (Atlanta: Scholars Press, 1987).

Schwab, M. *Le Talmud de Jérusalem* 11 vols. (Paris: Maisonneuve, 1871–90).

Scott, S.P. *The Code of Justinian* 2 vols. (New York, NY: AMS, 1973).

Shorey, P. *Plato, The Republic* LCL, 2 vols. (London: Heinemann and Cambridge, MA: Harvard University Press, 1937 and 1935).

Sparks, H.F.D. (ed.) *The Apocryphal Old Testament* (Oxford: Clarendon, 1984).

Stählin, O. *Clemens Alexandrinus: Stromata Buch I-VI* GCS vol. 52 (Berlin: Akademie-Verlag, 1960).

Strack, H. and Billerbeck, P. *Kommentar zum Neuen Testament aus Talmud und Midrasch* 5 vols. (München: Beck, 1922–61).

Sukenik, E.L. *The Dead Sea Scrolls of the Hebrew University* The Isaiah^b Scroll, War Rule and Thanksgiving Hymns (Jerusalem: Hebrew University Press, 1955).

Thackeray, H. St. J. (et al.) (eds.) *Josephus* LCL, 10 vols. (Cambridge, MA: Harvard University Press and London: Heinemann, 1926–65).

Thelwall, S. *The Writings of Tertullian* ANCL vol. 11 (Edinburgh: T & T Clark, 1869).

Thompson, R.C. *The Devils and Evil Spirits of Babylon* 2 vols. (London: Luzac, 1903–4).

Vaux, R. de and Milik, J.T. *Discoveries in the Judaean Desert VII: Qumran Grotte 4 II:I Archéologie.II. Tefillin, Mezuzot et Targums 4Q128-4Q157* (Oxford: Clarendon, 1977).

Vermes, G. (ed.) *The Dead Sea Scrolls in English* (Harmondsworth: Penguin, 1987).

Walker, A. *Apocryphal Gospels, Acts and Revelations* ANCL vol. 16 (Edinburgh: T & T Clark, 1870).

Wallis, R.E. *The Writings of Cyprian Bishop of Carthage* ANCL vols. 8 and 13 (Edinburgh: T & T Clark, 1868 and 1869).

Wendland, P. (ed.) *Hippolytus* GCS vol. 26 (Leipzig: Hinrichs, 1916).

White, A.N. Sherwin– *The Letters of Pliny: A Historical and Social Commentary* (Oxford: Clarendon, 1966).

Wilson, W. *The Writings of Clement of Alexandria* ANCL vols. 4 and 12 (Edinburgh: T & T Clark, 1867 and 1869).

II. Select Secondary Sources

Aalen, S. " 'Reign' and 'House' in the Kingdom of God in the Gospels" *NTS* 8 (1961–2) 215–40.

Achinger, H. "Zur Traditionsgeschichte der Epileptiker–Perikope Mk 9, 14–29 par, Mt 17, 14–21 par, Lk 9, 37–43a" in A. Fuchs (ed.) *Probleme der Forschung* (Wein: Herold, 1978) 114–23.

Achtemeier, P.J. "Gospel Miracle Tradition and Divine Man" *Int* 26 (1972) 174–97.

— "Miracles and the Historical Jesus: A Study of Mark 9.14–29" *CBQ* 37 (1975) 471–91.

— "The Origin and Function of the Pre–Marcan Miracle Catenae" *JBL* 91 (1972) 198–221.

— "Toward the Isolation of Pre–Markan Miracle Catenae" *JBL* 89 (1970) 265–91.

Aitken, W.E.M. "Beelzebul" *JBL* 31 (1912) 34–53.

Alexander, W.M. *Demonic Possession in the NT* (Edinburgh: T & T Clark, 1902).

Ambrozic, A.M. "New Teaching With Power (Mk.1.27)" in J. Plevnik (ed.) *Word and Spirit: Essays in Honour of David Michael Stanley* (Willowdale, Ontario: Regis College, 1975) 113–49.

Annen, F. "Die Dämonenaustreibungen Jesu in den synoptischen Evangelien" *TB* 5 (1976) 107–46.

— *Heil für die Heiden: Zur Bedeutung und Geschichte der Tradition vom besessenen Gerasener (Mk 5,1-20 parr.)* (Frankfurt am Main: Knecht, 1976).

Argyle, A.W. "The Meaning of ἐξουσία in Mark 1, 22–27" *ExpTim* 80 (1968–9) 343.

Attridge, H.W. *First Century Cynicism in the Epistle of Heraclitus* (Missoula: Scholars Press, 1976).

Aune, D.E. "Magic in Early Christianity" *ANRW* II.23.2 (1980) 1507–57.

Baarda, T. "Gadarenes, Gerasenes, Gergesenes and the 'Diatesseron' Tradition" in E. Ellis and M. Wilcox (eds.) *Neotestamentica et Semitica* (Edinburgh: T & T Clark, 1969) 181–97.

Bächli, O. " 'Was habe ich mit Dir zu schaffen?' Eine formelhafte Frage im A.T. und N.T." *TZ* 33 (1977) 69–80.

Bacon, B.W. "The Markan Theory of Demonic Recognition of the Christ" *ZNW* 6 (1905) 153– 8.

Baird, M.M. "The Gadarene Demoniac" *ExpTim* 31 (1919–20) 189.

Baltensweiler, H. " 'Wer nicht uns (euch) ist, ist Für uns (euch)!' Bemerkungen zu Mk 9,40 und Lk 9,50" *TZ* 40 (1984) 130–6.

Barrett, C.K. Bammel, E. and Davies, W.D. (eds.) *Donum Gentilicum: NT Studies in honour of David Daube* (Oxford: Clarendon, 1978).

Barrett, C.K. *The Holy Spirit and the Gospel Tradition* (London: SPCK, 1947).

Bartlett, D.L. *Exorcism Stories in the Gospel of Mark* (Ph.D. Thesis: Yale University, 1972).

Batdorf, I.W. "Interpreting Jesus since Bultmann: Selected Paradigms and their Hermeneutic Matrix" in K.H. Richards (ed.) *SBLSP* (Chico: Scholar Press, 1984) 187–215.

Bauernfeind, O. *Die Worte der Dämonen im Markusevangelium* (Stuttgart: Kohlhammer, 1927).

Baumbach, G. *Das Verständnis des Bösen in den synoptischen Evangelien* (Berlin: Evangelische Verlagsanstalt, 1963).

Beasley–Murray, G.R. *Jesus and the Kingdom of God* (Grand Rapids: Eerdmans and Exeter: Paternoster, 1986).

— "Jesus and the Spirit" in A. Descamps and A. de Halleux (eds.) *Mélanges Bibliques en hommage au R.P. Béda Rigaux* (Gembloux: Duculot, 1970) 463–78.

Beauvery, R. "Jésus et Béelzéboul (Lc 11,14–28)" *Assemblées du Seigneur* 30 (1963) 26–36.

Becker, J. "Wunder und Christologie" *NTS* 16 (1969–70) 130–48.

Becker-Wirth, S. "Jesus triebt Dämonen aus (Mk 1, 21–28)" *Religionsunterricht an höheren Schulen* 28 (1985) 181–6.

Behm, J. *Die Handauflegung im Urchristentum* (Darmstadt: Wissenschaftliche Buchgesellschaft, 1968).

Benko, S. "Early Christian Magical Practices" in K.H. Richards (ed.) *SBLSP* (Chico: Scholars Press, 1982) 9–14.

Best, E. *Disciples and Discipleship. Studies in the Gospel of Mark* (Edinburgh: T & T Clark, 1986).

— "Exorcism in the NT and Today" *Biblical Theology* 27 (1977) 1–9.

— *Following Jesus* (Sheffield: JSOT, 1981).

— *The Temptation and the Passion: The Markan Soteriology* (Cambridge: Cambridge University Press, 1965).

Betz, H.D. "The Early Christian Miracle Story: Some Observations on the Form Critical Problem" in R.W. Funk (ed.) *Early Christian Miracle Stories* Semeia 11 (Missoula: SBL, 1978) 69–81.

— "The Formation of Authoritative Tradition in the Greek Magical Papyri" in B.F. Meyer and E.P. Sanders (eds.) *Jewish and Christian Self-Definition* (Philadelphia: Fortress, 1982) III, 161–70.

— "Introduction to the Greek Magical Papyri" in H.D. Betz (ed.) *The Greek Magical Papyri in Translation* Vol. 1: Texts (Chicago: Chicago University Press, 1986) xli–liii.

— "Jesus as Divine Man" in F.T. Trotter (ed.) *Jesus and the Historian: In Honor of Ernest Cadman Colwell* (Philadelphia: Westminster, 1968) 114–33.

Betz, O. "The Concept of the So–Called 'Divine–Man' in Mark's Christology" in D.E. Aune (ed.) *Studies in NT and Early Christian Literature* (Leiden: Brill, 1972) 229–40.

— "Das Problem des Wunders bei Flavius Josephus im Vergleich zum Wunderproblem bei den Rabbinen und im Johannesevangelium" in O. Betz, K. Haacker and M. Hengel (eds.) *Josephus-Studien* (Göttingen: Vandenhoeck & Ruprecht, 1974) 23–44.

— "Jesu Heiliger Krieg" *NovT* 2 (1958) 116–37.

— "Miracles in the Writings of Flavius Josephus" in L.H. Feldman and G. Hata (eds.) *Josephus, Judaism and Christianity* (Leiden: Brill, 1987) 212–35.

— and Grimm, W. *Wesen und Wirklichkeit der Wunder Jesu* (Frankfurt am Main: Peter Lang, 1977).

Black, M. *An Aramaic Approach to the Gospels and Acts* (Oxford: Clarendon, 1967).

— "The Messiah in the Testament of Levi xviii" *ExpTim* 60 (1948–9) 321–2.

Bligh, J. "The Gerasene Demoniac and the Resurrection of Christ" *CBQ* 31 (1969) 383–90.

Böcher, O. *Christus Exorcista: Dämonismus und Taufe im Neuen Testament* (Stuttgart: Kohlhammer, 1972).

— *Dämonenfurcht und Dämonenabwehr. Ein Beitrag zur Vorgeschichte der christlichen Taufe* (Stuttgart-Mainz: Kohlhammer, 1970).

— *Das Neue Testament und die dämonischen Mächte* (Stuttgart: Katholisches Bibelwerk, 1972).

Boers, H. *Who Was Jesus? The Historical Jesus and the Synoptic Gospels* (San Francisco: Harper & Row, 1989).

Bokser, B.M. "Wonder-Working and the Rabbinic Tradition. The Case of Hanina ben Dosa" *JSJ* 61 (1985) 42–92.

Bonner, C. "The Story of Jonah on a Magical Amulet" *HTR* 41 (1948) 31–7.

— *Studies in Magical Amulets Chiefly Graeco-Egyptian* (Ann Arbor: University of Michigan Press, 1950).

— "The Technique of Exorcism" *HTR* 36 (1943) 39–49.

— "The Violence of Departing Demons" *HTR* 37 (1944) 334–6.

Borg, M.J. *Conflict, Holiness and Politics in the Teachings of Jesus* (New York and Toronto: Mellen, 1984).

— *Jesus, A New Vision: Spirit, Culture and the Life of Discipleship* (San Francisco: Harper & Row, 1987).

— "A Renaissance in Jesus Studies" *TToday* 45 (1988) 280–92.
— "What Did Jesus Really Say?" *BibRev* 5 (1989) 18–25.
Boring, M.E. "Criteria of Authenticity. The Lucan Beatitudes As a Test Case" *Forum* 1 (1985) 3–38; revised as "The Historical–Critical Method's 'Criteria of Authenticity': The Beatitudes in Q and Thomas as a Test Case" in C.W. Hedrick (ed.) *The Historical Jesus and the Rejected Gospels* Semeia 44 (Atlanta: Scholars Press, 1988) 9–44.
Bornkamm, G. *Jesus of Nazareth* (London: SCM, 1960).
— "Πνεῦμα ἄλαλον. Eine Studie zum Markusevangelium" in *Geschichte und Glaube* II (München: Chr. Kaiser, 1971) 21–36.
— Barth, G. and Held, H.J. *Tradition and Interpretation in Matthew* (London: SCM, 1982).
Bousset, W.G. and Gressmann, H. *Die Religion des Judentums im Späthellenistischen Zeitalter* (Tübingen: Mohr, 1966).
Bowker, J. *The Targums and Rabbinic Literature* (Cambridge: Cambridge University Press, 1969).
Bowman, J. "David, Jesus the Son of David and Son of Man" *Abr-Nahrain* 27 (1989) 1–22.
— "Exorcism and Baptism" in R. H. Fischer (ed.) *A Tribute to Arthur Vöörbus: Studies in Early Christian Literature and its Environment* (Chicago: Lutheran School of Theology, 1977) 249–63.
— "Solomon and Jesus" *Abr-Nahrain* 23 (1984–5) 1–13.
Brière, J. "Le cri et le secret. Signification d'un exorcisme. Mc 1,21–28" *Assemblées du Seigneur* 35 (1973) 34–46.
Brown, P. "The Rise and Function of the Holy Man in Late Antiquity" *JRS* 61 (1971) 80–101.
— "Sorcery, Demons, and the Rise of Christianity from Late Antiquity into the Middle Ages" in M. Douglas (ed.) *Witchcraft, Confession and Accusations* (London: Tavistock, 1970) 119–46.
— *The World of Late Antiquity* (London: Thames and Hudson, 1971).
Brox, N. "Das Messianische Selbstverständnis des Historischen Jesus" in K. Schubert (ed.) *Vom Messias zum Christus* (Wien–Freiburg–Basel: Herder, 1964) 165–201.
Bryant, H.E. "Note on Luke xi. 17" *ExpTim* 50 (1938–9) 525–6.
Büchler, A. *Types of Jewish-Palestinian Piety* (London: Jews College, 1922).
Bühner, J.-A. "Jesus und die antike Magie. Bemerkungen zu M. Smith, Jesus der Magier" *EvT* 43 (1983) 156–75.
Bultmann, R. *History of the Synoptic Tradition* (New York: Harper & Row, 1976).
— "The Problem of Miracle" *Religion in Life* 27 (1957–8) 63–75.
Burger, C. *Jesus als Davidssohn: Eine Traditionsgeschichtliche Untersuchung* (Göttingen: Vandenhoeck & Ruprecht, 1970).
Burkill, T.A. "Concerning Mk. 5.7 and 5.18–20" *ST* 11 (1957) 159–66.
— "The Historical Development of the Story of the Syrophoenician Woman (Mark vii: 24–31)" *NovT* 9 (1967) 161–77.
— "Mark 3.7–12 and the Alleged Dualism in the Evangelist's Miracle Material" *JBL* 87 (1968) 409–17.
— *Mysterious Revelation: An Examination of the Philosophy of St. Mark's Gospel* (New York: Cornell University Press, 1963).
— "The Notion of Miracle with Special Reference to St. Mark's Gospel" *ZNW* 50 (1959) 33–48.
— "The Syrophoenician Woman: The Congruence of Mark 7.24–31" *ZNW* 57 (1966) 123–37.
Busse, U. *Die Wunder des Propheten Jesus* (Stuttgart: Katholisches Bibelwerk, 1977).
Calvert, D.G.A. "An Examination of the Criteria for Distinguishing the Authentic Words of Jesus" *NTS* 18 (1971–2) 209–19.
Caragounis, C.C. "Kingdom of God, Son of Man and Jesus' Self-Understanding" *TynBul* 40 (1989) 2–23, 223–38.
Carlston, C.E. "A *Positive* Criterion of Authenticity" *BR* 7 (1952) 33–44.
Carr, D. "Narrative and the Real World: An Argument for Continuity" *History and Theory* 25 (1986) 117–31.
— *Time, Narrative and History* (Bloomington: Indiana University Press, 1986).
Casas, G.V. "Los Exorcismos de Jesus: Posesos y Endemoniados" *Biblia y Fe* 2 (1976) 60–76.

-- "Jesús El Exorcista" *Biblia y Fe* 6 (1980) 28–40.

Cave, C.H. "The Obedience of Unclean Spirits" *NTS* 11 (1964–5) 93–7.

Chadwick, G.A. "Some Cases of Possession" *The Expositor* 6 (1892) 272–81.

Charlesworth, J.H. "The Historical Jesus in the Light of Writings Contemporaneous with Him" *ANRW* II.25.1 (1982) 451–76.

-- *The NT Apocrypha and Pseudepigrapha: A Guide to Publications, with Excursuses on Apocalypses* (Metuchen, NJ: American Theological Library Association and Scarecrow Press, 1987).

--*The Pseudepigrapha and Modern Research* (Missoula: Scholars Press, 1976).

Chilton, B.D. "A Comparative Study of Synoptic Development: The Dispute between Cain and Abel in the Palestinian Targums and the Beelzebul Controversy in the Gospels" *JBL* 101 (1982) 553–62.

-- "Exorcism and History: Mark 1:21–28" in D. Wenham and C. Blomberg (eds.) *Gospel Perspectives* 6, (Sheffield: JSOT, 1986) 253–71.

-- *The Kingdom of God in the Teaching of Jesus* (Philadelphia: Fortress Press, 1984).

-- *Profiles of a Rabbi, Synoptic Opportunities in Reading about Jesus* (Atlanta: Scholars Press, 1989).

Comber, J.A. "The Verb θεραπεύω in Matthew's Gospel" *JBL* 97 (1978) 431–4.

Corrington, G.P. "Power and the Man of Power in the Context of Hellenistic Popular Belief" in K.H. Richards (ed.) *SBLSP* (Chico: Scholars Press, 1984) 257–61.

Craghan, J.F. "The Gerasene Demoniac" *CBQ* 30 (1968) 522–36.

Cranfield, C.E.B. "St. Mark 9.14–29" *SJT* 3 (1950) 57–67.

Crasta, P.M. *Miracle and Magic: Style of Jesus and Style of a Magician* (Th.D. Thesis; Rome: Pontificia Universitas Gregoriana, 1985).

Cratchley W.J. "Demoniac of Gadara" *ExpTim* 63 (1951–2) 193–4.

Dalman, G. *The Words of Jesus* (Edinburgh: T & T Clark, 1902).

Danker, F.W. "The Demonic Secret in Mark: A Re–examination of the Cry of Dereliction (15, 34)" *ZNW* 61 (1970) 48–69.

Daube, D. *The NT and Rabbinic Judaism* (Salem: Ayer, 1984).

-- 'Ἐξουσία in Mark 1.22 and 27" *JTS* 39 (1938) 45–59.

Davies. T.W. *Magic, Divination and Demonology Among the Hebrews and Their Neighbours* (London: Clarke and Leipzig: Spirgatis, 1897).

Day, P.L. *An Adversary in Heaven* (Atlanta: Scholars Press, 1988).

Deissmann, A. *Bible Studies* (Edinburgh: T & T Clark, 1901).

-- *Light from the Ancient East* (London: Hodder and Stoughton, 1910).

Delobel, J. (ed.) *Logia: Les Paroles de Jésus - The Sayings of Jesus* (Leuven: Leuven University Press, 1982).

Dermience, A. "Tradition et rédaction dans la péricope de la Syrophénicienne: Marc 7,24–30" *RTL* 8 (1977) 15–29.

Derrett, J.D.M. "Contributions to the Study of the Gerasene Demoniac" *JSNT* 3 (1979) 2–17.

-- "Law in the NT: The Syrophoenician Woman and the Centurion of Capernaum" *NovT* 15 (1973) 161–86, reprinted with further annotations in his *Studies in the NT* I (Leiden: Brill, 1977) 143–69.

-- "Legend and Event: The Gerasene Demoniac: An Inquest into History and Liturgical Projection" in E.A. Livingstone (ed.) *StudBib 1978* II (Sheffield: JSOT, 1980) 63–73 reprinted with further annotations in his *Studies in the NT* III Misdrash, Haggadah, and the Character of the Community (Leiden: Brill, 1982) 47–58.

-- "Spirit–possession and the Gerasene Demonaic" *Man* (n.s.) 14 (1978) 286–93.

Detweiller, R. and Doty, W.G. (eds.) *The Daemonic Imagination: Biblical Texts and Secular Story* (Atlanta: Scholars Press, 1990).

Diaz, J.A. "Questión sinóptica y universalidad del mensaje cristiano en el pasaje evangélico de la mujer cananea" *CB* 20 (1963) 274–9.

Dibelius, M. *From Tradition to Gospel* (London: Clarke, 1971).

Dieterich, A. *Abraxas: studien zur religionsgeschichte des später altertums* (Leipzig: Teubner, 1891).

Dilthey, W. *Gesammelte Schriften* 12 vols. (Leipzig and Berlin: Teubner and Göttingen: Vandenhoeck & Ruprecht, 1958).

Dodds, E.R. "Supernormal Phenomena in Classical Antiquity" in his *The Ancient Concept of Progress and Other Essays in Greek Literature and Belief* (Oxford: Clarendon, 1973) 156–210.

Dodds, G.R. *The Greeks and the Irrational* (Berkeley: University of California Press, 1971).

Domeris, W.R. "The Office of Holy One" *Journal of Theology for Southern Africa* 54 (1986) 35–8.

Douglas, M. *Purity and Danger: An Analysis of Concepts of Pollution and Taboo* (Harmondsworth: Penguin, 1970).

— *Witchcraft, Confession and Accusations* (London: Tavistock, 1970).

Downing, F.G. *Jesus and the Threat of Freedom* (London: SCM, 1987).

— "The Social Contexts of Jesus the Teacher: Construction or Reconstruction" *NTS* 33 (1987) 439–51.

Dozent, P.P. "The Temptation Stories and Their Intention" *NTS* 20 (1974) 115–27.

Dschulnigg, P. *Sprache, Redaction und Intention des Markus-Evangeliums* (Stuttgart: Katholisches Bibelwerk, 1984).

Dudley, D.R. *A History of Cynicism from Diogenes to the Sixth Century A.D.* (Hildesheim: Georg Olms, 1967).

Duling, D.C. "The Eleazar Miracle and Solomon's Magical Wisdom in Flavius Josephus's *Antiquitates Judaicae* 8.42–49" *HTR* 78 (1985) 1.25.

— "The Promises to David and their Entrance into Christianity – Nailing Down a Likely Hypothesis" *NTS* 20 (1974) 55–77.

— "Solomon, Exorcism, and the Son of David" *HTR* 68 (1975) 235–52.

— "The Testament of Solomon: Retrospect and Prospect" *JSP* 2 (1988) 87–112.

— "The Therapeutic Son of David: An Element in Matthew's Christological Apologetic" *NTS* 24 (1978) 392–410.

Dunn, J.D.G. *Christology in the Making* (SCM, London, 1980).

— *Jesus and the Spirit* (London: SCM, 1975).

— "Matthew 12:28/Luke 11:20 – A Word of Jesus?" in W.H. Gloer (ed.) *Eschatology and the New Testament* (Peabody: Hendrickson, 1988) 31–49.

— "Spirit-and-Fire Baptism" *NovT* 14 (1972) 81–92.

— "Spirit and Kingdom" *ExpTim* 82 (1970–1) 36–40.

— *Unity and Diversity* (London: SCM, 1977).

— and Twelftree, G.H. "Demon-Possession and Exorcism in the NT" *Churchman* 94 (1980) 210–25.

Dupont-Sommer, A. "Exorcismes et Guérisons Dans les Ecrits de Qumrân" *VTSup* 7 (1959) 246–61.

— *The Jewish Sect of Qumran and the Essenes: New Studies on the Dead Sea Scrolls* (New York: Macmillan, 1955).

Easton, B.S. "The Beelzebul Sections" *JBL* 32 (1913) 57–73.

Edelstein, L. "Greek Medicine in its relation to Religion and Magic" *Bulletin of the History of Medicine* 5 (1937) 201–46.

Eitrem, S. *Some Notes on the Demonology in the NT* (Oslo: Brøgger, 1950).

Elliott, J.K. "The Synoptic Problem and the Laws of Tradition: A Cautionary Note" *ExpTim* 82 (1971) 148–52.

Evans, C.A. "Authenticity Criteria in Life of Jesus Research" *Christian Scholar's Review* 19 (1989) 6–31.

— "Jesus of Nazareth: Who Do Scholars Say That He Is? A Reivew Article" *Crux* 23 (1987) 15–19.

— *Life of Jesus Research: An Annotated Bibliography* (Leiden: Brill, 1989).

Everts, Wm.W. "Jesus Christ, No Exorcist" *BS* 81 (1924) 355–62.

Fabris, R. "Blessings, Curses and Exorcism in the Biblical Tradition" *Concilium* 178 (1985) 13–23.

Ferguson, E. *Demonology of the Early Christian World* (New York: Mellen, 1984).

Fiebig, P.W.J. "Neues zu den rabbinischen Wundergeschichten" *ZNW* 35 (1936) 308–9.

— "Zu den Wundern der apostelgeschichte" *'Aggelos': Archiv für neuetestamentliche Zeit-geschichte und Kulturkunde* 2 (1926) 157f.

Fiederlein, F.M. *Die Wunder Jesu und die Wundererzählungen der Urkirche* (Munich: Don Bosco, 1988).

Fischer, L.R. "Can this be the Son of David?" in F.T. Trotter (ed.) *Jesus and the Historian: Written in Honor of Ernest Cadman Colwell* (Philadelphia: Westminster, 1968) 82–97.

Fitzmyer, J.A. *A Wandering Aramean* (Missoula: Scholars Press, 1979).

Flammer, B. "Die Syrophoenizerin" *TQ* 148 (1968) 463–78.

Flusser, D. "Healing Through the Laying–on of Hands in a Dead Sea Scroll" *IEJ* 7 (1957) 107–8.

Fohrer, G. "Prophetie und Magie" *ZAW* 37 (1966) 25–47.

Freedman, D.N. "The Prayer of Nanonidus" *BASOR* 145 (1957) 31–2.

Fridrichsen, A. *The Problem of Miracle in Primitive Christianity* (Minneapolis: Augsburg, 1972).

— "The Conflict of Jesus with the Unclean Spirits" *Theology* 22 (1931) 122–35.

Fuchs, A. *Die Entwicklung der Beelzebulkontroverse bei den Synoptikern: traditions-geschichtliche und redaktionsgeschichtliche Untersuchung von Mk 3,22-7* (Linz: Studien zum NT und seiner Umwelt 5: 1980).

Fuchs, E. *Jesu Wort und Tat* (Tübingen: Mohr, 1971).

Fuller, R.H. *Interpreting the Miracles* (London: SCM, 1963).

— *The Mission and Achievement of Jesus* (London: SCM, 1954).

Funk, R.W. (ed.) *Early Christian Miracle Stories* Semeia 11 (Missoula: Scholars Press, 1978).

Gallagher, E.V. *Divine Man or Magician? Celsus and Origen on Jesus* (Chico: Scholars Press, 1982).

Gardiner, A.H. "Professional Magicians in Ancient Egypt" *Proceedings of the Society of Biblical Archeology* 39 (1917) 31–44.

Garrett, S.R. *The Demise of the Devil: Magic and the Demonic in Luke's Writings* (Minneapolis: Fortress, 1989).

Gärtner, R.B. "The Person of Jesus and the Kingdom of God" *TToday* 27 (1970) 32–43.

Gaston, L. "Beelzebul" *TZ* 18 (1962) 247–55.

— *Horae Synopticae Electonicae Word Statistics of the Synoptic Gospels* (Missoula: Scholars Press, 1973).

Geller, M.J. "Jesus' Theurgic Powers: Parallels in the Talmud and Incantation Bowls" *JJS* 28 (1977) 141–55.

George, A. "Note sur quelques traits lucaniens de l'expression 'Par le doigt de Dieu' (Luc XI, 20)" *Sciences ecclésiastiques* 18 (1966) 461–6; reprinted in his *Etudes sur l'oeuvre de Luc* (Paris: Gabalda, 1978) 128–32.

Georgi, D. "The Records of Jesus in the Light of Ancient Accounts of Revered Men" in L.C. McGaughtey (ed.) *SBL 1972 Proceedings* 2 vols. (Missoula: Scholars Press, 1972) II, 527–42.

Ghalioungui, P. *Magic and Medical Science in Ancient Egypt* (London: Hodder and Stoughton, 1963).

Gibbs, J.M. "Purpose and Pattern in Matthew's Use of the Title 'Son of David' " *NTS* 10 (1963–4) 446–64.

Giesen, H. "Dämonenaustreibungen – Erweis der Nähe der Herrschaft Gottes. Zu Mk 1,21-28" *Theologie der Gegenwart* 32 (1989) 24–37.

Girard, R. "Les démons de Gérasa" in *Le Bouc émissaire* (Paris: Grasset, 1982) 233–57.

Giversen, S. "Solomon und die Dämonen" in M. Krause (ed.) *Essays on the Nag Hammadi Texts in Honour of Alexander Böhlig* (Leiden: Brill, 1972) 16–21.

Gollancz, J. *The Book of Protection* (London: Henry Frowde, 1912).

Gonzáles, F.J.I. "Jesus y los demonios. Introduction cristologica a la lucha por la justicia" *Estudios Eclesiástcos* (Madrid) 52 (1977) 487–519.

Goodenough, E.R. *Jewish Symbols in the greco-Roman Period* 13 vols. (New York: Pantheon Books for the Bollingèn Foundation, 1953–68).

Goodwin, G.W. *Fragment of a Graeco-egyptian Work Upon Magic* (Cambridge: Macmillan, 1852).

Goshen–Gottstein, M.H. "The Psalms Scroll (11QPs^a): A Problem of Canon and Text" *Textus* 5 (1966) 22–33.

Grant, R.M. *Miracle and Natural Law in Graeco-Roman and Early Christian Thought* (Amsterdam: North–Holland Publishing Company, 1952).

— "Quadratus, The First Christian Apologist" in R.H. Fischer (ed.) *A Tribute to Arthur Vööbus: Studies in Early Christian Literature and its Environment, Primarily in the Syrian East* (Chicago: The Lutheran School of Theology, 1977) 177–83.

Grayston, K. "Exorcism in the NT" *Epworth Review* 2 (1975) 90–4.

— "The Significance of the Word *Hand* in the NT" in A. Descamps and A. de Halleux (eds.) *Mélanges Bibliques en hommage au R.P. Béda Rigaux* (Gembloux: Duculot, 1970) 479–87.

Green, W.S. "Palestinian Holy Men: Charismatic Leadership and Rabbinic Tradition" *ANRW* II.19.2 (1979) 619–47.

Grelot, P. "La Priére de Nabonide (4 Q Or nab)" *RevQ* 9 (1978) 483–95.

Grundmann, W. *Der Begriff der Kraft in der neutestamentlichen Gedankenwelt* (Stuttgart: Kohlhammer, 1932).

Guillmette, P. "La forme des récits d'exorcisme de Bultmann. Un dogme à reconsidérer *Eglise et Théologie* 11 (1980) 177–93.

— "Mc 1, 24 est-il une formule de défense magique?" *ScEs* 30 (1978) 81–96.

— "Un enseignement nouveau, plein d'autorité" *NovT* 22 (1980) 222–47.

Guttmann, A. "The Significance of Miracles for Talmudic Judaism" *HUCA* 20 (1947) 363–406.

Gutwenger, E. "Die Machterweise Jesu in formseschichtlicher Sicht" *ZKT* 89 (1967) 176–90.

Hadas, M. and Smith, M. *Heros and Gods: Spiritual Biographies in Antiquity* (New York: Harper & Row, 1965).

Hammerton–Kelly, R.G. "A Note on Matthew 12.28 par. Luke 11.20" *NTS* 11 (1964–5) 167–9.

Harrington, D.J. "The Jewishness of Jesus: Facing Some Problems" *CBQ* 49 (1987) 1–13.

Harvey, A.E. *Jesus and the Constraints of History* (London: Duckworth, 1982).

Hasler, J.I. "The Incident of the Syrophoenician Woman (Matt. xv.21–28, Mark vii.24–30)" *ExpTim* 45 (1933–4) 459–61.

Hawkins, J. *Horae Synopticae* (Oxford: Oxford University Press, 1909).

Hawthorn, T. "The Gerasene Demoniac: A Diagnosis Mark v.1–20. Luke viii.26–39. (Matthew viii.28–34)" *ExpTim* 66 (1954–5) 79–80.

Hay, L.S. "The Son-of-God Christology in Mark" *JBR* 32 (1964) 106–14.

Hedrick, C.W. "The Role of 'Summary Statements' in the Composition of the Gospel of Mark: a Dialog with Karl Schmidt and Norman Perrin" *NovT* 26 (1984) 289–311.

Heil, M. "Significant Aspects of the Healing Miracles in Matthew" *CBQ* 41 (1979) 274–87.

Heitmüller, W. *Im Namen Jesu* (Göttingen: Vandenhoeck & Ruprecht, 1903).

Hendrickx, H. *The Miracle Stories of the Synoptic Gospels* (London: Geoffrey Chapman and San Francisco: Harper & Row, 1987).

Hengel, M. *The Charismatic Leader and His Followrs* (Edinburgh: T & T Clark, 1981).

— *Jews, Greeks and Barbarians: Aspects of the Hellenization of Judaism in the pre-Christian Period* (London: SCM, 1980).

— *Judaism and Hellenism: Studies in their Encounter in Palestine During the Early Hellenistic Period* (London: SCM, 1974).

— *Son of God: The Origins of Christology and the History of Jewish-Hellenistic Religion* (London: SCM, 1976).

Hermann, I. " '. . . dan ist das Gottesreich zu euch gekommen': Eine Homilie zu Luk 11, 14–20" *BibLeb* 1 (1960) 198–204.

Herrmann, L. "Les premiers exorcismes juifs et judéo–chrétiens" *Revue de L'Université de Bruxelles* 7 (1954–5) 305–8.

Hiers, R.H. *The Historical Jesus and the Kingdom of God* (Gainesville: University of Florida Press, 1973).

— *The Kingdom of God and the Synoptic Tradition* (Gainsville: Florida University Press, 1970).

— "Satan, Demons, and the Kingdom of God" *SJT* 27 (1974) 35–47.

Hinnels, J.R. "Zoroastrianism Saviour Imagery and its Influence on the NT" *Numen* 16 (1969) 161–85.

Hock, R.F. "Simon the Shoemaker as an Ideal Cynic" *GRBS* 17 (1976) 41–53.

Holladay, C.R. *Theois Aner in Hellenistic Judaism* (Missoula: Scholars Press, 1977).

Hollenbach, P.W. "Jesus, Demoniacs, and Public Authorities: A Socio–Historical Study" *JAAR* 49 (1981) 567–88.

Hopfner, T. *Griechisch-Ägyptischer Offenbarungszauber* 2 vols. (Leipzig: Hassel, 1921 and 1924).

Horsley, R.A. *Jesus and the Spiral of Violence: Popular Jewish Resistance in Roman Palestine* (San Francisco: Harper & Row, 1987).

— "Popular Messianic Movements Around the Time of Jesus" *CBQ* 46 (1984) 471–95.

— "Popular Prophetic Movements at the Time of Jesus Their Principal Features and Social Origins" *JSNT* 26 (1986) 3–27.

— *Sociology and the Jesus Movement* (New York: Crossroad, 1989).

Howard, J.K. "New Testament Exorcism and its Significance Today" *ExpTim* 96 (1985) 105–9.

Howard, V. *Das Ego Jesu in den synoptischen Evangelien* (Marburg: N.G. Elwert, 1975).

Hull, J.M. *Hellenistic Magic and the Synoptic Tradition* (London: SCM, 1974).

Hultgren, A.J. *Jesus and His Adversaries: The Form and Function of the Conflict Stories in the Synoptic Tradition* (Minneapolis: Augsburg, 1979).

Hunt, A.S. "A Greek Cryptogram" *Proceedings of the British Academy* 15 (1929) 127–34.

— "An Incantation in the Ashmoleon Museum" *JEA* 15 (1929) 155–7.

— "The Warren Magical Papyrus" in S.R.K. Glanville (ed.) *Studies Presented to F. Ll. Griffith* (London: Egypt Exploration Society, 1932) 233–40.

Huntress, E. " 'Son of God' in Jewish Writings Prior to the Christian Era" *JBL* 54 (1935) 117–23.

Huppenbauer, H.W. "Belial in den Qumrantexten" *TZ* 15 (1959) 81–9.

Iersel, B.M.F. van *'Der Sohn' in den Synoptischen Jesusworten* (Leiden: Brill, 1964).

Jayne, W.A. *The Healing Gods of Ancient Civilizations* (New York: University Books Inc., 1962).

Jeremias, J. *Jerusalem in the Time of Jesus* (London: SCM, 1969).

— *NT Theology* (London: SCM, 1971).

— *The Parables of Jesus* (London: SCM, 1972).

Jonge, M. de. "Christian Influence in the Testaments of the Twelve Patriarchs" *NovT* 4 (1960) 182–235.

— "The Main Issues in the Study of the Testaments of the Twelve Patriarchs" *NTS* 26 (1980) 508–24.

— "Once More: Christian Influence in the Testaments of the Twelve Patriarchs" *NovT* 5 (1962) 311–19.

— "Recent Studies on the Testaments of the Twelve Patriarchs" *SEA* 36 (1971) 77–96.

— *Studies on the Testaments of the Twelve Patriarchs: Text and Interpretation* (Leiden: Brill, 1975).

— "The Testaments of the Twelve Patriarchs and the New Testament" *SE* 1 (1959) 546–56.

Jongeling, B. (et al.) *Aramaic Texts From Qumran* I (Leiden: Brill, 1976).

Kallas, J. *The Significance of the Synoptic Miracles* (London: SPCK, 1961).

— *Jesus and the Power of Satan* (Philadelphia: Westminster, 1968).

Kampling, R. "Jesus von Nazaret – Lehrer und Exorzist" *BZ* 30 (1986) 237–48.

Käsemann, E. "Die Heilung der Besessenen" *Reformatio* 28 (1979) 7–18.

— "Lukas 11, 14–28" in his *Exegetische Versuche und Besinnungen* 2 vols. (Göttingen: Vandenhoeck & Ruprecht, 1960) I, 242–8.

Kasper, W. (et al.) *Teufel, Dämonen, Besessenheit* (Mainz: Matthias-Grünewald, 1978).

Kazmierski, C.R. *Jesus, the Son of God: A Study of the Markan Tradition and its Redaction by the Evangelist* (Würzburg: Echter, 1979).

Keck, L.E. "Mark 3.7–12 and Mark's Christology" *JBL* 84 (1965) 341–58.

Kee, H.C. *Medicine, Miracle and Magic in NT Times* (Cambridge: Cambridge University Press, 1986).

— *Miracle in the Early Christian World* (New Haven and London: Yale University Press, 1983).

— "Satan, Magic, and Salvation in the Testament of Job" in G. McRae (ed.) *SBLSP* 2 vols. (Cambridge, MA: SBL, 1974) I, 53–76.

— "The Terminology of Mark's Exorcism Stories" *NTS* 14 (1967–8) 232–46.

Kelly, H.A. *Towards the Death of Satan* (London: Chapman, 1968).

Kertelge, K. "Jesus, seine Wundertaten und der Satan" *Conc* 1 (1975) 168–73.

— *Die Wunder Jesu im Markusevangelium: Ein redaktionsgeschichtliche Untersuchung* (München: Kösel, 1970).

— "Die Wunder Jesus in der neueren Exegese" *TB* 5 (1976) 71–105.

King, L.W. *Babylonian Magic and Sorcery* (London: Luzac, 1896).

Kingsbury, J.D. *Matthew: Structure, Christology, Kingdom* (London: SPCK, 1976).

— "Observations on the 'Miracle Chapters' of Matthew 8–9" *CBQ* 40 (1978) 559–73.

Kirchschläger, W. "Engel, Teufel, Dämonen. Ein biblische Skizze" *BLit* 54 (1981) 98–102.

— "Exorzismus in Qumran?" *Kairos* 18 (1976) 135–53.

— *Jesu exorzistisches Wirken aus der Sicht des Lukas: Ein Beitrag zur lukanischen Redaktion* (Klosterneuberg: Österreichisches Katholisches Bibelwerk, 1981) 45–54.

— "Wie über Wunder reden?" *BLit* 51 (1978) 252–4.

Kissinger, W.S. *The Lives of Jesus: A History and Bibliography* (New York and London: Garland, 1985).

Klein, G. "Der Synkretismus als theologisches Problem: Apg 19, 11–20" *ZTK* 64 (1967) 50–60.

Kleist, J.A. "The Gadarene Demoniacs" *CBQ* 9 (1947) 101–5.

Kloppenborg, J.S. *The Formation of Q* (Philadelphia: Fortress, 1987).

Knox, W.L. "Jewish Liturgical Exorcism" *HTR* 31 (1938) 191–203.

Koch, D.-A. *Die Bedeutung der Wundererzählungen für die Christologie des Markusevangeliums* (Berlin and New York: de Gruyter, 1975).

Kolenkow, A.B. "A Problem of Power: How Miracle-Doers Counter Charges of Magic in the Hellenistic World" in G. MacRae (ed.) *SBLSP* (Missoula: Scholars Press, 1976) 105–10.

— "Relationships between Miracle and Prophecy in the Greco–Roman World and Early Christianity" *ANRW* II.23.2 (1980) 1470–1506.

Kraeling, C.H. "Was Jesus Accused of Necromancy?" *JBL* 59 (1940) 147–57.

Kremer, J. "Besessenheit und Exorzismus. Aussagen der Bibel und heutige Problematik" *BLit* 48 (1975) 22–8.

Kruse, H. "Das Reich Satans" *Bib* 58 (1977) 29–61.

Kuhn, H.W. *Ältere Sammlungen im Markusevangelium* (Göttingen: Vandenhoeck & Ruprecht, 1971).

Kümmel, W.G. *Promise and Fulfilment: The Eschatological Message of Jesus* (London: SCM, 1969).

Lamarche, P. "Les miracles de Jésus selon Marc" in X. Léon-Dufour (ed.) *Les Miracles de Jesus selon le Nouveau Testament* (Paris: Seuil, 1977) 213–226.

— "Le Possédé de Gérasa" *NRT* 90 (1968) 581–97.

Lambrecht, J. "Le possédé et le troupeau (Mc 5, 1–20)" *RCIAfr* 33 (1968) 557–69.

Langdon, S. "An Incantation for Expelling Demons from a House" *ZA* 2 (1925) 209–14.

Langton, E. *Essentials of Demonology: A Study of Jewish and Christian Doctrine Its Origin and Development* (London: Epworth, 1949).

— *Good and Evil Spirits* (London: SPCK, 1942).

Lattey, C. "The Messianic Expectations in 'The Assumption of Moses'" *CBQ* 4 (1942) 9–21.

Latourelle, R. "Authenticité historique des miracles de Jésus: Essai de criteriologie" *Gregorianum* 54 (1973) 225–62.

— *The Miracles of Jesus* (New York: Paulist, 1988).

— "Originalité et Fonctions des miracles de Jésus" *Gregorianum* 66 (1985) 641–53.

Leaney, R. "Dominical Authority for the Ministry of Healing" *ExpTim* 65 (1953–4) 121–3.

Légasse, S. "L'épisode de la Cananéenne d'après Mt 15,21–28" *BLE* 73 (1972) 21–4.

— "L' 'homme fort' de Luc xi 21–22" *NovT* 5 (1962) 5–9.

Leivestad, R, *Christ the Conqueror: Ideas of Conflict and Victory in the NT* (London: SPCK, 1954).

— *Jesus in His own Perspective* (Minneapolis: Augsburg, 1987).

Léon-Dufour, X. (ed.) *Les miracles de Jésus selon le NT* (Paris: Seuil, 1977).

— "L'épisode de l'enfant épileptique" *La formation des évangiles* (Burges: Desclée de Brouwer, 1957) 94–100.

Lewis, E.L. "Christ and Unclean Spirits" *Theology* 23 (1931) 87–8.

Limbeck, M. "Beelzebul – eine ursprünglich Bezeichnung fur Jesus?" in K.H. Schelkle (ed.) *Worte Gottes in der Zeit* (Düsseldorf: Patmos, 1973) 31–42.

— "Jesus und die Dämonen. Der exegetische Befund" *BK* 30 (1975) 7–11.

— "Satan und das Böse im NT" in H. Haag (ed.) *Teufelsglaube* (Tübingen: Katzmann, 1974) 271–88.

Lindars, B. "Jesus and the Pharisees" in C.K. Barrett, E. Bammel and W.D. Davies (eds.) *Donum Gentilicium: NT Studies in Honour of David Daube* (Oxford: Clarendon, 1979) 51– 63.

— and Smalley, S.S. (eds.) *Christ and Spirit in the New Testament* (Cambridge: Cambridge University Press, 1973).

Ling, T. *The Significance of Satan* (London: SPCK, 1961).

Loader, W.R.G. "Son of David, Blindness, Possession, and Duality in Matthew" *CBQ* 44 (1982) 570–85.

Loos, H. van der *The Miracles of Jesus* (Leiden: Brill, 1965).

Lorenzmeier, T. "Zum Logion Mt 12, 28; Lk 11, 20" in H.D. Betz and L. Schottroff (eds.) *Neues Testament und christliche Existenz: Festschrift für Herbert Braun* (Tübingen: Mohr, 1973) 289–304.

McArthur, H.K. (ed.) *In Search of the Historical Jesus* (London: SPCK, 1970).

McCasland, S.V. *By the Finger of God* (New York: Macmillan, 1951).

— "The Demonic 'Confessions' of Jesus" *JR* 24 (1944) 33–6.

— "Portents in Josephus and in the Gospels" *JBL* 51 (1932) 323–35.

— "Religious Healing in First Century Palestine" in J.T. McNeill, M. Spinka and H.R. Willoughby (eds.) *Environmental Factors in Christian History* (Chicago: University of Chicago Press, 1939) 18–34.

— "Signs and Wonders" *JBL* 76 (1957) 149–52.

McCown, C.C. "The Christian Tradition as to the Magical Wisdom of Solomon" *JPOS* 2 (1922) 1–24.

— "The Ephesia Grammata in Popular Belief" *TPAPA* 54 (1923) 128–40.

McEleney, N.J. "Authenticating Criteria and Mark 7.1–23" *CBQ* 34 (1972) 431–60.

MacDonald, D.R. (ed.) *The Apocryphal Acts of Apostles* Semeia 38 (Decatur: Scholars Press, 1986).

Macintosh, A.A. "A Consideration of Hebrew גער" *VT* 19 (1969) 471–9.

MacLaurin, E.C.B. "Beelzebul" *NovT* 20 (1978) 156–60.

MacRae, G. "Miracle in *The Antiquities* of Josephus" in C.F.D. Moule (ed.) *Miracles: Cambridge Studies in Their Philosophy and History* (London: Mowbray, 1965) 127–47.

Maher, M. "Recent Writings on the Miracles" *New Blackfriars* 56 (658, 1975) 165–74.

Malina, B.J. and Neyrey, J.H. *Calling Jesus Names. The Social Value of Labels in Matthew* (Sonoma, CA: Polebridge, 1988).

Mann, C.S. "Wise Men or Charlatans" *Theology* 61 (1958) 495–500.

Manrique, A. "El endemoniado de Gerasa" *Biblia y Fe* 8 (1982) 168–79.

Margoliouth, D.S. "The Syrophoenician Woman" *The Expositor* 22 (1921) 1–10.

Martin, A.D. "The Loss of the Gadarene Swine" *ExpTim* 25 (1913–14) 380–1.

Marwick, M. (ed.) *Witchcraft and Sorcery: Selected Readings* (Harmondsworth: Penguin, 1970).

Mastin, B.A. "Scaeva the Chief Priest" *JTS* 27 (1976) 405–12.

Mateos, J. "Térmnios relacionados con 'Legión' en Mc 5,2–20" *Filologia Neotestamentaria* 1 (1988) 211–15.

Maynard, A.H. "TI EMOI KAI ΣOI" *NTS* 31 (1985) 582–6.

Mead, G.R.S. *Apollonius of Tyana: The Philosopher-Reformer of the First Century AD* (New York: University Books, 1966).

Metzger, B.M. "Names for the Nameless in the NT. A Study in the Growth of Christian

Tradition" in P. Granfield and J.A. Jungman (eds.) *Kyriakon: Festschrift Johannes Quasten* 2 vols. (Münster, Westfalen: Aschendorff, 1970) I, 79–99.

–– "A Magical Amulet for Curing Fever" in B.M. Metzger (ed.) *Historical and Literary Studies: Pagan, Jewish and Christian* (Leiden: Brill, 1968) 104–10.

–– "St. Paul and the Magicians" *Princeton Seminary Bulletin* 38 (1944) 27–30.

Meyer, B.F. *The Aims of Jesus* (London: SCM, 1979).

–– "Objectivity and Subjectivity in Historical Criticism of the Gospels" in his *Critical Realism and the NT* (Allison Park: Pickwick, 1989) 129–45.

Meyer, P.W. "The Problem of the Messianic Self–Consciousness of Jesus" *NovT* 4 (1961) 122–38.

Meyer, R. *Das Gebet des Nabonid* (Berlin: Adademie–Verlag, 1962).

Meynet, R. "Qui donc est 'le plus fort?' analyse rhétorique de Mc 3, 22–30; Mt 12, 22–37; Luc 11, 14–26" *RB* 90 (1983) 334–50.

Milik, J.T. " 'Priére de Nabonide' et Autres écrits d'un cycle de Daniel. Fragments Aramées ·de Qumrân 4" *RB* 63 (1956) 407–15.

Mills, M.E. *Human Agents of Cosmic Power in Hellenistic Judaism and the Synoptic Tradition* (Sheffield: JSOT, 1990).

Miyoshi, M. *Der Anfang des Reisesberichts Lk.9.51-10.24* (Rome: Biblical Institute, 1974).

Montefiore, C.G. *Rabbinic Literature and Gospel Teachings* (London: Macmillan, 1930).

Montgomery, J.A. "Some Early Amulets from Palestine" *JAOS* 31 (1911) 272–81.

Moore, G.F. *Judaism in the First Centuries of the Christian Era, the Age of Tannaim* 3 vols. (Cambridge, MA: Harvard University Press, 1948–50).

Moule, C.F.D. (ed.) *Miracles. Cambridge Studies in their Philosophy and History* (London: Mowbray, 1965).

Mussner, F. *The Miracles of Jesus: An Introduction* (Notre Dame: University Notre Dame Press, 1968).

–– "Eine Wortspiel in Mk 1, 24?" *BZ* 4 (1960) 285–6.

Neirynck, F. "Mt 12,25a/Lc 11,17a et la rédaction des évangiles" *ETL* 62 (1986) 122–33.

–– "Words Characteristic of Mark: A New List" *ETL* 63 (1987) 367–74.

Nestle, E. "Jüdische Parallelen zu neutestamentlichen Wundergeschichten" *ZNW* 8 (1907) 239–40.

Neusner, J. *From Politics to Piety: The Emergence of Pharisaic Judaism* (Englewood Cliffs: Prentice Hall, 1972).

–– *Messiah in Context* (Philadelphia: Fortress, 1984).

–– "New Problems, New Solutions: Current Events in Rabbinic Studies" *SR* 8 (1979) 401–18.

–– *The Rabbinic Traditions about the Pharisees Before 70* 3 vols. (Leiden: Brill, 1971).

Neyrey, J.H. "The Idea of Purity in Mark's Gospel" ' in J.H. Elliott (ed.) *Social-Scientific Criticism of the NT and its Social World* Semeia 35 (Decatur: Scholars Press, 1986) 91–128.

Nickelsburg, G.W. (ed.) *Ideal Figures in Ancient Judaism* (Missoula: Scholars Press, 1980).

Nilsson, M.P. *Die Religion in den griechischen Zauberpapyri* (Lund: Gleerup, 1948).

Nkwoka, A.O. "Mark 3: 19b–21: A Study on the Charge of Fanaticism Against Jesus" *Biblebhashyam* 15 (1989) 205–21.

Noack, B. *Satanas und Soteria* (København: Gads, 1948).

Nock, A.D. "Greek Magical Papyri" *JEA* 15 (1929) 219–35.

Nyberg, H.S. "Zum Grammatischen Verständnis von Matth. 12, 44–45" *ConNT* 2 (1936) 22–35; reprinted 13 (1949) 1–11.

Oakman, D.E. "Rulers' Houses, Thieves and Usrupers: The Beelzebul Pericope" *Forum* 4 (1988) 109–23.

O'Day, G.R. "Surprised by Faith: Jesus and the Canaanite Woman" *Listeneing* 24 (1989) 290–301.

Odegard, D. "Miracles and Good Evidence" *RelS* 18 (1982) 37–46.

Oesterley, W.O.E. "The Demonology of the OT Illustrated by Ps. 91" *The Expositor* 16–18 (1907) 132–51.

Oesterreich, T.K. *Possession Demonical and Other* (London: Kegan Paul, Trench, Trubner, 1930).

Oster, R.E. Jr. *A Historical Commentary on the Missionary Success Stories in Acts 19.11-40* (Ph.D. Thesis, Princeton Theological Seminary, 1974).

Owen, E.C.E. "Δαίμων and Cognate Words" *JTS* 32 (1930–1) 133–53.

Peabody, D.B. *Mark as Composer* (Macon, GA: Mercer University Press, 1987).

Perels, O. *Die Wunderüberlieferung der Synoptiker in ihrem Verhältnis zur Wortüberlieferung* (Stuttgart, Berlin: Kohlhammer, 1934).

Perrin, N. *The Kingdom of God in the Teaching of Jesus* (London: SCM, 1963).

Pesch, R. *Der Besessene von Gerasa* (Stuttgart: Katholisches Bibelwerk, 1972).

— *Jesu ureigene Taten?* Ein Beitrag zur Wunderfrage (Freiburg, Vienna: Herder, 1970).

— "The Markan Version of the Healing of the Gerasene Demoniac" *Ecumenical Review* 23 (1971) 349–76.

— " 'Eine neue Lehre aus Macht': Eine Studie zu Mk 1,21–28" in J.-B. Bauer (ed.) *Evangelienforschung* (Graz–Wein–Köln: Styria, 1968) 241–76.

— "Ein Tag vollmächtigen Wirkens Jesu in Kapharnahum (Mk 1,21–34, 35–39)" *BibLeb* 9 (1968) 61–77, 114–28, 177–95.

Peters, T. "The Use of Analogy in Historical Method" *CBQ* 35 (1973) 475–82.

Peterson, E. Εἶς Θεός. *Epigraphische, formgeschichtliche und religionsgeschichtliche Untersuchungen* (Göttingen: Vandenhoeck & Ruprecht, 1926).

Petterson, O. "Magic-Religion: Some Marginal Notes to an Old Problem" *Ethos* 22 (1957) 109–19.

Petzke, G. "Die historische Frage nach den Wundertaten Jesu, dargestellt am Beispiel des Exorzismus Mark. IX. 14–29 par" *NTS* 22 (1976) 180–204.

Pimental, P. "The 'unclean spirits' of St Mark's Gospel" *ExpTim* 99 (1988) 173–5.

Pokorný, P. "The Temptation Stories and Their Intention" *NTS* 20 (1974) 115–27.

Polhill, J.B. "Perspectives on the Miracle Stories" *RE* 74 (1977) 389–99.

Polkow, D. "Method and Criteria for Historical Jesus Research" in K.H. Richards (ed.) *SBLSP* (Atlanta: Scholars Press, 1987) 336–56.

Praeder, S. *Miracle Stories in Christian Antiquity* (Philadelphia: Fortress, 1987).

Preisendanz, K. "Die griechischen und lateinischen Zaubertafeln" *AP* 11 (1935) 153–64.

— "Neue griechische Zauberpapyri" *Chronique d'Egypte* 26 (1951) 405–9.

— "Zur Überlieferungsgeschichte der spätantiken Magie" *Aus der Welt des Buches: Festgabe zum 70. Geburtstag von Georg Leyh* (Leipzig: Harrassowitz, 1950) 223–40.

Pryke, E.J. *Redactional Style in the Marcan Gospel: A Study of Syntax and Vocabulary as Guides to Redaction in Mark* (Cambridge: Cambridge University Press, 1978).

Rankin, H.D. *Sophists, Socratics and Cynics* (Beckenham, Kent: Croom Helm, 1983).

Reif, S.C. "A Note on גער" *VT* 21 (1971) 241–2.

Reiner, E. "Surpu: A Collection of Sumerian and Akkadian Incantations" *Archiv für Orientforschung* Beiheft 11 (1958).

Reitzenstein, R. *Hellenistische Wundererzählungen* (Leipzig: Teubner, 1963).

— *Poimandres: Studien zur Griechisch-Ägyptischen und Frühchristlichen Literatur* (Leipzig: Teubner, 1904).

Remus, H. "Does Terminology Distinguish Early Christian from Pagan Miracles?" *JBL* 101 (1982) 531–51.

— "Magic or Miracle? Some Second-Century Instances" *SecCent* 2 (1982) 127–56.

— *Pagan-Christian Conflict Over Miracle in the Second Century* (Cambridge, MA: Philadelphia Patristic Foundation, 1983).

Riesenfeld, H. "De fientliga andarna Mk 9,14–29" *SvExA* 22–3 (1957-8) 64–74.

Riga, P. "Signs of Glory: The Use of 'Sēmeion' in St. John's Gospel" *Int* 17 (1963) 402–24.

Rist, M. "The God of Abraham, Isaac, and Jacob: A Liturgical and Magical Formula" *JBL* 57 (1938) 289–303.

Rodd, C.S. "Spirit or Finger" *ExpTim* 72 (1960-1) 157–8.

Rohde, E. *Psyche: The Cult of Souls and Belief in Immortality Among the Greeks* (London: Routledge and Kegan Paul, 1925).

Roloff, J. *Das Kerygma und der irdische Jesus. Historische Motive in den Jesus-Erzählungen der Evangelien* (Göttingen: Vandenhoeck & Ruprecht, 1970).

Ross, J.M. "The Decline of the Devil" *ExpTim* 66 (1954-5) 58–61.

— "Epileptic or Moonstruck?" *BT* 29 (1978) 126–8.

Rüsch, E.G. "Dämonenaustreibung in der Gallus–Vita und bei Blumhardt dem Älteren" *TZ* 34 (1978) 86.

Russell, D.S. *The Method and Message of Jewish Apocalyptic* (London: SCM, 1964).

Russell, E.A. "The Canaanite Woman and the Gospels (Mt.15.21–28; cf. Mk.7.24–30)" in E.A. Livingstone (ed.) *StudBib 1978* 2 vols. (Sheffield: JSOT, 1980) II, 263–300.

— "A Plea for Tolerance (Mk. 9.38–40)" *IBS* 8 (1986) 154–60.

Sabugal, S. *La Embajada mesiánica de Juan Bautista Mt 11,2-6 = Lc 7,18-23)* (Madrid: SYSTECO, 1980).

Safrai, S. and Stern, M. (eds.) *The Jewish People in the First Century* 2 vols. (Assen: Van Gorcum and Philadelphia: Fortress, 1974 and 1976).

Sahlin, H. "Die Perikope vom gerasenischen Besessenen und der Plan des Markusevangeliums" *ST* 18 (1964) 159–72.

Samain, J. "L'accusation de magie contre le Christ dans les Evangiles" *ETL* 15 (1938) 449–90.

Sanders, E.P. *Jesus and Judaism* (London: SCM, 1985).

Sanders, J.A. *The Dead Sea Psalms Scrolls* (Ithaca: Cornell University Press, 1967).

Santo, C. de "The Assumption of Moses and the Christian Gospel" *Int* 16 (1962) 305–10.

Schenk, W. von "Tradition und Redaktion in der Epileptiker–Perikope Mk 9,14–29" *ZNW* 63 (1972) 76–94.

Schenke, L. *Die Wundererzählungen des Markusevangeliums* (Stuttgart: Katholisches Bibelwerk, 1974).

Schille., G. *Die Urchristliche Wundertradition: Ein Beitrag zur Frage nach dem irdischen Jesus* (Stuttgart: Calwer, 1967).

Schindler, C.J. "Demonic Possession in the Synoptic Gospels" *Lutheran Church Quarterly* 1 (1928) 285–414.

Schlatter, A. "Das Wunder in der Synagogue" *Beiträge zur Förderung christlicher Theologie* 16 (5, 1912) 49–86.

Schlosser, J. "L'exorciste étranger (Mc, 9.38–39)" *RevScRel* 56 (1982) 229–39.

Schmithals, W. "Die Heilung des Epileptishen" *ThViat* 13 (1975–6) 211–34.

— *Wunder und Glaube. Eine Auslegung von Markus 4, 35–6, 6a* (Neukirchen–Vluyn: Neukirchener–Verlag, 1970).

Schubert, K. "Wunderberichte und ihr Kerygma in der rabbinischen Tradition" *Kairos* 24 (1982) 31–7.

Schultz, W. "Ephesia Grammata" *Philologus* 68 (1909) 210–28.

Schürer, E. *The History of the Jewish People in the Age of Jesus Christ* 3 vols. (Edinburgh: T & T Clark, 1973–1987).

Schwarz, G. " 'Aus der Gegend' (Mk V. 10b)" *NTS* 22 (1976) 215–6.

— "ΣΥΡΟΦΟΙΝΙΚΙΣΣΑ–ΧΑΝΑΝΑΙΑ (Markus 7.26/Matthäus 15.22)" *NTS* 30 (1984) 626–8.

Schweizer, E. "Anmerkungen zur Theologie des Markus" in *Neotestamentica et Patristica. Eine Freundesgabe Herrn Professor Dr. Oscar Cullmann* NovTSup 6 (Leiden: Brill, 1962) 35–46.

— "Er wird Nazoräer heissen (zu Mc 1,24; Mt 2,23)" in W. Eltester (ed.) *Judentum, Urchristentum, Kirche* (Berlin: Töpelmann, 1964) 90–3.

— "Towards a Christology of Mark?" in J. Jervell and W.A. Meeks (eds.) *God's Christ and His People* Studies in Honour of Nils Alstrup Dahl (Oslo: Universitetsforlaget, 1977) 29–42.

Segal, A.F. "Hellenistic Magic: Some Questions of Definition" in R. van den Broek and M.J. Vermaseren (eds.) *Studies in Gnosticism and Hellenistic Religions Presented to Gilles Quispel on the Occasion of his 65th Birthday* (Leiden: Brill, 1981) 349–75.

Sellew, P. "Beelzebul in Mark 3: Dialogue, Story, or Sayings Cluster?" *Forum* 4 (1988) 93–108.

Shae, G.S. "The Question on the Authority of Jesus" *NovT* 16 (1974) 1–29.

Sider, R.J. "The Historian, The Miraculous and Post–Newtonian Man" *SJT* 25 (1972) 309–19.

Simonis, W. *Das Reich Gottes ist mitten unter euch* (Düsseldorf: Patmos, 1986).

Skehan, P.W. "A Fragment of the 'Song of Moses' (Deut.32) From Qumran" *BASOR* 136 (1954) 12–15.

Slingerland, H.D. *The Testaments of the Twelves Patriarchs: A Critical History of Research* (Missoula: Scholars Press, 1977).

Smalley, S.S. "Spirit, Kingdom and Prayer in Luke–Acts" *NovT* 15 (1973) 59–71.

Smart, J.D. "Jesus, the Syro–Phoenician Woman – and the Disciples" *ExpTim* 50 (1938–9) 469–72.

Smith, G. "Jewish, Christian, and Pagan views of Miracle under the Flavian emperors" in K.H. Richards (ed.) *SBLSP* (Chico: Scholars Press, 1981) 341–8.

Smith, J.Z. "Towards Interpreting Demonic Powers in Hellenistic and Roman Antiquity" *ANRW* II.16.1 (1978) 425–39.

–– *Map is not Territory. Studies in the History of Religions* (Leiden: Brill, 1978).

Smith, M. *Jesus the Magician* (London: Gollancz, 1978).

–– *Palestinian Parties and Politics that Shaped the OT* (New York and London: Columbia University Press, 1971).

–– "Prolegomena to a Discussion of Aretalogies, Divine Man, the Gospels and Jesus" *JBL* 90 (1971) 174–99.

Somerville, J.E. "The Gadarene Demoniac" *ExpTim* 25 (1914–4) 548–51.

Stanton, G.N. "On the Christology of Q" in B. Lindars and S.S. Smalley (eds.) *Christ and Spirit in the NT* (Cambridge: Cambridge University Press, 1973) 27–42.

Starobinski, J. "An Essay in Literary Analysis – Mark 5.1–20" *Ecumenical Review* 23 (1971) 377–97.

–– "The Gerasene Demoniac" in R. Barthes (et al.) *Structural Analysis and Biblical Exegesis* (Pittsburgh: Pickwick, 1974) 57–84.

–– "The Struggle with Legion: A Literary Analsysis of Mark 5.1–20" *New Literary History* 4 (1973) 331–56.

Starr, J. "The Meaning of Authority in Mark 1.22" *HTR* 23 (1930) 302–5.

Stein, R.H. "The 'Criteria' for Authenticity" in R.T. France and D. Wenham (eds.) *Gospel Perspectives* I (Sheffield: JSOT, 1980) 225–63.

–– "The Proper Methodology for Ascertaining a Markan Redaction History" *NovT* 13 (1971) 181–98.

–– "The 'Redaktionsgeschichtlich' Investigation of a Markan Seam (Mc.1.21f.)" *ZNW* 61 (1970) 70–94.

Steinmueller, J.E. "Jesus and οἱ παρ' αὐτοῦ (Mk. 3:21–21)" *CBQ* 4 (1942) 355–9.

Stewart, J.S. "On a Neglected Emphasis in NT Theology" *SJT* 4 (1941) 293–301.

Stock, A. "Jesus and the Lady from Tyre. Encounter in the Border District" *Emmanuel* 93 (1987) 336–9, 358.

Stone, M.E. (ed.) *Jewish Writings of the Second Temple Period* (Philadelphia: Fortress and Assen: Van Gorcum, 1984).

Storch, W. "Zur Perikope von der Syrophönizierin. Mk 7, 28 und Ri 1, 7" *BZ* NF 14 (1970) 256–7.

Strack, H.L. *Jesus die Häretiker und die Christen nach den ältesten jüdischen angaben* (Leipzig: Hinrichs, 1910).

Strange, W.A. "The Sons of Sceva and the Text of Acts 19.14" *JTS* 38 (1987) 97–106.

Strugnell, J. "More Psalms of 'David'" *CBQ* 27 (1965) 207–16.

Sturch, R.L. "The Markan Miracles and the Other Synoptics" *ExpTim* 89 (1977–8) 375–6.

Sugirtharajah, R.S. "The Syrophoenician Woman" *ExpTim* 98 (1986) 13–15.

Suhl, A. "Der Davidssohn im Matthäus–Evangelium" *ZNW* 5 (1968) 57–81.

–– "Überlegungen zur Hermeneutik an Hand von Mk 1,21–28" *Kairos* 26 (1984) 28–38.

Tagawa, K. *Miracles et Évangile* (Paris: Presses Universitaires de France, 1966).

Talmon, S. "Messianic Expectations at the Turn of the Era" *Face to Face* (New York) 10 (1983) 4–12.

Taylor, B.E. "Acts 19.14" *ExpTim* 57 (1945–6) 222.

Tcherikover, V. *Hellenistic Civilization and the Jews* (New York: Atheneum, 1977).

Theissen, G. *The First Followers of Jesus* (London: SCM, 1978).

–– "Itinerant Radicalism: The Tradition of Jesus Sayings from the Perspective of the Sociology of Literature" *Radical Religion* 2 (1975) 84–93, a translation of "Wanderradikalismus" *ZTK* 70 (1973) 245–71.

— "Lokal– und Sozialkolorit in der Geschichte von der syrophönikischen Frau (Mk.7.24–30)" *ZNW* 75 (1984) 202–25.

— *Miracle Stories of the Early Christian Tradition* (Edinburgh: T & T Clark, 1983).

Thompson, R.C. *Semitic Magic: Its Origins and Development* (London: Luzac, 1908).

Thompson, W.G. "Reflections on the Composition of Mt.8.1–9,34" *CBQ* 33 (1971) 365–88.

Tiede, D.L. *The Charismatic Figure as Miracle Worker* (Missoula: Scholars Press, 1972).

Torczyner, H. "A Hebrew Incantation against Night–Demons from Biblical Times" *JNES* 6 (1947) 18–29.

Trevijano, R. "El transfordo apocaliptico de Mc 1, 24.25; 5, 7.8 y par." *Burgense* 11 (1970) 117–33.

Trocmé, E. "Is There a Marcan Christology?" in B. Lindars and S.S. Smalley (eds.) *Christ and Spirit in the NT* (Cambridge: Cambridge University Press, 1973) 3–13.

— *Jesus and his Contemporaries* (London: SCM, 1973).

Tuckett, C. (ed.) *The Messianic Secret* (London: SPCK and Philadelphia: Fortress, 1983).

Turner, C.H. "Markan Usage: Notes Critical and Exegetical, on the Second Gospel" *JTS* 25 (1924) 377–85, 26 (1925) 12–20, 145–56, 225–40, 337–46.

Twelftree, G.H. *Christ Triumphant: Exorcism Then and Now* (London: Hodder and Stoughton, 1985).

— "ΕΙ ΔΕ . . . ΕΓΩ ΕΚΒΑΛΛΩ ΤΑ ΔΑΙΜΟΝΙΑ . . ." in D. Wenham and C. Blomberg (eds.) *Gospel Perspectives* 6 (Sheffield: JSOT, 1986) 361–400.

— "Jesus in Jewish Traditions" in R.T. France and D. Wenham (eds.) *Gospel Perspectives* 5 (Sheffield: JSOT, 1984) 289–341.

— "The Place of Exorcism in Contemporary Ministry" *Anvil* 5 (1988) 133–50.

— "Temptation of Jesus" in J.B. Green and S. McKnight (eds.) *Dictionary of Jesus and the Gospels* (Downers Grove: IVP, 1992).

Vaganay, L. "Les accords négatifs de Matthieu–Luc contre Marc: L'Episode de l'enfant épileptique (Mt. 17, 14–21; Mc.9,14–29; Lc.9,37–43a)" in *Le probléme synoptique: Une hypothése de travail* (Tournai: Desclée, 1957) 405–25.

Venkowski, J. "Der gadarenische Exorzismus. Mt 8,28–34 und Parr." *Communio Viatorum* 14 (1971) 13–29.

Vermes, G. "Essenes–Therapeutai–Qumran" *The Durham University Journal* 52 (1960) 97–115.

— *The Dead Sea Scrolls: Qumran in Perspective* (London: Collins, 1977).

— "Hanina ben dosa" *JJS* 23 (1973) 28–50, 24 (1973) 51–64.

— *Jesus the Jew* (Glasgow: Fontana, 1976).

— *Jesus and the World of Judaism* (London: SCM, 1983).

— *Post–Biblical Jewish Studies* (Leiden: Brill, 1975).

Vögtle, A. "The Miracles of Jesus against their Contemporary Background" in H.J. Schultz (ed.) *Jesus and His Time* (Philadelphia: Fortress, 1971) 96–105.

Vollenweider, S. " 'Ich sah den Satan wie einen Blitz vom Himmel fallen' (Lk 10:18)" *ZNW* 79 (1988) 187–203.

Volz, P. *Die Eschatologie der jüdischen Gemeinde im neutestamentlichen Zeitalter* (Hildesheim: Olms, 1966).

Walker, W.O. "A Method for Identifying Redactional Passages in Matthew on Functional and Linguistic Grounds" *CBQ* 39 (1977) 76–93.

Wall, R.W. " 'The Finger of God' Deuteronomy 9.10 and Luke 11.20" *NTS* 33 (1987) 144–50.

Wansbrough, H. "Mark iii. 21 – Was Jesus out of his mind?" *NTS* 18 (1971–2) 233–5.

Weber, J.C. Jr. "Jesus' Opponents in the Gospel of Mark" *JBR* 34 (1966) 214–22.

Weder, H. "Wunder Jesu und Wundergeschichten" *VF* 29 (1984) 25–49.

Wee, B.C. "The Syrophoenician Woman – Mark 7.24–30; New Testament in the light of the Old" *Compass* 18 (1, 1984) 38–40.

Weinreich, O. *Antike Heilungswunder. Untersuchungen zum Wunderglauben der Griechen und Römer* (Giessen: Töpelmann, 1909).

Weiss, W. *"Ein neue Lehre in Vollmacht." Die Streit- und Schulgespräche des Markus-Evangeliums* (Berlin and New York: de Gruyter, 1989).

Wenham, D. "The Meaning of Mark iii. 21" *NTS* 21 (1975) 295–300.

White, L.M. "Scaling the Strongman's 'Court' (Luke 11.21)" *Forum* 3 (1987) 3–28.

Wilhems, E. "Der fremde Exorzist: Eine Studie über Mark 9.38" *ST* 3 (1949) 162–71.

Wilkinson, J. "The Case of the Bent Woman in Luke 13.10–17" *EQ* 49 (1977) 195–205.

–– "The Case of the Epileptic Boy" *ExpTim* 79 (1967–8) 39–42.

Wink, W. "Jesus as a Magician" *USQR* 30 (1974) 3–14.

–– "Jesus' Reply to John Matt 11:2–6/Luke 7:18–23" *Forum* 5 (1989) 121–8.

Wire, A.C. "The Structure of the Gospel Miracle Stories and their Tellers" in R.W. Funk (ed.) *Early Christian Miracle Stories* Semeia 11 (Missoula: Scholars Press, 1978) 83–113.

Wrede, W. "Zur Messiaserkenntnis der Dämonen bei Markus" *ZNW* 5 (1904) 169–77.

Wünch, R. (ed.) *Antike fluchtafeln* (Bonn: Markus und Weber, 1912).

–– *Antikes zaubergerät aus Pergamon* (Berlin: Reimer, 1905).

Yamauchi, E.M. "Magic in the Biblical World" *TynBul* 34 (1983) 169–200.

–– "Magic or Miracle? Diseases, Demons and Exorcisms" in D. Wenham and C. Blomberg (eds.) *Gospel Perspectives* 6 (Sheffield: JSOT, 1986) 89–183.

Yates, J.E. "Luke's Pneumatology and Luke 11.20" *SE* II Pt. I (1964) 295–99.

–– *The Spirit and the Kingdom* (London: SPCK, 1963).

Yates, R. "Jesus and the Demonic in the Synoptic Gospels" *ITQ* 44 (1977) 39–57.

–– "The Powers of Evil in the NT" *EQ* 52 (1980) 97–111.

Zerwick, M. "In Beelzebul principe daemoniorum (Lc.11,14–28)" *VD* 29 (1951) 44–8.

Index of Biblical Passages

Old Testament

Genesis
1.4	67
6.1–4	50
12–15	43
32.11	44

Exodus
4.22–3	150
8.19	108
14.9	116
19.13	44
23.20	116
23.23	116
23.30	110
31.18	108
32.34	116
33.2	116

Numbers
16.3–5	68
19.11	144
19.16	144

Deuteronomy
9.10	108
28.12	44
31.29	44
32.5	94
32.8	223
32.17(LXX)	105
33.27–8	110

Joshua
6.26	33
22.24	61

Judges
2.14	44
11.12	61, 64
16.16(B)	68

1 Samuel
16	37, 44, 51
16.16	60
16.23	60
18.10	60

2 Samuel
7	183
7.11	183
7.12–14	150
7.14	152
16.5–14	63
16.10 (LXX)	63
19.16–23	63
19.22 (LXX)	63

1 Kings
8.3	105
17	63
17.18	61, 63, 64
19.5	116
19.7	116
22.16 (LXX)	33

2 Kings
1.2	105
3.13 (LXX)	63
4.9	68

1 Chronicles
28.11–19	108

2 Chronicles
6.2	105
35.21	63

Ezra
1.2	105
1.26	186
5.11	105

5.12	105	35.6	101, 103, 119
6.9	105	35.8	144
6.10	105	42.7	101
7.12	105	42.16	101
7.21	105	42.18–20	101
7.23	105	43.8	101
		53.12	111
Nehemiah		61.1	101, 119, 120
1.4	105	63.15	105
1.5	105	65.1–5	73
2.4	105		
2.20	105		
		Jeremiah	
Psalms		1.5	67
2.7	152	23.5	183
8.3	108	27.6f.	44
90.17	44	33.15	183
92.1	187		
95.5 (LXX)	105		
105.37 (LXX)	105	*Ezekiel*	
106.16 (LXX)	68	8.1	108
136.26	105	11.5	108
146.7b–8a	119		
151	37, 38		
151.3–4	37	*Daniel*	
		2.18	105
Isaiah		2.19	105
9.5 (LXX)	183	2.27	18
11.10	183	2.37	105
24–27	223	2.44	105
24.21	219	3.25	150
24.21f.	223	4.34	105
24.22	223	5.23	105
29.18	101	10.13	223
29.18–19	120		
32.1–20	182		
32.3	101	*Habakkuk*	
35.1–7	205	3.11	105
35.5	101, 103, 119		

New Testament

Matthew		4.11	vii, 114, 115
1.20	65	4.13	65, 214
2.2	186	4.23	103, 166
2.23	65, 68	4.24	101, 128, 138
3.13	65	4.24–5	128, 138
4.1–11	55	5.38–9	179
4.1	vii, 103, 114	6.25–32	214
4.2	vii, 114	7.16–17	29
4.3	170	7.18–23	208
4.6	151	7.22–3	167
4.10	115	7.22	167

7.28	102		220, 227
7.28f.	58	12.24	40, 98, 104, 161, 176, 178, 198
8–9	72	12.24ff.	214, 215
8.4	103	12.25	98
8.5–13	145	12.25–9	220
8.8	176	12.25–30	106
8.9	109, 154	12.26	109
8.16	101, 177	12.27	16, 32, 39, 47, 104, 107, 109,
8.16–17	128, 138		217, 218
8.20	214	12.27–8	106
8.27	59	12.27–30	100
8.28	101, 200	12.28	3, 98, 106. 107, 108, 109, 111,
8.28–34	72		121, 127, 137, 160, 161, 164,
8.29	61, 82, 83, 86, 186		167, 168, 170, 217, 218, 219,
8.29b	220		222, 223, 224, 228
8.33	59, 101, 176	12.28ff.	66
8.34	59	12.29	13, 111, 138, 167, 168, 170,
9.1–8	168		186, 219, 221
9.8	59, 102	12.30	107, 111
9.26	59	12.38	104
9.27–31	102	12.38–42	179
9.27	184	12.39	94, 170
9.32	101	12.43	11, 135
9.32–3	101, 102, 138, 146, 148	12.43–5	13
9.32–4	98, 99, 100, 102	12.45	119
9.33	59, 102, 103	12.46ff.	177
9.34	104	13.16–17	119
10	123	13.24–30	220, 222, 224
10.1	122, 167	13.36–43	221, 222
10.7	167	13.45	65
10.1–15	vii, 55, 122	13.47–50	222
10.1–14	123	13.53–8	166
10.25	105	13.54	58
11–13	120	15.21–8	88
11.2–6	vii, 55, 118, 119, 179, 208,	15.22	90, 101, 184
	219, 228	15.25	103
11.4	119, 168	15.31	59, 102
11.4–6	101, 121	16.1	104
11.5	119, 167, 170	16.1–4	170
11.6	120	16.23	115
11.12	119	17.18	59, 60, 71, 96
11.18	200, 208	17.26	103
11.21–3	167, 168, 170	19.25	58
11.24–6	129	20.30	65, 184
12.9–14	168	20.31	184
12.15–16	128, 138	21.11	65
12.22	3, 101, 102, 103, 138, 146,	21.12–17	179
	148, 162, 177	21.14	102
12.22–3	101, 178	22.33	58
12.22–7	99	22.34	69
12.22–8	102	22.46	58
12.22–30	vii, 55, 98, 99–100, 137	24.24	202
12.22–32	115	24.27	127
12.22–37	98	24.41	221
12.23	59, 102, 176, 180, 181, 184,	24.42	111

25.1–46	222
25.31–46	221
26.61	65
26.69	65
27.63	201, 202
28.3	127
28.5	65

Mark

1–8.26	45
1	88
1.1	81
1.9	65
1.9–13	116
1.10–11	186
1.11	117
1.12	vii, 58, 103, 114
1.12–13	55
1.13	vii, 114, 115, 116, 117
1.14	88
1.14–15	117, 166, 168
1.15	218
1.21	65
1.21–2	57, 58, 166
1.21–8	vii, 3, 55, 57–8, 76, 138, 144, 147, 166
1.21–34	59
1.22	58
1.23	58, 61, 81, 93, 146, 147, 154
1.23–5	154
1.23–7	60, 74
1.23–8	58, 71, 76
1.24	61, 62, 63, 64, 66, 67, 68, 81, 148, 149
1.24–5	83
1.25	62, 68, 69, 70, 84, 153, 154, 157, 160, 162
1.26	93, 96, 155, 156
1.26–8	70
1.27	2, 57, 58, 59, 71, 95, 176
1.27–8	58, 59
1.29	58
1.29–31	3, 56, 138
1.31	96
1.32	101, 128
1.32–4	59, 128, 138
1.34	69, 70, 103, 128
1.39	103, 128, 138, 166
1.40	94
1.40–5	3
1.43	103
1.45	79
2.1	79, 214
2.1–12	3, 166, 168, 179
2.1–3.6	58

2.3	145
2.5	94
2.7	2
2.12	59
2.15	79
2.18–3.6	168
2.27	169
3.1–5	179
3.1–6	3, 55, 166, 168
3.7–12	59, 128, 129, 138
3.7	129
3.8	129
3.11	61, 62, 66, 81, 93, 147, 149, 151, 154
3.14	79
3.14–15	167
3.15	103, 124, 125
3.17–19	74
3.19–21	98, 100, 178
3.19–35	116
3.21	100, 104, 176, 177, 178, 214
3.22	98, 103, 104, 106, 112, 140, 161, 176, 178, 180, 198, 199, 208
3.22–6	99
3.22–7	vii, 55, 98, 99–100, 137
3.22–30	98
3.23	103, 112, 116, 198
3.23b–26	113
3.23–7	106
3.26	116
3.27	89, 100, 111, 112, 113, 138, 167, 168, 170, 219, 221
3.28	161
3.30	79, 98, 176, 177, 178, 198, 199
3.31	100, 177
3.31–5	100, 104
4.13	79
4.15	116
4.34–6.44	166
4.35–41	74
4.35–5.43	58, 74
4.38–9	138
4.39	69
4.41	2, 59, 78, 166
5	74, 75, 76, 155, 164
5.1–17	73
5.1–20	vii, 3, 55, 72, 73–74, 77, 92, 138, 144
5.2	80
5.2ff.	93
5.2–5	92
5.3	80, 112
5.3–4	144
5.3–5	80
5.5	80

5.6	61, 80, 81	7.1–23	89, 179
5.6–7	146	7.24	89
5.7	33, 60, 62, 63, 64, 81, 82, 83,	7.24–31	89
	147, 149, 151, 152, 163	7.24–30	vii, 3, 55, 76, 88, 145, 146
5.7f.	86	7.24–8.26	88
5.7–9	154	7.25	58, 89, 93, 146, 147
5.7–13	81	7.25–6	148
5.8	62, 77, 83, 84, 95, 153	7.26	89, 90, 103
5.8–9	162	7.27	90
5.8ff.	160	7.27–8	90
5.9	39, 84, 85, 153, 154	7.29	160, 162
5.10	86	7.30	59
5.10ff.	210	7.31–7	3
5.10–12	154	7.33	158
5.10–13	83	7.34	162
5.11ff.	164	7.35	112
5.11–13	155	7.36	69, 79
5.12	86	7.37	59
5.13	70, 71, 74, 96	8.7	2
5.14	59, 78, 176, 177	8.11	116, 170
5.15	59, 78, 80, 101, 155, 173	8.22–6	3, 84, 154
5.16	78, 80, 101	8.22–10.52	84
5.16–20	78	8.23	158
5.17	59, 78, 80	8.32	71
5.18	79, 80, 101	8.33	116
5.18–20	74, 78, 79	8.38	81
5.19	79, 80	9	93, 156
5.20	59, 79, 80, 148	9.7	81
5.21–43	3	9.14	93
5.23	94; 159	9.14–19	92
5.28	94	9.14–20	92
5.33	61, 147	9.14–29	vii, 3, 55, 74, 76, 91, 92, 125,
5.34	94		138, 144, 145
5.36	94	9.17	93
5.40	103	9.17–18	92, 93
5.41	96, 162	9.18	92, 97, 103
5.43	59, 69	9.18–19	94
6.1–6	166	9.19	92, 93, 94, 97
6.2	58	9.20	60, 61, 92, 93, 94, 146
6.3	2	9.21–2	92, 93
6.7	122, 124, 125	9.21–7	92
6.7–12	vii, 55, 122, 123, 221	9.22	60
6.7–13	124	9.22–3	94
6.11	123	9.23	59, 97
6.12	167	9.24	94, 97
6.13	97, 103, 125	9.25	26, 92, 93, 95, 96, 153, 157,
6.14–16	208		161, 162, 164
6.30	vii, 122, 125	9.26	71, 155, 160
6.45	58	9.26–7	71, 96
6.45–8.26	166	9.28	59, 103
6.49	60	9.28–9	92, 96, 97, 166
6.51	59	9.29	97, 163
6.53–6	59	9.37–43	91
6.56	84	9.38	16, 40, 42, 52, 103, 125, 139,
7	146		218

9.38f.	224
9.38–9	40
9.38–40	40
9.38–41	97, 109
9.39	42
9.40	40, 43, 107
9.49f.	218
10.2	116
10.21	214
10.24	58
10.26	58
10.28–30	214
10.32	58, 88
10.46–52	3
10.47	65
10.48	69
10.52	94
11.11	65
11.15	103
11.15–19	179
11.18	58
12.5	103
12.6	81
12.8	103
12.15	116
12.18	103
12.34	58
13.32	81
14.1	88
14.16	2
14.36	81
14.43	58
14.61	81
14.67	65
14.69	65
15.1	58
15.19	147
15.39	81
16.6	65
16.12	221
16.17	222
16.18	186
17.14–21	91

Luke

1.36	67
2.4	65
2.39	65
2.40	65
4	vii
4.1	114
4,1–13	55
4.2	vii, 114

4.2–13	103
4.3	170
4.10–11	151
4.13	vii, 114, 115
4.16–30	166
4.16	65
4.22	58
4.31	65
4.31–2	166
4.31–7	57
4.31–44	57
4.32	58, 104
4.33	61, 147
4,35	70, 71, 96
4.36	59, 176, 177
4.38–9	56, 120, 138
4.39	138
4.40–1	128, 138
4.41	61, 138
4.44	128, 138
5.5	94
5.8	147
5.9	59
5.17–26	168
5.26	59
5.33	104
6.6–11	168
6.16–19	138
6.17–19	128
6.43–5	29
7.1–10	103, 145
7.7	176
7.8	109
7.16	59, 102
7.18	119
7.18–23	vii, 55, 103, 118, 119, 179, 219, 228
7.19	119
7.20–1	119
7.21	118, 119, 120, 121, 224
7.22	98, 119, 168, 170
7.23	120
7.33	200, 208
7.36–50	179
8.2	85, 119
8.3	112
8.12	114
8.19ff.	177
8.19–21	214
8.25	59
8.26	86
8.26–39	72, 73
8.27	200
8.28	60, 61, 82, 83
8.29	80, 86, 112, 208

8.31	86, 154		219, 222, 223, 224, 228
8.34	59, 176	11.20ff.	66
8.35	59	11.20–23	100
8.36	101	11.21	98, 112, 186
8.37	59	11.21f.	138, 219
8.56	59	11.21–2	13, 111, 168, 170
9	123	11.22	167
9.1	122	11.23	107, 111
9.1–6	vii, 55, 122	11.24–6	11, 13, 95, 112, 135
9.2	167	11.26	119
9.11–12	123	11.27–8	214
9.37	104	11.29	170
9.42	61, 96	11.29–32	103, 179
9.43	59	11.36	127
9.49	16, 52, 125, 139	11.37	104
9.49f.	224	11.38	104
9.49–50	40, 109	12.5	186
9.50	40, 43, 107	12.15	112
9.51–19.28	126	12.33	112
10	123	12.44	111, 112
10.1	125	13.10–17	56, 138
10.1–7	214	13.11	56
10.1–11	vii, 55, 122, 124	13.12	56
10.4	123, 124	13.16	56, 112, 114
10.9	124, 167	13.17	102
10.13–15	167, 168, 170	13.22	138
10.17	125, 140	14.33	112
10.17–19	122, 125	15.21–2	119
10.17–20	vii, 55, 122–3, 124, 125, 224	16.1	112
10.18	66, 114, 120, 126, 127, 221, 224, 228	16.16	98
		17.24	127
10.19	125, 126, 186	18.31	104
10.19–20	123, 186	19.8	112
10.23–4	119	19.34	119
10.25	104	19.45–8	179
10.27	104	19.45	65
11.9	16	19.48	58
11.14	3, 59, 101, 103, 138, 146, 148, 162, 176, 177, 178	20.21	103
		20.40	58
11.14–15	99, 100	20.41	104
11.14–23	vii, 55, 98, 137	22.3	221
11.14–26	98	22.20	104
11.14–20	99	22.23	115
11.15	98, 104, 161, 176, 178, 198	22.31	221
11.15ff.	214	22.35	123
11.16	104	22.47	104
11.17	98	22.54	104
11.17–23	99–100, 106	23.18	60
11.18	109, 114	23.35	104
11.19	32, 39, 47, 104, 107, 109, 217, 218		
		John	
11.19–20	106	1.45	65
11.20	3, 98, 106, 107, 108, 109, 110, 111, 121, 127, 137, 160, 161, 164, 167, 168, 170, 217, 218,	2.4	63
		2.12	214
		2.13–25	179

2.23	170	16.17	52, 82, 140
4.46–54	141	16.18	140, 161
4.54	170	17.31	96
6.69	67	19	31, 33, 66
7.20	176, 177, 199, 200, 208	19,11–40	30
8.48	176, 177, 198, 199, 200, 208	19.12	119
8.48–9	200	19.13	31, 32, 33, 34, 42, 52, 66, 119,
8.48–52	199		137, 139, 163
8.49	208	19.13–19	30, 34, 84
8.52	199, 208	19.13–20	16, 30
9.1–41	166	19.14	30, 31
9.6	158	19.15	51, 119
9.17	141	19.16	119
10.20	100, 176, 177, 178, 199, 200,	26.24–5	200
	208		
10.21	101, 176	*Romans*	
10.38	169	8.17	193
10.41	208		
11.31	42	*1 Corinthians*	
11.41–2	163	10.20	105
12.18	170	14.5	200
12.31	222	14.13–19	200
14.30	142, 222	14.23	200
16.11	142, 222		
17.1	111	*2 Corinthians*	
17.15	222	4.10	193
17.21	111		
18.30	203	*Galatians*	
20.30	141, 170	3.1	105
		6.17	192, 193
Acts			
2.22	65, 170	*Ephesians*	
2.24	96	6.12	50
2.32	96		
2.40	94	*Philippians*	
3.2	23	2.15	94
3.6	65	3.10	193
3.14	67		
3.26	96	*Colossians*	
4.6	31	1.24	193
4.10	34		
4.27	67	*1 Thessalonians*	
4.30	67	5.27	163
4.32	112		
5.15f.	178	*1 Timothy*	
5.34–9	180	4.1	186
8.18–19	42		
10.34–43	129	*Hebrews*	
10.36–43	129	1.5	152
10.38	65, 128, 129, 138, 170, 215		
12.15	200	*James*	
13.10	206	5.14–15	163
13.11	115		
13.33–4	96	*1 Peter*	
16.16–18	30, 221	2.12	203

2.14	203
4.15	203, 204
2 Peter	
2.4	223
1 John	
2.20	67
4.6	186
Jude	
6	223
Revelation	
3.7	67
4.5	127

8.5	127
8.13	167
9.5	220
9.20	105
11.19	127
14.4	42
14.11	220
16.18	127
18.7	220
18.10	220
18.15	220
20.1–3	223
20.10	66, 220
22.6	67

Index of Ancient Literary Sources

Dead Sea Scrolls

Cairo Damascus Document
(*CD*)

| 5.17b–19 | 199 |
| 6.1 | 67 |

Genesis Apocryphon 51, 52, 159
(*1QapGen*)

19	51
20	42, 43, 44, 51, 157, 158, 160
20.26	46
20.28–9	68
20.29	46

The War Scroll (*1QM*)

12.1	105
12.2	105
14	44
14.5ff.	45
14.10	68
15.end	50
18.1–5	108

Thanksgiving Hymns (*1QH*)

| 3.34 | 105 |
| 9.11 | 45 |

Fragment (*1QHf*)

| 4 | 45 |
| 4.6 | 68 |

The Manual of Discipline (*1QS*)

| 3.9 | 49 |
| 4.6 | 44 |

| 4.18f. | 219 |
| 10.13 | 105 |

Florilequim
(*4QFlor*)

	183
1.7	188
1.11	183

*4QPsDan A*ᵃ (= *4Q243*)

| | 82, 151 |

Psalms Scroll
(*11QPs*ᵃ)

27.2	37
27.3	37
27.4	37
27.10	37

(*11QPsAp*ᵃ)

1.2	38
1.4	38
4.4	38, 41

Temple Scroll
(*11QTemple*)

48.11–13	144
49.5–21	144
50.3–8	144

| *4QTherapeia* | 16, 38 |

The Prayer of Nabonidus 17, 46
(*4QPrNab or 4QsNab*)

Apocrypha and Pseudepigrapha

Letter of Aristeas   126

Baruch
  4.7   105

2 Baruch
85.10   219

Ben Sirach
45.6   67
47.11   184

1 Enoch   49
10.4   183, 188
10.4ff.   219
10.4–6   223
10.11f.   219
10.11–13   223
10.12   223
10.12f.   223
12–14   154
18.14–9.2   223
19.1   223
21.6f.   223
21.6–10   223
37–71   187
55.4   183, 187
90.23–4   223
90.23–7   223

4 Ezra
  5.50–5   219
14.10·   219

Martyrdom of Isaiah
  2.4–5   199

Jubilees   16, 21, 49, 160, 209, 215, 226
  5.6–10   223
10   51, 52, 154
10.4–9   223
10.5   51
10.5–9   223
10.5–10   223
10.8   51
10.10   157
10.12   157
10.17   51
16.33   186
48.9–11   199

1 Maccabees
  2.57   184

2 Maccabees
15.23   105

Assumption of Moses   188
  9.1   188
  9.7   188
10.1   66, 183, 188, 220
10.3   66, 188, 220
10.7   188

Sibylline Oracles
  3.63   186
  3.73   186

Psalms of Solomon 183, 184
17   184
17.21(23)   183
17.21(23)–46   183

Testament of Solomon 17, 18–19, 21, 35, 36, 47,
                         48, 52, 184, 226
1   18
1.5–7   35
1.6   39
2.9   39
5.7   39
5.9   39
5.10   39
11.5   38
11.6   39
15.13–15   18
16.6   39
18.6–37   39
18.16   39
18.23   39
18.25   39

Wisdom of Solomon
  2.13   151
  2.16b–18a   151

Tobit   16, 21, 39, 49, 52, 160, 209,
                         226
  6.17   109
  8.3   157
13.11   105

Testaments of the Twelve Patriarchs

Testament of Reuben
6.5–12   185
6.10–12   183, 185
6.12   185

Testament of Levi
18.3   186
18.6–7   185
18.11f.   183
18.11b–12   185
18.12a   186
18.12b   186

Testament of Judah
24   185
25.3.   183, 188
25.3b   186

Testament of Zebulon
9.8   183, 186

Testament of Dan
5.10f.   183, 187
5.10–11a   187

Early Christian Literature

Acts of Andrew   20
6   144
13   148

Apostolic Constitution
VIII.7   33

Arnobius
Adversus Gentes
I.46   140, 206

Dio Chrysostom
Discourse
32.2   28–29
32.9–11   28–29

Clement of Alexandria
Stromata
6.16.133   108

Cyprian
Testimonia
3.37   203

Eusebius
History of the Church
1.9.3   34
4.3.2   195, 204

Proof of the Gospel
3.2   203
3.3   205
3.4.31   203

Hippolytus
Refutations
6.34   105
7.15   141
7.20   141

Irenaeus
Adversus Haereses
2.23.3–4   195
2.32.4   34

Jerome
Letter
108.13   144

Acts of John
'The Destruction of the
Temple of Artemis' 148

Justin Martyr
Apology
1.6   34
1.35   34
1.48   34
2.6   140

Dialogue with Trypho
30.3   34, 140
69   195, 205
76.6   34. 140
85.2   34, 140

*Nag Hammadi
Codex IX*
3.70   35

Origen
Contra Celsum
  I.6   33, 139, 195, 196
  I.28   195
  I.38   141, 195, 196
  I.60   141
  I.67   139
  I.68   27, 32, 195, 196, 205
  III.24   33
  III.50   32
  IV.34   33
  VI.41   207
  VIII.25   105

Acts of Peter   75
  2.4.11   20, 26, 74, 148

Pistis Sophia
  102.255   141
  102.258   141
  130.332–5   141

Tertullian
Scorpiace
  12.3   203

Acts of Thomas
  3.31.–3   95
  5.44f.   148
  5.45   61
  8.75–81   93

Gospel of Thomas
  35   111, 112

Other Ancient Writers

Athenaeus
Deipnosophists
  4.157b   29
  11.502c   29

Codex Justinianus
  IX.18.7   203

Codex Theodosianus
  IX.16.4   203

Demosthenes
Orations
  47.45   198

Diodorus Siculus
History
  2.18   201
  15.76   28
  26.5   76

Diogenes Laertius
Lives of Eminent Philosophers
  1.15   28
  1.19   28
  6.13   28
  6.101   29
  6.103   28, 29
  6.103–105   28
  6.104   28
  6.104–105   28

Epictetus
Discourses
  1.1.16   64
  1.22.15   64
  1.27.13   64
  2.19.16   64
  2.19.17ff.   64
  3.20.15   29
  3.22.26   64

Homer
Iliad
  5.77   32
  16.234   32
  16.605   32

Josephus   16, 21, 31, 36, 37, 47, 49, 52,
                  157, 180, 209, 213, 214, 226

Against Apion
  1.71   90

Antiquities of the Jews
  2.167–70   136
  6.160   37
  6.165   37
  6.166   37
  6.168   37, 178
  6.169   37
  6.211   37
  7.265   63

8.36–9	36	31	148
8.42–9	139		
8.45	36, 139	Philosophies for Sale	
8.45ff.	82	2.11–12	206
8.46f.	41		
8.46–9	39, 50, 52, 139	Peregrinus	
8.47	26, 96	10–11	30
8.48	74	13	190
8.49	25, 26, 36, 155	15	69
8.182	36	16	30
8.190	36		
9.19	105	*Pausanias*	
18.2–10	213	ii.xii.2	32
18.23–5	213		
18.63f.	180		
18.63–64	196	*Philo of Alexandria*	
18.85–7	213	De Gigantibus	
18.124	83	7–8	50
20.97	179	16	50
20.97–8	213		
20.97–9	180	Quod Deus immutibilis sit	
20.102	213		16, 21, 49, 63, 64
20.167	213	133–9	64
20.169	213	138	64
20.188	213		
20.224–51	31	In Flaccum	
		36	60, 144
The Jewish War		40	144
1.10	180		
2.8	158	*Pseudo Philo*	16, 21
2.117–9	213	Liber Antiquitatum Biblicarum	
2.259	202, 213		49
2.261–3	213	60	33, 34, 52, 139, 183
2.433	213		
3.41	180	*Philostratus*	23, 24, 226
3.233	85	Life of Apollonius of Tyana	
3.289	85	1.2	24
3.458	85	1.3	23
3.485	85	3.38	26, 75, 95, 146, 148
4.13	85	3.40	26
6.114	31	3.45	25
7.253	213	4.20	25, 36, 60, 70, 74, 81, 95, 96,
7.437–41	213		148, 156, 158, 160
		4.45	25
Lucian of Samosata 16, 21, 157, 226		5.13	25
Alexander		6.7	25
1	190	7.38	27
2	190	7.39	24, 27, 206
		8.7	24, 207
Disowned			
6	148	*Plato*	28, 47
		Phaedo	
Philopseudes		81a	201
11	70		
16	70, 95, 148		

The Republic
364b–365a   27
398a   75
444b   201

Pliny
Natural History
28.37   158
28.86   75
31.18–24   137

Pliny the Younger
Letters
   X.96   194
   X.96.3   204

Seneca
Epistulae Morales
LXXXVII.25   29

Suetonius
Life of Claudius
25.4   196

Life of Nero
16.2   193

Tacitus
Annals
.15.44   34, 204
15.44.3–8   193

Rabbinic Literature

Mishnah
Berakot
   5.5   211

Taʿanit
   3.8   150

Ketubot
   13.1–2   *31*

Kelim   144

Oholot
   17.5   *31*

Tosefta
Ḥullin
   2.22f.   139
   2.22–3   140, 192

Jerusalem Talmud
Berakot
   1.9d   23

Maʿaser Šeni
   5.56a   23

Šabbat
   14.4   140
   14.4.14d   139

Šeqalim
   4.48a   32

ʿAboda Zara
   2.2   139, 140

Babylonian Talmud

Berakot
   17b   150
   34b   23, 160, 211
   51a   85

Šabbat
   104b   192

Pesaḥim
   112a   151
   112b   23, 36, 51, 75
   112b–113a   148

Taʿanit
   24b   150, 160

Ḥagiga
   15b   150
   16a   150

Giṭṭin
   69a   75
   90a   192

Baba Meṣiʿa
   59b   170, 179

Sanhedrin
   43a   140, 141
   67a   192

93b	179
98a	179

Šebuʿot

15b	158

ʿAboda Zara

27b	139, 140

Ḥullin

86a	150

Meʿila

17b	23, 48, 70, 178, 211

Sifra Leviticus

26.6	183, 187

Numbers Rabbah

19.8	43

Ecclesiastes Rabbah

1	23

Pesiqta Rabbati

5	63
36	183, 187, 188
40b	50

Papyri

Papyri Graecae Maqicae

I.162	84
III.420	158
IV	82
IV.1017–19	85
IV.1067f.	82
IV.1227	139
IV.1243ff.	70
IV.1248	39
IV.1254	95
IV.1294	96
IV. 1500	67
IV.2984ff.	67
IV.3007–86	32
IV.3013ff.	70
IV.3019	41, 83, 160, 161
IV.3019f.	139
IV. 3019ff.	106
IV.3019–20	82
IV.3024f.	95
IV.3024–25	96
IV.3033	38, 83
IV.3033ff.	67
IV.3034ff.	33
IV.3037	84
IV.3037ff.	112
IV. 3039	83
IV.3039ff.	84
IV.3045	83
IV.3046	82
IV.3045–49	67
IV.3052	83
IV.3056	83
V.46	82

V.99–171	38
V.103ff.	67
V.122–33	38
V.247–304	38
VII.331	95
VIII.6f.	67
VIII.13	66, 67, 68
XII.63f.	82
XII.72	82
XIII.171	95
XIII.242ff.	84, 154
J.383	193

P. Leiden

I.348[22]	38

P. London

II.438.19	201

P. Oslo

1.153	83
1.161f.	69

P. Oxyrhynchus

1665.5f	76
3275.40	83
3275.46	83
3295.19	83
3295.24	83

P. Warren

25f.	38

Index of Authors

Aalen, S. 98, 233
Achinger, H. 91, 233
Achtemeier, P.J. 54, 58, 74, 91, 93, 97, 142, 166, 209, 219, 233
Aitken, W.E.M. 105, 106, 233
Aland, K. 108, 231
Alexander, W.M. 140, 233
Allan, G. 65
Allegro, J.M. 229
Allen, W.C. 66
Allison, F.G. 229
Ambrozic, A.M. 57, 233
Anderson, A.A. 229
Anderson, H. 58, 63, 78, 89, 91, 168, 169, 178
Annen, F. 72, 86, 233
Argyle, A.W. 103, 233
Arnold, C.E. 50
Attridge, H.W. 28, 233
Audollent, A. 70, 229
Aulen, G. 7
Aune, D.E. 41, 63, 64, 84, 139, 153, 158, 159, 160, 162, 163, 169, 190, 191, 197, 202, 207, 233, 234
Avigad, N. 229

Bächli, O. 64, 233
Baarda, T. 72, 233
Bacon, B.W. 233
Baillet, M. 229
Baird, M.M. 73, 233
Baltensweiler, H. 40, 110, 233
Bammel, E. 211, 216, 233, 242
Banks, R. 129
Barrett, C.K. 54, 61, 108, 110, 154, 163, 182, 187, 188, 189, 199, 209, 211, 216, 222, 233, 242
Barrett, P.W. 50
Barth, G. 60, 76, 90, 120, 235
Barthélemy, D. 229
Barthes, R. 246
Barlett, D.L. 74, 77, 233
Barton, G.A. 186
Bartsch, H.W. 6
Batdorf, I.W. 6, 7, 233
Bauer, J.-B. 244
Bauernfeind, O. 62, 63, 64, 67, 68, 73, 81, 233

Baumbach, G. 115, 233
Baumgarten, J. 37
Beare, F.W. 65, 94, 121, 123, 124, 203
Beasley-Murray, G.R. 107, 110, 115, 117, 218, 233
Beauvery, R. 234
Becker, J. 185, 234
Becker-Wirth, S. 57, 234
Behm, J. 44, 234
Bell, H.I. 33, 83, 229
Bellinzoni, A.J. 53
Benko, S. 196, 234
Berger, K. 141, 149, 168
Berger, P.L. 8
Bermann, D. 209
Bertram, G. 82
Beskow, P. 207
Best, E. 43, 58, 59, 65, 84, 89, 91, 98, 106, 111, 115, 116, 128, 129, 136, 142, 177, 178, 234
Betz, H.D. 16, 38, 131, 229, 234, 242
Betz, O. 37, 142, 170, 218, 234
Bickermann, E. 105
Bietenhard, H. 143
Bigg, C. 204
Billerbeck, P. 61, 63, 65, 66, 109, 124, 126, 158, 162, 182, 183, 184, 187, 232
Black, C.C. 54, 55
Black, M. 42, 79, 80, 89, 93, 119, 162, 185, 223, 234
Blackburn, B. 68, 213
Blass, F. 70, 89, 109
Blau, L. 158, 229
Bligh, J. 234
Bloch, M. 132, 133
Block, M. 37
Blomberg, C. 11, 18, 50, 57, 131, 136, 138, 140, 143, 147, 153, 154, 155, 219, 236, 247, 248
Böcher, O. 11, 86, 142, 153, 220, 234
Böhlig, A. 35, 238
Boers, H. 234
Bokser, B.M. 23, 234
Bonnard, P. 40, 65
Bonner, C. 6, 35, 84, 155, 234
Bonnet, M. 231

Borg, M.J. 3, 6, 170, 171, 175, 209, 217, 219, 234, 235
Boring, M.E. 131, 235
Bornkamm, G. 7, 58, 60, 76, 90, 120, 235
Borrois, G.A. 14
Borsch, F.H. 214
Bourghouts, J.F. 229
Bousset, W. 67, 136, 184, 186, 213, 214, 235
Bovon, F. 73, 246
Bowie, E.L. 23, 24
Bowker, J. 235
Bowman, J. 35, 183, 199, 200, 235
Braude, W.G. 229
Braun, H. 7, 201, 242
Breech, J. 7
Briére, J. 59, 235
Broek, R. Van den 195, 197, 245
Brooke, G.J. 184
Brown, P. 34, 47, 235
Brown, R.E. 199
Brown, S. 115
Brownlee, W.H. 68
Brox, N. 235
Bruce, F.F. 32, 82, 129, 180, 196
Bryant, H.E. 235
Bryce, H. 229
Büchler, A. 178, 235
Büchsel, F. 112
Bühner, J.-A. 207, 209, 215, 235
Buchanan, G.W. 7
Buck, H.M. 63, 64
Bulmer, R. 181
Bultmann, R. 6, 7, 10, 19, 20, 41, 42, 48, 55, 67, 68, 75, 86, 89, 90, 91, 92, 93, 100, 103, 104, 107, 110, 121, 124, 126, 137, 155, 163, 167, 168, 169, 172, 180, 199, 216, 218, 219, 222, 233, 235, 239
Bundy, W. 72, 74
Burger, C. 102, 183, 235
Burket, W. 27
Burkill, T.A. 62, 64, 69, 73, 79, 81, 83, 89, 235
Burrows, M. 229
Busse, U. 235
Butts, J.R. 110

Cadbury, H.J. 119
Cadoux, C.J. 126
Caird, G.B. 123, 124, 126
Calvert, D.G.A. 235
Calvin, J. 158
Canary, R.H. 132
Cangh, J.-M. van 98, 108
Caquot, A. 46
Caragounis, C.C. 107, 108, 111, 218, 235
Carlson, C.E. 106, 107, 115, 235

Carr, D. 132, 235
Carr, E.H. 132
Carr, W. 49, 50
Carson, D.A. 50, 112
Casas, G.V. 235, 236
Cave, C.H. 236
Cave, S.V. 73
Chadwick, G.A. 60, 236
Chadwick, H. 27, 229
Charles, R.H. 186, 229
Charlesworth, J.H. 3, 6, 16, 18, 19, 187, 216, 219, 229, 236
Chilton, B.D. 57, 98, 112, 170, 236
Chwolson, D. 139
Cohoon, J.W. 230
Collins, J.J. 186, 209, 211
Colson, F.H. 230
Colwell, E.C. 234, 238
Comber, J.A. 236
Conolly, R.H. 34
Conybeare, F.C. 11, 18, 24, 25, 230
Conzelmann, H. 7, 115, 120
Cook, M.J. 104
Corrington, G.P. 190, 206, 236
Coulton, C.C. 194
Craghan, J.F. 78, 236
Cranfield, C.E.B. 72, 113, 236
Crasta, P.M. 236
Cratchley, W.J. 236
Creed, J.M. 107, 119
Crehan, J.H. 2
Cremer, H. 41
Crombie, A.C. 135
Crosby, H.L. 230
Cross, F.M. 17, 37, 230
Crossan J.D. 14, 100, 111, 221
Cullmann, O. 59, 245
Cupitt, D. 1, 2

Dahl, N.A. 245
Dalman, G. 72, 110, 183, 184, 218, 236
Danby, H. 230
Danker, F.W. 236
Daube, D. 96, 211, 233, 236, 242
Davies, T.W. 75, 236
Davies, W.D. 211, 216, 233, 242
Day, P.L. 11, 236
Debrunner, A. 70, 89, 109
Dehn, G. 72, 81
Deissmann, A. 41, 83, 84, 95, 112, 193, 236
Delcor, M. 37
Delebecque, E. 30
Delling, G. 36, 230
Delobel, J. 54, 98, 108, 236
Denis, A.-M. 19, 230

Derenbourg, J. 192
Dermience, A. 88, 236
Derrett, J.D.M. 56, 63, 72, 75, 77, 80, 84, 85, 86, 90, 122, 143, 144, 236
Descamps, A. 44, 107, 110, 162, 233, 239
Detweiler, R. 72, 236
Diaz, J.A. 236
Dibelius, M. 10, 11, 19, 20, 72, 74, 100, 106, 129, 155, 172, 236
Diehl, E. 230
Dieterich, A. 236
Dilthey, W. 133, 237
Dix, G. 190
Dodds, E.R. 20, 24, 30, 237
Dods, M.R. 230
Domeris, W.R. 67, 237
Doty, W.G. 72, 236
Douglas, M. 181, 235, 237
Downing, F.G. 28, 29, 53, 103, 230, 237
Dozent, P.P. 237
Drewermann, E. 57, 72, 88, 91, 98, 114, 122, 146
Driver, G.R. 46, 75
Dschulnigg, P. 54, 237
Dudley, D.R. 28, 29, 237
Dufton, F. 88
Duling, D.C. 2, 18, 19, 35, 36, 74, 183, 184, 237
Dunn, J.D.G. 4, 11, 59, 108, 109, 110, 118, 120, 121, 136, 138, 140, 142, 149, 150, 151, 152, 161, 162, 168, 177, 209, 213, 216, 217, 218, 219, 224, 237
Dupont-Sommer, A. 17, 44, 230, 237
Durkheim, E. 190
Dzielska, M. 23
D'Alviella, Count 75

Easton, B.S. 124, 237
Ebstein, E. 61
Edelstein, L. 237
Edgar, C.C. 14
Edwards, R.A. 66, 111
Egger, W. 128
Eissfeldt, O. 183, 186
Eitrem, S. 11, 13, 57, 70, 95, 139, 142, 158, 160, 191, 237
Elliott, J.H. 237, 243
Ellis, E.E. 72, 233
Eltester, W. 68, 245
Engelbrecht, J. 136
Enslin, M. 7
Epstein, I. 192, 230
Evans, C.A. 2, 130, 131, 216, 237
Everts, W.W. 140, 237

Fabris, R. 237
Fascher, E. 153, 176

Feldman, L.H. 15, 16, 37, 234
Fenner, F. 158
Ferguson, E. 11, 24, 237
Ferguson, J. 24
Feuerbach, L. 3, 4
Fiebig, P.W.J. 10, 48, 49, 146, 160, 162, 230, 237, 238
Fiederlein F.M. 238
Filson, F.V. 40, 65
Finkelstein J. 230
Fischer, L.R. 238
Fischer, R.H. 195, 235, 239
Fitzmyer, J.A. 16, 17, 46, 68, 72, 82, 114, 119, 122, 126, 151, 230, 238
Flammer, B. 238
Flew, A. 133, 136
Flusser, D. 44, 110, 149, 178, 238
Foakes Jackson, F.J. 32
Foerster, W. 86, 126, 186, 230
Fohrer, G. 150, 238
Fowler, H.N. 220
France, R.T. 119, 131, 132, 166, 246, 247
Frazen J. 75
Freedman, D.N. 238
Freedman, H. 230
Frend, W.H.C. 194
Frerichs, E.S. 182
Freyne, S. 14, 22, 180, 209, 211
Fridrichsen, A. 8, 61, 62, 70, 121, 139, 159, 167, 169, 170, 204, 206, 207, 216, 238
Frye, R.M. 134
Fuchs, A. 91, 98, 233, 238
Fuchs, E. 173, 238
Fuller, R.H. 8, 60, 102, 103, 142, 182, 183, 184, 238
Funk, R.W. 6, 70, 89, 109, 132, 219, 234, 238, 248

Gadamer, H.G. 134
Gaechter, P. 40
Gager, J. 35
Gallagher, E.V. 190, 204, 205, 207, 213, 238
Galling, K. 186
Gardiner, A.H. 238
Gardiner, P. 133
Garrett, S.R. 30, 190, 191, 199, 206, 238
Gärtner, R.B. 219, 238
Gaster, M. 18, 19
Gaster, T.H. 230
Gaston, L. (*HSE*) 54, 55, 59, 80, 89, 90, 96, 103, 105, 106, 119, 238
Geller, M.J. 16, 68, 80, 139, 144, 191, 238
George, A. 238
Georgi, D. 238
Gerhardsson, B. 102
Ghalioungui, G. 238

Gibbs, J.M. 102, 238
Giesen, H. 57, 238
Gifford, E.H. 230
Ginzberg, L. 230
Girard, R. 72, 238
Giversen, S. 35, 238
Gloer, W.H. 111, 237
Gnilka, J. 56, 57, 72, 88, 91, 98, 122, 128, 129
Gonzáles, F.J.I. 238
Goodenough, E.R. 35, 173, 238
Goodwin, G.W. 230, 238
Goppelt, L. 7, 65
Goshen-Gottstein, M.H. 37, 239
Goulder, M. 98
Granfield, P. 104, 243
Grant, F.C. 72
Grant, M. 136, 169
Grant, R.M. 25, 136, 195, 230, 239
Grayston, K. 2, 44, 239
Green, J.B. 247
Green, W.S. 239
Greeven, H. 129, 147
Grelot, P. 239
Grenfell B.P. 230
Gressmann, H. 67, 184, 235
Griffith, F.L. 230, 240
Grimm, W. 234
Grobel, K. 58
Grundmann, W. 41, 60, 61, 147, 153, 167, 205, 239
Güttgemanns, E. 77
Guelich, R.A. 45, 57, 58, 68, 72, 88, 98, 114, 117, 122, 128, 129, 149, 177
Guerlac. H. 135
Guillemette, P. 57, 64, 71, 239
Gulick, C.B. 230
Gummere, R.M. 230
Gundry, R.H. 94, 101
Gurewicz, S.B. 37
Guttmann, A. 220, 239
Gutwenger, E. 239

Haacker, K. 37, 234
Haag, H. 242
Hadas, M. 239
Hadidian, D.Y. 134
Haenchen, E. 30, 32, 41, 180
Hahn, F.C. 68, 82, 123, 124, 142
Hahn, H.C. 66
Halleux, A. de 233, 239
Halleux, R.P. de 44, 107, 110, 162
Halliday, W.R. 24
Hamm, M.D. 56
Hammerton-Kelly, R.G. 108, 239
Hanse, H. 198
Hardy, B. 132

Harmon, A.M. 16, 230
Harnack, A. 5, 6, 11, 12, 66, 140
Harrington, D.J. 6, 14, 16, 17, 230, 239
Harris, M.J. 196
Hartel, G. 230
Harvey, A.E. 7, 48, 49, 61, 68, 107, 120, 136, 137, 149, 152, 189, 209, 210, 211, 215, 239
Harvey, V.A. 2, 132, 133
Hasler, J.I. 239
Hata, G. 37, 234
Hauck, F. 60
Hawkins, J.C. 54, 59, 101, 115, 119, 126, 239
Hawthorn, T. 73, 239
Hay, L.S. 239
Hedrick, C.W. 128, 131, 235, 239
Heikel, I.A. 231
Heil, M. 239
Heitmüller, W. 44, 239
Held, H.J. 26, 76, 90, 120, 235
Hemer, C.J. 81
Hendrickx, H. 57, 239
Hengel, M. 14, 15, 24, 37, 105, 109, 124, 125, 149, 150, 173, 211, 213, 215, 234, 239
Hennecke, E. 19, 20, 34, 148, 231
Henrichs, A. 232
Herford, R.T. 192, 231
Hermann, I. 239
Herrmann, L. 239
Herzog, R. 146, 191
Hick, J. 216
Hickling, C. 77, 214
Hicks, R.D. 231
Hiers, R.H. 7, 110, 169, 170, 239
Hill, D. 65, 104, 168
Hinnells, J.R. 240
Hock, R.F. 240
Hodgson, P.C. 5
Hoffmann, P. 66, 124, 125
Hogarth, D.G. 32
Holladay, C.R. 213, 231, 240
Hollander, H.W. 185
Hollenbach, P.W. 6, 7, 130, 143, 145, 179, 240
Holtz, T. 111
Honoré, A.M. 103
Hooker, M.D. 77, 115, 214
Hopfner, T. 240
Horner, G. 231
Horsley, G.H.R. 231
Horsley, R.A. 6, 7, 28, 129, 240
Houlden, L. 49
Howard, J.K. 240
Howard, V. 12, 95, 164, 240
Hull, J.M. 9, 10, 13, 18, 48, 60, 62, 86, 153, 157, 158, 197, 206, 240
Hultgren, A.J. 98, 240

Hume, D. 133, 136
Hummel. R. 104
Hunt, A.S. 230, 240
Hunter, A.M. 126, 170
Huntress, E. 240

Iersel, B.M.F. van 240
Isaac, E. 187

Jackson, J. 231
James, M.R. 231
Jannasch, W. 44
Jayne, W.A. 240
Jellicoe, S. 126
Jeremias, A. 158
Jeremias, G. 38, 232
Jeremias, J. 14. 31, 32, 73, 85, 88, 90, 104, 110, 111, 114, 118, 121, 122, 123, 124, 125, 126, 127, 142, 162, 164, 168, 169, 178, 221, 240
Jervell, J. 47, 245
Johnson, A.R. 86
Johnson, E.A. 2
Johnson, S.E. 153
Jones, H.S. 60, 69, 83
Jonge, M. de 185, 186, 187, 231, 240
Jongeling, B. 16, 17, 18, 159, 231, 240
Joüon, P. 111
Jühlicher, A. 117
Jungmann, J.A. 104, 243

Käsemann, E. 2, 65, 94, 142, 167, 240
Kallas, J. 9, 169, 240
Kampling, R. 173, 240
Kasper, W. 240
Kazmierski, C.R. 129, 240
Keck, L.E. 129, 240
Kee, H.C. 8, 9, 16, 17, 20, 24, 27, 41, 44, 45, 46, 49, 57, 65, 68, 69, 73, 75, 81, 95, 103, 115, 141, 146, 169, 171, 179, 196, 197, 205, 207, 211, 220, 231, 240, 241
Kelly, H.A. 241
Kennedy, J.M. 45
Kermode, F. 204
Kertelge, K. 7, 8, 57, 58, 59, 70, 74, 77, 89, 91, 92, 106, 148, 241
Kiev, A. 179
Kilburn, K. 230
Kilpatrick, G.D. 65
King, L.W. 44, 241
Kingsbury, J.D. 2, 72, 102, 183, 213, 241
Kirchschläger, W. 11, 137, 205, 241
Kissinger, W.S. 6, 7, 241
Kittel, G. 42
Kittel, R. 231
Klausner, J. 179, 183, 192

Klein, G. 241
Kleist, J.A. 241
Klijn, A.F.J. 14
Kloppenborg, J.S. 102, 114, 126, 241
Klostermann, E. 40, 60, 84, 86, 115
Knibb, M.A. 187, 223, 231
Knox, W.L. 33, 241
Koch, D.-A. 57, 68, 241
Koester, H. 138, 142, 169, 215
Koetschau, P. 231
Kolenkow, A.B. 179, 191, 241
Kozicki, H. 132
Kraeling, C.H. 198, 208, 241
Krause, N. 35, 238
Kremer, J. 12, 241
Kruse, H. 241
Kümmel, W.G. 6, 53, 54, 66, 103, 107, 110, 124, 126, 149, 218, 241
Kuhn, H.W. 241

Labuschagne, B. 231
Lacocque, A. 18
Lagrange, M.-J. 93
Lake, K. 32, 231
Lamarche, P. 57, 241
Lambrecht, J. 241
Lampe, G.W.H. 1
Langdon, S. 241
Langton, E. 11, 84, 126, 241
Latourelle, R. 9, 56, 72, 87, 88, 91, 97, 131, 138, 153, 158, 241
Lattey, C. 241
Lauterbach, J.Z. 192, 231
Lawlor, H.J. 231
Leaney, A.R.C. 40, 211, 241
Lee, B.J. 175
Leeuw, G. van der 191
Légasse, S. 146
Leivestad, R. 9, 169, 170, 182, 189, 216, 218, 219, 241, 242
Léon-Dufour, X. 57, 166, 241, 242
Lessing, G. 4
Lewis, E.L. 242
Leyh, G. 244
Liebermann, S. 15
Lietzmann, H. 193, 194
Lightfoot, J.B. 231
Lightfoot, R.H. 59, 78, 80
Limbeck, M. 113, 242
Lindars, B. 65, 111, 120, 163, 199, 211, 216, 242, 246, 247
Ling, T. 242
Linnemann, E. 127
Lipsius, R.A. 231
Livingstone, E.A. 77, 236, 245

Loader, W.R.G. 183, 242
Locke, J. 120
Loewe, H. 231
Lohmeyer, E. 59, 72, 116
Lohse, E. 158, 184, 231
Loos, H. van der 8, 33, 59, 84, 86, 92, 146, 158, 159, 169, 176, 242
Lorenzmeier, T. 242
Liddell, H.G. SJ, 60, 69, 83
Lühramm, D. 123
Luck, G. 191, 231
Luz, U. 70

MacDonald, D.R. 19, 242
Macintosh, A.A. 46, 242
Mack, B.L. 7, 57
Mackey, J.P. 3
MacLaurin, E.C.B. 98, 105, 242
Macleod, M.D. 230
MacMahon, J.H. 231
MacRae, G. 241, 242
Maher, M. 136, 242
Mair, L. 190, 191
Malherbe, A.J. 28, 231
Malina, B.J. 98, 191, 242
Mandelbaum, M. 132
Mann, C.S. 7, 56, 72, 100, 146, 242
Manrique, A. 72, 242
Manson, T.W. 103, 123, 126
Manson, W. 105, 119
Marcus, R. 105, 231
Margoliouth, D.S. 242
Marin, A.D. 242
Marsh, J. 7
Marshall, I.H. 4, 5, 65, 72, 111, 118, 119, 120, 123, 124, 169
Marwick, A. 134, 135
Marwick, M. 190, 242
Marxsen, W. 59, 65, 89
Mastin, B.A. 31, 242
Mateos, J. 85, 242
Mauser, U.W. 116
Maynard, A.H. 62, 152, 242
McArthur, H.K. 242
McCasland, S.V. 36, 62, 139, 153, 242
McConnell, S. 101
McCown, C.C. 18, 19, 32, 231, 242
McEleney, N.J. 242
McEwin, J.S. 140
McGaughtey, L.C. 238
McKnight, S. 114, 247
McNeill, J.T. 242
McRae G. 241
Mead, G.R.S. 242
Mearns, C. 98, 187, 219

Meeks, W.A. 47, 245
Mehlmann, J. 198
Meier, J.P. 3
Mendelsohn, I. 13, 206
Metzger, B.M. 32, 97, 104, 123, 242, 243
Meyer B.F. 4, 7, 27, 28, 38, 131, 234, 243
Meyer, E. 134
Meyer P.W. 243
Meyer, R. 243
Meyers, E.M. 14
Meynet, R. 98, 113, 243
Michaelis, W. 140
Michaels, J.R. 203
Michel, O. 81
Micklem, E.R. 159
Milik, J.T. 17, 187, 229, 231, 232, 243
Millar, F. 15
Miller, D.G. 134
Milligan, G. 32, 41, 60, 76, 82, 83, 93
Milligan, J.D. 135
Mills, M.E. 9, 16, 19, 35, 243
Milot, L. 56
Mink, L.O. 132
Miyoshi, M. 243
Mohlberg, C. 194
Montefiore, C.G. 72, 74, 231, 243
Montgomery, J.A. 85, 231, 243
Moore, C.H. 231
Moore, G.F. 182, 223, 243
Morenz, S. 44
Morris, L.L. 152, 206, 215
Moule, C.F.D. 3, 79, 127, 242, 243
Moulton, J.H. 32, 41, 60, 76, 82, 83, 93
Munz, P. 132
Murray, A.T. 231
Mussner, F. 8, 68, 131, 168, 243

Nagakubo, S. 14
Naveh, J. 16, 231
Neirynck, F. 54, 78, 80, 89, 98, 129, 243
Nestle, E. 108, 231, 243
Neusner, J. 16, 49, 178, 182, 209, 231, 243
Newton, C.T. 32
Neyrey, J.H. 98, 105, 191, 242, 243
Nicholson, F.W. 158
Nickelsburg, G.W.E. 22, 209, 211, 243
Niebuhr, R.R. 3
Nielsen H.K. 169
Nilsson, M.P. 243
Nineham, D.E. 33, 80, 88, 90, 91, 97, 117, 129, 149, 216
Nkwoka, A.O. 98, 177, 243
Noack, B. 11, 243
Nock, A.D. 229, 243
Nolan, B.M. 183

Norman, A.P. 132

Oakman, D.E. 6, 98, 243
Odegard, D. 136, 243
Oepke, A. 66
Oesterley, W.O.E. 243
Oesterreich, T.K. 11, 243
Olafson, F. 132
Oldfather, C.H. 232
Oldfather, W.A. 232
Oppenheimer, A. 180
Oster, R.E. 30, 32, 33, 244
Otto, R. 112, 143, 170
Oulton, J.E.L. 231
Owen, E.C.E. 244
O'Brien, P.T. 50, 162
O'Day, G.R. 88, 243
O'Neil, E. 28

Pancaro, S. 200
Pannenberg, W. 7, 133, 134
Parker, S.T. 79, 143
Passmore, J. 132
Paulus, H. 4
Peabody, D.B. 54, 244
Pelikan, J. 2
Penella, R.J. 23
Perels, O. 244
Perrin, N. 54, 107, 110, 128, 142, 168, 239, 244
Pesch, R. 40, 45, 56, 57, 58, 59, 64, 72, 78, 88, 89, 91, 95, 98, 114, 122, 128, 129, 131, 135, 142, 173, 244
Peters, T. 134, 244
Petersen, N.R. 74
Peterson, E. 59, 244
Petitpierre, R. 1, 2
Petrie, S. 103
Petterson, O. 244
Petzke, G. 23, 92, 93, 97, 244
Pimental, P. 60, 244
Plevnik, J. 57, 233
Ploeg, J.P.M. van der 38, 232
Plummer, A. 93, 105
Pokorny, P. 244
Polag, A. 103, 119
Polhill, J.B. 244
Polkow, D. 130, 131, 244
Praeder, S. 244
Pratten, B.P. 230
Preisendanz, K. 19, 232, 244
Preisker, H. 85, 200
Pritchard, J. 232
Procksch, O. 67
Pryke, E.J. 54, 59, 78, 80, 83, 90, 128, 145, 147, 178, 244

Puech, E. 38, 232

Quasten, J. 104, 243
Quispel, G. 245

Rackham, H. 232
Radice, B. 232
Rahlfs, A. 232
Rambaut, W.H. 232
Rankin, H.D. 29, 244
Ratschow, C.H. 13
Reif, S.C. 244
Reifferscheid, A. 232
Reimarus, H. 4
Reiner, E. 244
Reiser, M. 43
Reith, G. 230
Reitzenstein, R. 67, 244
Remus, H. 153, 191, 195, 204, 206, 244
Rengstorf, K.H. 65
Rice, G.E. 57
Richards, J. 1
Richards, K.H. 6, 7, 131, 190, 196, 206, 233, 234, 236, 244, 246
Richardson, A. 8, 142
Riches, J. 7
Ridderbos, H. 169
Riesenfeld, H. 244
Riga, P, 244
Rigaux, R.P.B. 44, 233, 239
Rist, M. 244
Rivkin, E. 209
Roberts, A. 232·
Robinson, J.M. 3, 9, 35, 69, 142, 232
Robinson, W.C. 70
Rodd, C.S. 244
Rodkinson, M.L. 232
Rohde, E. 70, 244
Rohde, J. 115
Rolfe, J.C. 232
Roloff, J. 244
Rosen, G. 145
Rose, H.J. 191
Ross, J.M. 40, 244, 245·
Rüsch, E.G. 245
Russell, D.S. 50, 182, 188, 245
Russell, E.A. 40, 245

Sabourin, L. 49
Sabugal, S. 118, 245
Safrai, S. 14, 178, 245
Sahlin, H. 73, 245
Samain, J. 201, 202, 207, 245
Sanday, W. 126

Sanders, E.P. 7, 27, 28, 38, 104, 182, 189, 191, 218, 234, 245
Sanders, J.A. 37, 232, 245
Santo, C. de 245
Sawyer, H. 59
Schaeder, H.H. 65
Scheidweiler, F. 34
Schelkle, K.H. 242
Schenk, W. von 91, 97, 245
Schenke, L. 57, 245
Schille, G. 8, 245
Schillebeeckx, E. 11
Schindler, C.J. 245
Schlatter, A. 126, 245
Schlosser, J. 40, 42, 245
Schmidt, C. 232
Schmidt, K.L. 58, 83, 128, 232, 239
Schmithals, W. 245
Schnackenburgh, R. 222
Schnapp, F. 185
Schottroff, L. 242
Schramm, T, 104, 123, 138
Schreckenberg, H. 16
Schreiber, J. 54, 106
Schürer, E. 14, 16, 18, 19, 31, 32, 35, 72, 179, 182, 188, 196, 245
Schürmann, H. 57, 72, 91, 94, 115, 119, 120, 122, 169
Schubert, K. 210, 235, 245
Schuller, E.M. 232
Schultz. H.J. 49, 247
Schultz, W. 245
Schulz, S. 104, 115, 119, 124
Schwab, M. 232
Schwarz, G. 90, 245
Schweitzer, A. 2, 4, 5, 7, 8, 174, 216
Schweizer, E. 33, 40, 58, 59, 65, 68, 69, 80, 86, 89, 91, 100, 106, 107, 128, 129, 149, 150, 164, 168, 169, 245
Scott, R. 60, 69, 83
Scott, S.P. 232
Scott, W. 169
Seccombe, D.P. 120
Seebas, H. 67
Seesemann, H. 62
Segal, A.F. 195, 197, 245
Sellew, P. 98, 245
Sellin, G. 126
Sevenster, J.N. 14, 169
Shae, G.S. 245
Shanks, H. 57
Shorey, P. 232
Sider, R.J. 136, 245
Simon, M. 230
Simonis, W. 245

Simpson, R.T. 103
Skehan, P.W. 37, 245
Slingerland, H.D. 185, 246
Smalley, S.S. 120, 162, 242, 246, 247
Smalley, W.A. 37
Smart, J.D. 246
Smith, G. 246
Smith, J.Z. 11, 47, 181, 191, 246
Smith, M. 10, 14, 37, 49, 137, 191, 192, 193, 194, 195, 196, 197, 198, 201, 203, 204, 206, 207, 235, 239, 246
Somerville, J.E. 246
Speyer, W. 24
Spinka, M. 242
Stählïn, O. 232
Stanley, D.M. 57, 233
Stanton, G.N. 77, 120, 171, 196, 246
Starky, J. 37
Starobinski, J. 72, 73, 246
Starr, J. 246
Stauffer, E. 109, 153, 164
Steck, O.H. 66
Stein, R.H. 54, 58, 59, 74, 89, 90, 97, 100, 119, 131, 132, 221, 246
Steinmueller, J.E. 100, 246
Stern, M. 14, 245
Stewart, J.S. 246
Stock, A. 57, 72, 88, 98, 114, 122, 246
Stock, K. 79
Stone, M.E. 17, 35, 246
Storch, W. 246
Strack, H.L. 61, 63, 65, 66, 109, 124, 126, 158, 162, 182, 183, 184, 187, 192, 232, 246
Strange, J.F. 14, 57
Strange W.A. 30, 31, 246
Strauss, C. Levi- 72
Strauss, D.F. 4, 5, 8, 72, 142
Streeter, B.H. 126
Strugnell, J. 246
Sturch, R.L. 246
Sugirtharajah, R.S. 88, 246
Sukenik, E.L. 232

Täger, F. 24
Tagawa, K. 57, 246
Talbert, C.H. 4
Talmon, S. 37, 246
Tatum, W.B. 7
Taylor, B.E. 31
Taylor, D.B. 65
Taylor, V. 41, 58, 61, 72, 74, 79, 80, 86, 88, 89, 90, 93, 97, 100, 106, 111, 120, 125, 128, 141, 149, 153, 168, 176, 246
Tcherikover, V. 14, 246
Telford, W. 213

Thackeray, H. St. J. 16, 80, 105, 232
Theissen, G. 8, 28, 30, 47, 59, 73, 75, 85, 88, 90 94,
    102, 143, 144, 176, 211, 213, 214, 219, 246, 247
Thelwall, S. 232
Thraede, K. 22
Tiede, D.L. 51, 215, 247
Tilborg, S. van 104
Tödt, H.E. 66, 94
Torczyner, H. 247
Trebilco, R.R. 82
Trevijano, R. 62, 247
Trites, A.A. 162, 163
Trocmé, E. 247
Troeltsch, E. 132, 133
Trotter, F.T. 234, 238
Tuckett, C.M. 28, 69, 70, 247
Turner, C.H. 54, 88, 247
Turner, H.E.W. 94, 130
Turner, M.M.B. 112
Turner, N. 63, 67, 89, 101, 109
Twelftree, G.H. 1, 8, 11, 12, 14, 30, 38, 39, 43, 50,
    52, 56, 60, 62, 65, 66, 82, 86, 92, 110, 114, 115,
    122, 125, 131, 135, 136, 138, 140, 141, 143,
    147, 148, 153, 154, 155, 161, 180, 192, 196,
    213, 215, 219, 220, 222, 237, 247

Ullendorff, E. 223, 231

Vaganay, L. 247
Vassiliadis, P. 54
Vaux, R. de 229, 232
Venkowski, J. 247
Vermaseren, M.J. 195, 197, 245
Vermes, G. 9. 15, 16, 17, 43, 131, 142, 146, 149,
    150, 152, 161, 170, 178, 179, 180, 181, 209,
    210, 211, 232, 247
Verseput, D.J. 183
Vögtle, A. 247
Vöörbus, A. 195, 235, 239
Vollenweider, S. 127, 247
Volkmar, P. 69
Volz, P. 182, 247

Walker, A. 232
Walker, W.O. 55, 247
Wall, R.W. 108, 247
Wallis, R.E. 233

Wansbrough, H. 177, 247
Weatherhead, L. 73, 84
Weber, J.C. 104, 247
Weder, H. 247
Wee, B.C. 88, 247
Weinreich, O. 159, 247
Weiss, B. 69
Weiss, J. 43
Weiss, W. 59, 247
Wellhausen, J. 42, 66
Wendland, H.-D. 44, 233
Wengst, K. 85
Wenham, D. 11, 18, 50, 57, 131, 132, 135, 136,
    138, 140, 143, 147, 153, 154, 155, 166, 170,
    177, 180, 192, 196, 213, 219, 236, 246, 247, 248
Whigham, P. 29
White, A.N. Sherwin- 194, 195, 204, 233
White, L.J. 6
White, L.M. 98, 247
Whittaker, G.H. 230
Wilcox, M. 72, 233
Wild, R.A. 50
Wilhems, E. 248
Wilkinson, J. 56, 248
Williamson, R. 16
Willoughby, H.R. 242
Wilson, G.H. 37
Wilson, W. 233
Wink, W. 11, 50, 119, 207, 248
Winter, P. 85, 196, 207
Wire, A.C. 248
Wissowa, G. 232
Woodhouse, W.J. 32
Woude, A.S. van der 231
Wrede, W. 62, 69, 70, 78, 79, 89, 90, 248
Wright, R.B. 183
Wünsch, R. 70, 139, 248

Yadin, Y. 229
Yamauchi, E.M. 8, 11. 18, 32, 39, 50, 248
Yates, J.E. 248
Yates, R. 117, 170, 248
Young, R. 136

Zeitlin, I.M. 182
Zerwick, M. 248

Index of Names and Subjects

Abraham 35, 43–44, 46, 47, 51, 157, 158, 160, 210, 214, 215, 226
Abrasax 39
Abyss 73
Acts of the Apostles 30–34
Acts of Pilate 34
'Adjure' 32–34, 36, 39, 82, 96, 139, 142, 149, 161, 163–164, 227
Agrath 23, 151
Amulet(s) 35, 36, 39, 44, 51, 95, 96, 157
Analogy, principle of 132, 133, 134
Anaxagorus 24
Antithsenes 28
Angels 18, 35, 39, 50, 62, 95, 115, 116, 126, 187, 188, 221, 223
Apocrypha
— New Testament 19–21
Apollonius of Tyana 16, 21, 23–27, 46, 47, 48, 52, 70, 74, 96, 146, 148, 156, 158, 159, 160, 227
Artemis 32
Azazel 154, 187, 188, 223

Baalshamaim 106
Baalzebub 105
Babylonian material 33, 44, 50, 75, 95, 157, 158, 160, 226
Baptist, John the 29, 55, 118–121, 167, 170, 200, 210, 219, 224
Beelzebul 40, 61, 98–113, 149, 181, 198, 199,
— Charge 61, 62, 104–106, 138, 149, 161, 176, 178, 181, 198, 199, 200, 208
— Controversy 16, 98–113, 115, 116, 126, 135, 137, 138, 146, 148, 177, 178, 182, 196, 217, 219, 220, 226
Belial 38, 45, 184
Beliar 185, 186, 187
Beth She'arim 14
Blindness 84, 101, 102, 119, 120, 154, 158
Bowls, incantation 85, 139, 144

Charismatic figures 22–40, 46, 52, 178, 179, 181, 209–213, 226
Church
— of England 1

— of Scotland 13
Coherence, criterion of 121, 130, 135
Correlation, principle of 132
Cross 142
Cynics 28–31, 47, 52, 59, 210, 211, 214, 226

Dating material 15–17
Daniel 35
David 35, 37–38, 44, 63, 157, 183, 189
Dead Sea Scrolls 15, 16, 17, 21, 37, 38, 43–47, 49, 52, 68, 82, 105, 108, 151, 152, 160, 183, 187, 189, 209, 226
Demoniac(s) 60, 71, 76, 143–145
Demoniac in synagogue 57–71, 76, 138, 144, 146, 147
Demonic 60
Demonology 11, 18, 73
Demon-possession 3, 11, 13, 14, 17, 18, 25, 26, 36, 60, 75, 84, 85, 93, 96, 101, 104, 105, 109, 111, 112, 128, 143, 144, 148, 149, 152, 156, 176, 177, 178, 181, 198, 199, 201, 207
Demon(s) 11, 17, 19, 23, 26, 37, 38, 40, 41, 46, 51, 69
— adjure/binding 33, 34, 39, 51, 68, 69, 70, 80, 83, 84, 95, 96, 112, 128, 163–164, 227
— confrontation with exorcist 20, 23, 25, 34, 36, 39, 61, 71, 76, 80, 81, 92, 144, 146–148, 156, 173
— consternation of 60, 61, 81, 92, 148, 173, 220
— defeat/control 23, 25, 34, 35, 36, 37, 38, 43, 44, 48, 50, 51, 52, 59, 86, 141, 162, 184, 207, 208, 220, 221, 228
— existence 8, 49–50
— foreign gods 105
— habitat 26, 76, 86, 93
— homeless 95
— messianic confession 61, 62, 68, 149, 151, 152
— multiform 85, 86
— name in incantations 95
— nature/work 13, 18, 25, 26, 35, 69, 85, 92, 101, 102, 144, 198
— plead leniency 75, 86, 154–155, 156
— protection from 39
— rebuking 45, 46, 69, 95–96, 138

— return of 25, 26, 95, 96
— self-defence 34, 51, 63, 64, 68, 82, 83, 152, 154
— spell on Jesus 82, 152
— transferred 51, 74, 75, 86, 155, 157
— violence of 26, 34, 70, 71, 96, 97, 144, 146, 155–156, 226
— vocalizing distress 27, 226
— voices of 1, 26, 70, 81, 84, 85, 128, 154
— words of 36, 51, 62, 63, 65–68, 81, 82, 83, 148–152, 226
worshipping Jesus 61, 81, 147
see also Spirit(s)
Demythologizing 6
Disciples 4, 42, 92, 94, 106, 107, 113, 125, 130, 135, 141, 144, 211, 217, 228
— of the Baptist 119, 120, 121, 224
— as exorcists 97, 122–127, 166, 167, 221, 228
— failures as exorcists 92, 93, 94, 96, 97
— mission of 55, 80, 122–127, 167, 221
— of rabbis 40, 179
Divination 30
Diviner 18
Dosa, Hanina ben 22, 23, 36, 46, 145, 150, 151, 160, 181, 209, 210
Doubt, methodological 132

Echeles 29
Egyptian material 50, 157, 159, 160, 226
Eleazar 36, 39, 47, 50, 74, 96, 139, 155, 157, 210, 214, 226
Empedocles 49
Enoch 154
Ephesian Grammata 32
Ephesus 30, 31, 32, 198
Epileptic Boy 91–97, 138, 144, 145
Eschatological events 49, 102–103, 119, 121, 168
Eschatology 110, 121, 168, 173, 184, 188, 209
— and defeat of demons 83, 86
— exorcism 46, 103, 108, 127, 173, 217–224, 227, 228
— and miracles 121, 219
Essenes 15, 158
Exorcism
— by blowing 27–28
— definition 13
— from a distance 26, 76, 90, 141, 145–146, 156, 173, 226
— of places 13
— proof of 20, 25, 26, 74–76, 155, 164, 173
— techniques 13, 26, 27
Exorcist(s) 22–47
— Babylonian 33, 44, 50, 75, 95, 158, 160, 226
— Gentile 31
— Jewish 16, 18, 36, 39, 40, 47, 106, 107, 109, 139, 157, 161, 162, 163, 178, 217, 226

— mendicant priests 47
— wandering 23, 26, 27–34, 59, 213, 226, 228

Fear and amazement 57, 58, 59, 71, 78, 80, 102, 103, 147, 176–177, 181, 220
Finger of God 98, 108, 110, 127, 165, 167, 170, 217, 222, 228
Fish 39
Funerary inscriptions 14

Gadarene demoniac 72–87, 144, 146, 156, 200, 208
Galilee/Galilean 14, 15, 17, 22, 28, 29, 31, 58, 65, 85, 150, 166, 168, 179, 180, 211, 214, 215
Gamaliel 145, 146
Gentile Mission 88, 90, 130

Hand 25, 35, 44, 50, 96, 108, 138, 158, 168, 188, 223
Hands, laying on of 44, 46, 52, 157, 158, 159, 173
Hasidim 151, 178, 209–212
Hermes 51, 66
Historical method 2, 8, 14, 53, 130–135, 206
Historicity 2, 53, 58, 61, 72, 76, 83, 84, 88, 90, 98, 103, 106, 108, 110, 118, 121, 130, 131, 132, 134, 135, 137, 138, 145, 146, 148, 149, 161, 164, 176, 177
'History' of power-authority 51
Holy individuals 34, 47, 51, 67–68, 148, 149, 150, 217
Honi 49, 150, 160, 209, 210
Holy Spirit 106, 108, 110, 120, 127, 137, 138, 167, 173, 217, 218, 219
— eschatological 217, 218, 228
— as power authority 98, 109, 161, 164, 165, 173, 217, 219, 228
Hyrcanus, Eliezer ben 49, 170

_I_, emphatic 61, 95, 108, 109, 164
Incantation(s) 26, 27, 32, 33, 34, 35, 36, 38, 44, 51, 52, 67, 69, 70, 82, 85, 95, 96, 139, 140, 153, 156, 159, 160, 161, 162, 163, 164, 172, 173, 177, 195, 205, 206, 217, 226
Incidental transmission, criterion of 103, 134, 135, 144
Insanity 5, 60, 77, 104, 176, 177, 200
Ipsissimus sensus 131
Ipsissima verba 131

Jacob 35
Jerome 105
Jesus
— authority of 58, 59, 71, 109, 120, 159, 173, 227
— baptism of 116, 117, 135, 185
— a charismatic 209–212, 214, 215, 227

— demon-possessed 198–201
— earthly 2
— eschatological charismatic 215
— eschatological prophet 189
— fanatic 177
— Galilean 179–180
— a hasid 9, 178, 209–212
— historical 2, 6, 10, 11, 17
— Holy One of God 67, 68, 148, 149
— mad 104, 176–178, 199
— magician 10, 105, 176, 190–207, 213, 214, 227
— Messiah 48, 62, 79, 81, 120, 121, 152, 176, 182–189, 213, 214, 215, 218, 227
— name 32, 33, 34, 40, 41, 42, 43, 56, 62, 64, 65, 66, 97, 139, 140, 141, 148, 161, 217, 224, 225, 226, 227
— of Nazareth 3, 64–66, 67, 68, 140, 148, 149, 214
— necromancer 208, 212, 213, 227
— peripatetic 213, 214, 228
— prophet 179, 189, 209
— quest(s) for 4, 6, 7
— a 'Samaritan' 198–201
— self understanding 55, 118, 171, 216–224
— teacher 6
— techniques as exorcist 69–70, 143–165, 178, 217
— violent exorcisms 70, 71, 96, 97, 155, 156, 226
John, Gospel of 100, 141–142, 189, 199–201, 222
Jonah 35

Kingdom
— of God 106–110, 119, 120, 121, 124, 125, 142, 166–171, 173, 188, 189, 211, 217–219, 224, 227, 228
— of Satan 106, 125, 168, 170, 227, 228

L 126
Legion 39, 76–77, 85–86

Madness, *see* Insanity
Magic 17, 25, 27, 35, 41, 70, 153–154
— definition 10, 153–154, 190–191
— Hellenistic 9
Magician(s) 44, 51, 92, 159, 190, 193, 194, 197, 201–204, 206–207
Magic and miracle 190–1
Magical Papyri 16, 21, 32, 33, 38–39, 47, 50, 51, 52, 69, 82, 96, 112, 139, 141, 157, 158, 160, 210, 214, 226
Mark 2
— priority of 53
Mastema 154
Mechanical aids 20, 46, 157–159, 164, 173, 177, 205, 227
Megara 139

Meir, Rabbi 150
Meleager of Gadara 29
Menedemus 29–30
Menippus of Gadara 29
Mental illness 143
Messianic age 66, 82, 101, 103, 109, 119, 121, 179, 182–189, 219, 220, 227
Messianic expectations 182–189, 219–220, 227
Messianic prophets 136, 179, 180, 202
Miracle(s) 4, 5, 6, 7, 8, 10, 49, 84, 120, 136, 172, 173, 178
— of the Baptist 208
— counterfeit 5, 137, 159, 200, 202, 204, 205
— and eschatology 120, 169, 189, 219, 224
— and exorcism 7, 8
— Greek stories 10, 24, 27, 49, 51
— of Jesus 6, 7, 9, 78, 120, 136, 159, 169, 179, 195, 197, 198, 202, 203, 205, 211, 219, 224, 225
— in John's Gospel 141–142
— in Judaism 10, 22, 49, 137, 172, 179, 181, 210, 220
— and magic 27, 159, 190, 195, 197, 200, 202, 203, 205, 206, 207
— and message of Jesus 4, 119, 120, 141, 166–171, 207, 210, 211
— problem of 4, 5, 6, 8, 25, 27, 131, 136–137
— significance of 5, 27, 59, 119, 120, 141, 163, 169, 170, 171
— as signs 4, 9, 56, 116, 140, 141, 169, 170, 171, 179, 189, 202, 224
— stories of Jesus 3, 4, 8, 9, 10, 91, 92, 102, 103, 131, 137, 166, 168, 172, 173, 176
— workers 24, 25, 27, 49, 51, 52, 137, 159, 196, 226
Moses 35, 51
Most High God 17, 43, 82, 186
— Jesus son of 149
Multiple attestation 130, 132
Music 37, 139, 157
Myth 5, 6, 133

Nakdimon 160
Name, use of 30, 32–36, 38, 39, 40–43, 52, 56, 61, 66, 67, 81–84, 92, 95, 97, 139, 140, 148, 152, 153, 154, 159–162, 164, 178, 192, 217, 224, 225, 226, 227
Narrative and historicity 131–132
Necromancy 29, 208, 212, 213
Noah 51, 215

Oenomaus of Gadara 30
Ornias 18, 35

Palestinian Judaism 14
Panthera, Jesus ben 192

Parable(s) 106, 171
— of the Net 222
— of the returning spirits 13
— of the Sheep and the Goats 222
— of the Strong Man 13, 98, 111–113, 117, 135, 138, 167, 170, 219, 227, 228
— of the Wheat and the Tares 220, 221, 222–224
Peregrinus of Mysia 29, 30, 190
Pharisees 15, 40, 49, 104, 106, 107, 116, 117, 140, 178, 200, 211
Pigs 71, 72–77, 85, 86, 154, 155, 156, 157, 164, 172, 177, 226
Power-authority
— for exorcism 20, 22, 23, 34–35, 38–40, 42–44, 51, 68, 106–109, 152, 159, 160, 161, 163, 164, 165, 173, 178, 200, 217, 225, 227, 228
— demonic 200, 208
— God 106, 165
Prayer 13, 150, 162–163, 166, 211, 222
— in exorcism 13, 17, 20, 44, 51, 52, 97, 159, 160, 162–164, 211, 227
Principalities and powers 49
Proof of exorcism 20, 25, 26, 74, 75, 155, 164, 173
Prophet(s) 64, 67, 145, 171, 209, 214
— Christian 29–30, 139, 167–168
— the Baptist 210
— false 139, 179, 190, 192, 202
— messianic 109, 136
Psalms 37–38, 187
Pythagoras 23, 49

Q 54, 55, 65, 66, 98, 101, 102, 103, 104, 106, 107, 108, 109, 110, 111, 115, 116, 119, 120, 123, 124, 126, 138, 170, 178, 219
Quadratus 195, 197, 204, 206, 207
Qumran Community and Scrolls, *see* Dead Sea Scrolls

Rab 150
Rabbis 46, 52, 59, 70, 109, 137, 139, 140, 151, 158, 159, 161, 181, 183, 188, 209, 210, 211, 212, 213, 227
Rabbinic literature 10, 16, 21, 22–23, 43, 47, 49, 50, 63, 150, 151, 157, 160, 169, 178, 179, 184, 200, 209, 210, 226
Rebuking evil 45, 46, 68, 69, 95, 115, 138
Ring (finger) 35, 36, 39, 157
Roots 36, 43, 157

Sarah 43, 44, 46
Satan 38, 44, 45, 55, 105, 106, 109, 115, 116, 117, 151, 178, 181, 184, 185, 186, 188, 198, 199, 207, 214, 223, 227

— cross and defeat 142, 222
— defeat of 45, 50, 55, 98, 106, 108, 111, 112, 113, 114, 115, 117, 125, 126, 127, 142, 168, 170, 186, 187, 188, 189, 219–224 227, 228
— falling 126, 127
— two stage defeat 223–224, 228
Scepticism 2
Sceva 31, 32
— sons of 16, 30, 31, 32, 42, 47, 66, 139, 210, 226
Scribes 29, 58, 104, 180, 200, 210
Semyaza 223
Seventy (Two) disciples 126
— Mission of 123, 125
— Return of 115, 125, 140
Simeon ben Yose 23, 46, 48, 158, 160, 178, 227
Socrates 28
Solomon 18–20, 35–36, 38, 39, 51, 52, 82, 139, 160, 183
Son of David 18, 35, 66, 102, 182, 183, 184, 220, 227
Son of God 9, 66, 81, 82, 141, 147, 149, 150–152
Sounds in incantations 39, 51
Spells 27, 69, 70, 75, 160, 163, 193, 195
Spirit(s) 17, 18, 22, 28, 35, 37, 38, 44, 45, 49, 50, 55, 66, 67, 73, 75, 140, 186, 187
— of the dead 75
— deaf and dumb 95, 157, 162
— demonic 83
— of divination 30
— the divine 37
— dumb 92, 103, 138
— of error 186
— eschatological 217, 218, 228
— evil 1, 8, 13, 18, 34, 36, 37, 38, 43, 44, 45, 46, 49, 75, 95, 97, 119, 120, 136, 138, 140, 152, 154, 157, 160, 162, 182, 183, 184, 186, 198, 199
— of holiness 185
— of infirmity 55, 56, 138
— of Judas Iscariot 1
— kindly 95
— unclean 60, 83, 89, 118, 124, 144, 162, 168, 176, 198, 199
— of understanding and sanctification 186
— wicked 185
see also (Demons)
Spirit/finger saying 98, 108–110, 127, 165, 167, 170, 217, 222, 228
Spittle 141, 158
Stada, ben 192
Strange Exorcist 16, 40–43, 47, 52, 97, 107, 109, 125, 139, 210, 218, 224, 226
Supernatural, the 20
Synoptic(s)
— healing stories 3
— traditions 8

Synoptic Problem 53–54
Syrophoenician woman and daughter 88–90, 138, 144, 145, 146, 156

Taxo 188
Temalion, ben 23, 48, 158
Temptations, the 55, 111, 112, 114–117, 126, 191
Transfering demons 51, 75, 76, 86, 154, 155, 157, 226

Vowels in incantations 39

Water 26, 28, 43, 50, 51, 63, 75, 76, 86, 93, 141, 146, 155, 157, 186

Zakkai, Johanan ben 43, 49
Zeno Papyri 14